AGENTS
OF
INFLUENCE

AGENTS OF INFLUENCE

Pat Choate

ALFRED A. KNOPF NEW YORK 1990

This Is a Borzoi Book Published by Alfred A. Knopf, Inc.

Library of Congress Cataloging-in-Publication Data
Choate, Pat.
Agents of influence.
   Includes index.
   1. United States—Foreign economic relations—
Japan.   2. Japan—Foreign economic relations—United
States.   3. Lobbyists—United States.   4. Foreign
agents—United States.   I. Title.
HF1456.5.J3C55   1990   337.73052   90-53118
ISBN 0-394-57901-1

Manufactured in the United States of America
Published October 8, 1990
Reprinted Once
Third Printing, November 1990

For Betty and Frank Choate

A JAPANESE VIEW

"Influence in Washington is just like in Indonesia. It's for sale."

—*Japan Economic Journal*

A BRITISH VIEW

"America has the most advanced influence-peddling industry in the world. Washington's culture of influence-for-hire is uniquely open to all buyers, foreign and domestic . . . its lawful ways of corrupting public policy remain unrivaled."

—*The Economist*

AN AMERICAN VIEW

"The real scandal in Washington is not what is done illegally, but what is done legally."

—*The New Republic*

A DUTCH VIEW

"A big part of the problem is that Americans can be bought so easily."

—*Dutch writer Karel van Wolferen*

CONTENTS

Foreword   xi

Introduction   xv

1. JAPANESE INFLUENCE
   ONE   Japan's Political Victories   3
   TWO   America the Vulnerable   15
   THREE   Japan's Political Mind-set   28

2. JAPANESE LOBBYING
   FOUR   Washington's Revolving Door   49
   FIVE   Japan Buys Washington   64
   SIX   Japan Takes Television   77

3. JAPANESE POLITICKING
   SEVEN   Hidden Interests   109
   EIGHT   The Politicians' Politician   121
   NINE   Grass-roots Politicking   132

4. JAPANESE PROPAGANDIZING
   TEN   Japan's Six Excuses   147
   ELEVEN   The Japanese Wurlitzer   163
   TWELVE   Japan on Japan   181

Conclusion   200

Appendix A   Former Federal Officials
                Who Later Represented
                Foreign Interests   208

Appendix B   Japan's Registered Foreign
                Agents in America   250

Notes   257

Acknowledgments   281

Index   283

Illustrations will be found following page 136

FOREWORD

JAPAN IS RUNNING an ongoing political campaign in America as if it were a third major political party. It is spending at least $100 million each year to hire hundreds of Washington, D.C., lobbyists, super-lawyers, former high-ranking public officials, public relations specialists, political advisers,—even former presidents. It is spending another $300 million each year to shape American public opinion through its nationwide local political network.

Better financed, more extensive, and more effective than either U.S. political party or any domestic industry, union, or special interest group, Japan's campaign for America serves one very important purpose: to influence the outcome of political decisions in Washington, D.C., that directly affect Japanese corporate and economic interests, decisions where every day hundreds of millions of dollars—and cumulatively billions of dollars—are on the line.

By knowing about these decisions ahead of its U.S. competitors, by using its network of well-connected insiders and lobbyists in Washington, D.C., by unleashing its grass-roots political network, by shaping the coverage of economic issues by journalists, and by mobilizing its opinion leaders in universities and think tanks, the Japanese are able to use their purchased political influence in America as a critical element of their corporate and national strategies.

This political game goes on daily and has for more than two decades. The victories scored by Japan include consumer electronics, supercomputers, machine tools, ball bearings, optical fibers, satellites, rice, biotechnology, air transport, telecommunications, semiconductors, legal and financial services, among dozens of others. No American industry—regardless of how competitive—is safe.

In politics, as in business, Japanese strategy follows a simple and predictable pattern: protect your own domestic market from foreign penetration and capture as much of your competitor's market share as possible. The Japanese strategy succeeds largely because of fundamental political differences between Japan and America.

Japan, for instance, does not tolerate its top government officials becoming other nation's top lobbyists. America does.

Japan does not permit its politicians or its political parties to accept donations from any foreigner, foreign corporation, or organization controlled by foreigners. America does.

Japan does not allow foreign interests to stage-manage "grass-roots" political campaigns among its people. America does.

Japan does not depend upon other nations to finance its thinking about Japan's long-term role in the world economy. America does.

Japan does not allow other nations to manipulate the curricula taught to its elementary, high school, and college students. America does.

In short, America tolerates foreign interference in its domestic affairs. But Japan does not. This basic political difference is a major reason why Japan's trade negotiators and companies succeed, while America's fail. It reflects the cumulative personal and professional decisions made by hundreds of Americans who constitute an important segment of this nation's governing class.

To put the matter in perspective, when John Maynard Keynes resigned from Britain's Treasury in 1919 after playing a key role in the negotiations over the Treaty of Versailles, he was faced with a problem of how to earn a living. His previous government salary had been £1,200 a year, and Keynes, never in his life averse to making money, naturally hoped to make more. He was offered the chairmanship of the British Bank of Northern Commerce, which was controlled by two prominent Scandinavian industrialists. For working only one day a week, he would have been paid £2,000 per year. But Keynes felt that he could not accept. "I am sure they want me," he wrote his father, "because they think I shall be of use to them with the Treasury and the Foreign Office; whereas in fact I am not at all disposed to play the foreigners' game against our own departments." In today's Washington, such a standard of political rectitude seems hopelessly antique.

The declining civic virtue described in this book reflects an *American* weakness. It is not the result of villainy by the Japanese or any other foreign interest. America's foreign competitors merely use the legal opportunities and services presented in America by Americans to maximize their economic and political advantage here. Any indignation about undue foreign influence in America's internal affairs, therefore, should focus on those Americans who have supported the progressive cheapening—even the fundamental corruption—of the value of national service that used to guide the conduct of our public life.

Naturally, many of those who serve as agents of influence for foreign interests—particularly those who once served in the United States government—object to any inspection of what they are now doing and its consequences for America. Many foreign corporations and governments share those objections.

Their criticism takes three forms. First, they claim that the examination of foreign influence over America's political and economic system smacks of "McCarthyism." But the issue is not about patriotism or ideology. It is about systemic, identifiable, virulent political corruption—all entirely legal and widely tolerated, at least in official Washington.

Second, the critics allege that the analysis of Japan's politicking, lobbying, and propagandizing in America somehow constitutes "Japan bashing," or perhaps even "racism." Of course, some Americans are racist and some bashing of Japan does occur. But the vast majority of the accusations of racism and Japan bashing are little more than cynical gambits offered up to discredit legitimate American concerns and enforce self-censorship.

Japan's political efforts are cited herein mainly because the Japanese have the most extensive, sophisticated, and successful political-economic machine in the United States. Other countries are now mimicking it by establishing similar webs of influence in America. An examination of Japan's political activities here, therefore, provides a convenient guide to the broader trend.

Finally, some protest the examination of foreign lobbying, politicking, and propagandizing on the ground that Japanese and other foreign interests merely "play the game by American rules." Their point is that if the "game" permits Washington insiders to peddle influence to the highest bidder, foreigners should be allowed to bid. My point is the "game" itself is harmful to American interests and requires basic reform.

Foreign interests are, and should be, entitled to as much representation in Washington as they can afford. After all, the political stakes for them are as high—sometimes higher—as they are for domestic interests. What is at issue here is the nature and form of such representation.

Any reform of the "game," particularly those I propose in the concluding chapter, must be applied equally to domestic and foreign interests. The corruption of America's political principles by domestic interests is no less destructive than by foreign interests, and no more desirable.

The real issue is whether the manipulation of America's political and economic system by Japanese and other foreign interests has reached the point that it threatens our national sovereignty and our future, and, if so, what do we do about it.

INTRODUCTION

THE ALFALFA CLUB is one of Washington's most exclusive and least known organizations. The sole purpose of this oddly named group of America's most powerful men (and only men) is to gather once a year at a Washington hotel for a private black-tie dinner where members exchange political jests.

Among the 670 men who attended the seventy-sixth annual dinner in 1989 were President George Bush, Vice President Dan Quayle, the Supreme Court justices (absent Sandra Day O'Connor), the Bush cabinet, the Joint Chiefs of Staff, congressional leaders, business titans, former federal officials, and scores of other Washington power brokers.

Senator Lloyd Bentsen, chairman of the Senate Finance Committee and the 1989 Alfalfa Club president, drew the biggest laugh of the evening. Bentsen opened with a story about his wife's reaction that day when he told her that he was going to meet with the great political and economic powers who hold America's future in their hands. "Oh," she said, "you're going to Tokyo?"

In truth, Bentsen's anecdote was no joke. America is selling its economy to Japan and surrendering to the political and economic control that always accompanies such ownership. Between 1980 and 1988, Japanese direct investment in the United States increased by more than 1,000 percent. Already, the Japanese:

- Own $285 billion of America's direct and portfolio assets.
- Control more than $329 billion of U.S. banking assets (a 14 percent share of the U.S. market).

- Control more than 25 percent of California's banking assets and 30 percent of its outstanding loans.
- Possess more real estate holdings in the United States than the members of the European Community (EC) combined.
- Routinely purchase 30–40 percent of U.S. Treasury securities.
- Trade up to 25 percent of the daily volume on the New York Stock Exchange.
- Produce nearly 20 percent of the semiconductors sold in the United States; more than 30 percent of the automobiles; almost half the machine tools; and a majority of the consumer electronics, among dozens of other goods and services.

Of course, foreigners have long invested in the United States. In the nineteenth century, British capital helped develop America. British, Dutch, and Canadian investors still have significant American holdings. But in the 1980s, Japan's investments in America expanded more rapidly than any other nation's. By 1995, Japan will have become the largest foreign investor in America. By 1999, Japanese investors will hold more American assets than Britain, Holland, and Canada combined.

To protect and promote their investments, Japanese proprietors are erecting a complex infrastructure of political influence throughout America. It is being used to co-opt politicians, shape public opinion, finance political campaigns, silence or isolate critics, and blackball appointees to high federal positions. Already, Japan's involvement in America's internal affairs is so extensive that U.S. trade policies are often shaped more by Japanese than American interests.

Ever since the arrival of Citizen Genêt in 1793, foreign interests have regularly sought to influence politics and public opinion in the United States. The Greek Lobby, for instance, has been able to sway U.S. relations with Turkey, Greece's neighbor and rival. For many years, Chiang Kai-shek's China Lobby dominated American thinking on China. The Israeli Lobby has a powerful voice in America's Middle East policymaking. The Irish Lobby has long helped influence American policies on Northern Ireland.

But of all nations, Japan understands best that political power in America is a commodity that can be acquired by the highest bidder. Of all nations, Japan has been willing to pay the most to shape America's attitudes and actions. Of all nations, Japan wields the most striking power over America's economic and trade policies. And of all nations, Japan succeeds best at using its political strength in America to gain economic benefits for itself.

One reason that Japan has such a commanding political presence in the United States is that it hires so many American lobbyists, political advisers, and public relations representatives. While Britain, Japan, the Netherlands, and Canada are—in that order—the four largest investors in the United States, in 1990 Japan employed one and a half times as many Washington lobbying, public relations, and law firms (92) to speak on its behalf as Canada (55), twice as many as Britain (42), and thirteen times as many as Holland (7).

Japan's political efforts in America also differ substantially in approach from those of other nations. Japan's American political machine is a continuous enterprise stretching from coast to coast. Its foundation rests on diplomacy, lobbying, politicking, and propagandizing—each delicately crafted and systematically integrated with the others. By contrast, Canada and the nations of Western Europe still rely heavily on traditional diplomacy to influence U.S. economic and trade policies. Like their American counterparts, most Canadian and European firms retain Washington representatives only when they need assistance on such specific matters as fighting U.S. Customs tariff rulings.

While the Japanese have almost unimpeded access to America's political and economic system, their own system remains largely closed to Americans. Former U.S. trade officials, for example, can lobby for almost anyone, domestic or foreign. But former officials of the Japanese government are, for the most part, simply unwilling to work for an American company.

Of equal political importance, the Japanese are reluctant to criticize their government to foreigners. Paul Krugman, the prominent international economist from the Massachusetts Institute of Technology, notes that while everyone knows that Japan's protectionist policies on rice are costly to its consumers, "I have had the experience of finding Japanese economists *from the private sector* refuse to acknowledge that the rice policy is costly, even in informal conversations. When pressed hard, they explained that they did not feel it was their place to criticize their government to a foreigner."

While Japan claims that its market is open, foreigners sell relatively little there. Japanese imports of manufactured goods as a percent of gross national product are about half that of the United States and less than a third that of Germany and other members of the European Community. Japan also claims that its economy is wide open for investment. In practice foreign investors face endless hidden obstacles. Fewer than thirty Japanese companies are sold to foreigners annually, and most of these are small, insignificant, or in deep trouble. Although America's economy is twice the size of Japan's, total U.S. direct investment in Japan is less than $17 billion—roughly one-fifth the amount of Japanese direct investment in America.

In short, Japanese firms can invest and sell in America, but American firms find it difficult to invest and sell in Japan. Japanese companies can actively participate in American politics, but American companies are unable to do the same in Japan. Japan can hire Americans to publicly criticize U.S. policies, but the Japanese are unwilling to do the same for foreigners, even in private. As a result, Japan has both a strategic economic advantage and a strategic political advantage over American companies.

The purpose of Japan's American political machine is to preserve these advantages. Its goals are sixfold:

- To keep the American market open for Japanese exports.
- To smooth the way for additional Japanese purchases of key American assets.
- To prevent discovery or criticism of Japan's adversarial trade practices.
- To neutralize the political opposition of Japan's American competitors.
- To influence America's trade policies toward Japan, as well as its policies toward Europe and other nations where Japan has significant economic interests.
- To force the integration of the U.S. and Japanese economies to the point where America will be politically and economically unable to confront Japan's mercantile policies.

Following Japan's successful example, the Koreans, the Taiwanese, and several European countries are now creating their own political machines in America. Their goal: to advance their interests in America and counter Japan's growing influence over the U.S. government.

Although Japan's American political machine is run from Tokyo, it is staffed overwhelmingly by Americans. The cost is more than $400 million a year—an amount roughly equal to the combined total expenditures of the 1988 House and Senate congressional elections. At least $100 million of Japan's political outlays goes to Washington lobbyists, super-lawyers, and political advisers. The remaining $300 million is spent to expand a pro-Japan state and local political network.

These monies finance a variety of activities designed to shape the attitudes of the American people and the actions of their government. To mold the thinking of tomorrow's leaders, for instance, Japanese institutions finance the preparation and distribution of teaching materials used in hundreds of U.S. grade schools, high schools, and universities to educate American students about Japan. Much of this material is nothing but Japanese propaganda.

Most recently, Japan has bought five colleges in America—Regis College and Loretto Heights College in Colorado and Warner Pacific College, Salem College, and Tokyo International University in Oregon—and is establishing a sixth in a suburb of Washington, D.C. Ten to twenty years from now, Japanese graduates of these colleges will be managing the assets that Japan is now busily acquiring in America.

To influence the public debate over America's policies toward Japan, the Japanese fund a growing number of the policy institutes and scholars who supply elected and appointed U.S. officials with ideas and policy positions. While the integrity of these scholars is generally beyond question, significant Japanese funding often has the effect of amplifying one particular set of views about which policies America should adopt. Already, Japan finances virtually all of the U.S.-Japan study programs operated by American universities and think tanks. At the same time, it systematically attacks both the substance of any criticism of its trade positions and the professional standing of the critics themselves.

To shape the positions of American trade associations, Japanese companies have joined dozens of these organizations and now, as a matter of course, set their policy and lobbying agendas. In addition, the Japanese regularly operate front groups that advocate pro-Japan positions; they control the operations of these shadowy political coalitions through a vast network of American distributors, suppliers, contractors, and local partners. American companies that need access to Japan's markets are told by the Japanese to make a public show of supporting Japan's positions in congressional testimony and elsewhere.

To influence national politics, Japan has put on its permanent payroll many leaders from both political parties and many of the top political advisers to the President, members of Congress, governors, and mayors. Japanese corporations now help finance both the Republican and Democratic parties, and Japanese business interests make large political action committee (PAC) donations to congressional candidates. Japanese companies regularly indoctrinate their U.S. employees on how to vote in elections and encourage them to lobby Congress for positions that favor Japanese interests.

To influence state and local decision making, Japan has established a grass-roots network that includes dozens of Japanese chambers of commerce and five regional associations of U.S. governors and Japanese business leaders. In addition, Japan has sixteen consulates and trade offices strategically positioned throughout the United States. At the insistence of their government, Japanese companies are donating hundreds of millions of dollars to local civic and social projects as a means of influencing Congress through its constituents, friends, and local supporters.

To prejudice the trade and economic decisions of the President of the United States, Japan threatens to withhold financing for the federal government's huge deficits. In 1989, this economic blackmail was so obvious that President Bush publicly cautioned Americans not to complain too loudly about Japanese investment and trade practices lest Japan withhold new funds.

To sway Washington decision makers, Japan fields an army of hundreds of lobbyists. Many of these lobbyists were previously federal officials, just as many current federal officeholders were once Japanese lobbyists. The money Japan spends annually on its Washington effort exceeds the combined budgets of the U.S. Chamber of Commerce, the National Association of Manufacturers, the Business Roundtable, the Committee for Economic Development, and the American Business Conference—Washington's five most influential business organizations.

Japanese penetration of the American political system is now so deep that its integrity is threatened. In their own country, the Japanese call this sort of money politics "structural corruption." In this case, it means that so many advocates of Japan's position are involved in decision making that the ultimate outcome is structurally biased in Japan's favor.

Japan now wields so much political power in America that it can, in effect, veto much legislation that it dislikes. It can ignore almost any U.S. law or policy that it finds inconvenient. It can politically overwhelm virtually any combination of American companies, unions, or other interests that it opposes.

Today, Japan plays a major role in shaping American public policy on everything from tariff rates to federal support for such critical technologies as semiconductors and high-definition television (HDTV). Indeed, Japan now plays a critical role in devising the policies that will determine which U.S. industries will survive and which will not, which parts of the country will grow and which will decline, which jobs will remain and which will disappear.

While no one doubts that Japanese and other foreign interests are entitled to representation in Washington, one may raise fair questions about its nature and form:

- Should former high-ranking U.S. officials—people who are privy to the intimate details of Washington's economic and trade strategies—be permitted to lobby for Japanese and other foreign economic rivals?
- Should Japanese and other foreign corporations be allowed to operate political action committees and involve themselves in the financing, even indirectly, of American elections?
- Should Japan be allowed to conduct secret propaganda programs in America?
- Has Congress become too susceptible to the political pressure generated by Japanese corporations?
- How pervasive is Japan's support of American think tanks and the scholars who generate the ideas for America's political candidates, elected officials, and policymakers?
- Does Japanese investment, lobbying, politicking, and propagandizing threaten the national sovereignty of the United States?

Whatever the answers to these questions, the central point of this book is that the ultimate responsibility for any domestic transfer of political power from American to foreign hands resides with Americans, not with the Japanese or any other nation.

If the standards for post-government employment of high officials permit a revolving-door corruption that is harmful to American interests, the responsibility for changing those standards rests with the American people, and not with the foreign interests that profit from them.

If the activities of those in the pay of foreign interests are too hidden, the responsibility for putting the public spotlight on what they do rests with inquisitive American media, an investigative American government, and a vigilant American public.

If the nation invests too little in educating American elementary- and secondary-school students about world history, geography, languages, and economics, the fault lies not with Japan for filling that vacuum with its self-serving propaganda, but with us for permitting it.

If huge federal budget deficits are forcing America to borrow too much and to sell off too many of its productive assets, then the burden for budget reform lies with American lawmakers, businesses, and taxpayers, not with foreign lenders and investors.

If American business and government are so disengaged from each other that foreign economic rivals can exploit the resulting political vacuum, then the responsibility for establishing a closer and more cooperative relationship falls on U.S. corporations and American officials, not with the foreign governments and their companies.

In a sense, this book is not about Japan or any other foreign interest. It is about a fundamental problem with American governance—one that allows foreign interests to assume a dangerously large role in America's politics and policymaking through political manipulation.

The responsibility for correcting this problem is exclusively our own. After all, America and its government belong to us.

Recall Deep Throat's advice on how to unravel Watergate: "Follow the money." It's not a bad way to understand Japan's growing political influence in America.

In Part 2, this book follows Japan's money to Washington insiders and ex-officials. In Part 3, it examines how Japan now sponsors American trade associations and front-group coalitions, and helps fund both U.S. political parties. In Part 4, it reveals how Japan sustains a massive economic propaganda program in America that includes efforts to shape the way educators in thousands of U.S. schools teach our elementary- and secondary-school students about Japan.

Japan gets full value for the political money it spends in America. To illustrate the point, Part 1 begins with a look at recent Japanese political victories in Washington.

1.
JAPANESE
INFLUENCE

Chapter One

JAPAN'S POLITICAL VICTORIES

CAN AMERICAN BUSINESS succeed in today's fiercely competitive global markets by offering the world's lowest-priced, highest-quality products, and by aggressively marketing and servicing these products?

Sadly, no. For those companies that want to succeed in the 1990s, producing the best is no longer good enough.

In addition to the five classic economic strategies—price, quality, innovation, marketing, and service—there now is a sixth: politics. In today's economy, what cannot be won in the marketplace can be acquired through brute political power in the back halls of government.

In contemporary America there is no lack of opportunity to gain the economic upper hand through political maneuvers. Surprisingly, however, only a handful of American companies devote serious attention to this sixth dimension of competition. Fewer than 30 percent of the CEOs of America's 150 largest corporations even *try* to affect the international trade and economic policies of their own government. Virtually none devote any attention to the trade and economic policies of the foreign countries where they operate.

By contrast, the top executives of major Japanese and European firms seem to spend half to three-quarters of their time shaping the international and domestic policies that affect their businesses. As a result, their companies are able to influence—if not dictate—the economic and trade policies of their own governments. As these companies increase their presence in the U.S. market, they are seeking comparable influence over the American government.

Foreign companies bring to America an understanding of the special

3

link between political influence and economic advantage. Together with their home governments, these foreign corporations have hired thousands of U.S. lobbyists, academics, political advisers, public relations consultants, and former high-ranking government officials to help them turn America's most basic trade policies to their advantage.

Altogether, 161 countries employ some 3,500 foreign agents registered in Washington—a majority of whom work on trade issues. There are perhaps twice that many who are unregistered foreign lobbyists. Those in the pay of foreign interests now can be found in virtually all of Washington's inner sanctums. In the process, a great deal of political power in the United States is being transferred from American to foreign hands.

Japan's American political machine is by far the best-staffed, best-organized, and best-financed of any nation's. According to public records, 140 Japanese government agencies and companies employed American lobbying and propaganda firms in 1990.

This kind of political muscle pays off. Time after time, it has enabled Japanese interests to manipulate the policies of the U.S. government to their own benefit, despite the damage done to American workers and industries. Four recent examples illustrate Japan's growing political influence in America.

VICTORY NO. 1: TRUCKS

In 1989, the Japanese politically trounced Ford, Chrysler, and General Motors on a key U.S. tariff ruling. Japan's victory now deprives the U.S. Treasury of more than $500 million a year in duties and adds that much to the federal budget deficit.*

The Japanese government sets "voluntary quotas" on the number of passenger cars that its manufacturers can export to America. But no such quota exists for truck exports. Japanese manufacturers can send as many trucks to the United States as they like.

The only hitch: there is a big difference in U.S. tariff duties between passenger cars (2.5 percent) and light trucks (25 percent). Throughout the early and mid-1980s, Japanese manufacturers were quite willing to pay higher duties on truck exports; after all, their car export quotas were full. By 1987, however, transplanted Japanese automotive factories in America were producing so many cars in the United States that there

---

* This amount is precisely double what was authorized in 1990 for the Federal Trade Adjustment Assistance Act—the principal means by which Washington assists those workers and communities that have lost jobs due to imports.

was little need for the Japanese to ship over additional cars. That meant that car export quotas were going unfilled. To exploit the tariff rate differential, the Japanese hit on the idea of reclassifying light trucks as cars.

In the spring of 1988, when this abuse of U.S. tariff regulations became apparent, the Customs Service began a review process, inviting comments from interested parties. The Japanese soon mounted an intense lobbying campaign.

In the summer of 1988, this campaign went public when Congressman William Dannemeyer (R-Calif.) drafted a "Dear Colleague" letter that would be sent to William von Raab, then Commissioner of Customs. The letter urged that no changes be made in Customs regulations affecting the import of foreign trucks, most of which, of course, are Japanese. In July 1988, thirty members of the House of Representatives and eleven senators signed the letter and sent it to von Raab. But von Raab refused to preempt the formal decision-making process of the Customs service.

One of Japan's responses was to expand their lobbying team. In October 1988, for instance, Suzuki hired Robert Thompson, a well-connected Republican lobbyist who had been an aide to Vice-President George Bush in the early 1980s.

On January 4, 1989, Customs ruled that the light trucks could not be classified as cars. As von Raab notes:

> These vehicles are built on truck bodies. They have truck characteristics. Most are built in truck divisions. Most are built in truck factories. They are advertised as trucks, off-road vehicles, vans or vehicles that can carry cargo. For years, the Japanese have certified them as trucks when importing them into the United States. Even my grandmother can go into a parking lot and tell the difference between a passenger car and a truck. These are trucks.

Dannemeyer and his colleagues summoned von Raab to Capitol Hill to explain why they had initiated the review process in the first place. Sitting in on the meeting with the Members' blessing was John Rehm, who had been General Counsel in the White House Office of the Special Representative for Trade Negotiations during the Johnson Administration. Rehm's law firm represented Japanese and other foreign automotive interests, plus American automobile importers. Together, the Congressmen and Rehm badgered von Raab about the reclassification issue.

Japan reacted swiftly. During a January 1989 meeting of the Finance Ministers of the world's seven leading industrial nations, the Japanese

Minister of Finance persuaded his German and British counterparts to approach Treasury Secretary Nicholas Brady and ask for an official reconsideration. (Ironically, the first reported complaints about von Raab's decision were attributed to the German Finance Minister, even though Japan—the main force behind the opposition—was the primary source of imported trucks in the United States.) Brady swiftly complied. Within nine days of the Customs announcement, the ruling was suspended.

To kill the ruling altogether, Japan's American lobbyists and representatives of the Japanese government met with officials from the Office of the U.S. Trade Representative, the White House, and the Department of the Treasury. Japanese automakers financed a public relations campaign in Washington and around the country, alleging that von Raab's ruling would do enormous harm to U.S. consumers by upping truck retail prices. (Actually, the price of American-made trucks would not have been affected.) Automotive importers flooded Congress with angry letters. Japanese Embassy officials lobbied friends in the Administration and Congress. The government of Japan implied that an unfavorable ruling could do great harm to long-term U.S.-Japan relations.

In a rare show of political unity, the heads of Chrysler, Ford, and General Motors—Lee Iacocca, Donald Petersen, and Roger Smith—sent a joint letter to the President and Congress urging that the Customs ruling be preserved. The Big Three made similar arguments in newspaper advertisements and in meetings with key Administration officials. Their lobbyists pleaded with every member of Congress who would see them. Their dealers sent thousands of letters to Capitol Hill. But their efforts were wasted.

Japan had more political strength in Washington than Ford, Chrysler, General Motors, and their dealerships combined. Within forty-five days of von Raab's ruling, the Treasury Department overturned the Customs Service decision and reclassified light truck imports as passenger cars.

Moreover, the Administration made yet another important concession to the Japanese. It agreed to classify these trucks as passenger cars for the purpose of tariff assessments *and then reclassify them as trucks* for sale once they were inside the United States. The purpose of this elaborate bureaucratic two-step was to enable the vehicles to meet the Environmental Protection Agency's fuel-efficiency standards, which are lower for trucks than they are for cars. Nor do these vehicles have to meet federal emissions standards and safety requirements for cars, which are also lower for trucks than they are for cars.

In the end, Japan avoided more than $500 million a year in import duties. Most important for Japan, it was neither asked nor forced to make a single trade concession of its own.

VICTORY NO. 2: NATIONAL SECURITY

In 1988, Japan defeated American efforts to punish one of its largest companies for selling restricted military technology to the Soviet Union.

In the 1970s and early 1980s, the United States was able to track Soviet submarines by placing acoustic devices on the floor of the world's oceans. As a result, the United States enjoyed a considerable—though secret—strategic advantage. Then Soviet spies, including the notorious Walker family, obtained technical specifications that revealed the limits of these devices. The Soviets realized that they would need to equip their subs with silent propellers.

But the Soviets needed restricted propeller-silencing technology and they were able to obtain it from Japan's Toshiba Machine Company and Norway's Kongsberg Vaapenfabrikk. That technology has since allowed the Soviets to produce ultra-quiet submarines. These Soviet submarines, loaded with multiple-warhead missiles, can now creep undetected so close to the U.S. coast that they could destroy most of America's strategic arsenal before it could be launched. Defense experts believe that the cost of repairing the damage done to America's submarine defenses will exceed $30 billion.

When this security breach was revealed in 1987, Toshiba and Kongsberg faced a political firestorm in the United States. Toshiba was widely condemned and the Japanese government was criticized harshly for failing to enforce international agreements that prohibit sales of critical military technologies to the Soviets. Conservative members of Congress smashed a Toshiba cassette player with sledgehammers on the grounds of the Capitol—an event that was replayed many times on Japanese television as an example of "Japan bashing."

Dozens in Congress demanded that Japan pay for the damages to U.S. security. A clear congressional majority appeared to support a complete ban on Toshiba sales in the United States. In June 1987, the Senate voted 92–5 to impose sanctions as part of a larger trade bill. The House voted to ban the sale of Toshiba products in U.S. military exchange stores and prepared to prohibit Toshiba products throughout America.

The Norwegian government responded by forcing the reorganization of Kongsberg and limiting its future activities to military products for Western governments. The Japanese response was more modest. Both the chairman and the president of Toshiba Corporation resigned, and the firm sent pro forma letters of apology to American officials. But there was no thought of offering to pay for any damages to American security.

Moreover, Japan and Toshiba mounted a massive campaign to kill the pending sanctions. The government of Japan warned that any sanctions would do great, perhaps irrevocable, harm to long-term U.S.-Japan relations. (As we shall see, Japan makes the same claim whenever the U.S. sales of any of its prominent corporations are threatened.) Toshiba hired a small army of prominent Washington insiders to lobby on its behalf. Among them: ex-Nixon aide Leonard Garment, ex-congressmen Jim Jones (D-Okla.), and Burton Wides, a lawyer-lobbyist who had been a top aide to Senator Edward Kennedy (D-Mass.). Jones and Garment billed Toshiba at what the media later revealed were "regular hourly rates anticipated to be in excess of $500."

While Washington lobbyists worked directly for the Japanese on this case, Toshiba's case was also argued—albeit more subtly—by state and local officials. At Toshiba's request, mayors, state officials, and governors with company facilities in their jurisdictions lobbied their congressional representatives to oppose the sanctions.

Toshiba told its 4,000 American employees that congressional action could imperil their jobs. Soon, Congress began to receive thousands of letters from Toshiba's workers and their families, pleading that sanctions not be imposed on their employer.

Toshiba also enlisted the aid of U.S. companies that used Toshiba components in their own products. A "SWAT team" of lobbyists from Tektronix, Apple Computers, Sun Microsystems, Hewlett-Packard, American Telephone & Telegraph, and Compaq worked to eliminate any ban on the sales of products that used Toshiba components. Another team, headed by Andrew Manatos, Assistant Secretary of Commerce in the Carter Administration, worked to get a similar exemption on products manufactured by Toshiba but sold under American labels, such as copiers and car telephones.

A senior executive from a large American company that took Toshiba's side explains:

We were outraged by what Toshiba had done and told them so. Half of our products, however, contained Toshiba components. The only alternative sources were made in Japan by Japanese companies. We looked quietly for other suppliers in Japan, but no one would sell to us. Our ox was about to be gored. Like it or not, we had to lobby against the sanctions. Otherwise, we could have been put out of business.

But Toshiba's strongest ally was the Reagan Administration, which made killing the sanctions one of its top legislative priorities in 1987 and 1988. Administration officials told one member of Congress after another that the sanctions would do enormous damage to long-term U.S.-Japan relations.

Soon after the Administration announced its opposition to the Toshiba sanctions, however, new revelations about Toshiba appeared. In September 1987, the Defense Intelligence Agency and the Central Intelligence Agency told Congress about three other Toshiba sales to Soviet bloc nations.

These new cases quickly became known as Toshiba Two, Three, and Four. Toshiba Two was the purported 1979 sale to Czechoslovakia—then a principal corridor for shipping Western technology to the Soviets—of an entire computer-chip manufacturing plant. Toshiba Three was the alleged 1986 sale to East Germany of an advanced computer-chip assembly line. Toshiba Four was a 1987 agreement by Toshiba's top officers to sell East Germany additional advanced semiconductor technology.

Members of Congress charged Toshiba with sacrificing U.S. and Japanese national security for quick profits. Toshiba countered by calling its critics "racists" and "Japan bashers." The CIA was accused of pursuing a vendetta against Japan.

Reagan Administration officials tried to persuade the press that none of these incidents had ever happened. Its lobbyists claimed:

- Toshiba Two had been a legal sale of a transistor plant to Czechoslovakia in 1979.
- Toshiba Three never happened.
- Toshiba Four—which would have been legal—was only a *proposed* sale of a printed circuit board plant to East Germany. The idea was supposedly abandoned because of the political controversy surrounding Toshiba One.

Congressman Duncan Hunter (R-Calif.) and others say that Toshiba and its lobbyists were lying. Hunter arranged for Guy DuBois, then head of the CIA's technology transfer division, to brief Congress on the matter. DuBois provided what Hunter and other attendees say was "conclusive evidence" of the Toshiba sales. By this time, however, many key members had been pressured so heavily to oppose the Toshiba sanctions that they refused even to attend the intelligence briefings.

As a vote on the sanctions neared, Toshiba seemed certain to face some form of retribution. The Reagan Administration, scenting defeat, shifted gears. It tried to ensure that any sanctions ultimately imposed would be trivial in their effect. In early February 1988, Richard Armitage, Assistant Secretary of Defense, sent Congress a letter claiming that it was difficult to assess the "actual damage" caused by the Toshiba diversion. Armitage attempted to minimize the effects of Toshiba's actions, saying that, while the company's subsidiary had given the Soviets production capacity, the Soviets "had initiated R&D of advanced marine propeller designs between 1979–1982." What Armitage did not say was that the Soviets lacked the production capacity to exploit this research—until Toshiba sold it to them.

Despite the Administration's efforts, a majority in Congress still favored a strong response. So on March 29, 1988, the Administration played its final card. Congress received a letter from Secretary of State George Shultz, Secretary of Commerce William Verity, and Deputy Secretary of Defense William H. Taft IV, claiming that any punishment of Toshiba would "have a chilling effect on the excellent cooperation we are now receiving from the Governments of Japan and Norway in uncovering past diversions and halting illegal exports."

In other words, if Congress punished Toshiba, Japan might permit other illegal exports to the Soviets.

Toshiba's lobbying, Japan's diplomacy, and the Administration's opposition defeated efforts to punish the corporation in any meaningful way. While its machine tool subsidiary was to be prohibited from selling any products in the United States for a period of two years beginning in August 1988, the Reagan and Bush administrations both deferred enforcement of the ban. And though Toshiba sales to the federal government were also banned, sales of Toshiba products that were unavailable from other sources were still permitted. So were sales of Toshiba components—parts that are included in innumerable Pentagon-purchased products.

Because of reporting loopholes in federal lobbying laws, no one knows precisely how much money was spent to beat the sanctions. Senior congressional staff who followed the sanctions battle estimate that the Japanese laid out as much as $20 million and U.S. companies another $30 million. Public records reveal that the law firms that provided Toshiba with the services of former Deputy USTR William Walker—Mudge, Rose, Guthrie, Alexander & Ferdon—and of Leonard Garment and Jim Jones—Dickstein, Shapiro & Morin—were paid more than $12 million, largely to work on the sanctions issue and trade concerns.

Regardless of whether the total bill was $50 million or $500 million, the price was a bargain for Toshiba, which stood to lose $3 billion in U.S. sales for each of three years. Toshiba's victory was also a bonanza for Japanese taxpayers, since the cost of repairing the damages to both the American and the Japanese submarine detection systems will be borne by American taxpayers.

VICTORY NO. 3: RICE

Rice produced in Japan costs at least seven times more than rice harvested in the United States. Yet Japan blatantly excludes imports of American rice through a maze of legal and regulatory barriers.

American rice growers estimate that they could capture a minimum of $2 billion of the Japanese market with minor effort, if only Japan's import barriers were lowered. Under U.S. trade law, American rice producers can secure federal help in prying open the Japanese market by initiating a three-step process. Step one is for the U.S. industry to file a petition documenting foreign protectionism. Step two is for the government to use that petition as the basis for an investigation. Step three—if the study finds that foreign protectionism exists—is for the government to negotiate the reduction of these trade barriers or, if this fails, to retaliate.

In 1986 and again in 1988, American rice processors took the first step in this process and filed a petition with the U.S. Trade Representative which documented Japan's exclusion of rice imports. Soon after the first petition was filed, leaders from Japan's ruling Liberal Democratic Party sent the President a letter saying that U.S. actions would threaten long-term U.S.-Japan relations. The Japanese legislators predicted that if the matter was even discussed in talks between the two countries

> grave political problems would arise, and cause serious anxiety and confusion among the Japanese people. Furthermore, we fear that, should this happen, the long-standing friendship between the United States and Japan may seriously be impaired.

Simultaneously, Japan's giant association of agricultural cooperatives— the *nokyo*—moved into action. With $51 billion in annual revenues, the *nokyo are* Japanese agribusiness. They own one of the world's largest banks and also one of the world's largest insurance companies. Zenchu, the political coordinating center of the *nokyo*, hired Washington lobbyists to fight the rice millers' petition.

The *nokyo* also mounted a public relations campaign with the American press and U.S. farm organizations. The *nokyo's* message to the Reagan Administration: any discussion of rice trade would violate basic cultural sensitivities in Japan, since rice farming played an intimate role in Japanese culture. Again and again, the *nokyo* pointed out that Japan was already "a very stable market, and the largest customer for U.S. farm products."

American producers of wheat, soybeans, and other crops were warned that their Japanese customers might look elsewhere if Japan was forced to open its market to U.S. rice exporters. The message: urge Congress to go slow. In the end, the major U.S. farm organizations did not support the rice millers. In fact, the heads of the American Agricultural Movement, the North Dakota Wheat Commission, and the Colorado Wheat Administrative Committee publicly opposed the rice millers' petition.

Japan's lobbying and politicking worked. In both 1986 and 1988, the U.S. Trade Representative refused to initiate an investigation into Japan's exclusion of American-grown rice. Once the USTR refused to act, the case was closed.

To add insult to injury, Japan will not allow American rice to be shown to Japanese consumers. At a March 1990 international food fair outside Tokyo, the Japanese government forced U.S. officials to remove the American rice exhibited in the United States Rice Council's booth. The excuse: Japanese officials said displaying the handful of rice in the American booth violated Japan's trade and food control laws.

VICTORY NO. 4: CONSTRUCTION

Although American builders are among the most competitive in the world, Japan has kept them out of its booming construction market and has scuttled American firms' efforts to get market-opening help from their own government.

Japan's exclusionary practices were highlighted in 1987, when it refused to permit American firms, the most experienced airport builders in the world, to participate in its $6 billion Kansai Airport project. Senator Frank Murkowski (R-Alaska) and Congressman Jack Brooks (D-Tex.) responded by introducing a bill to bar Japanese construction companies from operating in U.S. federally funded construction projects as long as American companies were excluded from Japan.

The proposed legislation prompted a new spate of U.S.-Japan negotiations. In the midst of these talks, Commerce Secretary Malcolm Baldrige, whose department headed the U.S. negotiating team, was killed in a freak rodeo accident. During the confusion that surrounded the naming of Baldrige's successor, Japanese lobbyists with strong White House connections used their influence to block the promotion to Under

Secretary for International Affairs of J. Michael Farren, the Commerce Department official who was handling the construction negotiations. On the eve of the final round of negotiations, Farren resigned. His departure threw the American effort into chaos. Simultaneously, the Japanese quietly told the Administration that unilateral U.S. action might damage long-term U.S.-Japan relations.

This familiar diplomacy-and-lobbying formula again enabled the Japanese to evade any serious challenge to their exclusionary practices. Though a ban on Japanese participation in federally financed construction projects was included in a late 1987 continuing appropriations resolution, which was signed in August 1988, it was in effect for less than a year. And while Japanese companies were forbidden to bid on federally funded construction at U.S. airports for five years, this restriction was lifted by USTR Carla Hills in the spring of 1990.

Japan promised to permit American contractors to bid on seventeen construction projects. In context, however, this means almost nothing. Japan awards almost 500,000 public works contracts each year. The fact that seventeen of these projects will be open to U.S. bidders is insignificant: Japan made no guarantees that contracts would be *awarded* to U.S. firms, even if they offered the best and lowest bids. Two years after their promise was made, the Japanese government has issued construction licenses to only twenty-six foreign firms. Of these, twenty-three have tie-ups with Japanese companies—though only a handful of them actually have contracts. And the contracts they have must be shared with Japanese partners. Meanwhile, Japanese companies continue to operate throughout the United States with virtually no restrictions.

Japan scored dozens of similar victories in the 1980s—in supercomputers, machine tools, ball and roller bearings, optical fibers, satellites, biotechnology, air transport, telecommunications, alcoholic beverages, semiconductors, legal and financial services, and the transfer of "cutting edge" technology such as that embodied in the FSX fighter plane.

In each of these victories, a strikingly familiar pattern emerges. When Japan has a competitive good or service, government-sanctioned cartels destroy their foreign competitors with cutthroat pricing. This predatory pricing is subsidized by cartel arrangements, by charging Japanese consumers up to twice the overseas price for the same good, and, sometimes, by paying secret, illegal kickbacks to U.S. importers.

When American firms offer a competitive good or service, such as telecommunications or construction, the Japanese market remains tightly closed. If an American company protests, it is intimidated. If Congress moves to take action, Japan makes the issue a test of U.S.-Japan relations. For the most part, the State Department can be expected to endorse Japan's position in Washington's inner councils for foreign policy reasons; the National Security Council for geopolitical reasons; and the Office of Management and Budget, the Council of Economic Advisers, the Justice Department, and the Treasury Department for economic and ideological reasons.

If there are bilateral trade negotiations, Japan stalls long enough for its industries to prevail. In virtually every instance, Japan hires prominent ex-officials of the American government and leading U.S. politicians to plead its case with their friends in government and the press.

By now, this is an old formula. Still, it works for Japan. One of the best measures of its success is the fact that other nations are adopting it.

No American industry—regardless how competitive—is safe. Unless major changes are made in the integrity, priorities, and processes of U.S. trade policymaking—and unless they are made soon—Japan and other nations are sure to score dozens of additional victories in the 1990s.

Chapter Two

AMERICA THE VULNERABLE

HUNDREDS OF Washington's power elite now work to advance Japan's political and economic interests in America. Nothing comparable is found in the capital of any other nation. Any of the elites in Japan, Korea, France, Germany, or Britain who did the same would be considered, and treated as, social lepers.

How did this come to be? Why do so many of America's best and brightest—people who come to Washington to fight for conservative or liberal causes—stay on after their public service to work for overseas interests? Moreover, how do they justify working on behalf of foreign countries in those cases where it is clear that their victories can only occur through American losses? The answer: money and ideology.

A revealing example of "Washington ethics" in action is contained in the scandal that rocked the Department of Housing and Urban Development (HUD) in the late 1980s.

In early 1989, congressional hearings revealed that, over the previous decade, much of the HUD money available for low-income housing was allocated on the basis of insider relationships. The technique was simple. A lobbyist or consultant with special connections to the Reagan Administration, the Republican Party, or a high-ranking HUD official would ask the HUD Secretary or his top aides for a funding priority. Once the project was approved, the influence peddler would be paid a huge fee.

The ethical mind-set among many insiders is revealed in their responses to the HUD scandal. In July 1989, for instance, the topic arose at a private dinner party in Washington's fashionable Cleveland Park. Among the guests were a prominent Washington lawyer-lobbyist, several other lobbyists, their spouses, an ex-congressman, and a corporate executive.

One guest condemned the immorality of HUD's influence peddlers, who had siphoned money earmarked to house the poor. Another sneered at the hypocrisy of James Watt, the ultraconservative former Secretary of the Interior, who publicly denounced HUD's activities but took $400,000 for using his political connections to get three HUD projects funded.

The lawyer-lobbyist, however, had a somewhat different perspective. "I only wish," he said, "that I could have gotten in on the deal. Everything that Watt and the others did was legal. And as far as I'm concerned, if it's legal, it's okay."

This lobbyist really had his finger on the pulse of Washington: "If it's legal, it's okay" is the ethical standard that now prevails.

In the 1980s, more than a hundred high-ranking federal officials, including several members of Congress, were forced out of office for their involvement in ethically questionable activities. Many others were investigated. Some were convicted. A handful went to prison.

Yet all of those who were evicted or convicted were punished for running afoul of bribery or perjury statutes. *Only one person* was convicted of violating government ethics laws—and his conviction was overturned in 1989.

The bizarre nature of these laws is illustrated by the fact that executive branch officials are prohibited from accepting as much as a soft drink from an American company or lobbyist. Yet the law permits these same officials to be lavishly wined and dined by the Japanese and other governments even when they are being lobbied.

Given the loopholes, there are virtually no post-government rules for those in Congress or their staff. Until late 1989, Congress exempted itself from most of the ethics legislation applied to the other branches of government—just as Congress had earlier exempted itself from the laws on occupational safety, fair labor standards, and civil rights.

Absent tough federal ethics laws and post-government employment rules, the prevailing ethics in Washington are those of the legal profession. The lobbying game is played by "lawyers' rules," largely because many, if not most, of Washington's 40,000 lobbyists—and more than a third of Congress—are attorneys.

One Washington lawyer notes that a major problem with legal ethics, particularly as they apply to lobbying, can be traced to the corrupting influence of the adversarial system of law. The lawyer explains:

Although very few lawyers actually practice in court, the adversary proceeding is the context in which almost all law is practiced. For example, you advise your client on tax matters to do what he thinks he can get away with in a lawsuit. So even though the tax lawyer may never enter court, he's always got his eye on the adversary proceeding, which provides the guideline.

In an adversarial proceeding, the role of the lawyer is to represent his or her client to the hilt and thus to help the client prevail. Whether the lawyer's client really is selling a defective product is irrelevant. All that matters is whether the prosecution or the plaintiff can prove to the satisfaction of the court (or a jury) that the defendant is "guilty"—that is, selling the defective product and doing it knowingly. The same lawyer notes:

> The truth is irrelevant in court. If the truth is adverse to the client, the lawyer is ethically prohibited from revealing the truth to anybody, most of all the court. Everything that a lawyer says in connection with his client, therefore, is a distortion. In the main, the lawyer's fiduciary obligation requires him to be silent about some things and vocal about others. Consequently, the truth is textured.

In America's adversarial legal system, such distortions are expected. In a structured court proceeding, each side presents its case. Distortions can be challenged and defended. In principle, the process allows a neutral judge or jury to arrive at the truth.

No similar structure for arriving at the truth exists for lobbying. The "judge" is a member of Congress, a congressional staffer, or a federal official. Often this judge is neither neutral nor knowledgeable about the rules of the game—namely, that everybody distorts. The physical absence of an opposing side allows distortions to go unchallenged. Moreover, many advocates do not reveal on whose behalf they are speaking.

The lawyer-client relationship of the adversarial court proceeding has been grafted on to the lobbyist-client relationship. In the process, many lawyer-lobbyists have learned to adhere to the adversarial standards of the courtroom. They proceed as if they had a fiduciary and ethical responsibility to help their client win at all costs, even when winning for a foreign company or government runs counter to the interests of the nation.

The Washington attorney observes, "My hunch is that most of these lawyer-lobbyists not only would harm the country but would feel professionally or ethically obligated to do so in pursuit of their client's interests."

These attitudes are reinforced, of course, by big rewards—financial, social, and political. In this regard, Washington today is like Wall Street more than a century ago, when Jay Gould and Jim Fisk attempted to corner the market in gold, ultimately precipitating a financial panic. At a congressional inquiry in 1870, a year after Fisk and Gould's attempted coup, one highly placed witness was asked his opinion of the participants' patriotism. The witness responded that Fisk, Gould, and their co-conspirators in the Grant Administration were "all apparently very patriotic, but most of them wanted to make money."

As Richard Harwood, ombudsman for the Washington *Post*, notes, "Washington has but two great obsessions: the Redskins and money. More than a trillion dollars a year pours in for redistribution by the politicians, which accounts for the perpetual porcine glint in our eyes."

Harwood adds, "We're uncommonly obsessed with bucks on a personal level as well. We didn't become the richest metropolis in the world on food stamps and secondhand clothes."

Just as Wall Street has been transformed by the actions of takeover kings and financial wizards looking for a fast buck, the flow of lobbying money has changed Washington from a charming Southern city into a glitzy citadel of conspicuous personal consumption. The result is a mercenary culture where aberrant behavior is tolerated, where ethical standards perpetually recede, and where the acceptable limits of lobbying are continually expanded.

From 1979 to 1984, for instance, attorney Michael Abbell led the Justice Department's efforts to extradite alleged drug dealers and criminals back to the United States. Six months after he left office, he went to work for the reputed bosses of Colombia's Cali cocaine cartel.

Abbell's new job was to use his contacts, skills, and knowledge to keep Cali's drug traffickers from being extradited. But Abbell has done even more for his clients. He has lobbied Congress and the American Bar Association to weaken U.S. extradition treaties. He has tried to arrange a deal with the Justice Department for his Colombian clients. He has testified as an expert witness in Spanish courts *against* a request by his old office to extradite a detained cartel leader to America for trial.

Still, Abbell is no renegade. The ruling attitude in Washington has become "everybody does it"—everybody leaves his or her old government job and sells his or her inside knowledge and personal contacts to the highest bidder. The current rationale: "And why not me?"

The void created by collapsing ideals of public service and civic virtue has been filled by a pervasive cynicism. Many now see public service as nothing more than a booster rocket on a one-way journey to wealth and power as a Washington insider. And one of the quickest ways to make big money is to represent foreign interests.

A 1986 General Accounting Office (GAO) survey revealed that seventy-six former federal officials had become registered foreign agents. Among these were eight special assistants to the President, five assistants to the President, two deputy assistants to the President, one presidential counselor, one deputy White House press secretary, one chief of staff to the Vice President, a chairman and a vice chairman of the U.S. International Trade Commission, two Deputy U.S. Trade Representatives, six senators, nine representatives, twelve senior Senate staff, five senior House staff, and four retired generals.

All told, these ex-officials represented 166 foreign clients from fifty-two countries and two international entities. Almost one-third of them went to work for Japan.

But this is only the tip of the iceberg. Hundreds of other Americans are lobbying, politicking, and propagandizing on behalf of Japan and other foreign interests. For example, the GAO report does not include those who lobbied for the domestic affiliates of foreign companies, since they are exempted from having to register with the Justice Department. Nor does it include lawyers who are similarly exempted if their work can be construed as part of the practice of law—even if those same activities, performed by nonlawyers, would require registration. Consultants and advisers who do not lobby are also exempted from registration requirements.

GAO admits that its review was based on incomplete federal personnel records. So, at best the report paints a partial picture.

Partly to fill this information gap, Appendix A of this book includes a compilation—also inexhaustive—of 200 officials who went on to work for Japan and other foreign interests between 1980 and 1990. It identifies the former government position(s) of these ex-officials, their current employers, and their foreign clients. As far as available records permit, it also lists how much these ex-officials (or their firms) were paid.

As these numbers suggest, Washington's ethos of greed and personal selfishness has spawned a large cadre of well-connected influence peddlers who are anxious to sell anyone, foreign or domestic, any help they need—so long as the price is right.

America is increasingly vulnerable—politically and economically—to Japan's growing ability—and willingness—to force Americans to do its bidding. Sometimes Japan acts subtly. Sometimes it does not.

Japan's greatest source of influence over America is the nation's debilitating dependence on Japanese funds to finance the federal budget deficit. Just before President Bush left for Tokyo in February 1989 to attend the funeral of Emperor Hirohito, he was asked what he would say to those Americans concerned that the Japanese are "buying and owning too much of the United States economy." Bush's response:

> Don't get so concerned over foreign ownership that you undermine the securities markets in this country. We have horrendous deficits, and foreign capital joins domestic capital in financing these deficits.

The President was only repeating in public what Japan's diplomats and politicians have been saying in private for years: Japan will refuse to finance America's huge federal budget deficits if the American government takes a hard line on trade with the Japanese.

Financing America's federal budget deficit is only one of several ways that Japan is flexing its political and economic muscle in America. The growing dependence of American firms on Japanese high-technology components is another.

Japanese politician Shintaro Ishihara, former Minister of Transport in the Nakasone cabinet, explains how this works in *The Japan That Can Say "No,"* the controversial book he co-authored with Sony chairman Akio Morita. Ishihara says that, while American know-how can develop advanced technologies, America cannot use its own know-how, simply because it lacks advanced production capacity. That capacity, Ishihara says, is in Japan.

Ishihara advocates using Japan's high-technology production capacity as political leverage against America. He writes:

> If, for example, Japan sold [microprocessor] chips to the Soviet Union and stopped selling them to the U.S., this would upset the entire military balance. . . . The more technology advances, the more the U.S. and the Soviet Union will become dependent upon the initiative of the Japanese people—this is getting crazy now, but the point is clear.

The point is indeed clear.

When Congress considered sanctions against Toshiba in 1988, for instance, those American companies that were dependent on Toshiba components—mainly semiconductors—had a simple political choice to make: lobby Congress on Toshiba's behalf or risk going out of business.

Similarly, Japanese semiconductor manufacturers used their economic leverage in 1987 and 1988 to undermine the U.S.-Japan Semiconductor Agreement. In 1986, Japan's government agreed that by 1991 foreign semiconductor manufacturers would be allowed to have slightly more than a 20 percent share in Japan's previously closed markets. The government of Japan also promised to put an end to the illegal dumping practices of Japanese chip makers.

The very next year, the Japanese engineered a worldwide shortage of computer chips. Suddenly, availability tumbled and prices soared. Alan Wolff, counsel for the Semiconductor Industry Association of America (SIAA), reports that many U.S. companies were on the verge of going under because they were unable to get the chips they needed to manufacture their products.

The ability to control both prices and availability gave Japanese manufacturers the weapon they needed to erode American support for the semiconductor agreement. What Japan did, cleverly, was to create and exploit a major rift within the U.S. electronics industry—between semiconductor producers (SIAA) and users (computer companies). Because of its market dominance, Japan had the power to strong-arm American firms into making long-term commercial arrangements that they would otherwise reject.

Many of the American companies that felt the shock of the chip shortage sought help from Congress. Senator Pete Wilson (R-Calif.) said that Japanese suppliers offered to sell DRAMs (dynamic random access memory chips) to U.S. firms only if the companies would transfer their "proprietary technology" (generally patents and other manufacturing secrets) to the Japanese DRAM manufacturer.

In March 1988, Wilson announced that the Japanese Ministry of International Trade and Industry (MITI) had approached a U.S. chip manufacturer, offering the firm guaranteed access to the closed Japanese market. The catch was that the American firm would have to come out in public with a denunciation of the bilateral semiconductor accord.

Once Wilson revealed this scheme, MITI predicted that the shortages would vanish. They soon did. But the federal government—then actively involved in opposing potential sanctions against Toshiba—took no follow-up action against either Japan or its chip makers.

More recently, flamboyant Texas entrepreneur T. Boone Pickens has felt the lash of Japan's leverage politicking. In late 1988, the Union Bank of California (UBC) expressed an interest in providing Pickens' company, Mesa, with an unrestricted, revolving $50 million credit line. (UBC is owned by the Bank of Tokyo.)

In early April 1989, UBC and Mesa executives met in Dallas and worked out the deal. A UBC executive informed Mesa that the Dallas

office of the bank was satisfied with the arrangement and had recommended approval of the bank's participation to the California office.

Just as the UBC-Mesa negotiations were being concluded, Pickens
announced that his Boone Company, a privately held investment vehicle,
had purchased a 20 percent stake in Koito Manufacturing Company, one
of Japan's biggest producers of auto parts. As Koito's largest stockholder,
Pickens asked for three seats on its board of directors. Koito responded
by denying the request, then hiring investigators to dig up information
about Pickens' private dealings.

Pickens' UBC credit line suddenly disappeared. Mesa officials say that
in late April an embarrassed bank official called to say that the deal was
off because "a Japanese voice in California had vetoed UBC's participation
in Mesa's line of credit due to Boone Co.'s recent investment activity in
Japan."

There is a basic arithmetic to America's financial vulnerability to economic blackmail. The federal budgets of the 1980s more than tripled the
national debt, from less than $950 billion in 1980 to more than $3.1
trillion in 1990. Since 1987, foreign lenders—especially the Japanese—
have financed the bulk of the budget deficit. So long as such deficits
continue, America's political vulnerability to overseas lenders can only
increase.

In California, Japanese banks already hold 25 percent of the state's
banking assets and 30 percent of all outstanding loans. Economist David
Hale of Kemper Financial Services estimates that Japanese banks could
have a similar market share nationwide by the mid-1990s.

By controlling—or at least holding a major position in—the U.S. financial system, the Japanese are in a position to know the most intimate
plans of the majority of American corporations. They will also have a
major influence over which companies get money and which do not. This
will give Japan even greater behind-the-scenes leverage.

Japan's economic and political influence will be exerted through its
powerful Finance Ministry. As a routine matter, six of Japan's largest
banks—Dai-ichi Kangyo, Sumitomo, Fuji, Mitsubishi, Sanwa, and Mitsui—meet regularly with Finance Ministry officials. According to the *Far
Eastern Economic Review*, the agenda of these meetings includes "setting
deposit rates and many other banking matters." The meetings are kept
secret "to avoid possible anti-trust action by Japan's Fair Trade Commission."

Foreign lenders now hold so much federal debt, and foreign owners
now hold so many American assets, that they want, and expect, a say
about America's economic, trade, and political policies. The deeper

America goes into debt, and the more assets it sells, the louder and more insistent this voice will become.

The federal government's dependence on foreign capital explains a great deal about President Bush's solicitous attitude toward the Japanese, who now annually finance roughly a third of the federal budget deficit. If the banks and governments of Japan and Europe stopped funding this deficit, the President would either be forced to ask Congress for much higher taxes or be required to make politically unpopular spending cuts.

As long as the President and Congress are unwilling to make tough decisions about the federal budget, Japan and Europe will have enormous political leverage over America.

Ideology is a major source of America's vulnerability. Until very recently, the American Establishment was obsessed with anti-Communism. It still advocates hard-line free trade. This myopia legitimates the ongoing sacrifice of America's economic interests in the name of foreign policy and defense considerations that often have only the most specious connections with the containment and rollback of Communism.

Other nations, particularly Japan, are acutely aware of America's ideological fixations. Moreover, they know how to turn these passions to their advantage. A 1988 American Enterprise Institute study of U.S.-Japan relations quotes Kanji Nishio's observation that America's obsession with the cold war had allowed Japan to

> conduct a diplomacy that exploited and totally used the U.S. Even
> if Japan was asked to take some responsibility, we could get away
> with avoiding it and simply pursue our own economic interests.

Free trade is the ideal way to expand world commerce. Without question, free markets and the decentralized allocation of resources are the most efficient means to organize production and distribution. In *theory*, the concepts of perfect competition and comparative advantage translate into a global economic order in which no single company can monopolize world prices and no one government can improve the overall welfare of its citizens by interfering with the production and allocation of goods and services. In *theory*, should a government interfere in trade—perhaps with subsidies or other protectionist supports—it could actually harm the welfare of its citizens.

While there is theory, there is also reality. And the reality of global commerce is that others, particularly Japan, refuse to adopt the free trade model. As a result, there is a widening gap between how the world should operate under free trade theory and how it actually does. It now appears, for instance, that much of the postwar global expansion may have been generated less by free trade and more by the fact that the United States consistently lowered its barriers to foreign imports, and at a much faster rate than other nations lowered theirs. Moreover, hindsight shows us that global expansion is also partly due to the transfer of U.S. financial and technological aid, which accelerated the rebuilding of war-torn European and Asian economies. In effect, lower trade barriers and continuing technology transfers operated as a massive, unappropriated foreign aid program.

In the 1980s, the intellectual bedrock of the hard-line "free traders"— the idea that free trade benefits a nation regardless of whether it is "fair"— was shaken by events that cannot be explained by traditional notions. Japan defied theory: it openly restricted imports, subsidized exports, and became the world's richest per capita industrial nation. Other countries, like Korea and Taiwan, are taking the same tack, and are beginning to benefit accordingly.

Still, some of America's most influential economists deny either that this is happening or that it makes a difference. During the mid-1980s debate on industrial policy, for instance, Charles Schultze, chairman of the Council of Economic Advisers (CEA) in the Carter Administration, wrote, "Japan does not owe its industrial success to its industrial policy. Government is unable to devise a 'winning' industrial structure." In 1989, Herbert Stein, chairman of the CEA in the Nixon Administration, wrote that America should forget about its trade deficit because it does us no harm. Stein also said the "inflow of capital and ownership of assets in the U.S. by foreigners is not a cause of dangerous dependence that is a political or security danger to us." In 1990, Stein went a step further in a *Wall Street Journal* article in which he argued that it was irrelevant if America had become the world's number two economic power.

Only now is a new trade theory emerging that explains the obvious: perfect competition does not exist. In the real world, a monopoly—or a small number of firms operating as an oligopoly—can restrict output, raise prices, and generate higher profits. They then can use these elevated profit levels to gain a permanent, global hold on an industry. Higher profits, of course, come at the expense of foreign customers and competitors. Yet a beggar-thy-neighbor approach to national prosperity can succeed and does, economically as well as politically.

MIT's Paul Krugman, a leading international economist and the principal architect of the new strategic trade theory, notes that this new thinking opens "the possibility that government intervention in trade via import restrictions, export subsidies, and so on may under some circumstances be in the national interest after all."

While this new thinking about trade may reflect the reality of how the world actually works, it also offers a huge potential for abuse. Ironically, the dogma of free trade represents an enormously powerful—and beneficial—force, because it keeps the potential greed of special interests in check.

Yet this same orthodoxy inhibits an open discussion over strategic trade policy. Deviations from neoclassic economic theory are inevitably derided as "industrial policy" or "picking winners and losers." Critics of free trade theory are invariably labeled "protectionist." In the process, slogans replace thought and dogma substitutes for policy.

America requires new thinking about how a generally correct model of trade should be revised to reflect a subtly altered international situation. Unfortunately, official U.S. devotion to orthodox economic theory gives Japan and others innumerable opportunities to dismiss legitimate criticism and turn America's ideology back on its negotiators.

When the United States moved to confront Japan in 1989 for blocking sales of American satellites, supercomputers, and timber, Shigeo Muraoka, the Japanese Vice Minister for International Trade and Industry, announced that his country was considering filing a complaint under the General Agreement on Tariffs and Trade "because the U.S. action seriously undermines the spirit of free trade." Muraoka's maneuver so badly tangled the U.S. initiative that it forced USTR Carla Hills to explain repeatedly why American actions were not violating free trade principles.

Today, America's elites are as paralyzed by old thinking about trade as Japan's elites are paralyzed by their own domestic power politics. As a result, America is unable to adapt its trade policies to the changing global commercial order.

Another important cause of America's vulnerability is the fact that Japan and other foreign interests have virtually unlimited opportunities to influence the nation's trade policymaking, in part because so many U.S. institutions and people are involved.

In the executive branch, trade decision making is divided among the Office of the U.S. Trade Representative, the Office of Management and Budget, the Council of Economic Advisers, the Treasury Department, the State Department, the Commerce Department, and twelve other major agencies. By the late 1980s, some 6,000 bureaucrats had some say over trade matters.

A parallel split of authority exists within Congress. Before it was put to a final vote, the Omnibus Trade and Competitiveness Act of 1988 involved two hundred members of Congress from twenty-two separate committees and subcommittees. The final bill ran some 1,300 pages.

Struggles for power are relentless. The Department of Agriculture wants to negotiate agricultural trade. The Department of Transportation expects to deal with airline and international transport agreements. The Department of Defense handles co-production arrangements. The Interior Department insists on leading negotiations that concern foreign sales of federal coal. The Treasury Department has sole authority to deal with shifts in exchange rates. The Department of Commerce is responsible for promoting American exports. The Export-Import Bank decides when to provide low-interest financing for exports. The Overseas Private Investment Corporation chooses when to insure investments abroad.

The constant battle for political turf among these agencies gives Japan unlimited opportunities for gamesmanship. Clyde Prestowitz, formerly counsel to the Secretary of Commerce, says that the Office of the USTR initially hesitated to support a semiconductor dumping case against Japan because it would strengthen the Department of Commerce's role in American trade matters. Conversely, when Nippon Telegraph and Telephone (NTT) failed to live up to its 1981 agreement to increase procurement of foreign goods, the USTR pressed hard for specific purchasing targets. Commerce opposed the policy. As it turns out, NTT had cultivated key Commerce officials, some of whom went on Japan's payroll when they left the government.

America does not have one trade policy: it has dozens, each of which reflects the limited bureaucratic concerns of individual federal agencies. In principle, the Office of the USTR has the responsibility to assemble an overall U.S. trade strategy and coordinate America's trade negotiations. But it has little authority to enforce consistent or even supportive action by other agencies.

Furthermore, the Office of the USTR is badly funded and thinly staffed. In 1985, it was unable to pay the $85 monthly subscription fee for the daily Japanese-language newspaper needed by the office staff to keep up with events in Tokyo. Japanese publishers sent the paper free of charge since they thought America's trade negotiators should know what they were reporting. The USTR still has only one and a half full-time funded positions for staff who focus on bilateral U.S.-Japan trade issues. In all, its staff totals 140.

When the federal government does try to create and implement national trade policies, it is shackled by time-consuming interagency negotiations, excessive numbers of classifications for traded goods, burdensome licensing procedures, and a bias toward litigation. In practice, this leads to more bureaucrats, more lawyers, more advocates, more rules, and slower action.

The complex processes and fragmented structure through which America crafts and administers its trade policies give Japan countless openings to influence U.S. decision making. It can stall and delay government action, usually with impunity. The status quo dominates. And maintaining the status quo of relatively open American markets and relatively closed foreign markets is one of the main political objectives of most of America's trading partners.

For example, America's anti-dumping and anti-subsidy laws are a potentially powerful tool for confronting predatory foreign anti-competitive practices. But these tools only work if they are applied in a timely manner. Even after repeated streamlining, these remedies are so time-consuming, costly, and uncertain that they are used only as a last, desperate resort.

Under current law, American companies are entitled to relief if foreign competitors' exports are subsidized by their governments, or if foreign manufacturers sell their goods in the United States at a price below fair market value. (In the latter case, the foreign firm is said to be "dumping" its goods on the American market.)

To exercise its rights, an American industry must file a well-documented petition with the Commerce Department. If Commerce concludes that a review of the case is merited, the International Trade Commission (ITC) conducts a study. If the ITC finds, first, that either dumping or government subsidies exist and, second, that the U.S. industry has been injured by these activities, it sends a positive finding back to Commerce. At that point, Commerce decides whether to impose a duty to offset the dumping or subsidy. If it chooses to impose a duty, it must also calculate the amount to be collected. Finally, the Customs Service, which is located in the Treasury Department, collects these duties.

One former lobbyist fairly well summed up the current state of American trade policymaking and administration:

What we lobbyists want is something complex, time-consuming, and abstract. Our goal is to bill hours rather than craft a rational national policy. That's the job of government. We *like* the current structures and processes.

He might have added: so do America's foreign competitors.

Chapter Three

JAPAN'S POLITICAL MIND-SET

A QUICK WAY to understand Japan's political activities in America is to learn how the Japanese practice politics in their home country.

A skilled tutor for such learning is Shigezo Hayasaka. For almost two decades, he was an intimate adviser to former Prime Minister Kakuei Tanaka, Japan's "god of votes" and political shogun. Hayasaka—who served as Tanaka's secretary, political director, and spokesman—says he has "seen things that should not be seen and heard things that should not be heard."

One of Hayasaka's responsibilities was to raise and distribute funds for Tanaka supporters. He says that even a freshman member of the ruling Liberal Democratic Party (LDP) must raise at least 100 million yen a year ($600,000) through private contributions to pay staff and to meet other political expenses. More senior members require as much as 200 million yen ($1.2 million). Leaders like Tanaka secure the loyalty of their followers by helping them raise that money. Hayasaka recalls going among Tanaka's supporters with a large satchel of yen—containing the equivalent of roughly $1.5 million—and distributing the cash. He says that during heated elections some of the recipients were so grateful "they had tears in their eyes."

Where does this money come from?

Most of it flows from Japanese companies, agricultural interests, and business associations, particularly the Keidanren (the Japan Federation of Economic Organizations). The amounts these groups contribute are staggering. The Keidanren alone gives the LDP nearly $100 million a year. Its member companies provide many times more. In the 1990 elections, the LDP raised more than $1 billion from the Keidanren and other business interests.

Official reports from the Japanese government show that, between the spring of 1988 and the spring of 1989, contributions from business and private individuals to Japanese political officials exceeded $2 billion. Knowledgeable Japanese observers say the actual amount was twice that. By contrast, in the United States, with twice the population of Japan, the combined cost of the 1988 presidential, Senate, and House elections was only $803 million. On a per capita basis, ten times more is spent on national elections in Japan than in America.

Apparently, even $4 billion is sometimes not enough in Japanese politics. In the 1990 election, the LDP—putting up its headquarters as collateral—borrowed $100 million from Japanese banks. In cash emergencies, politicians also seek insider stock tips, gifts of stock, and preferential treatment on the purchase and sale of land.

What does all this money buy? What do LDP contributors expect in return?

Simple. They want closed markets, political protection by Japan's powerful career bureaucrats, influence with the government, and intelligence about the prospective policies of foreign governments.

Because of its money politics, Japan has one of the most corrupt political systems in the world. Five times since the mid-1950s, the Japanese government has been shaken by revelations of payoffs and scandals. Although Prime Ministers like Tanaka—and, more recently, Noboru Takeshita—were embarrassed by public exposure and forced from office by internal LDP struggles, Japan's blatant money politics continues essentially unchanged.

The practices necessary for survival in Japan's system have shaped the political attitudes of Japanese business leaders. Not surprisingly, they have brought these attitudes with them to America. Their experiences in Tokyo help explain why they are willing to spend so much money in Washington and why they hire so many Washington insiders to represent their interests. The Japanese see politics as an integral part of business. For them, buying influence and information is simply another cost of doing business. And compared with the prices in Tokyo, influence buying in Washington is a bargain.

The Recruit scandal that forced Prime Minister Noboru Takeshita to resign in 1989 provides a rare inside glimpse into Japan's money politics.

It reveals much about the political mind-set that Japanese corporations have brought to America. It also shows the lengths to which Japanese companies will go to gain the upper hand in economic conflicts.

The Recruit affair—coupled with the recent works of authors Karel van Wolferen, James Fallows, Clyde Prestowitz, and Chalmers Johnson—also reveals a political system so paralyzed that it could not offer real trade reciprocity to other nations *even if it wanted to*. Instead, Japan's government and corporations have hired American lobbyists and public relations firms to deflect U.S. criticism about Japan's closed markets and sidetrack any meaningful political response.

The Recruit Company was a high-flying Japanese telecommunications, job placement, and publishing conglomerate. Its president, Hiromasa Ezoe, was an outsider in the ultimate insider society. He bought his way in. Recruit, which published guides for job seekers, bribed officials of the Labor Ministry to keep restrictive rules on how companies could announce job openings, thereby creating a market for its publications. Recruit is also alleged to have bribed Hisashi Shinto, chairman of Nippon Telegraph and Telephone—the world's largest company—to obtain special telephone circuits, some of which Recruit then sold to other concerns.

To gain the favor of Japan's ruling elite, Ezoe lavished enormous gifts of cash and insider stock on hundreds of Japanese politicians and bureaucrats. He awarded stock and money to journalists and political commentators. Ezoe gave extravagantly. Then Prime Minister Takeshita received more than $2 million. In fact, so many politicians in the LDP took money and stock from Ezoe that the party had enormous trouble finding someone untainted by Recruit money to replace Takeshita.

What is unusual about the Recruit affair is not that Ezoe bought influence: virtually all Japanese companies do that. Recruit is unusual because Ezoe gave so much to so many so indiscreetly that his bribery became a public scandal. In the process, the affair uniquely highlighted Japan's mix of money, politics, influence peddling, bribery, and insider relations.

One of the most important revelations of the Recruit affair was just how much Japan remains an insider society.

Now, as in centuries past, the Japanese import the best products, technology, and ideas from the outside world, while excluding the outsiders themselves. A newcomer—whether a foreigner or a parvenu Japanese businessman like Ezoe—must go to extraordinary lengths to penetrate the inner sanctum of those who rule Japan and control the many licenses, permits, and approvals needed to do business. The rights of the established village, clan, academic clique, or political faction are always primary.

Consider the network of family, political faction, and business that dominates the Japanese construction industry. Former Prime Minister Takeshita's youngest daughter is married to the president of one of the Big Six Japanese construction contractors. Takeshita's eldest daughter is married to the son of the leader of the construction *zoku*, a group of forty of the most influential Japanese politicians with close ties to the construction industry. Takeshita's half brother is married to the daughter of the founder of the Fukuda Construction Company, one of the largest contractors in Japan. Former deputy cabinet secretary Ichiro Ozawa is married to another daughter of the founder of Fukuda Construction. Former Prime Minister Yasuhiro Nakasone's daughter is married to the heir apparent of Kajima Construction, Japan's largest contractor.

It is hardly surprising that the American construction industry has difficulty penetrating this clubby network.

The maze of family relationships found in the construction industry is not unique; it is the Japanese way, and it pervades the entire Japanese economy.

Most Japanese politicians, bureaucrats, and business leaders are also connected through one of the most exclusive alumni associations in the world: they are graduates of Tokyo University (Todai). More than 88 percent of the high-ranking bureaucrats in Japan's powerful Ministry of Finance are Todai graduates, as are 76 percent in the Foreign Ministry and 68 percent in the Ministry of Transport. Business is also largely run by Todai graduates. In the mid-1980s, 401 of the CEOs of the largest 1,454 Japanese firms were Todai graduates, and another 212 were graduates of either Kyoto University or Hitotsubashi University. At no time in American history did the Ivy League have such a lock on corporate and governmental power.

There is an extraordinary degree of movement within the Japanese elite between business, government, and politics. In government, only the "top of the class" (those who stay on to become Vice Minister or Vice Minister for International Affairs) retire in their mid-fifties. The rest retire sooner—mid-forties to early fifties. Once administrative officials are retired, many go to work as senior corporate executives in the industries they formerly supervised. The Japanese call this "descending from heaven." Japanese bureaucrats naturally see a close link between their own well-being and that of Japan's corporate interests.

The Recruit affair also revealed the extent to which the elites who govern Japan are caught up in a golden triangle. One leg consists of the top administrators who oversee the various government ministries. Another leg is the Liberal Democratic Party, which has controlled the Japanese Diet since the mid-1950s. The third leg is Japanese business.

Within this power triad, two conflicts prevail. One is internal to each of the legs. The Foreign Ministry, for example, often battles the Ministry of International Trade and Industry (MITI) over control of trade policy, just as the Ministry of Construction often fights the Transport Ministry for control over highway projects. The several factions that comprise the ruling LDP compete with each other for party dominance. Moreover, Japan's economic interests are often at odds with each other, trying to gain the political edge in their economic competition.

Another perpetual power struggle rages between bureaucrats, politicos, and business interests. In the 1960s, the nature of this conflict was transformed by the political rise of Kakuei Tanaka. Tanaka was a complete outsider. He was not educated at one of the elite universities. But he was a natural politician who understood how to collect and use money for political advantage.

Tanaka headed an LDP faction. Like most factions, it was less a crowd bound by political beliefs than a traditional Japanese leader-follower group competing for control of the party. Tanaka's primary role as faction leader was to raise money for his followers and increase their influence in the Diet.

Tanaka devised a new way to accomplish both ends. He urged his parliamentary supporters to develop specialized knowledge in a policy area and to establish close ties with the bureaucracy. The fruit of this strategy is the *zoku giin*, groups of mid-career LDP Dietmen who have or have had formal jurisdiction over policy areas and who maintain strong ties with the relevant agency bureaucrats. Using their political base in the Diet, the *zoku giin* are provided intelligence and political favors by the bureaucrats. Using their close ties to the ministry officials, they are able to obtain favors from the agencies for their private-sector supporters.

Tanaka's faction developed close, rewarding relationships first with the construction industry, and soon thereafter with the posts and telecommunications sectors, commerce and industry, and finance. Other factions within the LDP quickly copied Tanaka's techniques, and money soon poured into their political coffers as well.

What gives the *zoku giin* so much influence is the fact that many of the "*zoku* bosses" now control the key policy committees within the LDP's influential Policy Affairs Research Council (PARC), which advises the LDP leadership on policy and political matters. The chairmen of these committees have a specialized knowledge that often rivals or exceeds that of agency bureaucrats. Because in Japan's parliamentary system the proposals of the ruling LDP become law with little opposition, the decisions of these LDP policy committees are of enormous consequence to business.

.   .   .

Why is the Japanese political system so vulnerable to corruption and excessive business influence? The answer lies in the immense cost of vote gathering and the consequent need of Japanese politicians to raise private funding—not only for political purposes but also simply to carry out their official duties.

For example, the Japanese government gives each member of the Diet only enough funds to hire two or three employees. Since most Diet members need an additional sixteen to eighteen staffers, they are forced to seek money from private donors.

By way of comparison, suppose that U.S. congressmen not only had to raise their campaign funds from private political action committees but also depended upon special interests to pay for their official staff. This is precisely the current situation in Japan. Business buys favors by supplying Japanese politicians with the monies they need to finance their campaigns and to hire staff.

Although U.S. firms contribute heavily to political candidates, their efforts pale in comparison to what Japanese companies give their politicians. In July 1987, for instance, President Reagan held a Republican Party fund-raiser that generated $500,000. It was thought a great success. That very same evening in Tokyo, the Japanese construction industry hosted a gala for Prime Minister Takeshita and his LDP faction that raised $14 million.

Japanese corporations also gain influence with their government through gifts to politicians and bureaucrats. As one Japanese politician explains: "Japan is a gift-giving society. If someone does you a favor, then you are obligated to give a favor in return." The Japanese call this a "friendship gift."

Retiring government officials are often presented with cash gifts by Japanese companies. Van Wolferen reports that "even minor officials such as employees in a local office of a regional construction bureau may receive more than a million yen, and higher officials probably receive rather staggering sums."

In America, this would be considered bribery on a fee scale. Sometimes, the Japanese do draw a line between fund-raising and personal corruption. Two high officials from Japan's allegedly incorruptible bureaucracy were recently arrested for taking money from Recruit while still in office. One—Takashi Kato, the former Vice Minister of Labor— was accused of accepting $55,000 plus a $72,000 loan to buy stock on the basis of insider information.

The line between gifts and bribes in Japan is, at best, fuzzy. Former

Prime Minister Nakasone, for instance, admitted to receiving $300,000 in gifts from Recruit. His successor, Noboru Takeshita, confessed to accepting more than $2 million. Yet neither was arrested or indicted, since the sums were considered to be political contributions. By contrast, the former head of NTT and the two bureaucrats mentioned above were arrested and indicted for accepting the same type of gift. In their cases, the gifts were said to be bribes.

Often, bribes to officials come long after they provide favors—what Americans would call "deferred compensation." Japanese prosecutors report that Recruit offered stock to Vice Minister Kato a year and a half *after* he had blocked the passage of regulations that the company had opposed. Prosecutors alleged that Kato's stock was "intended and received" as payment for his previous action.

The Japanese practice of making delayed payments to officials for favors raises serious questions about the effectiveness of U.S. ethics laws, which allow former government officials to enter into a wide variety of financial arrangements with the Japanese almost immediately upon leaving office.

As a matter of course, the Japanese will try to make the friendship gift "guilt-free" to the recipient. Because giving cash to departing officials of the U.S. government is illegal, Japanese "gifts" often come in the form of one-time contracts for consulting, lobbying, writing a report or a speech—indeed, almost anything—soon after the officials leave office.

Over the past two decades, the Japanese have routinely given friendship gifts to former U.S. officials and members of their families. Most recipients are unaware that their friendship gift is, in effect, a quid pro quo payment for what the Japanese view as prior favors.

Perhaps the best-known friendship gift was Ronald Reagan's 1989 speaking trip to Japan, for which he was paid $2 million to deliver two twenty-minute speeches and appear at some events. One prominent Japanese politician's comment sums up the prevailing Japanese attitude:

> President Reagan protected Japan from the protectionists in Congress and permitted us to export to your market. He is popular with the Japanese people and we wanted him to know how much we appreciated what he had done for our nation.

Japanese Prime Ministers know that they will be unable to keep their public promises to open Japan's markets. They realize that if Japan were to offer real trade reciprocity to other nations, many powerful interest groups would band together to unseat them or, at the least, the delicate balance of power between Japanese agency bureaucrats, politicos, and business interests would be upset. For the Japanese, this is an intolerable prospect. As a result, Japanese trade negotiators cannot respond to other nations' trade concessions in any meaningful way.

In Japan, power is so diffused that no one man—or small group of men—can make a binding decision. Moreover, any position taken by one group (or faction) that damages another is unacceptable.

Because of internal political paralysis, Japan can do almost nothing to break its addiction to protectionist policies and aggressive export drives, regardless of the long-term harm to its relationship with the United States and other nations. Karel van Wolferen notes:

Although there is no convincing reason to suspect that the administrators have worked out a grand master plan for industrial domination of the world, what they are doing has the same effect as if there were such a plan. . . . Japan strives for industrial dominance because power is the only guarantee for safety . . . Hence the continued voracity for foreign market shares and foreign technology.

Japanese mercantilism is possible only because of the tolerance and support of the United States government. Indeed, whenever the European Community and other Asian nations have urged the United States to join them in forcing Japan to provide reciprocal trade concessions, the American government has consistently refused.

Instead of making internal political reforms and offering real trade reciprocity to other nations, Japan has launched a massive global political and propaganda offensive. The goal: to deflect foreign criticism, to insulate Japan from foreign pressures, to maintain the delicate domestic political balance of power, and to strengthen Japanese power and prestige abroad.

The only way that Japan can achieve these goals is by attaining effective political domination over the United States. This is why Japan is spending so much to buy the best legal and lobbying talent in America, to provide assured post-government employment for its American political friends, and to finance a vast cadre of apologists—some ideologues, some academics, some ex-officials, and some simply fast-guns-for-hire.

So far, the Japanese political strategy has been extraordinarily successful. For four decades, Japan has used the United States as its political shield against the world, even as Japanese industries have ravaged their American competitors. Japan has secured most of the de facto advantages of U.S. citizenship for its people and its companies, despite the fact that reciprocal rights are denied Americans in Japan. It was easy to do.

When Japanese businesses came to America in the postwar period, they found a political system far more open, far less Byzantine, and far less competitive than their own. They also discovered a governing bureaucratic elite that was far less worldly than its Japanese counterpart.

As outsiders, the Japanese were prepared to make the extraordinary effort that is required of newcomers in their own society. They were also able to buy the talents and connections of former high-ranking American officials to represent them in Washington. They learned that the price of becoming a political insider in America is a cut-rate bargain compared with similar costs in Japan.

Just as the Japanese have developed a score of products at home and then modified them for export to other countries, they also have refashioned their domestic political style for use in America in some interesting ways.

The Japanese are obsessed with secret intelligence. Secrecy, deceit, camouflage, and betrayal are such an integral part of Japanese politics and business that participants generally assume that there can and will be a vast difference between *tatemae* and *honne*—"the official story" and "the truth." To protect themselves in Japan, companies hire thousands of people to collect and analyze information about everyone connected with the political or economic networks relevant to their businesses.

The Japanese have brought their obsession with intelligence with them to America. Consequently, Japanese political and economic influence in America—as it is in Japan—is underpinned by superb information. Much as the Central Intelligence Agency monitors all that it can about other nations' intentions, the Japanese government and its companies monitor everything they can about the United States and its intentions. A great deal of the information that they collect is public. Some is private. Some is secret.

To collect and make sense of this information, Japan staffs its American political machine with thousands of analysts, advisers, and information gatherers, many of whom are Americans. Much of this intelligence gathering is done by Japanese companies. Herbert E. Meyer, vice chairman of the National Intelligence Council during the Reagan Administration, says that the Japanese trading companies have created a vast overseas information collection system. According to Meyer:

[E]very branch office of every trading company operates like an information vacuum cleaner, sucking in information . . . and even gossip. . . . Some of these trading company operations are substantial; the Mitsubishi intelligence staff in New York takes up two entire floors of a Manhattan skyscraper.

Meyer says that this information is "transmitted daily—sometimes hourly or even by the minute—back to Japan." It is shared with the trading companies' executives, business partners, and the government. Sometimes this information is highly classified. Bob Woodward reports in his book *Veil* that in 1982 the National Security Agency discovered that the Mitsubishi Corporation was sending back to Tokyo classified U.S. documents on the Middle East that it had obtained from an American consulting firm. Mitsubishi was never prosecuted.

A former American executive of a leading Japanese financial house says that Americans are simply too trusting. Gathering intelligence was a basic responsibility of the New York office where he worked, and he would regularly be told by his Tokyo superiors to get detailed, private information about American companies. To do this, someone would be sent to visit the American firm under the pretense that he was preparing a research report for potential Japanese stockholders. The real purpose was industrial espionage. Any information obtained was immediately forwarded to Tokyo, where it was given to the American firm's Japanese competitor—and often to MITI as well.

Normally, the Japanese will assign three or more firms to analyze a single problem or issue. Each firm will be asked to produce its own analysis. Many U.S. observers have commented—rather naïvely—that this redundancy reflects Japanese ineptitude or exploitation by Washington consultants. In reality, the Japanese are seeking the multiple views so they can distinguish between the official and the true story.

Their American intelligence gatherers give the Japanese a clear view of the inside workings of every major federal agency, every major congressional committee, both political parties, most trade associations, and virtually all the influential American think tanks. They also provide a steady stream of inside, advance information (the lifeblood of lobbying) about the personalities, relationships, alliances, conflicts, and organizations that shape events and opinions throughout America.

In 1988, during the final negotiations over trade law reform, a member of the House Ways and Means Committee received a call from the Japanese Embassy about a provision in the just passed Senate bill. It was to be discussed the following day by the Ways and Means Committee.

None of the members of that committee, however, had yet received a copy of the final Senate legislation—though the Japanese obviously had. The embassy had a copy hand-delivered to the congressman.

In late 1988, there was much speculation about who would be named to the position of U.S. Trade Representative. Although Carla Hills's name was never mentioned in the American press during this period, the Japanese knew she was the leading candidate weeks before she was appointed. One week prior to her appointment, a Japanese official bragged to an American friend that "the lady" who would be USTR was "most acceptable" to Japan. Two days before President Bush announced Hills's appointment, a Japanese newspaper broke the story in Tokyo.

What these examples illustrate is that Japan may now have the best political intelligence system in America. Certainly it rivals the information-gathering efforts of the Soviet KGB. It is comprehensive and systematic. It employs thousands of Americans, many of whom have direct access to the most intimate political information of virtually every important organization or network in this country.

This intelligence provides Japan with a powerful political tool. It enables the Japanese to know when, how, and with whom to act. It also accounts for much of Japan's political success in America in recent years.

Much of Japan's political accomplishment in the United States is also due to its success in getting prominent Americans to make its case.

Many of Japan's American spokespersons are academics who depend on Japanese money and access to Japanese institutions to support their careers. Others are American business people, governors, and state and local officials who seek to curry favor and investments by supporting Japan's positions—or by attacking its critics. Most of Japan's advocates, however, are American lawyers and lobbyists.

Dozens of these men and women were once cabinet officers, U.S. trade negotiators, military officials, members of Congress, and congressional staffers. Washington's "Japan Lobby"—super-lawyers, public relations advisers, international trade specialists, political consultants, pollsters, Japan specialists, academics, and free-lance influence peddlers—is now so vast and so well organized that it constitutes a virtual shadow government.

By hiring so many prominent Americans, Japan has ready and often exclusive access to the best expertise on any matter that comes before the U.S. government. Japanese interests have now established a financial relationship with each of the ten largest Washington law firms that specialize in trade matters. Because many of these paid advocates are also advisers to the President, the cabinet, and Congress, Japan is assured that its agenda is always considered in federal policy deliberations.

The employment of so many prominent Americans provides Japan with instant credibility for many of its positions. Few people, for example, ever have the tactlessness to suggest that the policy position of a former USTR, CIA Director, or Secretary of State may be nothing more than paid flackery.

Japan's hiring of Americans gives it effective political insulation against criticism. Just as many academics are reluctant to risk losing funding or vital access by offering real criticism, so do American critics of the Japan Lobby tend to tone down their comments because they are afraid to challenge the prominent, well-connected, and powerful American bankers, academics, and politicians who are Japan's representatives.

Similarly, Japan has muted partisan criticism of its political activities by spreading money generously among Republicans and Democrats. Politicians who question the practices or motives of Japan, and especially the Japan Lobby, automatically challenge key leaders within their own party—something only a few have the courage to do.

Japan now spends so much on lobbyists, consultants, and advisers that it is actually changing the post-government career paths of many federal officials. One former U.S. trade negotiator puts it bluntly:

> When people in government get ready to leave, they know where the money is. It's with the Japanese. Nobody who's looking at an opportunity to make $200,000 or more a year representing a Japanese company is going to go out of their way to hurt them while in office.

Such Japanese largess to political "friends" does not go unnoticed by many officials who are still in office. The Japan Lobby has a name for it: "the demonstration effect."

Although Japan's yearly $400 million expenditure on its American political machine is huge in absolute terms, it is trivial when compared with the annual $50 billion trade surplus that Japan maintains with the United States. Japan's companies send one-third of their exports to America. Its investors own more than $285 billion in American assets and, at present rates of investment, they will own five or ten times that amount within a decade. Japan depends on America to finance its national defense and to be its political protector. For what Japan has at stake, the political influence it buys for only $400 million a year would be a bargain at ten times the price.

. . .

The Japanese play politics for keeps. They stalk, intimidate, and smear their American critics. Clyde Prestowitz reports that after the publication of his book on U.S.-Japan trade relations, *Trading Places*, he was told by his hosts in five different cities that Japan's local consul general had discouraged them from inviting him to be a speaker at their programs.

Another critic who had a serious brush with Japanese intimidation is a recently retired partner in a large U.S. construction-related company. In 1986, he served as the chairman of a construction industry trade association. In that capacity, he testified before the U.S. Senate, urging members to pass legislation that would pry open Japan's closed construction market. Almost immediately, Japan retaliated against his company.

This man's company had a long and honored business relationship with a large Japanese firm. At the time of his testimony, the two companies were involved in a joint project in Latin America. After he testified, the Tokyo government put political pressure on the Japanese firm. The American executive says, "Our Japanese partner told us that, within less than a week of my testimony, they had been called by a senior official from the Japanese government and asked why a Japanese firm was associated with a U.S. firm that was criticizing Japan's policies on construction." In Japan, public contracts are a regular part of the spoils system. So the Japanese government holds life-and-death power over Japanese construction companies.

Very quickly, another senior partner in the U.S. construction firm was contacted by the Japanese. This man responded by asking his colleague to "calm down," which meant, of course, to shut up. Soon, most executives in the U.S. construction industry knew about the incident. The story of Japan's retaliation quickly chilled the American construction industry's public support for the proposed legislation.

Japan's goal, of course, was to stifle American criticism.

As one senior congressional aide notes: "The Japanese government knows that if punishment comes early, is applied sharply, and is well publicized, it will effectively silence most American critics."

The construction executive puts it another way: "It's hard to make a critical comment about Japan without committing business suicide." This goes far in explaining why the American business community in Japan is so reluctant to criticize Japan's closed markets.

The Japanese also bully their critics with smear campaigns. For example, they have few qualms about raising the matter of race whenever they are criticized. Indeed, in a remarkable outburst in April 1988, Hajime Tamura, Japan's powerful Minister of International Trade and Industry, publicly labeled the trade bill sponsored by Senator Lloyd Bentsen and Congressman Dan Rostenkowski (D-Ill.) (and, by implication,

Bentsen and Rostenkowski themselves) "racist." The Japanese know that Americans are quite race-conscious and that an easy way to ensure that an argument, criticism, or critic is ignored is to impute racial prejudice.

The Japanese and their apologists are also quick to vilify their opponents as "Japan bashers." While some Americans use the term in a jocular manner to mean "critic," the connotations in Japan are "racist," "enemy," or "extremist." As an epithet, it is increasingly used as a not so subtle means of discrediting critics and ignoring their criticism. More recently, Japanese spokespersons, including many unwitting Americans, have begun to equate criticism of Japan with McCarthyism.

Intimidation works. Smears of racism, Japan bashing, and McCarthyism are such a potent threat to most thoughtful people that they enforce a pernicious form of self-censorship. Those critics who do speak up are quickly isolated. Companies are reluctant to seek the aid of their government, even when their rights are being violated. Public officials fear that if they are too hard on the Japanese on behalf of American interests, they will lose the chance to make big money working for the Japan Lobby. They might even find themselves shunned by potential American employers who are afraid they could offend Japanese customers by hiring a "Japan basher."

Of all nations, Japan is the most adept at economic diplomacy. It succeeds, in part, because so many senior U.S. political appointees are so inexperienced. But Japan's success is also attributable to the peculiar penchant of American Presidents for "personal diplomacy."

Former Tanaka aide Shigezo Hayasaka observes, "American Presidents seem unable to grasp how little power Japanese Prime Ministers actually have. While personal diplomacy has gained important concessions for Japan, I think that it has done much less for the United States. Naturally, we will engage in personal diplomacy as long as the United States is willing."

During a substantial portion of the eight years of the Reagan Administration, Japan's economic diplomacy was conducted with a special artfulness. It was based on the unusually close friendship that Prime Minister Yasuhiro Nakasone developed with President Ronald Reagan— a friendship so close that it became celebrated as the "Ron-Yasu" relationship.

Time and again, Yasu asked his friend Ron for economic favors. In 1983, for instance, the American machine tool industry filed a petition with the U.S. International Trade Commission (ITC) alleging that the Japanese were selling computer-operated machine tools in America at an unfairly low price, a practice prohibited under international trade agreements. The ITC investigated, found the Japanese guilty as charged, and recommended that the President impose stiff tariff penalties on imported Japanese machine tools.

So Yasu called Ron. He asked him to deny relief to the American machine tool makers. Ron granted Yasu's wish, thereby allowing Japanese machine tool producers to consolidate their hold on the U.S. market.

In 1986, the Department of Transportation issued an order that would have required Japan Air Lines (JAL) to provide data about its cargo flights in the United States. Failure to comply could have resulted in fines, or even a ban on doing business in the United States.

At issue were arbitrary Japanese rules that required American airlines carrying cargo between Japan and Western Europe to unload half their cargo in Anchorage or, alternatively, to carry a reduced load of fuel, which also forced them to stop in Anchorage. Either way, the effect— really, the design—was to ensure that it took longer for U.S. planes to reach their final destinations. Since reciprocal demands were not imposed on JAL by the U.S. government, the Japanese cargo carrier had a strong, though artificial, competitive advantage. So the U.S. Department of Transportation responded with its cargo data requirements.

In April 1986, Yasu phoned Ron. Donald Regan, the President's chief of staff, took the call. Yasu asked Regan to have the airline matter dropped. Regan discussed the issue with Secretary of State George Shultz, whose staff then asked the Department of Transportation to drop the investigation on "foreign policy" grounds. The Transportation Department meekly complied.

By contrast, when Ron asked Yasu for favors on trade, all that he got were seven "market-opening packages" that, in retrospect, produced a tremendous amount of publicity and no noteworthy results.

Japan's diplomatic trump card is America's obsessive concern with the U.S.-Japan "relationship." Repeatedly, the Japanese have elevated contentious bilateral issues into tests of the soundness of "the relationship." Repeatedly, the United States has made political and economic concessions to preserve "the relationship." It is a uniquely Japanese form of brinkmanship. And, invariably, when America goes "eyeball to eyeball" with the Japanese, it is America that blinks. By contrast, there is no evidence that the Japanese have ever made more than a symbolic economic concession for the sake of "the relationship."

The U.S. State Department, which has assumed the role of Guardian of the Relationship, regularly takes Japan's side in trade and economic disagreements between the two nations. And just as regularly, U.S. economic interests are sacrificed on "foreign policy" grounds.

What makes this economic diplomacy so dangerous for American business is the latitude given executive branch officials to make decisions—including the authority to enter into secret trade agreements. Often these secret agreements, usually called "side letters" or "side agreements," are not even reported to the responsible committees of Congress, much less reviewed by them.

Yet these secret agreements can be of enormous consequence to American industry. In the Nixon Administration, a private compact was made with Japan on textiles. In the Carter Administration, one secret trade agreement sharply limited U.S. actions against Japanese television manufacturers who were ravaging American producers; another denied substantial tax benefits to American exporters and ultimately required a major revision of U.S. tax laws on trade. In the Reagan Administration, there were secret stipulations in the semiconductor agreement with Japan and secret provisions in the counterfeiting and piracy pacts signed with Singapore and Korea in the late 1980s.

Interestingly enough, these agreements are kept secret only from American business, Congress, the press, and the American public. They are *not* kept secret from the foreign companies that benefit from them.

In practice, covert diplomacy, inexperienced U.S. negotiators, and the willingness of foreign interests to hire ex-officials can be a deadly mix for American business.

Economic propaganda is a central element of Japan's trade programs. Indeed, one of the basic responsibilities of high-level MITI officials is to create a "cover story" that justifies the exclusion of foreign products from the Japanese market.

Some of Japan's economic propaganda is simply absurd. In 1978, the Japanese government refused to permit imports of American-made blood analyzers because, it asserted, the Japanese have "different" blood. In 1986, foreigners were not allowed to participate in the land reclamation portion of the Kansai Airport project because Japan has "different" dirt. That same year, MITI attempted to prevent American and European ski manufacturers from offering their products in Japan because Japan has "different" snow. In 1987, American garbage disposals were kept out of the Japanese market because Japan has a "different" sewage system. Also that year, American beef imports there were limited because Japanese intestines were longer than those of other people. In 1990, Japan tried to keep out American lumber exports, alleging the wood couldn't withstand Japanese earthquakes—which are "different" from those here.

Japan also excels at spreading disinformation. The FSX episode is a clear example. In 1988, the Pentagon and the State Department agreed to give Japan advanced technology that it would use to build a modified version of the F-16 fighter plane, a mainstay of the U.S. Air Force. In return, some of the work would be done by General Dynamics.

Critics pointed out that Japan had an enormous trade surplus with the United States and could buy a modified F-16 for one-third of what it would cost to build the FSX. Others, including Commerce Secretary Robert Mosbacher, objected to the arrangement because much of the technology being transferred to Japan could speed its entry into the passenger aircraft manufacturing industry—one of the few areas where American companies still have a commanding lead.

Japan's response was to claim that, from the start of the FSX negotiations, it had preferred to proceed on its own and had undertaken the arrangement only at the insistence of the U.S. government. American advocates of the deal echoed this message. Nevertheless, congressional opposition to the FSX deal mounted.

At one point in the spring of 1989, it appeared that opponents of the FSX venture had enough votes in the Senate to kill it. Japan quickly announced that if the United States Congress rejected the FSX agreement, it would seek a similar arrangement with European manufacturers. What this revealed, of course, was that Japan desperately wanted the FSX. It wanted the technology and it needed the know-how that experienced U.S. aerospace firms had. Technology is useless without know-how. Japan had been playing a game familiar to every American child: "Don't throw me in that briar patch!"

Japan is equally skillful at getting Americans to discredit those who criticize Japan. Clyde Prestowitz recalls that in the summer of 1989 he was approached by a Japanese diplomat who noted how sad it was that Prestowitz was being labeled a "Japan basher." The official suggested that Prestowitz try to diffuse such accusations by writing an article that criticized the views of Dutch journalist Karel van Wolferen, another chronicler of the trade tensions between America and Japan. The Japanese official offered to publicize the article and actually sent a newscaster from NHK, Japan's version of the BBC, to see Prestowitz. Prestowitz told the journalist he would have nothing to do with this divide-and-conquer technique.

That same summer, Alan Webber, managing editor of the *Harvard Business Review*, was approached by an American official in Tokyo who lamented how "the Gang of Four" were destroying the U.S.-Japan "relationship." The U.S. official suggested that Webber's publication go after these Japan bashers—after all, he said, something had to be done by responsible publications. "The Gang of Four," of course, were Prestowitz and van Wolferen, as well as the University of California's Chalmers Johnson, a historian of MITI and Japanese trade policy, and *Atlantic Monthly* writer James Fallows, based in Tokyo at the time, who had recently criticized Japan's industrial policies in articles and speeches.

In other words, the Japanese are as skilled at politics as they are at building world-class products. Their political skills have been honed in a fiercely competitive atmosphere, where rivals systematically use political influence, often corruptly, to gain the economic edge. And they have brought those skills and attitudes with them to America. As the following chapters will document, these skills, and the corruption they frequently produce, have been as indispensable to Japan's economic success as the quality of its products.

Japanese money politics works so well in America because so many prominent Washingtonians can be hired so easily. And all they ask in return is that people not pay too much attention to the source of their prosperity.

And just what is that source? Individual and corporate American taxpayers, for sure. But increasingly, much of it flows from foreign interests that employ thousands of lobbyists and advisers. In 1987 alone, registered foreign lobbyists officially reported receipts of more than $402 million from their foreign clients. The actual amount is, without question, many times that. Foreign political money is now a major force in the Washington economy.

2.
JAPANESE
LOBBYING

Chapter Four

WASHINGTON'S REVOLVING DOOR

WASHINGTON TODAY is reminiscent of London in the 1930s. The British writer Robert Byron spoiled many of his social relationships because of his fierce opposition to the policies of Nazi Germany. At elegant dinner parties in London, Byron would look at a man who was attempting to defend the appeasement policies of the Chamberlain government and ask in a loud, clear voice, "Are you in German pay?"

Though Byron's dinner invitations dried up, the social principle of his time has endured. As it was considered rude to suggest that a British gentleman might be in the service of the Germans, so it is also considered rude to suggest that the position of a distinguished American political figure, journalist, academic, or former federal official might reflect the fact that he is in the pay of the Japanese, the Koreans, the Greeks, the French, or some other foreign interest. As one Washingtonian says: "We prefer tidy dinner parties."

Consequently, Washington has learned to live by its own special rules, and one of the most important of these rules is simply this: you cannot impugn the motive behind someone's argument, only the argument itself. In today's Washington, it is considered bad form, even rude, to question someone's argument on the basis of his or her employment.

By hiring prominent Americans, foreign interests buy instant credibility for their positions. Just as children tend to believe the athletes who endorse cereals, public officials tend to believe their former colleagues. While adults know that athletes are paid to promote products, those in power are often unaware that the words of ex-officials represent little more than skillful, well-paid ventriloquism by foreign interests.

Unfortunately, dinner parties are not the only occasions where political

motives and employment go unidentified. By law, those who represent
foreign interests must register with the Justice Department. They must
attach a copy of their most recent registration statements to any testimony
they give before Congress. Yet an informal Department survey reveals
that fewer than 2 percent actually do so.

Washington's unquestioning acceptance of ex-officials' pronounce-
ments gives a sharp political advantage to the foreign interests for whom
they work. It allows these interests to befog an issue, raise doubts, and
delay or even prevent changes in American trade policy—including those
that are clearly in America's national interest.

Equally significant, government positions are now being filled by a
cadre of well-connected insiders who constantly shift back and forth
between officialdom and a more lucrative life as registered foreign agents.
For many, public service on behalf of American interests is simply a
sabbatical from their more permanent career as agents of influence for
foreign interests.

These ex-officials are highly effective in representing foreign clients
because they possess a special, intimate knowledge of the inside workings
of America's trade, investment, and related economic strategies. They
also have privileged access to friends, former colleagues, and former
subordinates who continue to hold high government office.

These ex-officials often provide their foreign clients with invaluable
insights during trade negotiations. They are even more useful as agents
of influence when U.S. trade negotiators are unaware that they are involved in the negotiations process. During the 1989 U.S.-Korea telecommunications trade negotiations in Seoul, for instance, U.S. officials ac-
cidentally found out that the government-to-government talks were being
monitored secretly by American attorney Terrence J. Fortune, until 1983
a State Department legal adviser and now an adviser to Korean interests.
During a break in the talks, U.S. negotiator Gordana Earp left the room
to look for an empty office in which to make a phone call. What she
found instead was Fortune in an office fitted with a one-way mirror that
overlooked the negotiation room. She also discovered that the Koreans
were secretly taping the sessions from the same room.

Because of their expertise, ex-officials are regularly sought out by the
media, where they can advance their clients' positions by writing editorial
pieces, appearing on television, and debating policy matters. When they
do so, they generally are identified as knowledgeable former government
officials—rarely as paid foreign agents.

A brief example. When Elliot Richardson appeared on the national
television program *It's Your Business* in April 1988, he was addressed
throughout the show as "Mr. Ambassador." His comments on the many

benefits of growing foreign investment in this country were accorded the respect due to one who was Ambassador to Great Britain, who has held three cabinet posts, and who has served in a score of other high-level government positions. Never mentioned was the fact that Richardson now represents other, very different interests—those of the Association for International Investment (AFII), for whom he is general counsel.

No one seriously questions whether ex-officials or others have the right to lobby or whether foreign interests have the right to be represented in Washington. The real issue is the nature of this representation and its effects on America's policymaking and political autonomy. At bottom, the issue is the same one addressed by James Madison in *Federalist* paper No. 10, which spells out the danger of the "mischiefs of factions"—organized groups whose common passions are "adverse to the rights of other citizens or to the permanent and aggregate interests of the community [nation]."

In Madison's day, the mischiefs of factions came primarily from domestic interests. Now they come from overseas as well.

America's top international and trade experts are becoming other nations' top advisers. Two of the six ex-Secretaries of State did work for foreign interests after they left office. Edmund Muskie, Secretary of State in the Carter Administration, has lobbied on behalf of Canadian and British clients. Another former Secretary of State, Henry Kissinger, heads an international consulting firm that has advised businessmen from Japan, Korea's giant Daewoo conglomerate, Fiat of Italy, and a Delaware-registered limited partnership that makes investments in China, among many others. (For whatever reason, Kissinger keeps his client list a closely guarded secret.)

Many other former senior officials of the State Department now staff Japan's American political machine. Virtually all these diplomats turned foreign agents reached public office through partisan politics—campaign work, financial contributions, or both; relatively few came up through the ranks of the Foreign Service. (See Appendix A.)

For many years, the Defense Department has been criticized for allowing a revolving door to operate between the military and U.S. defense contractors. What has received almost no attention, however, is the growing number of former Pentagon officials who sign up as advisers and who register as foreign agents for Japan and other countries.

For the six years that Richard Perle was Assistant Secretary of Defense for International Affairs, he had important influence over U.S. military assistance to Turkey, which receives some $600 million annually in such aid. In May 1988, one year after leaving office, Perle met with the Turkish Prime Minister and negotiated a contract for a new company he had conceived, International Advisers, Inc. The job: help Turkey acquire U.S. military and economic assistance. The fee to Perle's company was $875,000 a year for at least two years.

Retiring admirals and generals are also racing through the revolving door between public service and foreign lobbying. Among them: Admiral Daniel Murphy, onetime chief of staff to Vice President George Bush, has lobbied for Turkey and Morocco. Former Air Force generals Kelly Burke, Guy Hecker, and Thomas Stafford have formed a lobbying firm; among their clients is Japan's giant Sumitomo Corporation. One of the best-connected former military officers who have become Japan advisers is General William Dyke, commander of the U.S. Army in Japan until 1988. Dyke's wife was a national security adviser to George Bush when he was Vice President. She is now a White House staff member on the National Security Council. After Dyke retired in 1988, he was hired by Mitsubishi Heavy Industries (Japan's leading defense company) and Nissan. Mitsubishi executives say they rely on Dyke to provide "general advice" on a variety of matters. In late 1989, journalist Gene Marlowe reported that Nissan had hired Dyke to help it get access to technology for a multiple-launching rocket system developed by the U.S. firm LTV.

Naturally, Japan and other foreign interests most want ex-trade officials to advise and represent them on trade matters. As a result, the revolving door spins so fast, so frequently, and with such force that it has virtually incapacitated the agencies that spew forth these ex-officials.

In theory, the Office of the U.S. Trade Representative (USTR) is responsible for developing and coordinating U.S. trade policy and for leading trade negotiations. It sits in the Executive Office of the President, where its staff can coordinate the trade activities of the other departments of the federal government. Though the office is staffed by career trade specialists, it is headed by political appointees—the USTR, three deputies, and a general counsel. Since the inception of this office in the early 1960s, its top tier has been regularly depleted by the revolving door.

Between 1973 and 1990, one-third of the USTR officials who held principal trade positions left to become registered foreign agents. Of these, most did work for Japan. Half (four of eight) of those who served as the USTR later became lobbyists for foreign concerns. Of these, three went to work for Japan. All but two of those who served as the Office's general counsel—America's top trade lawyer—hired out as foreign agents when they left. Again, most worked for Japan.

In 1989, the top three American trade positions—the USTR and the two senior deputy USTRs—went to people who were working for Japanese and other foreign interests. Each was once a high-ranking federal official. Each represented overseas concerns after leaving government. Each spun the revolving door full circle by reentering public office. If history is a guide, moreover, one or more of the three will again represent foreign interests when they leave public office.

Carla Hills, the President's choice to be America's top trade negotiator, had been an Assistant Attorney General in the Nixon Administration and was HUD Secretary under Gerald Ford. In the mid-1980s, she worked as a registered foreign agent for Daewoo, a Korean conglomerate that makes autos, steel, ships, electronics, and heavy machinery and operates a major bank and construction company. In the late 1980s, Hills also lobbied for two Canadian timber companies. Just prior to entering office as the USTR, she was providing business and legal advice to Japan's Matsushita Corporation. Her husband is Roderick Hills, who represented C. Itoh, one of Japan's largest trading companies, when it was caught up in the Toshiba affair.

President Bush chose Julius Katz to be one of two senior Deputy USTRs. Prior to being named Hills's deputy, Katz, a former Assistant Secretary of State for Economic Affairs in the Nixon Administration, was head of the well-connected Government Research Corporation (GRC), a Washington-based public affairs firm, whose clients included the Japanese government, Hitachi, and Toyota.

As the other Washington Deputy USTR, Bush chose S. Linn Williams, a former general counsel at the Overseas Private Investment Corporation (OPIC), to focus on U.S.-Japan trade. His immediate prior position was representing Japanese clients as the partner who opened the Tokyo office of Gibson, Dunn & Crutcher, one of Los Angeles' largest law firms and a major firm representing Japanese interests.

The revolving door is only one of several ways that Japanese and other foreign interests acquire personal ties to the Office of the U.S. Trade Representative. They also maintain important connections through political insiders. For instance, Stanton Anderson was a senior White House and State Department official in the 1970s. Subsequently, he became one of Japan's top lobbyists. After the 1980 election, he directed the economics portion of the transition team that staffed the Reagan Administration.

In July 1985, after Clayton Yeutter was named USTR, lobbyists with foreign ties were responsible for organizing and staffing the USTR's Of-

fice. The three-person transition team consisted of Julius Katz, James
Lake, and William Walker. At the time, Katz was an international business consultant. Lake, a prominent Republican lobbyist, had been press
adviser to Reagan's 1984 campaign (as he had been in 1976 and 1980,
and would be for George Bush in 1988). Walker, another well-known
lobbyist, was President Ford's Deputy USTR. Less than a month after
the Republicans regained the White House in 1981, Walker had registered as a foreign agent. Among the clients he subsequently represented
were Toshiba, the Electronics Industries Association of Japan, the Hong
Kong Trade Department, the Korea Iron and Steel Association, the China
National Textiles Import & Export Association, and the Japan Aluminum
Federation.

In mid-1985, the Katz-Lake-Walker team took up their task, identi-
fying the people Yeutter would appoint to senior policy posts. They
interviewed those individuals who already held high negotiating and staff
positions. They proposed a reorganization of the Office that would have
eliminated virtually all these people, many of whom were hard-liners on
Japan, but the White House vetoed this controversial move. In the
meantime, the team got an intimate look at the innermost thinking,
strategy making, and vulnerabilities (e.g., personnel conflicts) of America's top trade agency.

One former employee at USTR recalls: "The way the transition was
handled was very uncomfortable for all of us. We knew that their decisions
would affect our careers. Because of their friendship with Clayton, we
also knew that we would be forced to see these lobbyists again many
times after the transition was over." How right he was.

Walker minimized the benefits of having served on the Yeutter transition team. He told the Baltimore *Sun* that it "was 'irrelevant' to any
dealings I might have with the Trade Office. I've had access to Clayton
for five years. Sure it's an advantage. . . . As with anything in Washington,
if you know people it's easier to do business with them."

By contrast, Lake spoke with the Washington *Post*'s Stuart Auerbach
in 1986 about the advantages of his access to Yeutter: "The Japanese
sought me out. Did I think it was odd? No. They knew I was a friend
of Clayton Yeutter. The Japanese work very hard to figure out who has
access and who can communicate their views." The views he chose to
communicate were those of Mitsubishi, Suzuki, the Japan Auto Parts
Industries Association, and the Japan Tobacco Institute.

Lake understated his access to Yeutter. The two had worked together
for many years. More important, Lake is one of Clayton Yeutter's closest
friends and advisers. Interviews and Lake's telephone logs reveal that
the two men spoke on the phone most days at 7:15 a.m. One former

USTR official said that "the staff constantly had to fight against Lake. Clayton was always saying, 'But Jim says this,' or 'Jim says that.' " This official adds that Lake was so involved in the USTR's work that he "was like an unpaid staffer."

The problem, of course, was that Lake *was* paid—but by the Japanese.

The Japanese scythe has also swept through the International Trade Commission (ITC), a little-known but important trade agency. The ITC advises the President and Congress about dumping, foreign subsidies, and the economic consequences of various policy choices. It also helps the Commerce Department calculate the level of tariffs placed on subsidized imports and on imports sold in the United States below their overseas cost of production.

Over the past two decades, many former ITC commissioners have become foreign agents. The most visible incident involved Daniel Minchew, ITC chairman during the late 1970s. While still serving on the ITC, Minchew, an ex-lobbyist for the government of Japan, negotiated a contract to represent Japanese business interests. The Japanese established a special organization to hire him. Unfortunately, Minchew's career as a foreign agent was cut short when he was sent to prison for crimes previously committed while working for Senator Herman Talmadge (D-Ga.).

Despite the public flap about Minchew and the revolving door, several other ITC commissioners have gone on to become foreign agents. Between 1973 and 1990, for example, six of the thirteen ITC commissioners who left this quasi-judicial, independent federal agency went to work as either foreign agents or advisers to foreign companies. Of these, three went to work for firms that represented the Japanese. (See Appendix A.)

The revolving door has done particular damage to the credibility of the Commerce Department. While the USTR is responsible for formulating and coordinating U.S. trade policy, the Commerce Department's International Trade Administration (ITA) is responsible for administering it. The ITA promotes U.S. exports, provides most of the basic data used to make federal policies on trade matters, and assists domestic companies that are hurt by imports.

The ITA is headed by an under secretary. In the 1980s, two of the four people who held this key trade post went to work for the Japanese after leaving office. Robert Herzstein, who served in the Carter Administration, was subsequently hired as an attorney by Komatsu, the Japanese construction equipment giant. Lionel Olmer, who served in the first Reagan Administration, later was taken on as an economic and political adviser for Nippon Telegraph and Telephone. Herzstein's and Olmer's post-government careers are hardly the exception for top ITA officials. Of the nineteen senior ITA officials who left the Department in the 1980s, nine later registered as foreign agents. Of these, Japan hired seven. (See Appendix A.)

Former ITA officials are invaluable acquisitions for foreign firms. Not only do they carry the standard clout and access keys of ex-officials; they also possess a special inside appreciation of the workings and strategies of American industry. ITA officials receive the Commerce Department's special industry analyses, the confidential reports of the private industry advisory councils, and classified information from the intelligence agencies. In complex trade negotiations, some companies even share their secret plans with ITA officials.

The movement of ITA officials through the revolving door onto foreign payrolls has often been disturbingly swift. In the early 1980s, Olmer, as head of the ITA, led U.S. efforts to open the Japanese telecommunications market to U.S. suppliers. Better than any other official in the federal government, he knew the capacities and strategies of American telecommunications companies. Olmer left ITA in the spring of 1985. That fall, he became an adviser to the chairman of Nippon Telegraph and Telephone, the company that controlled Japan's closed telecommunications market.

Also in the early 1980s, William Morris was the assistant secretary in ITA responsible for increasing U.S. exports. Soon after leaving office, Morris signed up to head Global USA, a newly formed company that represented several major Japanese companies. While representing Japanese interests, he also served on President Reagan's Commission on Industrial Competitiveness, where he chaired the task force on trade policy.

In 1986, Walter Lenahan, the principal Commerce Department negotiator in ongoing textile negotiations, resigned on Friday, February 7. On Monday, February 10, he went on the payroll of Mudge, Rose, Guthrie, Alexander & Ferdon—the law firm that represented Hong Kong in these same negotiations.

In 1986 and 1987, one of the principal trade negotiations between Japan and the United States dealt with increasing Japan's purchases of automobile components from American suppliers. One of the key U.S. negotiators on this issue was H. P. Goldfield, Assistant Secretary of Commerce for Trade Development, who was responsible for these talks and also those on the Kansai Airport in 1986. Goldfield left office in the midst of the negotiations. Later, he went to work for a law firm where he became a foreign agent for Korean interests.

Once Goldfield left, the leadership for the talks went to his deputy. He was Deputy Assistant Secretary of Commerce Robert Watkins, who repeatedly resisted congressional pressure to take a firm approach in these talks. Later, Watkins actually solicited a job from Japanese auto parts manufacturers while he was still on the U.S. government's payroll.

Watkins' attempt to go through the revolving door was discovered and widely condemned, and he resigned. Later, he too became a paid adviser to Korean automakers. Another senior official of the Commerce Department during the negotiations—Clarence ("Bud") Brown, the Deputy Secretary and former Republican congressman from Ohio—became a lobbyist for Honda in the spring of 1989.

As Clyde Prestowitz notes of these brash attempts to cash in with the Japanese: "These are examples of a game that is sometimes played far more subtly at even higher levels and for much higher and more lucrative stakes."

The revolving door threatens not only the integrity of government institutions but also the viability of government compacts. One such compact is the landmark U.S.-Canada Free Trade Agreement (FTA), signed in 1988.

To oversee the FTA and resolve any disputes that may arise, the two countries created a bilateral commission. The FTA itself establishes procedures for the timely, nonbinding resolution of most disputes. If both parties agree, the commission can settle a dispute through binding arbitration. Most important, the treaty provides a binational mechanism to settle anti-dumping and countervailing duty disputes. In these matters, the findings of the commission are binding and cannot be appealed.

There are two key features to the dispute-settlement process. First, all decisions of the commission must be unanimous. Second, commission findings are "normally" to be based on the findings of panelists chosen to review the disputes. The selection of these panelists is of enormous consequence, not only to those involved in the disputes but also to the function of the basic agreement. So the two countries created a strict selection process. Panels will consist of five experts. Two must be Canadian citizens and two must be U.S. citizens. The fifth will be chosen by the other four. All panelists are expected to serve in their capacity as "experts," and not as representatives of either government.

In the spring of 1989, the U.S. government identified a pool of twenty-five American trade experts from which it would select these panelists.

Of the twenty-five, fourteen are either registered foreign lobbyists or senior partners in law firms that represent foreign interests. Together, these fourteen experts and their firms represented forty foreign companies from seventeen countries and the Commission of the European Community. Among the companies they represented, two were Canadian-owned; most of the others did business in Canada.

The selection of the pool of panelists suggests that America has few trade experts other than lobbyists or those in foreign pay.

While every President brings to his administration a few outstanding individuals, many of the second- and third-tier jobs in federal trade and economic policymaking are filled on the basis of political spoils and personal connections. Over the past two decades, a large number of positions at the level of deputy secretary, under secretary, assistant secretary, and deputy assistant secretary have been filled by people who are inexperienced, out of work, on their way to something better, or tightly bound to partisan ideology. Many have never worked in government or business; few have been involved in negotiations of any sort. While some are competent and energetic, most are, as Harvard professor Raymond Vernon observes, "tyros who need substantial exposure before they can make use of the empty desks and file cabinets they encounter when they take office."

A less charitable Washington insider says:

Many of America's appointed trade officials have taken no more interest in the substance of trade policy than Vanna White takes in solving the riddles on *Wheel of Fortune*. She just smiles, turns over the letters, and takes the money. They just smile, flip the pages of their briefing books, and cultivate a list of potential foreign clients.

The average tenure for these political appointees is roughly eighteen months. Most depart before they learn the intricacies of their positions. And a substantial portion leave to become lobbyists for foreign interests.

Certainly not all appointees have taken this career path. But hundreds have. And the revolving door through which they travel has seriously damaged the conduct and credibility of America's trade policymaking. It guarantees that there is little or no institutional memory in America's trade policymaking agencies. Predictably, Japan and other countries exploit this ignorance and the resulting lack of continuity and consistency.

Equally important, the shuffling between public office and private positions shortens the government careers of U.S. trade negotiators. Few of them have the time to develop a long-term perspective on American policy. While many "short-termers" are anxious to make a name for themselves before they go on to something better, virtually none remain long enough to complete international trade negotiations that may stretch over many years.

This impatience often allows other governments to extract unwarranted concessions from their American counterparts. If they get a tough U.S. negotiator, they can simply wait until a replacement arrives. With the rapid turnover in high government posts, this generally does not take long.

In the mid-1980s, for instance, the hard-won U.S.-Japan Semiconductor Agreement committed Japan to increase foreign chip makers' share of the Japanese market to slightly more than 20 percent by 1991. But once Japan signed the agreement, the political pressure was off. Predictably, the Japanese dragged their feet in fulfilling their part of the bargain. What they knew from years of experience was that those who negotiated the agreement would soon leave office, maybe even go to work for them. New faces in Washington would mean either new policies or a lack of enthusiasm for enforcing the old policies devised by their predecessors.

The Japanese strategy was soon rewarded. In October 1989, the new U.S. Trade Representative, Carla Hills, in effect canceled the Semiconductor Agreement on her first official trip to Tokyo. Although she urged the Japanese to live up to their obligations, she pointedly noted that she had not signed the agreement and did not philosophically support the type of trade targets the agreement called for. She also publicly stated that in negotiations with Japan the United States is interested in "process, not results."

The revolving door also creates doubts about the trustworthiness of American trade officials and U.S. trade processes. One former Japanese Embassy official says that when former U.S. officials come to them looking for a job, they are often expected to prove their worth by bringing "golden nuggets"—inside information that may be of use to the Japanese.

Journalist James Fallows reports that in 1989 two recently departed Commerce Department officials went to Tokyo looking for business. To woo clients, they offered to help Japanese companies circumvent the very regulations they had written while in office. Whether they deliberately wrote loopholes into the law in expectation of their future earnings potential can never be known. But the very fact that these former officials offered themselves to the Japanese in this way undermines American confidence in the integrity of U.S. trade policymaking and administration.

Because of this sort of incident, many U.S. companies, such as those in the semiconductor industry, are now unwilling to share information with their own government, lest it fall into the eager hands of foreign competitors. Many executives from U.S. auto parts companies, for instance, remain bitter that Robert Watkins, the lead American negotiator in the U.S.-Japan auto parts talks, offered his services to the Japanese even before the negotiations had been concluded. Some companies that shared proprietary information about their plans with the Commerce Department's industry advisory committees say they will never do so again. This loss of confidence cripples the industry advisory system that is supposed to provide federal policymakers the perspectives they need to formulate and negotiate American trade policy.

Finally, the revolving door is creating a cadre of officials whose views on trade matters have been shaped largely by their advocacy on behalf of Japan and other foreign interests. Longtime Washington attorney Harry McPherson explains it best: "Most lobbyists are not born with a position on catalytic converters. In developing the argument for their client's position, they often convince themselves of its truth."

McPherson's point is that many foreign agents actually come to believe what they have been paid to say. What makes this self-seduction so dangerous is that the revolving door has now come full circle in many instances. Indeed, as Appendix A documents, many government officials turned foreign agents now have returned to government—this time as America's top policymakers.

By hiring ex-officials, Japan acquires several important political advantages. One of the most important is regular, unrestricted access to American leaders. Washington's network of influence—based on a fraternity of professional credentials, political appointments, and social relationships—is composed primarily of former government officials who move effortlessly between public office and private advocacy. The revolving door is their stock-in-trade: it is their livelihood.

Most are members of the interlocking networks from which any Administration draws its policymaking team. Top foreign policy jobs, for example, are usually filled by people deemed acceptable to the Council on Foreign Relations. The Council of Economic Advisers is normally drawn from the ranks of academic economists. Key players at the Treasury Department come from the financial community. The defense and military communities provide most top Pentagon appointees. Trade officials come from a small circle of politicians, lawyers, lobbyists, and trade experts. The Commerce Department is often headed by a major political fund-raiser from corporate America.

Foreign firms witnessed the power of "access plus" in February 1988, at the founding dinner of the Association for International Investment (AFII). The dinner's keynote speaker was none other than James A. Baker 3rd, then Secretary of the Treasury. While most of the best established American trade groups lack the clout to secure the Treasury Secretary as their dinner speaker, Baker's appearance at the AFII dinner reflected his long-standing relationship with Elliot Richardson, AFII's founder: Baker served under Richardson in the Ford Administration, when Richardson was Secretary of Commerce.

Japanese and other foreign interests penetrate the influence networks of Washington in many ways. The easiest and most common method is simply to pay for this access. The only thing that varies in such arrangements is the form in which the foreign money is accepted.

Generally, the insider is hired as a lobbyist. To spare the individual the embarrassment of having to formally register as a "foreign agent," overseas interests can hire him as a "consultant" instead. More recently, the Japanese have found another canny way to accomplish the same goal: putting Washington insiders on the "advisory boards" of their firms and government agencies.

The Japanese also penetrate Washington influence networks by placing American insiders on the boards of their U.S. subsidiaries and foundations. A new wrinkle is to give American insiders an equity position in a business deal, or pay them to be the deal's broker. Thus, Japan swaps equity for influence.

The Japanese also put potential critics on their payrolls. Many ex-officials who would never consider lobbying or advising the Japanese on political matters readily agree to advise them on issues ranging from labor-management relations to the arts. Similar arrangements are sometimes made for spouses and children. Often, all these people do is open doors for the Japanese to friends who serve in the government. But what these people actually accomplish is frequently less important to the Japanese than the fact that they are on Japan's payroll—and will be inclined to keep any criticisms they may have of Japan to themselves. In short, Japan rewards its friends and suborns the silence of its critics.

Japan has bought so much "access plus" in Washington that it has become a major force in staffing the executive branch. The White House personnel office regularly seeks advice from experts and political friends about whom to appoint to various positions. Many of the people who advise the personnel office are on Japan's payroll, and naturally these operatives suggest their own friends—many of whom are a part of their own network of influence—for the coveted appointments.

Because of Japan's "access plus" in Washington, the government of Japan has superior intelligence about America's intentions, strengths, weaknesses, and negotiating strategies. One foreign lobbyist estimates that at least 80 percent of what he and others do is collect and analyze information for their foreign bosses. Like the others, his job is to identify the right thing to say to the right person at the right time.

He says that he and his colleagues

provide answers to such basic questions as "Who are the decision makers?," "Who is for or against various policy options?," "What are the political pressure points, and who can press them?," "What tactics and arguments should be used?," "When should foreign officials be brought in to speak to U.S. officials?," and "What is the most persuasive way for them to argue their case?"

What makes ex-officials so useful at intelligence gathering is their unique insights about the agencies where they once worked. Even when these ex-officials cannot obtain inside information, they can often pick up enough hints to make well-informed guesses. More recently, Japanese companies have begun to hire many key technical experts from America's trade agencies. This provides still more useful information and, not incidentally, sows subtle doubts about the integrity of American negotiators.

For example, in the midst of the 1990 U.S.-Japan talks on high-technology trade, Fujitsu, Ltd., the Japanese electronics company, hired David Olive, the State Department's principal expert on the substance of these negotiations. Olive had helped draft State Department position papers, attended interagency meetings, had access to confidential information shared by American companies, and knew the American negotiating strategy. Olive's new job was the number two position in Fujitsu's Washington office, where he would follow trade and economic issues in America, Canada, and Western Europe. According to a knowledgeable USTR official who worked with him, Olive knew the government's bottom-line trade position on such critical high-technology industries as semiconductors, telecommunications, and supercomputers. R. Michael Gadbaw, a Washington lawyer for the semiconductor industry, told the Washington *Post* that companies are now "reluctant to give the U.S. government basic data because it will go right to the Japanese."

Because they hire so many senior insiders and coordinate their collection of information, the Japanese actually have a better overview of what is happening in the federal government than all but a handful of those who serve in the Administration. The Japanese also end up knowing more than any of their lobbyists, consultants, or advisers do individually. Japan's inside track allows its firms and organizations to short-circuit U.S. government decisions long before most people in the bureaucracy even know that something is afoot.

Chapter Five

JAPAN
BUYS
WASHINGTON

JAPAN'S RISE from a defeated nation after World War II into a political superpower in America occurred in three distinct stages. The first was the immediate postwar occupation when Japanese interests in America were primarily represented by leading Americans with long-standing relationships with Japan and, ironically, the U.S. Departments of State and Defense. The second began in the early 1970s when Japan began to hire well-connected Washington, D.C., insiders as lobbyists and advisers. The final stage got underway in the late 1970s when Japan began to monitor Congress, hire ex-members of Congress and their staffs, and establish its broad-based, grass-roots political network.

The modern Japan Lobby traces its origin to the American occupation and General Douglas MacArthur's efforts to demilitarize and democratize Japan. Soon after he arrived in 1945, he purged the militarists and the ultranationalists from the ranks of government, gave women the right to vote, wrote a constitution that banned war, and initiated a short-lived but nevertheless modern union movement.

Within months of his arrival, MacArthur began a program to break up Japan's *zaibatsu*—the family-owned super-conglomerates that dominated Japan's prewar economy and fueled its militaristic and imperial ambitions. He ordered Mitsui, Mitsubishi, Sumitomo, and Yasuda (the four largest of the *zaibatsu*) to prepare for their breakup, and he ousted the *zaibatsu* families from their companies. MacArthur also conducted war trials. As part of that process, his staff identified those Japanese businessmen who were to be charged and tried for war crimes.

By the spring of 1947, MacArthur's staff had prepared a comprehensive plan to break up 300 massive Japanese companies that controlled more than 75 percent of Japan's economy. Nineteen hundred business executives at these companies were slated for punishment for war crimes. MacArthur's strategy was to build a democratic, capitalistic Japanese society by selling the *zaibatsu* companies to their workers, thereby creating what would have been the largest employee stock ownership program in history.

But MacArthur neglected to consider the clout of U.S. banks and U.S. companies with extensive holdings in Japan. He also forgot the long-standing relationships between the economic and cosmopolitan elites in the two countries. Mitsui, for example, had first done business in the United States when Ulysses Grant was President. Many leading Japanese politicians and industrialists had lived in and been educated in America.

U.S. banks had made prewar loans to Japanese corporations, and many U.S. companies were owed reparations and royalties. American investors saw lucrative opportunities to make Japan into the "workshop of Asia." Reparations, royalties, investments, future plans, and long-established business relationships all would be threatened if the *zaibatsu* were broken up, Japan's business elite purged, and old relationships destroyed.

Less than eighteen months after the occupation began, a loose confederation of American bankers, industrialists, and "old Japanese hands" from the State Department joined with their allies among Japan's elite and began an assault on MacArthur's proposed reforms. The umbrella organization for this effort was the American Council on Japan (ACJ), which was unofficially created in mid-1947 and formally established in June 1948 at the Harvard Club in Manhattan. The ACJ offered itself to the U.S. government as a group of informed Americans available to advise it on policies toward Japan.

The ACJ's principal organizers were Harry F. Kern, the foreign editor of *Newsweek*, Compton Pakenham, *Newsweek*'s Tokyo bureau chief, and James Lee Kauffman, a prominent New York lawyer who represented U.S. interests in Japan. Another founding member and an honorary cochairman was Joseph. Clark Grew, America's Ambassador to Japan from 1932 to 1941 and Under Secretary of State at the end of World War II. Historian Howard Schonberger writes that most of the ACJ backers "operated largely behind-the-scenes and often without acknowledgement of their affiliation with the ACJ."

Grew, Kern, and their associates had access to all the leading figures in the Truman Administration. They also had important links with the National Association of Manufacturers and the U.S. Chamber of Commerce, two of America's largest business organizations.

For the men of the ACJ, access was critical. Fortunately for them, it was a sure thing. At the time of the council's formation, America's foreign policy was tightly controlled by some of the ACJ's closest allies: a few American companies with international operations, a few wealthy families like the Harrimans, and a small cadre of wealthy men from Wall Street. Then Secretary of Commerce Averell Harriman was a principal in the investment firm Brown Brothers, Harriman. Harriman's banking partner was Robert Lovett, who was also Under Secretary of State. The Secretary of Defense was James Forrestal, a major figure at the investment bank of Dillon Reed. Harriman's sister, Mary Harriman Rumsey, was, with Vincent Astor, an owner of *Newsweek*.

Using Kern as the voice and *Newsweek* as the medium, the ACJ began its public attack on MacArthur's economic dissolution plans in June 1947. Kern wrote a widely circulated article claiming that MacArthur's plan would undermine American capitalist principles and remove from office those "disposed to cooperate with the United States against the internal and external Communist threat." Later, the Communists' defeat of Nationalist forces in China and the Korean War would be the rationale for the "reverse course," the Japanese term indicating American retrenchment in occupied Japan in the face of the onset of the cold war. In the beginning, however, the reverse course was motivated primarily by economic, ideological, and other political considerations.

In the late 1940s, Kern arranged for a succession of American diplomats and businessmen to meet privately with leading Japanese politicians. When Truman appointed Wall Street lawyer John Foster Dulles as special ambassador to negotiate a formal peace treaty with Japan, Kern and other ACJ backers met with him frequently and served as a backdoor channel to the Japanese elite.

Though MacArthur strongly resisted the ACJ's attempts to sidetrack his reforms, he was unable to match the group's political influence in Washington. ACJ policy position papers were adopted by the federal government almost verbatim, and MacArthur was ordered to implement them. In this way, the Japan Lobby was able to stop the purge of Japanese business leaders who had supported the Japanese military during the war and free those awaiting trial as war criminals.

Perhaps more important, it was able to prevent the breakup of the *zaibatsu* banks. This allowed the *zaibatsu* companies to reconstitute themselves in their present structure—the *keiretsu*, a group of companies linked through interlocking shareholders and a bank, a trading company, and an insurance firm at the center. The Japanese Finance Ministry controls these banks through administrative guidance. Rather than promoting a less controlled economy, the reforms actually created a situation where the government acquired even greater control.

The ACJ—which also convinced the American government to adopt a peace settlement permitting Japan to scuttle several other MacArthur reforms—disappeared soon after the 1952 elections. As an organization, it became redundant when John Foster Dulles, who sympathized with the ACJ's aims, was named Secretary of State. Kern left *Newsweek* in the mid-1950s to become an influence broker between American business, Japan, and the Saudis.

In the 1950s, the responsibility for America's Japan policy shifted from MacArthur and his band of reformers to Dulles and the State Department. What emerged was a special U.S.-Japan relationship. It is a relationship that historian Kenneth Pyle has called unprecedented, unequal, and nonreciprocal—one in which, he says, "Americans welcome Japanese *deference* and the Japanese welcome the *dependence* on the United States."

The principal architect of this unique relationship was Shigeru Yoshida, Japan's brilliant postwar Foreign Minister. Pyle writes: "Privately Yoshida reasoned, 'Just as the United States was once a colony of Great Britain but is now the stronger of the two, if Japan becomes a colony of the United States it will also eventually become the stronger.' "

Yoshida's goal was to win the peace for Japan. His bargaining chip: the U.S.-Soviet conflict. His tool: Japanese business. His approach: to make Japan a military protectorate of the United States and, in the process, gain unimpeded access to the rich American market.

In a series of farsighted negotiations, Japan concluded a national security pact in which the United States was obligated to defend Japan if attacked but in which Japan had no reciprocal obligation toward the United States. In exchange for American guarantees of long-term security, Japan agreed to provide America with military bases. As part of this arrangement, the State Department worked to keep U.S. markets open to Japanese exports, encouraged U.S. firms to make technology and aid available to the Japanese at very low cost, and gave Japan political protection against its American critics.

Yoshida's strategy assured Japanese security without the burden of massive defense expenditures. It facilitated the accelerated rebuilding of Japanese industry. And it got Japan virtually unimpeded access to the largest market and the best technology in the world.

This was and is the essence of the "special relationship" between Japan and the United States.

In his study of that period, chronicler John G. Roberts concludes:

The benefits that . . . [Japan] gained from this turn of events were far greater than those that could reasonably have been expected from victory. For Japan was later granted a free hand, economically, in large portions of the "Greater East Asia Co-Prosperity Sphere" it had conquered and lost, while enjoying unhindered access to the American market as well as to raw materials in most of the non-communist world.

By the late 1960s and early 1970s, the world economy was vastly changed. As a measure for fiscal discipline at home, the Nixon Administration flirted with wage and price controls and embraced free-floating exchange rates.

Equally important, the war in Vietnam had damaged the credibility of America's foreign policy establishment and altered Congress's attitude toward the prerogatives of the executive branch. These changed attitudes culminated in two milestones, one within months of the other: first, the resignation of President Nixon; second, the passage of the 1974 Trade Act. The Trade Act, clearly the turning point in the modern history of American trade policy, removed some of the executive branch's discretion on trade policy matters, giving Congress more extensive and direct participation in setting and administering trade policy.

Two decades ago, imports from Japan and other countries were beginning to take a heavy toll on dozens of American industries. In most cases, domestic companies were losing out to foreign goods that were simply better made and more competitively priced. But in other cases, with important consequences for American industry, foreign firms were prevailing only through the use of such illegal, anti-competitive practices as dumping and kickbacks to American importers. Meanwhile, foreign markets, particularly Japan's, remained closed to competitive American products. The effect of this was the wholesale destruction of entire American industries.

American officials' perception of a "special U.S.-Japan relationship" freed Japan from the normal international responsibilities of an independent nation—responsibilities that would have included financing its own defense and granting economic reciprocity to its trading partners. This special relationship quickly became too convenient for policymakers on either side to alter: the Americans were comfortable with Japanese deference and the Japanese were comfortable with their military, political, and economic dependence on the United States.

But the American companies that were ravaged by Japan's predatory trading policies were not so comfortable. Repeatedly, these firms and their workers petitioned Congress and the executive branch for stricter enforcement of America's trade laws. They wanted to use access to the U.S. market as a lever to pry open foreign markets for American exports.

And they urged Congress to become more activist on trade matters. Beginning in the late 1960s, these demands started to send political shock waves through Japan. For the Japanese, an activist Congress meant that diplomacy and the State Department's political protection could no longer guarantee the continued American indulgence of their economic practices.

Japan responded, not by opening its markets or changing its economic ways, but by hiring dozens of prominent former U.S. officials and politicians—what the Japanese press called "name-brand lobbyists"—to advocate its positions with Congress, trade agencies, and the press. One of those who carefully tutored the Japanese in their approach was Richard V. Allen.

The passage from high official to foreign agent was a rocky one for Allen. In the 1968 presidential campaign, he was Richard Nixon's chief adviser on foreign policy and national security. But once Nixon was elected, he named Henry Kissinger to the National Security Adviser post and placed Allen in a subordinate role. Within months, Kissinger, a master at bureaucratic infighting, had eased Allen off his staff. Allen soon joined another White House office as Deputy Assistant to the President for International Trade and Economic Policy.

While Allen's activities in that position went unnoticed at the time, they became quite controversial in 1980, when Allen was serving as chief adviser on foreign policy and national security to Ronald Reagan's presidential campaign. In the last days of the campaign, some articles appeared accusing Allen of using his prior White House position in the Nixon Administration to help Japan.

According to *The Wall Street Journal*, Allen wrote a series of letters in 1970 to his friend Tamotsu Takase, an adviser to many powerful Japanese business and political leaders, describing the flaws in Japan's Washington lobbying efforts. Allen urged Japan to create an American-led lobbying machine—advice that Japan would act on within a year's time.

The *Journal's* Jonathan Kwitny also reported that Allen had slipped the Japanese confidential information: a copy of a U.S. government proposal to restrict licensing agreements and the sale of technical information about videocassette recorders. (At the time, the videocassette industry was still dominated by American companies.)

Kwitny revealed that Allen just happened to have someone in mind to lead the Japanese lobbying campaign: Washington lobbyist David Fleming. Fleming was subsequently taken on by Nissan (then called Datsun) for a fee of $10,000 a month. After Fleming acquired the Nissan account, Allen wrote to him demanding half of his Nissan fee, "inasmuch as your introductions to Japan were arranged by me." Fleming's attorney reminded Allen that such a payment "could be considered a violation of the law." It would have been deferred compensation, Japan style. Fleming refused to have any part in such a payment and eventually was replaced by Allen.

Almost immediately after the Kwitny article was published, Allen took a leave of absence from the Reagan presidential campaign. Soon after Reagan won, the President-elect reviewed Kwitny's allegations, concluded that Allen had done no wrong, and appointed him to the position of National Security Adviser.

Beginning in the early 1970s, Japanese companies and the Japanese government hired dozens of prominent ex-officials to tutor and represent them. Among those engaged in the late 1970s was William Eberle, Special Trade Representative in the Nixon Administration, who—like Fleming—went to work for Nissan. Another was William A. Colby, ex-Director of the CIA, who became a well-paid consultant to the Political Public Relations Center, a small but well-connected Japanese political institute.

Though Japan did employ a few highly visible "name-brand lobbyists" in the early 1970s, most members of America's trade policy elite still shunned work as foreign agents. But that soon changed. The turning point came in the mid-1970s, when Japan signed up Harald Malmgren, Eberle's deputy in the Nixon and Ford administrations.

In the eyes of many, Malmgren is America's foremost trade authority. Brilliant, innovative, and politically astute, Malmgren was and remains widely respected in Congress and in policymaking circles. Soon after leaving his White House post, he began signing up well-paying foreign clients. Among his prizes was a $300,000 contract to help a group of Japanese television manufacturers who had been caught dumping television sets on the U.S. market. Other lucrative contracts followed. In 1979, he landed a $90,000 contract with the European Community (EC). The EC paid Malmgren to use his extraordinary access and insights to get advance intelligence about how America would implement the new multilateral trade agreement that emerged from the Tokyo General Agreement on Tariffs and Trade (GATT) negotiations. According to the contract itself, Malmgren's services for the EC were to "commence on the date the President notifies the Congress of his intent to enter into the Multilateral Trade Agreements and shall terminate when he formally transmits copies of the signed agreements to the Congress together with drafts of the implementing legislation." Malmgren's information and insights were sought by the EC to help them quietly lobby the Administration even as it was drafting the legislation that would be sent to Congress.

That same year, Malmgren signed a $52,000 contract to represent the

Japanese Whaling Association, whose members were coming under increasing criticism for killing an endangered species. The Japanese government also paid him $10,000 to provide information about the "problems that are likely to be discussed at the [1979] Tokyo summit meeting and of the approach to these problems that will be taken by the participants." The Japanese government certainly understood its own positions; what it wanted was advance insights about America's approach.

With these contracts, Malmgren crossed two important lines simultaneously. One line separated low-paying public service from high-priced lobbying. Malmgren's fees were high, even among top Washington lobbyists. The other line separated America's business interests from those of its foreign competitors. Malmgren, who had represented America's economic concerns abroad, now represented foreign business interests in America.

Malmgren's contracts and fees were a source of envy and a topic of conversation in Washington in the late 1970s. Malmgren's Justice Department registration statements were copied and distributed widely among the Washington trade elite. One former trade official remembers that his copy of Malmgren's registration had been photocopied so many times that it was almost illegible.

Malmgren's pathbreaking shift onto the payroll of foreign interests not only showed those trade experts who were still in government how much money could be made by lobbying for foreign interests; his continued acceptance in elite political circles made similar career moves seem respectable for other trade experts.

With dozens of foreign companies and governments expanding their political presence in America, unlimited opportunities were available to those who were willing to become foreign agents. A stream of senior trade officials soon joined Malmgren in Japan's expanding Washington corps. David Osborne wrote in *The New Republic* that "our best trade experts became their best lobbyists."

This stream became a flood in 1981, after the Carter Administration and many other Democrats were turned out of office. Senator John Culver (D-Iowa) signed on with Toyota. Senator Frank Church (D-Idaho), once chairman of the Senate Foreign Relations Committee, went with the Japan External Trade Organization (JETRO). Senator Abraham Ribicoff (D-Conn.) was hired by the Japan Center for Information and Cultural Affairs. Others engaged by Japanese interests were Stuart Eizenstat (for Hitachi), Carter's chief domestic policy adviser, and Richard Rivers (for Fujitsu), onetime general counsel to the U.S. Trade Representative.

In the mid-1980s, the flood grew to tidal proportions as the first wave of Reagan appointees left office to cash in. (Appendix A provides a partial documentation of those who made the transition from public servant to foreign agent.)

By hiring so many ex-officials, the Japanese now have the capacity to assemble teams of lobbyists that are carefully tailored to influence individual members of Congress. Quite often, the lobbyist assigned to contact a member will be a former staffer or key campaign aide. They are virtually assured of access and attention. To impress congressional staff members, the Japan Lobby will often send a well-known ex-official to discuss an issue with them. One aide says, "I'll admit it. I'm flattered to have an ex-cabinet officer ask to get on my calendar and come to my office to plead with me." Only a handful of American companies lobby in this sophisticated way.

The jealous, somewhat frantic competition to serve Japan among ex-officials and Washington lobbying organizations is well illustrated by an incident during a 1985 visit to Washington by a delegation of Japanese Dietmen. That October, the 200-member bipartisan Northeast-Midwest Congressional Coalition invited Susumu Nikaido, the vice president of Japan's ruling LDP, and his visiting delegation for a luncheon discussion on U.S.-Japan trade. Nikaido's host was Robert Dole (R-Kan.), then Senate Majority Leader.

A representative from the Coalition contacted Dole's office to ask whether the senator would extend the Coalition's invitation to Nikaido. Within one hour, Stanton Anderson—a former Nixon adviser and State Department official, and head of the lobbying firm of Anderson, Hibey, Nauheim & Blair—called the Coalition aide to determine the purpose of the meeting and the issues that would be discussed.

Within an hour and a half, a representative from Keefe and Company, another prominent lobbying firm with strong Democratic connections, called to say that *they* were in charge of Nikaido's visit and that the date for the Coalition luncheon would be Tuesday, October 8. Later that day, Gray and Company, a major lobbying company headed by prominent Republican Robert Gray, called to say that *they* were handling the arrangements for the Nikaido delegation, and that the luncheon would be on Wednesday, October 9. The Coalition office phoned the Japanese Embassy and asked the Japanese to coordinate the event.

Eventually, a time was arranged. On the day of the luncheon, Richard McElheny, the newly appointed senior vice president of Gray and Company, stationed himself at the door of the meeting room and began thanking members of Congress for coming to the event. McElheny may have forgotten that it was the members, and not his firm, who initiated the meeting.

Some members recognized McElheny as the recently departed Assistant Secretary of Commerce for Trade Development. What particularly outraged a number of them, though, was that McElheny seated himself at the luncheon's head table, which had only six chairs—three for members of the Japanese Diet and three for the congressional hosts. McElheny took the chair of a congressional host. Later, McElheny sent Coalition co-chairman Frank Horton (R-N.Y.) a letter that said, "I hope that you will forgive my presumption for joining you and the other Members at the head table, particularly since this was an event sponsored under the auspices of the Coalition. . . . I hope in no way you feel I over-stepped fair bounds during the luncheon, but if so, I sincerely regret that unintended result." While McElheny's Japanese clients may not have understood his faux pas, they did witness how well connected Gray and Company was with the United States Congress.

Japan has few difficulties finding well-connected lobbyists or advisers in Washington—primarily because these insiders seek out the Japanese. A former senior staffer in the U.S. office of Japan's Foreign Ministry explains how it works: A well-connected lobbyist will invite someone from the embassy or a Japanese corporate executive to lunch. Sometime during the meal the lobbyist will mention that he is now available for "representation" or will turn the discussion to a trade or other commercial problem that his firm is particularly well equipped to handle. The former official says that many of these applicants will prove their worth by bringing "golden nuggets." He also says that American firms that are already on the Japanese payroll constantly bring the Japanese ideas for new services they can offer. A basic goal of these companies, of course, is to "grow their accounts." This official says that one of Japan's major political tasks is selecting from among the many people and ideas it is offered.

As Japan expanded its lobbying efforts, it quickly came to appreciate the power and influence of the "invisible branch" of the federal government: congressional staff. Those who work on Capitol Hill are the Rumpelstiltskins of the policy and legislative process—they do much of the real work, and their elected bosses take the credit. As the traditional power and prerogatives of seniority have eroded in the post-Watergate era, members have taken on added responsibilities, and in the process more than a few have lost the time to think about many of the issues they are assigned. Each member of Congress now sits on an average of three committees. Each must vote on hundreds of legislative initiatives annually. Each must raise enormous campaign chests and, particularly in the House, each must campaign constantly.

Many members of Congress, of course, are experts on specific topics—Senator Sam Nunn (D-Ga.), for instance, is considered an authority on matters of defense. But other members care little for issues and a lot about being elected and reelected. Many are also obsessed about their place in the congressional power structure and spend endless time courting their congressional peers. For these members—who, by most accounts, comprise the bulk of Congress—whatever remains is simply detail. And for them, the staff handles the details.

Over the past decades, there has been a vast expansion in the number and the influence of congressional staff. In the 1930s, Senator Harry Truman had only two staff members. In the 1950s, Senator John F. Kennedy's staff consisted of Theodore Sorensen and two other assistants. Today, each U.S. senator has between fifteen and eighty aides.

These aides do research, draft legislation, negotiate with constituents, contributors, and the special interests, and strike deals with their counterparts in Congress and the executive branch. They also brief the press, write speeches, prepare questions for hearings, and advise their bosses on how to vote. In the process, many have become far more powerful than the members they serve. Hence the lobbyists' rule of thumb: convince the staff, and you've won nine-tenths of the legislative battle.

Time and again, Japan has found that the principal obstacle it faces in Congress is staff opposition. In the 1980s, therefore, Japan decided to expand its influence with congressional staff. As a starting point, a major Japanese research institute published a comprehensive study in 1984 of the role and career patterns of the 30,000 people who constitute the congressional staff.

The analysis is remarkably complete. It explains how staff come upon new ideas, the personal and working relationships among key committee staff, how staff broker legislation with each other, the relationships between staff and their congressional bosses, what motivates the staff (money, public service, or the opportunity for something better), educational backgrounds, their age distribution, and their individual levels of influence. It also identifies the limits of staff influence.

In addition, the study discusses what the Japanese call "the key watching points," including the work of certain senior staffers, how to spot new ideas that are gaining staff attention (what the report calls "floating ideas"), and the need to identify early on those staff coalitions being formed around specific pieces of legislation.

In one of its most telling points, the study emphasizes the need for Japan to cultivate those staff who seem destined for greater things. It notes that many top U.S. trade officials got their start as young lawyers on the Senate Finance Committee. Among those identified by name who had made this transition were Richard Rivers and Robert Cassidy, Jr., both of whom became foreign agents after stints with the USTR.

Lastly, the study notes that, while some people work for Congress their entire careers, many others join staffs to obtain experience, gain a reputation, or become a lobbyist. In 1988, some of the most intense opposition to ethics reform legislation came from senior congressional staff who objected to a provision that would impose post-government employment restrictions on them and on their bosses—restrictions that had covered executive branch officials for some time. On two separate occasions, sponsors of the bill met with dozens of congressional staffers to get their views on the proposed reforms. Discussions were so acrimonious that the meetings became, in the words of one House staff member, "just about as close as it gets to a staff riot."

A high-ranking Senate aide asked, "Why does anyone in their right mind think that I would put up with all this abuse, pettiness, low pay, and hard work if I couldn't make some real money when I leave this job?" In Washington parlance, "make some real money" means just one thing: become a lobbyist.

Japan understands these sentiments well. In 1988, Japan's leading business newspaper, *Nihon Keizai Shimbun*, ran a thirteen-part series on how Congress works: the personalities, the role of staff, the key pressure points, how coalitions are formed, and how action is advanced or stalled. Authors Kazutami Yamazaki and Masao Kanasashi expanded these articles into a book that is widely used as a guide for Japanese businesses coming to America.

Japan now courts congressional staff systematically. The Japanese Embassy has assigned four officials to befriend and keep tabs on congressional staffers—to know their responsibilities, backgrounds, likes, dislikes, personal ambitions, connections, relationships with their bosses, and their positions on policies.

The Japanese also make a point of wining and dining congressional staff. Each year, Japan's Ambassador throws parties to which a hundred or more congressional trade specialists are invited. Small lunches and dinners permit more detailed exchanges of views. Congressional staff members who work on trade and other matters of importance to Japan have standing invitations for all-expenses-paid fact-finding trips to Tokyo. Many other nations have followed Japan's lead and now offer the same "opportunities."

While such exchanges give U.S. officials and their staff useful new perspectives and contacts, they also give foreign sponsors a unique, uninterrupted opportunity to get their policy messages across. These opportunities have not gone unnoticed. One former senior congressional aide reports, "I can only identify two other administrative assistants, other than myself, who did not travel to Japan, Taiwan, or Korea at the expense of those governments."

Today, congressional staff increasingly turn to Japanese clients and Japanese companies after their government service. As Appendix A documents, Japan has also hired many former congressional staffers to act as its eyes, ears, and advocates on Capitol Hill.

Chapter Six

JAPAN TAKES TELEVISION

THE REVOLVING DOOR between public office and private gain has tainted the integrity and degraded the quality of U.S. trade policy—at an increasing cost to the American economy. Just how great this cost has been—and how tawdry the trade policy business has become—is revealed by the secret history of how Japan destroyed the American television industry.

This is a story of how Japanese manufacturers and the Japanese government first created an anti-competitive cartel and then reinforced it with diplomacy, fraud, and the influence of Washington insiders in a direct assault on the American consumer electronics industry. It is history, but it is also a crime story.

At a technology conference sponsored by the National Academy of Sciences in October 1988, Nobutoshi Akao, economic minister at Japan's Washington embassy, and Erich Spitz, executive vice president for research and development at Thomson CSF of France, were supposed to talk about international R&D cooperation. But their discussion soon degenerated into a debate over whether the United States should adopt Japanese or European technical standards for high-definition television (HDTV), an innovation that produces pictures with the sharpness of 35mm film and sound with the clarity of a compact disc.

Both men knew that the difference between today's television receivers and those of HDTV is so great that most of America's existing 160 million sets are likely to be replaced over the next decade. Similar changes would then take place in the markets for videocassette recorders, video cameras, and computer monitors. By one estimate, the market for HDTV in the United States alone will reach $20 billion a year by the end of the 1990s.

Akao and Spitz also knew that each HDTV will be crammed with scores of advanced microelectronic chips. Whoever dominates the HDTV market in the 1990s is virtually assured domination of the global semiconductor industry—as well as the upper hand in dozens of other industries that will depend on the next generation of advanced technology. Indeed, whoever controls production of HDTV will almost certainly dominate the high-technology industries of the next century.

Notably absent from the debate was any mention of the plans of the American television industry. Why? Because *there is virtually no American television industry.* By 1990, there was only one remaining American television manufacturer—Zenith—and it was under intense pressure to sell off its television division. Zenith stood alone because, between 1968 and 1988, a roster of some of the most distinguished names in American consumer electronics—Philco, Sylvania, Emerson, Motorola, RCA, Westinghouse, Admiral, GE, Magnavox, and many others—either went out of the television manufacturing business or were acquired by foreign competitors.

The decimation of the American-owned television industry can be traced directly to:

- A sustained, predatory attack by a cartel of Japanese television manufacturers operating with the knowledge and support of the Japanese government.
- Secret, illegal payments to American importers of Japanese products.
- A secret trade agreement that obliged the U.S. government to side with Japan against its own companies and workers.
- The covert transfer of "inside" information about proposed actions by the U.S. government.
- The metamorphosis of more than twenty high-ranking federal officials handling the television case into well-paid agents of influence for the Japanese.

This is the story of how it all happened.

Japan's assault on the American television and consumer electronics market dates back to 1956, when the largest Japanese manufacturers—who then held 90 percent of their own domestic market—formed the Home

Electric Appliance Market Stabilization Council, an illegal production cartel. The intent of the cartel's participating companies was twofold: to monopolize the domestic market for television receivers, radios, and other home electric products and to exclude foreign imports. Once their home market was secure, the Japanese would launch a drive against the far richer American market.

The Stabilization Council set minimum price levels for domestic sales of television and radio receivers; established profit margin levels for retailers (22 percent) and wholesalers (8 percent); boycotted nonmembers; and denied foreign companies critical access to Japanese distribution networks. At the same time, the council worked with the Japanese government to raise a protectionist wall of tariff and nontariff barriers to foreign imports.

The council and its member companies had just one problem: the Japanese Fair Trade Commission (JFTC). The JFTC had been created after World War II to enforce the antitrust laws imposed during the American occupation. In 1956, and again in 1966, the Fair Trade Commission filed cases against all the major consumer electronics manufacturers, with the exception of Sony. These charges included: illegally cartelizing the Japanese market; enforcing industry-wide high price levels; collusively setting rebates and profit margins for distributors; and collectively boycotting nonaffiliated wholesalers.

When the JFTC exposed these schemes, the Japanese manufacturers in effect pleaded "no contest." But they were never prosecuted, and they were never ordered to make any structural changes in their operations. In fact, the firms were allowed to continue their monthly meetings. Benign neglect of antitrust statutes was, in fact, the deliberate policy of the Japanese government.

The JFTC's charges—and its subsequent inaction—revealed a fundamental political conflict among Japan's government agencies. The bureaucrats of the JFTC advocated a Western-style, pro-competition approach in which the interests of *consumers* were taken into account. MITI, by contrast, advocated hardball industrial policies to advance the interests of domestic *producers* in global markets. MITI won the bureaucratic fight and in the early 1960s targeted consumer electronics as a key element in its national industrial policy.

The first step in Japan's targeting initiative was to acquire America's television technology, which was then state-of-the-art. In the 1950s, American television manufacturers were internationally minded. They were investing in European production facilities to get under Europe's tariff wall. But since the Japanese market was closed to them, the only way they could generate earnings in Japan was to license their technology to members of the newly formed cartel. Foolishly, they did. RCA, GE, and Westinghouse each licensed and then transferred its monochrome technology to members of the cartel. In 1962, RCA went one step further and licensed its color technology to the Japanese.

Once the Japanese had the U.S. technology, they were in a position to launch phase two of their plan: a full-scale assault on the very American companies that had licensed their technology to the Japanese.

In 1963, Japanese television manufacturers created the Television Export Council to set cartel policy. For day-to-day administrative guidance, they also created the Television Export Examination Committee.

One of the council's first actions was to require that cartel members provide, prior to any U.S. shipment, an "application for validation." The purpose of the application was to identify the Japanese manufacturer, the trading company, the U.S. purchaser, the merchandise's trademark, its model and model number, the quantity to be shipped, the unit price, and the U.S. customer's registration number. The customer registration number was critical. Cartel members were bound by their agreement to exclude U.S. customers not registered with the Export Council, and during some periods were not allowed to change customers during the term of the cartel agreement without the cartel's consent.

The cartel also established its own enforcement mechanisms: the authority to investigate violations lay in the hands of the Television Export Council and the Examination Committee. Potential financial penalties could equal the total value of any shipment.

The cartel members knew that their success depended on protection of their home market. Japanese consumers had to be gouged to provide higher profits. That was the only way to make up for the losses incurred by selling the same products abroad at artificially low prices. Thus, a de facto Market Stabilization Council was re-created. This time, however, the council operated in secret.

To administer its price fixing, the cartel formed three groups. The Tenth Day Group was a working committee comprised of executives from the television divisions of the cartel members. They met monthly (usually on the tenth day; hence the name) to review production schedules, technical details, and prices. If the Tenth Day Group could not resolve a problem, it passed the matter along to the Palace Group. This group consisted of more senior executives from the companies and met at Tokyo's Palace Hotel. If a problem lay beyond the decision-making authority of the Palace Group, it would be passed on to the Okura Group. This group, which met in the Okura Hotel—at the time, Tokyo's finest— consisted of the chairmen and presidents of the cartel companies. The Okura Group had the last word on all cartel activities.

Participating Japanese manufacturers agreed to maintain consistent domestic price and production schedules. The cartel set prices, production volumes, and shipments to the United States. Members also exchanged technical and commercial information. Government officials helped by ensuring that U.S. exporters were harassed by import safety inspectors. The Electronics Industries Association of Japan persuaded Japanese distributors not to handle certain American television products. American television exports to Japan soon fell precipitously. (In 1976, only 500 of the 5 million television sets sold in Japan were made by non-Japanese companies.) The result: Japanese manufacturers soon had such a stranglehold on their domestic market that they could sell a set for more than twice as much in Japan as they could abroad. (Typically, a Japanese set that sold for $350 in the United States would sell for a minimum of $700 in Japan.)

Once the manufacturers agreed upon a price, it was submitted to MITI, where it was approved and became known as the official "check price." But the check price was not the real price. According to the U.S. Justice Department, the Japanese manufacturers also had concocted a secret "double-pricing" scheme with the help of eighty American importers—among them Sears and Alexander's. Through this scheme, the Japanese paid U.S. importers secret rebates of roughly $40 for each Japanese set.

These illegal rebates were paid in several ways. Some Japanese manufacturers deposited money for their American co-conspirators in secret bank accounts in Switzerland, Hong Kong, or Japan. Others sent telegraphic transfers of money marked as "credits" for spare parts. Still others gave American importers extended payment terms for their purchases—and forgave the interest. Japanese firms also provided offsetting discounts on other merchandise sold to TV importers, as well as payments disguised as "market research."

The objective was to destroy the American industry by selling goods extraordinarily cheaply, often at prices far below production costs. To avoid detection by the U.S. government and lawsuits by American manufacturers, the participants in this scheme filed falsified documents with the Customs Service, citing their "check price" as the amount they had received for each set. By reporting the higher, fraudulent price, the Japanese manufacturers were forced to pay higher U.S. import duties.* There was no way for U.S. officials or American manufacturers to know

---

* This additional ad valorem duty was almost certainly less than the additional dumping duty would have been had the cartel members reported the true prices of their television sets sold in the United States.

how much American importers were actually paying for the Japanese goods. It was a nearly perfect crime.

With the help of these secret rebates, already low check prices, and high profits from sales in their closed domestic market, the Japanese could easily underprice their American competitors. Jobs in the U.S. television manufacturing industry fell 50 percent between 1966 and 1970. They dropped another 30 percent between 1971 and 1975, and 25 percent more between 1977 and 1981.

Even without the illegal rebates, the official check price for Japanese sets sold in the United States was so low that it constituted "dumping." When American manufacturers realized what the Japanese were doing, they sought protection under U.S. law.

In March 1968, the Import Committee of the U.S. Electronics Industries Association filed a petition with the Treasury Department alleging that television sets from Japan were being unfairly and illegally dumped on the U.S. market.

In June 1968, the Treasury Department began an investigation. It sent questionnaires to five major Japanese television manufacturers— Sony, Sharp, Matsushita, Toshiba, and Hitachi—seeking information about their American sales. Sears, J. C. Penney, and Singer were also questioned about their import arrangements. (Without this information, Treasury could not legally determine whether the Japanese were, in fact, dumping their products.)

The Japanese manufacturers and their American importers simply stonewalled the requests. The cartel members and their American partners knew that if their kickback arrangements were revealed, they would face fines and penalties totaling hundreds of millions of dollars. A year went by and nothing happened. When Treasury pressed its demand, the Japanese Embassy requested more time. So did Japan's American importers.

One way to frustrate the Treasury inquiry and avoid these fines was to shred the evidence. In October 1970, an executive of one U.S. importer wrote to his superior suggesting that the firm's files and back purchase orders be "purged." Another—perhaps more predictable—solution was to go on a legal counteroffensive. One of Matsushita's New York attorneys proposed filing suit against Treasury, challenging the antidumping investigation. The American attorney counseled his Japanese client that "litigation might provide protection against 'double pricing' exposure."

Such worries were premature. The double-pricing scheme went undiscovered for more than a decade—until Gambles Import, a U.S. importer of Japanese sets, voluntarily paid Customs duties on the real prices of the televisions it imported. In 1970, Treasury could only conclude that, on the basis of the "check prices" reported by the U.S. importers to Customs, there was clear evidence that the Japanese were dumping television sets on the American market.

Treasury referred its ruling to what is now the International Trade Commission (then the Tariff Commission). Finally, in March 1971, almost three years after the American manufacturers filed their complaint, the U.S. government issued an official finding that the Japanese were dumping.

By then, however, much damage was done.

America's television firms were badly hurt over the three years it took to get government action. More than half of them suffered heavy losses in 1968, 1969, and 1970—the direct result of Japanese dumping and U.S. governmental complacency. What they now needed—and needed quickly—was for the Treasury Department to calculate and collect the anti-dumping levies the law required to offset the cartel's advantage.

By law, this levy was to be calculated as the arithmetical difference between the "fair price"—what the Japanese were charging for comparable sets in Japan—and the price they were charging in the American market.

Calculating the levy involved a complex formula dependent on timely, accurate information from the Japanese about manufacturing and shipping costs, domestic price formulas, and a number of other factors. Equally important was that the levies would apply retroactively, but only from the date that the ITC's dumping appraisal was published—September 7, 1970. The cartel's illegal gains of prior years were, in effect, a windfall gain.

Years would go by before the Treasury Department came up with a number.

While the dumping investigation dragged on, American companies sought other legal remedies. In December 1970, the National Union Electric Corporation (NUE), whose products were sold under the brand names of Emerson and Dumont, filed a private antitrust suit against certain Japanese manufacturers, their trading companies, their U.S. subsidiaries, and several American importers. NUE charged that the Japanese and their American collaborators were engaged in a conspiracy to restrain competition and drive American firms—including its own—out of business. NUE asked the court to award it damages.

In 1974, Zenith filed a similar suit, challenging Matsushita's purchase of the entire Consumer Products Division of Motorola. It also filed a petition with Treasury in 1970, alleging that the Japanese were subsidizing export sales to the United States by rebating taxes back to the manufacturers. By exporting tax-free goods, the Japanese manufacturers could reduce the export price of their sets by 13 to 15 percent. American manufacturers, by contrast, had to pay American taxes on the products they sold. To level the competitive playing field, Zenith asked Treasury to impose a countervailing duty on Japanese imports equal to their tax rebates.

The first Zenith petition posed a difficult dilemma for the Treasury Department. Though the Japanese tax rebates were consistent with basic international trade agreements permitting reimbursement of consumption taxes on export goods, prior rulings of the U.S. Supreme Court had found tax rebates to be a subsidy. Zenith argued that these rulings required Treasury to act.

If Treasury ruled in Zenith's favor, similar countervailing duties could be imposed on most U.S. imports. To avoid a trade conflict with other countries, the United States would then be forced either to alter its tax system to conform to global trade treaties or to renegotiate the essential elements of those treaties.

Treasury chose a third option: it did nothing. Of its tens of thousands of employees in the early 1970s, only one official was assigned to administer America's countervailing duty laws. Although he worked hard, he was perpetually behind. This gave Treasury officials the opportunity to bury Zenith's papers amidst huge stacks of unexamined countervailing duty petitions.

One former U.S. trade negotiator recounts a fundamental government tenet of the late 1960s and early 1970s: "Our trade policy was to keep U.S. markets open and the Congress pacified."

In large measure, this policy reflected the attitudes of Richard Nixon and his National Security Adviser, Henry Kissinger. Neither had much interest in trade matters, except when they impinged on foreign or defense policies. Perhaps the best example of their approach to trade matters is the way they disposed of a 1968 Nixon campaign pledge to reduce Japanese textile imports.

Kissinger himself recalls the textile wrangle as "a case of low comedy, frustration, and near fiasco." In his memoirs, he writes that, in early 1969, Nixon ordered him to strike a deal with the Japanese on three matters: the deployment of nuclear weapons, the return of Okinawa, and the reduction of Japanese textile exports to the United States. Kissinger claims that he was unenthusiastic about linking Okinawa with textiles, which he saw as only "a transient domestic political problem."

Kissinger quickly established a secret negotiating channel with an

emissary of Japanese Prime Minister Eisaku Sato, bypassing the bu-
reaucracies of both nations. Together, Kissinger and the Japanese representative crafted a secret agreement to limit Japanese textile exports
to the United States.

Nixon and Sato approved this agreement at a White House meeting
in November 1969. But it was kept secret, since the strategy was to let
the accord surface publicly only later, as a product of staged negotiations.
Kissinger explains: "Since the solution had to emerge from a negotiation
that had not yet started, Sato could hardly indicate its outcome in advance. And it would impair the new relationship if it appeared that we
had traded Okinawa for concessions on textiles."

But there was a problem: MITI officials and Japanese politicians refused to accept *any* reduction in textile exports to the United States. So
for two years the United States and Japan held increasingly acrimonious
discussions. And for two years the issue went unresolved. Finally, with
the 1972 election only thirteen months away, Nixon threatened to impose
quotas on the Japanese textile imports under the 1917 Trading with the
Enemy Act, which gave him wide latitude to exclude certain imports.
The Japanese soon relented and agreed to limit their textile shipments
to the United States.

By that time, textiles were only one of many sources of political strain
between America and Japan. Indeed, many Japanese leaders still resent
the "Nixon Shocks"—the July 1971 announcement that America had
reestablished relations with China and the August 1971 unveiling of
America's New Economic Policy, which included floating exchange rates.
Japan had been consulted on neither. Japanese leaders also recall the 10
percent duty surcharge that Nixon unilaterally imposed on imports, as
well as the pressure that his Administration put on the Japanese government to revalue its currency.

Through clever diplomacy, Japan used these frictions to gain political
leverage with the Nixon Administration. Japanese officials knew that, as
the presidential election neared, Nixon wanted to appear as a strong,
successful international leader. In early 1972, Japan proposed that the
two nations delay discussions on a number of trade issues—including
television dumping. Japanese strategists realized that a year's delay would
strengthen the position of the Japanese television manufacturers—and
perhaps fatally weaken their American competitors. As is often the case,
politics dominated economics: the Nixon Administration blithely agreed
to the Japanese proposal.

This momentary truce was shaken in May 1972, when Treasury began
an internal review of the countervailing duty petition Zenith had filed
two years earlier. The Japanese, always alert to actions within the U.S.

bureaucracy, protested. In July, newly chosen Prime Minister Kakuei Tanaka asked for a summit meeting with Nixon to discuss trade problems and set the stage for a fresh line of diplomacy on such matters as Sino-Japanese relations. Nixon agreed to a two-day meeting in Honolulu in August 1972—barely two months before the elections.

To prepare for the summit, William Eberle and Harald Malmgren, then America's top trade negotiators, met with MITI officials at the Hakone Hot Springs resort near Tokyo. Kissinger went to Japan as well to iron out various summit details with Japanese leaders.

At the summit's conclusion, Nixon and Tanaka announced that the Japanese would buy more than $1 billion worth of American goods, would reduce barriers to American investment, would liberalize access to the Japanese distribution system, and would support a new round of GATT negotiations.

Their final communiqué said nothing about U.S. concessions to the Japanese. Neither did it mention the television dumping case.

Many lawyers and former executives from the U.S. television industry believe Nixon struck another secret deal with the Japanese—one in which he agreed to halt U.S. actions against the television cartel. Officials close to Nixon claim that his subsequent inaction on the television case simply reflected the low priority he accorded trade concerns, as well as his growing preoccupation with the Watergate scandal.

Whatever the real story, the Nixon Administration—and later the Ford Administration—did virtually nothing about the cartel's violations of U.S. trade laws. In particular, Treasury failed to collect anti-dumping duties. When the International Trade Commission began to investigate the double-pricing scheme in March 1976, Treasury even went so far as to refuse ITC investigators access to its files. Meanwhile, the Nixon and Ford Justice Departments stood by passively as American companies struggled with their antitrust suits against the Japanese cartel.

So little was done about countervailing duty petitions that a frustrated Congress gave Treasury a mandate: it had one year to rule on these duty cases. Those cases that were already pending would have to be decided within a year of the enactment of the 1974 Trade Act. And so on January 5, 1976—exactly one year to the day—Treasury denied Zenith's petition. Zenith was forced to make a court appeal.

The repeated, deliberate delays in enforcing U.S. trade laws hope-lessly undermined the strength and competitive position of American television companies. It also made them easy acquisition targets. In May 1974, Motorola sold its television operation to Matsushita. Magnavox was purchased by N. V. Philips, a well-known Dutch firm. Warwick Elec-tronics, until then one of America's largest private television manufacturers, was purchased by Sanyo. In less than a year, three other U.S. television companies were either acquired or forced out of business.

In 1968, there were twenty-eight American-owned television manufacturers in business. By the end of 1976, only six remained. Though weakened, these six companies persisted in their fight against the Japanese cartel.

But they were tilting at windmills.

When Jimmy Carter became President in 1977, he inherited the result of years of inaction on the television case. By then, six years' worth of anti-dumping levies had gone uncalculated and uncollected. Zenith's countervailing duty petition, rejected by Treasury in 1976, remained pending in U.S. Customs Court. The NUE (Emerson) and Zenith antitrust suits also awaited decision.

Meanwhile, GTE/Sylvania had petitioned the International Trade Commission, charging that the Japanese cartel had violated U.S. antitrust and predatory-pricing laws. If the ITC agreed, the U.S. government would have been forced to embargo *all* illegally imported televisions. Several unions also had petitioned Treasury to restrict Japanese television imports, citing international trade agreements that permitted such restrictions if a domestic industry faced irreversible damage as a result of dumping.

In addition, the Committee to Preserve American Color Television (COMPACT)—a coalition of the remaining U.S. television manufacturers and unions—had petitioned the federal government to issue a quantitative restriction on the import of all finished color televisions. This action, COMPACT maintained, was permissible under both U.S. law and the laws of the GATT whenever a domestic industry faced irreparable harm.

The double-pricing scheme soon began to unravel. In March 1976, the ITC initiated a preliminary investigation of the secret rebate program. The Justice Department also started an investigation.

The Japanese cartel faced a minefield of proceedings and investigations. It badly needed to strike a political accommodation with the U.S. government. It badly needed Harald Malmgren.

Malmgren was the perfect candidate to broker a favorable deal for the Japanese. Having previously served as Deputy Special Trade Representative for Presidents Nixon and Ford, he was intimately familiar with the television case. He had worked with Eberle to craft America's position for the Nixon-Tanaka summit in 1972. When he left government in the mid-1970s, Malmgren became a free-lance agent of foreign influence. In 1977, five cartel members—Hitachi, Mitsubishi Electric, Sanyo, Sharp, and Toshiba—hired him to solve their problems.

Under the terms of his employment with the Japanese, Malmgren was obliged to work closely with the government of Japan. In fact, his contract said, "In carrying out the responsibilities under the retainer agreement, [Malmgren] is required to work closely with MITI."

Malmgren quickly delivered. As the *Japan Economic Journal* reported: "In three short months, Mr. Malmgren was able to talk to all sides involved in the dispute, and work out a compromise that was later called the orderly marketing agreement for Japanese color TV exports to the U.S."

The Orderly Marketing Agreement (OMA) limited Japanese television exports to the United States to 1.75 million units a year for three years. But it allowed the Japanese to use their newly acquired U.S. base—the previously American-owned manufacturing companies they had purchased—to fill orders that exceeded the quota. And what they couldn't fill with their new U.S. facilities, they could always meet with the stockpile of Japanese-made televisions already sitting in American warehouses.

The American television companies that had licensing arrangements with the Japanese—GE and RCA—thought the quotas "a good compromise." Zenith and others opposed them, insisting that they would be able to compete fairly with Japan only if Treasury would collect anti-dumping duties—and thereby negate the cartel's predatory-pricing advantage.

Malmgren's OMA quota was imposed anyway.

But much more than the television quota was agreed to in those telling first days of the Carter Administration.

Carter's point man on trade was Robert Strauss, the newly appointed Special Trade Representative and the former chairman of the Democratic Party as well as a top fund-raiser for Democratic candidates. As Strauss himself admitted, he knew virtually nothing about trade negotiations.

In a March 1977 *Newsweek* article, Strauss put it this way: "I know something more than absolutely nothing, but less than a little." Two months later, Strauss proved his point. As part of the deal, he signed a secret side letter with the Japanese and agreed to provisions that would hamper American actions on the television case for years to come. Strauss committed the United States to:

- Limit the ITC investigation of predatory pricing by the Japanese cartel.
- Appeal an earlier ruling by the Customs Court in favor of Zenith.

(The Japanese rebate of consumption taxes had been ruled a bounty or grant that required the Treasury Department to impose a countervailing duty.)

- Liquidate anti-dumping duties expeditiously. (The Japanese understood this to mean that U.S. officials would settle for little or nothing.)
- Ignore monopolization charges against Japanese companies when they were acting domestically in accordance with the directives of the Japanese government. (This gave the cartel an inviolable sanctuary from which they could pursue their anti-competitive schemes.)
- Inform the Japanese government quickly of any significant findings arising from U.S. investigations on the television case, and be open to informal Japanese communications (that is, create a back channel).

Strauss was badly outnegotiated.

Foremost on the American negotiating agenda had been the multilateral GATT negotiations and Japan's continued participation in those talks. For Strauss and the U.S. trade negotiating office, bilateral issues like the television case were little more than hindrances to America's larger GATT agenda.

The Japanese, on the other hand, saw the GATT negotiations as merely a sideshow. They wanted firm control of specific end-use industries—especially the critical consumer electronics sector. Thanks to Strauss, the cartel achieved a political solution to most of its legal problems in a single bold stroke—and at virtually no cost. It now had everything it needed to complete its assault on what remained of the American television industry.

As Strauss had promised, the ITC dropped its investigation. A leading U.S. government figure in the case was Daniel Minchew, chairman of the International Trade Commission during the Carter Administration and a former lobbyist for the Japanese. While the GTE/Sylvania petition was under ITC review, Minchew was in Tokyo exchanging views about television dumping with the Vice Minister of MITI and members of the Diet. When Congress got word of this, Minchew was publicly reproached in a hearing of the House Ways and Means Subcommittee on Trade. While still ITC chairman—and before he later went to prison for unrelated criminal activities—Minchew negotiated a contract to lobby for the Japanese once again.

. . .

Dropping the ITC case was only one of many ways in which the federal government—following the pattern set by the Strauss agreement—sided with the Japanese cartel against America's own television industry. In quick succession, the government led a successful fight to overturn Zenith's favorable ruling in the Customs Court, thereby relieving the Japanese of countervailing duties. The Justice Department reviewed the Zenith and NUE antitrust cases and ruled—incredibly—that it found "no evidence of concerted predatory conduct intended to destroy and supplant the U.S. color TV industry, either at an earlier period of time or at the present time."

Treasury went through the pretense of beginning to collect dumping duties. Customs was to set a figure on how much the Japanese manufacturers and their importers owed. The Japanese knew, of course, that thanks to the Strauss agreement they owed nothing. But Customs and the other agencies were unaware of the agreement.

During the Nixon and Ford years, the Japanese had been able to frustrate the inquiry by refusing to provide the information needed to make the dumping calculations. In late 1977, however, the Customs Service realized that there was an easy way to accurately calculate such duties—even without Japanese cooperation. Customs could simply use the commodity tax collected by the Japanese government as the basis for estimating U.S. anti-dumping duties. The anti-dumping statutes had defined foreign market value in almost the same manner as the Japanese government defined the basis for its commodity taxes. Moreover, in the absence of timely and reliable information, the Commissioner of Customs had the legal authority to use the best source available. This was it.*

In December 1977, the Customs Service initiated Project Omega to calculate and assess the duties quickly. By early March 1978, it was ready. The bill was going to be enormous—almost $382 million for duties on televisions dumped between January 1972 and April 1977 alone. The fees were scheduled to be collected on March 31, 1978.

On March 20, 1978, the Customs Service sent a letter to its field offices ordering them to keep the pending duty bill secret. It was too late. Three days earlier, Robert Mundheim, general counsel of the Treasury Department, had informed the Japanese government on a "strictly confidential basis" about the proposed U.S. actions.

Mundheim told the Japanese that, while their companies might wish

---

* The wording of Japan's commodity tax law is roughly the same as the wording of U.S. anti-dumping law where calculations of duties are concerned. But under U.S. anti-dumping laws, there is an adjustment mechanism for different circumstances of sale that the Japanese commodity tax does not include. Therefore, the U.S. method results in some inflation. Still, it was the best information available to Customs officials.

to litigate the pending duties, "the law requires that the anti-dumping duties assessed be paid before the litigation begins." On the other hand, Mundheim wrote, "we would be prepared to work out an approach with the affected importers that would permit them to obtain a judicial ruling on the major legal aspects of Customs' action without first paying all of the duties that are likely to be assessed."

Nor did Treasury stop there in its efforts to help the Japanese. A Mundheim aide, Jordan Luke, was sent to coach a representative of the Japanese Embassy on how to obtain a Customs Court decision before the total amount of duty on all entries would have to be paid.

Naturally, the Japanese cartel was immediately informed of Mundheim's confidential letter to the Japanese government. The cartel's representatives and lobbyists soon besieged Treasury officials. Meanwhile, American manufacturers and Congress were told nothing.

Ten days after Mundheim's letter, the Japanese government officially protested the proposed collections. It also requested an emergency meeting between Treasury officials and lawyers from the Japanese cartel. The meeting was held the following day at Treasury. Twenty representatives from the cartel attended, as did a handful of Japanese Embassy officials. One embassy official drolly argued that Customs' anti-dumping determination could only be made with information supplied by the Japanese cartel. The cartel's American lawyers urged that the U.S. government not inform Congress, the press, or U.S. companies about what was being considered or the negotiations with the cartel. Treasury complied, enabling the cartel to orchestrate all the political leverage it needed during the critical next few days.

On March 30, the Japanese Ambassador met with Mundheim and Treasury Under Secretary Bette Anderson to voice the objections of the government of Japan. He urged a delay until the "propriety of using the proposed methodology" could be discussed between the two governments. The same day—one day before the levy collection was to take place—Treasury was deluged with phone calls from American importers who made emotional pleas and threats. One Puerto Rican distributor of Japanese television sets threatened to kill himself if high duties were assessed.

The Treasury Department quickly gave in. It agreed to reconsider its calculation procedures and to collect only $46 million in anti-dumping duties for the April 1972–June 1973 period. Because the Customs liquidation notices assessing the penalties had already been distributed for posting the next morning, overnight telexes had to be sent to each Customs office ordering them to adjust the notice before posting it.

Only then did Congress learn about the notices. Two of the most

powerful congressmen—Charles Vanik (D-Ohio), chairman of the House
Ways and Means Subcommittee on Trade, and Dan Rostenkowski
(D-Ill.), a senior member of the committee—lambasted Treasury, citing
its procedural delay and blatant disregard for the American television
industry. For years thereafter, both congressmen would press reluctant
Treasury officials to fully assess the anti-dumping duties owed by the
Japanese. But that was still to come. In 1978, the real challenge was
simply to ensure that Treasury collected the $46 million it had already
assessed.

Treasury's unexpected accommodation of the Japanese created chaos
within the Customs Service. Two weeks after the March 30 decision,
Customs staff lawyers sent an extraordinary joint letter to their superiors
asking for clarification of the Treasury decision. The letter complained
that Customs' lawyers were "discovering Treasury policy through the
often dubious representations of the affected parties."

The letter also reported what the Japanese were saying—namely, that
the assessment was merely provisional, no more than a political sop, and
that it would be mitigated (or settled) through informal, government-to-
government negotiations or relatively informal contacts between Japanese manufacturers and the Treasury Department. Customs' lawyers
were especially disturbed to see Mundheim express willingness in his
March 17 letter to defer collection. They protested: "Customs was not
only not in receipt of a copy of this letter, it was not aware of its existence
until Mr. Tanabe [of the Japanese Embassy] brought it to our attention."
Obviously, the Japanese knew much more about what was happening at
the highest levels of the Treasury Department than did the Customs
officials who were responsible for collecting the anti-dumping duties.

Soon after the March announcement, the Treasury Department again
acceded to Japanese political pressure, agreeing to find "better numbers"
for duty assessments. What was unclear to outsiders was what "better
numbers" meant. Was Treasury searching for yet another estimating
procedure or was it looking for a face-saving way to settle on the cheap?

While Treasury sought its "better numbers," the cartel and its American corporate partners tried to make an end run around the Justice
Department's fraud investigation. In 1978, they tried to slip into law an
amendment granting retroactive immunity to importers who had falsified
Customs documents. According to members of Congress, the amendment was drafted by the law firm of Baker and McKenzie, counsel
to Mitsubishi Electric, and introduced by Congressman Jim Jones
(D-Okla.), who would become a lobbyist for Toshiba when he left Congress some years later. The immunity ploy quickly collapsed once the
Washington *Post* revealed the scheme.

In April 1978, Japan presented to the State Department its objections to Zenith's suit against the U.S. government for not collecting countervailing duties from the Japanese television manufacturers.

The Japanese warned that if the Supreme Court ruled in Zenith's favor, the decision not only would damage U.S.-Japan trade but would also "adversely affect world trade generally." Specifically, the Japanese government predicted that a ruling for Zenith "could bring about a breakdown of the GATT system itself and seriously impair the chances for success in . . . multilateral international trade negotiations."

The State Department sent Japan's paper to Wade McCree, then U.S. Solicitor General, who passed it on—at the State Department's request—to Michael Rodak, then the clerk of the Supreme Court, for distribution to each of the nine justices.

After Rodak distributed the paper, he sent the following message back to McCree:

I am not aware of any rule of this Court which would permit correspondence of this nature to be received and distributed to this Court. If the Government of Japan wished to express its views concerning this case it should have filed a printed brief . . . as provided for in Rule 42 of the Rules of this Court.

What Rodak meant was that the Japanese government had no business petitioning the Supreme Court in such a manner and, more important, that the State Department and the Solicitor General had no business acting as conduits for the government of Japan.

On April 26, 1978, the Supreme Court heard arguments on the Zenith countervailing duty case. In the session, Justice Harry Blackmun reprimanded the Solicitor General for his role in Japan's attempt to intimidate the Court. The exchange between Blackmun and McCree went like this:

[JUSTICE BLACKMUN]: Mr. Solicitor General, could I ask a question which perhaps I shouldn't ask. It may be a little delicate, but at the request of the Department of State you distributed a communication from the government of Japan in this matter. . . .
What does this mean vis-à-vis this case?
MR. McCREE: I don't think it means anything as far as the duty of this Court is concerned here today. . . .
[JUSTICE BLACKMUN]: You do not regard it as a threat to this Court?
MR. McCREE: I do not and I certainly circulated it only because

it had been forwarded to us from the Department of State and we circulated it for what it was worth. . . .

[JUSTICE BLACKMUN]: In any event, you are here in good faith doing your best to uphold the position espoused by the government of Japan anyway?

MR. McCREE: Well, if the Court please, I regard my role here as seeking to uphold the construction that the Congress, that the Secretary of the Treasury has placed upon the statute committed to you to administer, and the client of the government here is the Secretary of State and not a foreign prince or potentate.

In the end, the Supreme Court voted 9–0 against Zenith.

A year and a half after Robert Strauss made his secret commitments, Dan Rostenkowski learned of them. At a Ways and Means hearing, he asked Strauss for a copy of the secret side agreement, which he was given for the record. Surprisingly, virtually none of the American manufacturers ever learned of it. More important, the U.S. government remained committed to its deal.

In late 1978, the Japanese stepped up the pressure for a political compromise on the dumping case. Their lobbyists besieged Congress and the Administration. Prime Minister Takeo Fukuda sent President Carter a personal letter protesting U.S. actions to collect anti-dumping duties.

The one thing that the cartel and its U.S. importers did not do was pay the levied anti-dumping duties. Treasury pressed for its money only gingerly. By the spring of 1979, Customs had collected only $5.6 million of the $46 million it was owed. Of that, $5 million came from Sears. The other defendants were not paying their fines.

In a September 1978 Ways and Means subcommittee hearing, Vanik lashed out at Mundheim: "If your Department has a claim through IRS on a taxpayer, you have him tied up before he can turn around. He has liens all over him to keep him from breathing until he pays up, or gets out, if that is the case." Vanik demanded the same treatment for the Japanese cartel.

Throughout 1978, working groups within Treasury and Customs struggled to come up with a "better number"—one acceptable to the Japanese. In December, Treasury found its "better numbers." The only obstacle to a settlement was Congress.

In December, Mundheim met with Congressman Vanik to solicit his support for a quick deal. Though the estimated television dumping duties for 1972 through April 1977 had been nearly $382 million (plus an additional $200 million for the two years that followed), Mundheim asked Vanik if he would agree to settle the entire dumping case for $50 million. Mundheim also wanted to settle the kickback fraud for $5 to $10 million. (Under the law as much as $1 *billion* in fines could have been levied.)

The congressman angrily rejected the Treasury proposal. If the Administration settled on the cheap, he said, he would oppose legislation that Treasury had been seeking to allow the United States to adopt the multilateral trade agreements that had been negotiated in Tokyo.

So Treasury returned to its traditional negotiating posture: it stalled. It also went back to the drawing board to find another set of "better numbers." This time, however, it relied on data provided by the Japanese cartel. Customs' staff lawyers now went into open revolt. In a group memo dated March 2, 1979, nine of the staff lawyers vigorously protested the limited nature of and unverifiable statistics employed in the new approach. They argued that the Japanese commodity tax was remarkably reliable and should be used to make the calculations. What they understood was that, while members of the Japanese cartel might lie to the U.S. government, they would not lie to Japanese tax authorities. More important, Customs' lawyers knew the Japanese commodity tax figure was reliable, because the Japanese television manufacturers had no reason to inflate the amount of taxes they had to pay.

While Treasury was trying to engineer a settlement, it moved with glacial speed to collect the duties it had assessed. In late 1978 and early 1979, Treasury repeatedly granted interest-free payment extensions. It even offered to accept 25 percent of the payment in cash and the balance in the form of an interest-free promissory note.

Treasury's passivity infuriated Vanik and Rostenkowski. They prodded Treasury to make a full and immediate collection. After all, the purpose of the anti-dumping levy was to offset the predatory-price advantage the Japanese had over the U.S. companies. The longer Treasury dallied, the more U.S. industry was harmed. In a March 19, 1979, letter, Vanik wrote Robert Chasen, Commissioner of Customs: "I am compelled to point out that Customs' solicitous regard for the potential adverse impact of a full cash collection upon importers is completely at odds with the lack of concern for the injury of the domestic industry which has characterized the entire history of this case."

The congressmen knew that once the GATT negotiations were completed and approved by Congress, much of their political leverage would be lost. And so, predictably, the Treasury Department withheld action on the television case until it was clear that the Trade Agreements Act of 1979 would become law.

To facilitate a political settlement, the cartel and the Carter Administration devised a clever ploy. A provision was eased into the Trade Agreements Act of 1979 that allowed the Customs Service to compromise U.S. claims and not be challenged in court *if* the deal was completed before January 1, 1980. In the same legislation, a disgusted Congress transferred the Treasury Department's authority to administer countervailing duty and anti-dumping laws to the Commerce Department. The effective date of this transfer would also be January 1.

In July 1979, the Customs Service created a Special Task Force on Japanese Televisions. Ted Hume, a Mundheim aide, was put in charge. His mandate: clear the slate. Hume and his team made every effort to engineer a solution before the New Year's deadline. On October 31, the Customs Service issued a news release about Treasury's intentions to make some "adjustments" to its March 31, 1978, assessments.

Vanik and Rostenkowski dug in their heels. They pressured Treasury Secretary William Miller not to settle the matter before the end of the year. At the same time, the U.S. Electronics Industries Association and COMPACT filed suit to enjoin Treasury from entering into a compromise or settlement prior to January 1.

Although Treasury did try to wrap up a deal before January 1, it missed the deadline. On January 2, the responsibility for assessing and collecting the anti-dumping duties shifted to the Commerce Department.

Any hope that Commerce would be more aggressive than Treasury in the television matter was soon dashed. In retrospect, it is hardly surprising: Commerce had the same political masters as did Treasury, and most of the same people continued to work on the case. The Treasury staff who had administered the dumping and countervailing duty program went to Commerce; Ted Hume went to the Office of the U.S. Trade Representative.

On January 3, 1980, Hume wrote one of his new bosses, USTR general counsel Robert Cassidy, Jr., a detailed status report on the television case. Hume criticized the use of the commodity tax approach. On the other hand, he acknowledged that the government did not know how much was owed as a result of the fraud cases being pursued by the Justice Department. He also noted that many importers were refusing to pay the assessments levied in March 1978 and that the Justice Department had filed six collection suits.

Hume told Cassidy that the Secretary of Commerce had the authority to settle the case and that "such compromises are relatively invulnerable from judicial attack, if orchestrated properly." He advised Commerce to move quickly and "involve as few people as possible. (It is critical to control the facts.)" Hume was given the job of orchestrating a compromise.

In March 1980, Hume went to Tokyo and met with MITI officials to discuss a settlement. Each side spoke of "better numbers" that ranged from $50 to $100 million. Eventually, they split the difference. The question was how to make this deal politically palatable in America.

On April 28, 1980, Homer Moyer, Commerce's general counsel, announced that the potential anti-dumping duties owed the United States were really only $138.7 million, and not the $382 million Treasury had been ready to assess in March 1978. He also revealed that the government had settled the matter for $77 million, and that Commerce would dismiss suits for the collection of duties assessed upon entries prior to July 1, 1973. Finally, he said that Commerce would abandon all other investigations, claiming that "the United States knows of no violation or potential violation of law relating to or arising from the importation, sale or exportation of television receivers."

The compromise was a major political and economic victory for the cartel. It was the settlement on the cheap that the Japanese had sought through Strauss's secret side letter of May 20, 1977. During the Reagan Administration, the magnitude of the Japanese victory became even more apparent. Of the final $77 million settlement, only $16 million was ever collected. By way of comparison, had the U.S. government not made deals and merely enforced the law, it would have collected a minimum of $1 billion.

Almost immediately after Moyer's announcement, COMPACT and Zenith filed suits challenging the settlement agreement. Both suits contended that it unlawfully forgave hundreds of millions of dollars in anti-dumping duties owed by the Japanese. Zenith argued that the Commerce Secretary, in fact, lacked the authority to make a settlement. Vanik agreed.

The government struck back against Zenith and COMPACT with a zeal it had never shown in its confrontations with the Japanese cartel. The Justice Department stonewalled requests for information, forcing Zenith and COMPACT to pry out the facts piecemeal through federal court orders. To price Zenith out of the litigation, Justice demanded that Zenith post $11.5 million as security, or an amount equal to 15 percent interest, for one year of the uncollected settlement. The court reduced this bond to $250,000.

Ultimately the COMPACT and Zenith cases hinged on whether the Commerce Secretary had the legal authority to settle the anti-dumping suit. In 1979, Congress had sharply limited the President's authority to

settle such cases. To the surprise of Zenith, COMPACT, and legal scholars, the court interpreted the law to mean that such authority was still
vested in the Commerce Secretary. Appeals were made to the Supreme
Court, which chose not to review the case. Zenith and COMPACT were
out of luck.

But the government wasn't satisfied with victory: it sought vengeance.
It sued Zenith to collect the $250,000 bond, ostensibly as compensation
for the interest lost while the suit was being tried. (By contrast, the
government decided not to collect the unpaid interest owed by the Japanese cartel and its importers, an amount worth millions to the Treasury.)

Zenith fought back, and in 1986 the Court of International Trade ruled
in Zenith's favor. In its newfound zeal, the Justice Department appealed
the ruling to the Court of Appeals. In July 1987, however, the lower
court decision was upheld. As one legal scholar notes, it was a bittersweet
victory for Zenith: it had won a minor skirmish but lost the greater battle.
After twenty years, the anti-dumping case was over.

As the anti-dumping proceedings wound down in the late 1970s, the
fraud investigation was shifting into high gear. In 1978, federal prosecutors took some of America's leading retailers before grand juries in Los
Angeles, Chicago, and Norfolk, Virginia.

In January 1979, Seymour Hersh broke the story about the grand jury
investigations on the front page of *The New York Times*. In the article,
a spokesman for the Japanese cartel blamed their American importers
for any crimes that may have been committed.

A Customs Service official also spoke to Hersh. He maintained that
"the most momentous aspect of the grand jury investigation was the
possibly enormous civil penalties facing the importing companies if they
were convicted of Customs fraud. Under this law, the civil penalties
theoretically could equal the total value of the goods fraudulently imported—at least $1 billion." Other Customs officials told Hersh that the
threat of such penalties provided the impetus for Treasury's fast-track
efforts to settle the dumping and civil fraud penalties.

Hersh's article was widely distributed in Congress. His revelations
about the alleged kickback scheme and Treasury's apparent empathy for
the Japanese manufacturers caused a political furor.

In March 1979, Alexander's, Inc., a large department store chain,
pleaded guilty to one count for its involvement in the television conspiracy. Alexander's received the maximum fine: $5,000.

Sears, America's largest retailer and importer of television sets, was
indicted on multiple counts. Sears was accused of filing fraudulent Customs documents to obscure kickbacks, rebates, and illegal credits from
Japanese manufacturers. The Justice Department also named thirty-

seven unindicted co-conspirators: Toshiba and eleven of its employees, Sanyo and six of its employees, and eighteen Sears employees and lawyers. The roster of unindicted co-conspirators included John Rehm, who had been the Special Trade Representative's top lawyer in the 1960s. All denied any wrongdoing.

In 1980, the Sears case went before the U.S. District Court for the Central District of California. By a twist of fate, the case was assigned to the court's chief judge, Manuel L. Real. Sears's litigator was a former assistant to Judge Real.

Early on, Sears quickly moved that the case be dismissed, asserting that the prosecutor had used inflammatory language about the Japanese and had made selective allegations before the grand jury. Judge Real dismissed the case. The Justice Department appealed the decision. In 1981, the U.S. Court of Appeals for the Ninth Circuit reinstated the indictment.

Again, Sears moved that the case be dismissed, this time because of a legal technicality. Again, Judge Real dismissed the case. The Justice Department appealed. In 1983, the Circuit Court again reinstated the indictment.

Sears found another legal technicality and again moved to have the case dismissed. Again, Judge Real complied. The Justice Department appealed. And again the Circuit Court reinstated the indictment. This time, however, the Circuit Court did something highly unusual: it ordered Judge Real to reassign the Sears case to another judge.

Rather than follow the court's order, Judge Real filed his own independent petition to the Supreme Court, asking that it prohibit his removal from the case. On December 1, 1986, Judge Real's petition was denied.

But Judge Real did not reassign the case. Instead, he directed both the Justice Department and Sears to file briefs addressing the question of whether the Circuit Court had the authority to order his removal from the case. The Justice Department appealed.

The case had now become a struggle between the two courts. The Circuit Court ordered the clerk of the court for the Central District of California to randomly select another judge within seven days. Judge Real appealed the order. The bottom line from the Circuit Court: in June 1987, it informed Judge Real that if the case was not reassigned "he might well be punished for contempt."

Judge Real got the message. In July 1987, the case was assigned to Senior District Judge A. Andrew Husak, who is semi-retired but occasionally takes a case.

Sears again petitioned for a dismissal, claiming that it had been denied a speedy trial. In January 1988, Judge Husak dismissed the indictment. For the fifth time, the Justice Department appealed to the Circuit Court. In September 1989, the Circuit Court sent the case back to trial. By this time, one of the government's key witnesses had died. The memory of another had faded. The Justice Department dropped its case.

The private antitrust suits by NUE and Zenith moved as slowly as the Sears case did. En route to trial, Zenith was sued for $1.2 billion by Japanese manufacturers who claimed—quite imaginatively—that Zenith was unfairly restraining their efforts to expand their American market share. The discovery process in this countersuit delayed matters for another two years.

In 1980, the antitrust case was finally brought to the summary judgment phase of pretrial proceedings. In a wild series of twists and turns during the evidentiary stage, the presiding judge ruled that the tenets of the Anti-dumping Act of 1916 were not applicable to the case because of certain technical differences between television sets sold in Japan and those sold in the United States. More critically, however, he ruled that key pieces of the NUE and Zenith evidence were inadmissible. Among those items that the judge would not allow:

- The Treasury Department's finding that the Japanese had engaged in dumping.
- The unanimous finding by the U.S. Tariff Commission that American firms had been injured by the cartel's dumping.
- Evidence of the vast differential between the prices the cartel was charging in Japan and those it charged in America.
- The Japanese Fair Trade Commission's finding that the cartel's actions had been anti-competitive.
- Business diaries, memoranda, minutes and agendas of meetings of the cartel companies' executives that showed how they acted in concert.
- Portions of the reports submitted by the plaintiffs' economic experts.

Absent this proof, the District Court dismissed the conspiracy case on the grounds of insufficient evidence.

NUE and Zenith appealed the ruling to the U.S. Court of Appeals for the Third Circuit. In late 1983, the Appeals Court ruled unanimously that a fact finder could reasonably conclude from the admissible evidence that:

- The Japanese manufacturers had agreed to stabilize prices of televisions in Japan.
- The domestic and international competitive situation for the Japanese television makers gave them a motive to enter into the alleged conspiracy.
- The Japanese entered into formal written agreements that established minimum prices (or check prices) for television sets sold for export to the United States.
- The Japanese allocated customers in the United States by means of the "five-company rule," pursuant to which each petitioner agreed to sell directly to only five customers in the United States (including each manufacturer's U.S. sales subsidiary).
- Japanese prices for televisions sold in the United States were substantially lower than prices for comparable televisions in Japan. In fact, these were "dumping prices" that might help support an inference of predatory intent.
- The Japanese firms deceived the American government as well as their own government about the prices charged in the United States by systematically giving secret rebates to U.S. purchasers. Each Japanese manufacturer, moreover, knew that its Japanese rivals were also giving rebates.

The Appeals Court ruled that this "amounted to sufficient evidence of the alleged conspiracy" to send the case to trial. Officials at Zenith and NUE were jubilant, thinking that they would finally be able to try their case. But their elation was premature.

The Japanese manufacturers asked the Supreme Court to overturn the decision of the Appeals Court and thereby end the case. In 1985, the Court agreed to undertake a review.

In a stunning blow to Zenith and NUE, the Justice Department filed a "friend of the court" brief on behalf of the *Japanese manufacturers*. In it, Justice made three arguments. First, it argued that the Japanese companies had acted legitimately. Their parallel low prices, claimed Justice, should be viewed as the result of independent action, rather than systematic collusion. (Ironically, the Justice Department's case against Sears had named several of the same Japanese companies as unindicted co-conspirators for paying kickbacks and filing false import documents on their television exports.)

Second, Justice argued that "activity that is compelled by a foreign sovereign should not lead to liability in a private antitrust suit." Justice claimed that the cartel's actions were legal because they were prompted by the Japanese government—the "devil made me do it" excuse. Here is the second irony: when American companies form an export cartel under U.S. law to export to Japan, the U.S. government has no objection if the firms are prosecuted under Japanese antitrust laws. In other words, while the Japanese television cartel was immunized from U.S. laws, a defensive U.S. cartel would have been vulnerable to certain prosecution.

Third, the Justice Department argued that a finding in favor of Zenith and NUE could harm U.S. foreign policy interests. To support this point, the Justice Department told the Supreme Court that "the Governments of Australia, Canada, France, Japan, the Republic of Korea, Spain and the United Kingdom have formally advised the Department of State of their concerns about the potential impact of the court of appeals' decision."

In this last argument, the U.S. government boldly affirmed what the American companies had alleged all along: that their survival was being recklessly endangered by the amorphous goals of U.S. foreign policy.

In a narrow 5–4 decision, the Supreme Court found insufficient evidence of a conspiracy and sent the case back to the Appeals Court to determine whether more evidence was available. The Appeals Court dismissed the antitrust suit, saying it was "somewhat confused" by the Supreme Court. In April 1987, the Supreme Court refused to hear a final appeal by the American companies.

At long last, the antitrust case was over. Japan's television cartel had won.

By the late 1980s, Japan dominated America's television and consumer electronics markets. The logical next step was to squeeze extra profits from this dominant position.

In 1989, New York Attorney General Robert Abrams revealed that Panasonic and Technics (both subsidiaries of Japan's Matsushita) had mounted a vertical price-fixing scheme in America. Matsushita, of course, was a founding member of the television cartel. The Panasonic/Technics scheme was hauntingly reminiscent of what the Home Electric Appliance Market Stabilization Council had pulled off in Japan in the 1950s.

Abrams revealed that between March 1988 and August 1989 the Japanese companies had forced their American retailers—among them, Best Products, K Mart, Montgomery Ward, Circuit City—to charge fixed minimum prices for their products. Though his charge referred only to the sixteen most popular products of Panasonic and Technics—VCRs, camcorders, cordless telephones, answering machines, and stereo equipment, among other items—Abrams said that the firms had, in earlier efforts, tried to set fixed prices on all three hundred items they sold in the United States.

Through their scheme, the firms artificially had raised their U.S. prices by 5 to 10 percent. Abrams said the price-fixing was administered "through an elaborate nationwide scheme involving scores of [Panasonic and Technics] sales executives pressuring thousands of retailers to comply with the scheme and monitoring the prices they actually charged."

To enforce this price-fixing effort, Panasonic directed its executives to keep all U.S. retailers of Panasonic goods in step with the firm's policies. Panasonic told its employees that "those dealers not adhering to company policy could 'create chaos in the marketplace' and would allow Panasonic to 'lose face with the entire industry.' "

The question that lingers is whether the rest of "the entire industry," as Panasonic called it, really did know about Matsushita's price-fixing activities. If they did not, then how could Panasonic "lose face"? More important, were other consumer electronics companies participating in similar vertical price-fixing schemes?

When Abrams confronted Panasonic and Technics, they immediately agreed to a settlement—without actually acknowledging wrongdoing. The settlement required the companies to stop price-fixing, to repay $16 million in overcharges to nearly 700,000 customers, and to pay another $2 million to the state for settlement administration costs.

The settlement also revealed:

- Lechmere, Inc., a retailer with stores in New York and other northeastern states, was told by Panasonic that it would "make an example of dealers charging below the 'go' price [the fixed price] and would terminate all or part of its shipments to noncomplying dealers."
- When Luria and Sons, a Florida retailer, undercut Panasonic's fixed price on a cordless telephone, four different Panasonic representatives threatened that Panasonic would cease doing business with noncomplying retailers.

As in Japan, this sort of price-fixing allows the manufacturer to gain an unearned monopoly profit, which can then be used to subsidize dumping and other anti-competitive behavior.

But the Japanese were able to extort monopoly profits from American consumers because America's own television industry in effect had been destroyed by two decades of illegal, anti-competitive behavior by the Japanese.

By the late 1980s, the one hope that remained for an American television manufacturing industry was the emergence of high-definition television (HDTV).

Both Zenith and RCA executives had faith that the HDTV technologies were as much an improvement over current television technology as color had been over black and white. Just as Americans replaced their black-and-white sets with color sets in the 1960s and 1970s, they seemed likely to replace their existing receivers with HDTV in the 1990s.

For Zenith and RCA, this pending switch to a new technology offered a unique opportunity to get back into the television business.

Japanese and European companies realized this, too. All were racing to develop a technical standard for HDTV, and pressing the Federal Communications Commission to adopt their individual HDTV standards for the American market. Yet in 1986, in another blow to the American companies, the State Department urged the FCC to adopt *Japanese* HDTV standards. The message from the State and Justice departments was that the federal government was not only indifferent but actually somewhat hostile to the fate of the remnants of the American television industry.

In 1986, RCA was bought by General Electric. GE then sold the RCA television subsidiary to Thomson, a French company. Today, RCA's old research facility is owned and operated by a new European owner, but it has drastically reduced the number of workers. That leaves Zenith as the sole U.S.-owned television manufacturer. It holds a 12 percent share of the American market and is barely breaking even. Zenith is attempting to quickly introduce a leading-edge HDTV system, but the American government remains indifferent to the company's fate and that of the industry. The bulk of the American market is supplied by American-based operations of foreign-owned companies.

In large measure, the collapse of the U.S.-owned television industry can be traced to the failure of the American government to stop the predatory practices of the Japanese cartel.

When confronted with Japanese subsidies, the federal government opposed its own industry's efforts to apply countervailing duties.

When faced with the cartel's anti-competitive behavior, the American government refused to mount an antitrust suit and it actively opposed those filed by private American companies. When presented with clear evidence of a kickback scheme and Customs fraud, the federal government scuttled an ITC investigation.

When the Japanese cartel engaged in massive dumping, the federal government took twelve years to provide relief to American companies—and then settled their claims for less than two cents on the dollar. Moreover, at critical moments, the federal government repeatedly leaked vital information to the Japanese government—information that it withheld from American companies and Congress.

The failure of the federal government to enforce the legal protections it owed to the U.S.-owned television industry was no accident. Nor was it the consequence of bureaucratic incapacity. Even at its worst, American government is not *that* incompetent. Rather, it was the direct result of deliberate, repeated delays—a crucial part of the strategy devised by the American agents of the Japanese cartel.

As of 1989, more than twenty former government officials with some responsibility for the television case had been hired directly by the Japanese television manufacturers or by the law firms and lobbying organizations that represent them. Many other ex-officials involved in this case have gone to work for related Japanese interests. Under existing ethics laws, this is entirely legal.

The decline and fall of the U.S.-owned television industry is an economic loss of historic proportions. During the 1980s, the U.S. market for VCRs alone generated more than $71 billion in sales for Japanese manufacturers, and added significantly to the U.S. trade deficit with Japan.

The loss of the American television industry also undermined the television parts industry—a producer of such integral components as semiconductors, which are also used in hundreds of other industries. The Commerce Department's own analysts have concluded that a key factor in the decline of the American semiconductor industry was the loss of U.S. television manufacturers, who were among its largest customers.

Much like falling dominoes, the decline of the semiconductor industry now threatens dozens of other related U.S. industries, such as supercomputers and advanced machine tools.

Japan's success in this bold attack—which catapulted it to global dominance in the electronics industry—has put Japan today in a position from which it can easily launch similar strikes against all the world's high-technology markets. HDTV is but one such industry.

3.
JAPANESE
POLITICKING

Chapter Seven

HIDDEN INTERESTS

IN JULY 1989, millionaire Texas chicken processor Lonnie Pilgrim passed out $10,000 gifts on the Texas Senate floor while legislation that he favored was pending. Pilgrim, who gave personal checks with the payee's name left blank to nine of the thirty-one state senators, said he was making political contributions, not paying bribes.

And in fact, as Travis County district attorney Ronnie Earle said of Pilgrim's antics: "It would be difficult to make it into a bribery case. In Texas, it's almost impossible to bribe a public official as long as you report it."

While the national laws on campaign financing are not quite as porous as those in Texas, they also leave enormous loopholes. Although federal election law prohibits a foreign national from making a direct or indirect contribution in any local, state, or federal election, the same law allows foreign-owned companies in the United States to operate political action committees (PACs) and make contributions as if they were American firms.

This means foreign companies can put money into American elections by creating U.S. subsidiaries and raising money from their U.S. employees. Many do. In the mid-1980s, Sony Corporation of America donated $29,000 to California legislators, hoping to help persuade them to repeal the state's unitary tax. In their book *Buying Into America*, Martin and Susan Tolchin reveal that a coalition of "mostly Japanese foreign investors" added another $108,000 to the pot.

In the 1980s, a hundred foreign companies used this loophole to create their own PACs, and contributed to the war chests of House, Senate, and even presidential candidates.

Reports from the Federal Election Commission reveal that foreign companies contributed more than $1.1 million in the 1985–86 election cycle and more than $2.8 million in the 1987–88 elections. One such PAC, which gave George Bush's campaign money, is an offshoot of a Middle East holding company. Another PAC, which donated money to Michael Dukakis' campaign, is the U.S. affiliate of a Greek company.

In the 1987–88 election cycle, most foreign PACs, including some controlled by Swiss, Belgian, Saudi, Dutch, and British companies, funneled their contributions to the reelection campaigns of powerful members of the Senate Finance Committee and the House Ways and Means Committee—those responsible for American trade and tax legislation.

While the contributions of foreign-controlled PACs must be reported to the Federal Election Commission, there are legal, and sometimes untraceable, ways for foreign monies to be slipped into political campaigns. One is through "soft money" financing. Under a loophole in existing federal election laws, corporations, unions, and individuals can make unlimited contributions to the state Republican and Democratic parties. These monies are exempt from federal regulation or public disclosure.

Fund-raising experts estimate that each party generated at least $50 million of this unreported "soft" money in the 1988 campaign. Only the party chiefs know how much of it came from the U.S. subsidiaries of foreign-owned corporations.

Like American companies, foreign firms can also give money to American politicians by paying them "honoraria" for making speeches or participating in panel discussions. Dozens of members accept such foreign largess. A foreign firm can also contribute to elected officials in a number of indirect ways: through a well-connected law firm, a public relations company, even an investment bank it has hired. Partners in these firms generally contribute handsomely to their firms' PACs. So although the money may flow into the firm from foreign sources, once it goes from the partner to the PAC it becomes as American as apple pie.

Another way for foreign interests to increase the campaign funds of their U.S. political friends is to encourage their American dealers or suppliers to establish a PAC. One of the most influential American PACs with strong foreign support is the Auto Dealers and Drivers for Free Trade PAC (AUTOPAC). AUTOPAC was formed in April 1981 as an independent PAC operated by American vehicle-importers. Under existing campaign laws, independent PACs can collect and spend unlimited amounts to elect or defeat a candidate *if* they operate without the cooperation or consultation of the candidate and his campaign operation.

The American dealers who organized and run AUTOPAC urge their members to contribute either $2 for every car they sell or $5,000 a year. Foreign manufacturers ask their American dealers to participate in the PAC. Robert M. McElwaine, president of the American International Automobile Dealers Association, says the foreign manufacturers provide "encouragement, not coercion." In the 1988 election cycle, AUTOPAC raised $4.5 million from U.S. foreign-vehicle dealers. Of this, $2.57 million went for political contributions; the balance was spent on "administrative costs."

Because it is an "independent," AUTOPAC maintains its own staff, conducts political polls, and publishes a newsletter. Since independents are prohibited from lobbying, AUTOPAC relies on its member dealers to make its political pitches to Congress and the Administration.

One of the messages that AUTOPAC sends to elected officials in Washington is that if they vote against "free trade," they may wind up on the PAC's political hit list. This is not an idle threat. AUTOPAC regularly targets elected officials and then spends hundreds of thousands of dollars to defeat them—often in the critical last moments of their campaigns. In a close race, this money can prove decisive.

The 1988 Florida Senate race, in fact, demonstrates the potency of the AUTOPAC threat.

Both candidates in the race—Democrat Buddy MacKay and Republican Connie Mack—were well-known members of the House of Representatives. Their race was so close that on election night none of the four major networks was able to call a winner. In the end, the race was decided by fewer than 31,000 votes.

MacKay lost. He now reflects: "I could overcome the fact that Florida has become a Republican state. I could deal with Mack outspending me two to one. I could even surmount having Michael Dukakis head the national ticket. What I could not overcome was the $326,000 that AUTOPAC spent against me in the last four days of the campaign."

MacKay was referring to a flurry of negative advertisements that AUTOPAC ran in the final moments of the election. MacKay ruefully adds: "In the final analysis, I was not beaten by Connie Mack. I was beaten by Tokyo."

In the 1987–88 election cycle, AUTOPAC spent a total of $1.4 million on just seven congressional races. Six of its seven "picks" won. Five of those six were Republicans.

While AUTOPAC has spent money on Democrats' campaigns, its heavy contributions—historically and recently—go overwhelmingly to Republican candidates. Overall, 83 percent of AUTOPAC's 1987–88 election cycle contributions went to Republicans. Predictably, Democrats criticize AUTOPAC as an adjunct finance committee of the Republican Party. They also criticize the organization for its relationship with foreign automotive manufacturers. In April 1989, Senators David Boren (D-Okla.), Bob Graham (D-Fla.), Richard Bryan (D-Nev.), and Harry Reid (D-Nev.) sent a joint letter to the Justice Department questioning whether AUTOPAC should be forced to register as a foreign agent:

> We believe that the level of political activity undertaken by the Auto Dealers PAC and the *prima facie* evidence of a principal-agent relationship between the members of the . . . PAC and the Japanese automobile manufacturers demand an investigation to determine whether the American people are being properly informed about the identity and agenda of the PAC.

Tom Nemet, an auto-import dealer and the founder of AUTOPAC, dismisses the notion that the PAC is either a Japanese or a Republican front as "hogwash." In the fall of 1989, the Justice Department refused to require AUTOPAC to register as a foreign agent. Bryan and others are now working to change campaign finance reporting standards to require organizations such as AUTOPAC to register as foreign agents.

The final irony of AUTOPAC, which supported Republicans in the 1988 election, lies in who represents it in Washington: the law firm of Patton, Boggs & Blow—for Thomas Boggs is the son of Hale Boggs, the late Democratic Majority Leader, and Lindy Boggs, a Democratic representative from the state of Louisiana. In a videotape sent to auto dealers, Boggs praises AUTOPAC and the political power that it creates. Even more ironic, another member of Boggs's firm is Ron Brown, chairman of the Democratic National Committee, whose job is to help Democrats win elections.

Over the past few decades, literally hundreds of groups have sprung up with names that hide the interests they represent. As a result, Congress, federal officials, and the press find it increasingly difficult to know just whom they are talking to—to say nothing of where their information is coming from.

A group called Friendship in Freedom, for instance, ran half-page ads in most major American newspapers during the summer of 1989. The ads extolled U.S.-Europe relations and urged readers to "use every opportunity to propagate in articles, interviews and speeches the common values of European and American civilisation." The ads gave a Washington address, noted that the program was a German initiative, and in very fine print stated that the "founders of this campaign are leading citizens of the Federal Republic of Germany." What the ad did not reveal was that the address was that of a Washington lobbying firm and that the campaign was propaganda paid for by the West German government.

American companies often do the same thing. In the mid-1980s, the U.S. Committee for Energy Awareness sponsored a $30 million advertising campaign to foster the use of nuclear energy. Half the funding came from some fifty utilities who went unacknowledged in the group's ad campaign.

Weak disclosure laws on political representation, coupled with slack enforcement, gives foreign interests unlimited opportunities to operate political "front groups" in Washington while the interests themselves stay in the political background.

No other nation is better at this political game of shadows-and-mirrors than Japan. The Japanese realize that most Americans resent any outside interference in domestic politics. So to deflect potential criticism, they hide most of their political activities behind front groups, trade associations, and ad hoc coalitions. This allows them to put "an American face" on their U.S. politicking.

In 1976, a major Japanese front group was exposed when the Justice Department filed a civil suit against the United States–Japan Trade Council and MITI's Japan Trade Promotion Office. The council had represented itself as an independent trade association. It lobbied, directly and indirectly, for open-door trade policies. Its budget was more than $500,000 annually. In 1973, it played a key role in Japan's efforts to eliminate the "Buy America" clause in the legislation authorizing the Alaska pipeline.

The Justice Department suit charged that the council, which for twenty years had represented itself as a nonprofit trade association whose American members were interested in U.S.-Japan trade, was actually "an organization using a trade association façade to conceal its foreign agent activities in this country in representing Japanese governmental interests."

Less than two months after the suit was filed, the United States–Japan Trade Council signed a consent decree by which it was required to notify all parties on council mailing lists of the lawsuit, inform congressional and governmental contacts, and amend its registration documents with the Justice Department to reflect its role as a foreign agent. As part of this arrangement, the council's director and its executive secretary— Noel Hemmendinger and Allen Taylor—issued a statement that conceded that:

the Council, from its inception, in 1957, has acted as an agent of
the Japanese Government, and . . . it has never been nor is it now
a trade association, nor has it been governed by its members. The
members of the Council were not and are not now members as
such, but merely subscribers to its publications and have no voice
in its operations. The Council receives almost all of its funds from
the Japanese Government, which exercises general supervision and
has ultimate control over its activities. In addition, [the Japan Trade
Promotion Office] served no purpose other than to transmit funds
between the Embassy of Japan and the Council so as to obscure
the connection between the Government of Japan and the Council.

The Japanese are quick learners. Since this incident, Japanese government and corporate concerns have worked through real U.S. advocacy
organizations. Japanese companies have joined hundreds of trade associations and regularly enlist the aid of American "political-establishment
figures" who lend credibility to their politicking.

In 1981, *The New York Times* revealed that Japanese interests had
gained a major voice in a Washington public-interest group called Consumers for World Trade (CWT). Unlike the sham memberships of the
United States–Japan Trade Council, the membership of CWT is real: it
helps finance the organization's work. In 1980, Japanese automotive companies began to enroll new members in CWT from among their American
employees—dealers, mechanics, and telephone operators, among others. Subaru paid the initial membership dues of $15 for 1,500 of its
employees. At one time, Subaru's employees represented more than half
of the organization's membership. Toyota and other Japanese companies
made direct corporate contributions. Meanwhile, CWT was the subject
of admiring newspaper articles that praised the lonely struggle of its
director to fight the "free trade" battle.

Since the early 1980s, CWT has been one of Washington's more active
advocates of open-door U.S. trade policies. It has opposed virtually every
measure that would limit access to the American market as a means of
forcing the Japanese to open their own markets. In 1987, it helped
organize grass-roots lobbying against what it termed the "protectionist"
features of the Omnibus Trade Bill. In 1987 and 1988, its president gave
seventeen speeches on trade matters. During those same years, CWT
testified before Congress six times.

Throughout the last decade, Japanese companies, particularly automotive manufacturers, have taken a growing interest in the organization.
One measure of this interest, and the financial support that has accom-
panied it, is CWT's annual award dinners. In recent years, the largest

contingents at these events have been lawyers and lobbyists who represent Japanese concerns, as well as officials from Japanese automotive manufacturers and their trade associations. Also well represented at these meetings are diplomats from other foreign governments and representatives of American retailers who depend on imported goods.

The Japanese have found that they can also lobby their positions by using their American subsidiaries to form U.S.-based lobbying groups, like the International Electronics Manufacturers and Consumers of America, Inc. (IEMCA). IEMCA was formed in March 1987 by the U.S. divisions of thirteen Japanese electronics companies, together with J. C. Penney and the National Office Machine Dealers Association, just as Congress began to draft what would become the decade's most sweeping trade legislation.

IEMCA's sole mission is "to actively promote the benefits of, and need for, a free and open trading system"—in America, of course. One of IEMCA's pamphlets says that it is "particularly concerned with changes to U.S. trade policies that restrict the availability of, or make more expensive, electronic components and products." At the time the pamphlet was released, the U.S. government had imposed sanctions on Japanese electronics manufacturers in response to illegal dumping activities in the U.S. semiconductor market and lack of access in Japan for American semiconductor companies. The Japanese were doing all they could to get the sanctions lifted.

IEMCA's principal activity is lobbying. As Congress considered the 1988 Trade Bill, the IEMCA executive committee coordinated the lobbying activities of its member companies. Lobbyists from affiliated companies met often and worked together closely. Although an officer of IEMCA says that the group sponsored no formal letter-writing campaigns, he notes that individual member companies did encourage their American employees to write their congressional representatives about the trade bill.

Because the member Japanese companies operate IEMCA through their U.S.-based subsidiaries, neither the subsidiaries nor IEMCA is required to register with the Justice Department as a foreign agent. IEMCA prefers to be seen as an American effort, in which the Japanese companies "behave like Americans."

America has thousands of other trade associations. Many have offices in Washington. Like IEMCA, most of them lobby. The majority of these groups are associations of American-owned U.S. companies. Some—like the Japan Automobile Manufacturers Association (JAMA)—are comprised entirely, or almost so, of foreign companies doing business in America. Others—like the American International Automobile Dealers of America (AIADA)—are made up of American dealers and distributors for foreign manufacturers. Still others—like IEMCA—are formed by the U.S.-based subsidiaries of foreign companies.

Japanese companies have joined all the U.S. trade associations they can. By doing so, they gain valuable insights into the activities of their American competitors. They also acquire a powerful voice in the associations' politicking. In this way, Japan can advance its political positions while wrapping "stars and stripes" around its lobbying activities. By contrast, American firms are unable to gain comparable access in Japan to various trade organizations and standards-setting bodies.

Equally important, membership in these organizations enables the Japanese to mute domestic political criticism about their trade practices and forestall association demands for strong political action by the federal government. Historically, trade associations have been political rallying points for American companies, allowing them to advocate tough trade positions while reducing the risk of foreign retaliation against individual companies. This role is now being progressively destroyed. Why? American companies tend to act as organizations pursuing profits for shareholders. By contrast, Japanese companies tend to act in concert with some sense of the need for mutual protection, or at least "Japanese identity." It is a very rare thing indeed when a Japanese company in an American trade association advocates a political position opposed by the Japanese government—or allows such a position to go unchallenged. Since trade associations depend heavily on consensus, this means the Japanese are acquiring an effective veto over the activities of many associations of "American" industry.

Witness, for example, the increasingly obvious schizophrenia in the trade policy positions of the Semiconductor Equipment and Materials Industries (SEMI) association. SEMI is composed of companies that supply equipment, materials, and services used in manufacturing semiconductors. According to the organization, its four principal missions are to hold trade shows, provide a forum for developing international standards for the industry, conduct technical and educational seminars, and work with government agencies throughout the world "to create a sympathetic regulatory climate for our industry and facilitate the removal of unfair trade barriers."

As Japanese domination of the semiconductor industry has grown, so, too, has its presence in SEMI. Today, the organization finds itself increasingly torn between American corporate members who are critical of Japan's anti-competitive semiconductor policies and Japanese members whose goal is to quash any such criticism.

SEMI's problems were underscored in October 1989, when an executive from one of its American-owned member companies—LSI Logic—was preparing to leave for a SEMI conference in Hawaii, where he was to deliver one of a number of speeches. SEMI executives requested that the LSI officer, like others slated to address the conference, submit an advance copy of his speech. A second LSI executive reports that

> the day before [he] left for Hawaii, Friday, October 6th, I received a call from a SEMI executive. He said that the Japanese who had read the advance draft were very concerned that it was too aggressive. . . . He asked that references to U.S. equipment suppliers who had encountered a loss of technology to Japanese partners in joint ventures be removed, and, if possible, the whole criticism of a joint-venture strategy with the Japanese be omitted. He also asked that comments on Japan's nationalistic (as opposed to global) manufacturing and trade strategy be toned down.

Indirect pressure was also applied to LSI. A distributor from Japan contacted LSI's Japanese representative to ask that the speech be toned down. The distributor felt that his business might be affected by the speech. When the LSI executive got to Hawaii, he was met by a SEMI delegation who said that the speech was "yet another example of Japan bashing." They warned that if the talk was given without modification, "some of the Japanese in the audience would probably walk out."

In the end, the LSI official gave his speech. Later, he discovered that the Americans on the conference steering committee had asked for advance copies of the Japanese presentations, just as the Japanese were receiving copies from U.S. speakers, but were refused.

Japan is constantly looking for new ways to stay in the background while American surrogates do its politicking. One of the more sophisticated approaches is to create or join well-organized and well-financed ad hoc lobbying coalitions. When done skillfully, this puts an American face on foreign politicking in America. More important, it provides a double cloak with which to conceal foreign lobbyists—one for the coalition, the other for the trade association.

An example of how this works is the Pro Trade Group (PTG). The group is composed of what the *Japan Economic Journal* terms Japan's "natural" political allies—that is, "large multinational U.S. corporations with an overriding interest in free trade, organized consumers and retailers attracted by low-priced, high-quality Japanese goods, and major exporters of agricultural products and machinery."

Almost a third of those on PTG's master membership list are Washington law firms and public affairs agencies that represent Japanese interests. Many of the organizations have substantial Japanese sponsorship. Consumers for World Trade, for example, is a PTG member. IEMCA is also a member, as are other groups made up largely of the U.S. subsidiaries of Japanese companies. Other associations that help to comprise the PTG, including AIADA, have important indirect links to Japanese manufacturers.

In all of its lobbying and public relations, PTG has presented itself as a group "representing U.S. exporters, importers and consumers, manufacturing, agricultural, retailing, service and civic interests." This is how the PTG generally is described when its positions or representatives are quoted in the press or appear on television. All along, this image has been an ideal lobbying cover. As one lobbyist associated with PTG says: "What quickly happened after Pro Trade was formed was that people would go up to the Hill, say they represented PTG, and give out PTG's position papers. What they did not do was tell members or staffers what law firms they worked for, or which clients they and their firms represented."

In the Pro Trade Group, as in any lobbying coalition, the critical issue is how the group defines its political positions. Small working committees prepare draft position papers that are circulated for comments and a sign-off by all members. Obviously, whoever chairs the working group—or drafts the position papers—has enormous influence over the eventual outcome.

The lobbyist notes:

There are two groups in Washington—the big group that writes the letters and the little group that signs them. Everyone wants to be part of the little group. But Pro Trade turned all that around: the little group wrote the letters and the big group signed them. The problem, however, was that the little group was controlled by Japanese and other foreign lobbyists.

Indeed, the key working groups in the Pro Trade Group—Super 301 (market access), 201 (import relief), and anti-dumping and countervailing—are chaired by well-connected Washington lawyer-lobbyists whose law firms represent Japanese and other foreign clients. Bruce Aitken, who chaired the 301 committee, for instance, represents the government of Thailand, and his firm represents the Automobile Importers of America. The clients of his law firm include Toyota, Volvo of America, Saab, and NEC Electronics (USA), Inc. In the summer of 1989, the person who drafted Pro Trade's anti-dumping position paper was Noel Hemmendinger—the former director of the United States–Japan Trade Council and a registered lobbyist for several Japanese companies.

The Pro Trade Group was formed in early 1986 as an offshoot of the World Trade Forum's speakers' bureau. The bureau did not lobby, though some of its members wanted to form a larger coalition to address trade legislation that had begun to emerge in Congress in 1986. The original strategy of the coalition was to bring together all the different interests that opposed protectionism, hold seminars, and promote open trade policies. They would publish a series of position papers that reflected agreement among all the members. With these papers in hand, PTG would then conduct a public relations and lobbying blitz. For visibility in the media, the coalition steering group hired Kostmayer Communications to prepare a public relations game plan. For political credibility, PTG members with high-level executive branch connections informed the White House of the group's agenda. Shortly thereafter, President Reagan singled out the Pro Trade Group in prepared remarks before a Washington meeting of business groups interested in open-door trade policies.

In early 1988, the coalition mounted a well-coordinated public attack on the pending Omnibus Trade Bill. PTG arranged a press conference at which businessmen from two leading American companies (Caterpillar and Tektronix, Inc.) and lobbyists from two leading U.S. trade associations (National Grange and the American Business Conference) announced that a weak dollar and rising imports had ended the need for major trade law reform. At almost the same moment, many of the associations that comprised the Pro Trade Group issued statements that contained the same basic message.

As these statements might indicate, the Pro Trade Group lobbied to eliminate any provisions in the trade bill that would provide for U.S. trade retaliation against countries that closed their markets to U.S. exports. In their place, PTG pushed a narrow, technical piece of trade legislation that contained four basic features: authority for the President to negotiate in the Uruguay GATT trade talks; modification of the U.S. tariff code so that it was harmonized with those used by other leading industrial nations; looser export-control regulations; and better protection for U.S. intellectual properties (patents, copyrights, and trademarks). These were the same positions advocated by the Administration and many other foreign governments—particularly Japan.

Throughout the 1988 fight over the Omnibus Trade Bill, the Pro Trade Group was a visible, formidable presence on Capitol Hill. It played an important part in successful efforts to eliminate provisions in the bill requiring registration of foreign investment and banned imports from foreign companies that regularly violate U.S. laws.

Some of the provisions Pro Trade opposed became law. But American trade laws are only as effective as their enforcement. As the *Japan Economic Journal* pointed out: "Frequently, a law restrictive for international trade can have its teeth pulled when the key percentages, quotas, and tariffs are established." In 1989, defanging the Omnibus Trade Act became one of Pro Trade's principal goals. It lobbied the Administration not to enforce the "Super 301" provisions and sent federal officials guides on how this could be done. It circulated position papers that argued for a weakening of U.S. anti-dumping laws. It urged Congress not to consider new legislation to force disclosure of foreign investment.

Japan has certainly defanged recent U.S. trade legislation. After Congress created the "Super 301" authority, under which the Administration must annually name the worst offenses among unfair foreign trade practices, the USTR announced in 1989 that it would take action on only three among dozens of industries in which Japan prevents fair market access for U.S. firms. Even if Japan ultimately opened those markets, the value of trade progress for American firms would amount to less than two percent of the U.S. trade deficit.

The ultimate defanging came in 1990, when the Administration accepted hollow promises from Japan to open markets in the three troubled industries. Japan pursuaded the Administration not to name *any* of its industries under the 1990 Super 301 authority. By inducing U.S. government inaction, Japan and its U.S. lobby have reversed the thrust of the landmark 1988 Trade Act, much of which was drafted in response to Japan's unfair trade practices.

Many wholly U.S.-owned American companies and many distinguished economists supported Pro Trade's positions. Other American corporations and equally distinguished economists took precisely the opposite side. But the positions in this matter are irrelevant. Most of the lawmakers who were petitioned by Pro Trade were unaware that part of the organization's financing came from Japan and other foreign interests, and that many Americans making these presentations were in foreign pay. The only way policymakers could have learned this vital information was by making a tortuous search through Justice Department files. Even then, not all the information needed to see who is really speaking for whose interests is available. Pro Trade operates like the rest of the political game is now played in Washington.

Chapter Eight

THE POLITICIANS' POLITICIAN

MANY JAPANESE BELIEVE that their American investments give them the right to participate actively in U.S. elections. This attitude is reflected in an article by economist Keitaro Hasegawa published by *Chuo Koron* in 1988. Hasegawa argues that Japan now has so much invested in the United States that it has a direct interest in who wins presidential elections: Japan "cannot stand by uninterested in changes of government in the United States."

This interest, according to Hasegawa, "doesn't end with the general interest of the idly curious." Rather, he says, Japanese companies must "provide direct and indirect support to promote formation of an [American] administration that will be of value to the free market economic system." Hasegawa explains:

> This necessitates becoming involved in an unexpected variety of political activities, including the formation of PACs in [Japan's] U.S. subsidiaries to provide election funds, and efforts to mobilize the local employees of [Japan's] American subsidiaries.

In the 1988 election cycle, the Japanese were afraid that a Dukakis Administration would disrupt the coziness of the Ron-Yasu years. Investment banker Jeffrey Garten and others document how the Ministry of Finance took actions to prop up the American dollar and finance the American deficit which are irrational by any economic standard and make sense only from a political perspective. Their purpose was to aid a GOP victory.

In 1988, the Japanese also invested money directly in both political

parties. Through its American subsidiary, the Japanese electronics conglomerate NEC sponsored an "International Guests Project" at both the
Democratic and Republican conventions. The Tokyo Electric Power
Company also donated funds to this project—$5,000 for the Republicans
and $25,000 to the Democrats.

At the urging of Charles Manatt, chairman of the Democratic National
Committee in the mid-1980s and now a Washington political adviser to
NEC, NEC also gave $25,000 to both the Democratic and Republican
parties. Manatt's law firm represents numerous Japanese clients, including Toyota.

Party leaders like Manatt are ideal agents of influence for Japan because of their special access to the White House, Congress, national
power brokers, and inside political information. Manatt's metamorphosis
from party executive to foreign lobbyist is now the rule, rather than the
exception. Indeed, one of the fastest ways to build a clientele for a law
firm is to be a major official of either political party.

Some party leaders lobby on Japan's behalf even while in office. Frank
Fahrenkopf, who chaired the Republican National Committee from 1983
until early 1989, arranged meetings in 1987 for his client, Toyota, with
top officials in the Reagan Administration.

When the Democratic National Committee held its election for a new
chairman in the spring of 1989, both the final candidates had been lobbyists for the Japanese, and both their law firms were lobbying for a roster of
leading Japanese companies. Jim Jones, a former congressman from Oklahoma, had represented Toshiba Corporation, and his law firm, Dickstein,
Shapiro & Morin, had five additional foreign clients. Ron Brown, who became the chairman of the Democratic National Committee, had represented twenty-one Japanese electronics companies. Brown's law firm,
Patton, Boggs & Blow, represented two other Japanese clients, as well as
eleven additional foreign interests from nine other countries.

In sum, many of America's top political consultants have become Japan's top political advisers and lobbyists.

As Hedrick Smith observes in *The Power Game*, political campaigns have
become "a perpetual-motion machine"—an unbroken chain, one following another without interruption, where "mercenary consultants of the
campaign follow the winners right into office."

Because so many policy matters are decided on the basis of political
rather than substantive considerations, these advisers have an immense
influence over government decision making. They are ideal agents of
influence for foreign interests, who can gain access to the same invaluable

political information and advice that is given American officeholders. At the same time, foreign interests are assured that, when the big decisions are made, their representative is usually sitting at the elbow of an elected official.

These advisers' special edge in the access-and-influence-peddling business stems from the fact that they are not covered by *any* of the federal ethics statutes. It is entirely legal for them to be on a foreign payroll before, during, and immediately after a political campaign. Many are. Because they are part of the political entourage of the President and other elected officials, they have the "access plus" enjoyed by only a handful. Because they are the politicians' politicians who help put—and keep—elected officials in office, some of them can call in virtually any political favor they desire.

Lobbying has become so lucrative for political mercenaries that many now work in campaigns less for the salary than as a means to establish the inside relations, contacts, and visibility needed to attract lobbying clients. Many, in fact, take no salary as campaign officers so that they can continue to bill their lobbying clients. This is a big money game, and much of this money comes from Japanese and other foreign clients.

In today's spoils politics, even those political advisers who are fired can still get rich. John Sears, for instance, was terminated as Ronald Reagan's campaign manager in 1980. But he remained a part of the Republican brotherhood of influence. Less than four months after Reagan was sworn into office, the Japan Automobile Manufacturers Association signed him for $10,000 a month.

The makeup of George Bush's and Michael Dukakis' presidential campaign staffs in 1988 reveals how pervasively foreign interests have penetrated the American political process. Stuart Spencer, for instance, was Vice President Dan Quayle's political handler during the campaign. Spencer—a name partner in Hecht, Spencer & Associates and one of President Reagan's closest political advisers—is also a well-paid foreign agent. One of his former clients was the government of South Africa, which paid him $350,000 to lobby against economic sanctions in 1984 and 1985. Another Spencer client was Manuel Noriega, when he was head of Panama's drug-corrupted government. Former Ambassador to Costa Rica Francis McNeil testified before the Senate Foreign Relations Committee in 1988 that the Reagan Administration turned a blind eye on Noriega's drug dealings because of his usefulness to the Administration's covert war against Nicaragua.

In 1985 and 1986, Panama's leader paid Spencer's firm $360,000 to help him clean up his image. Another politico who worked on the Noriega project was Joel McLeary, the former Democratic Party national treasurer who was then associated with the Sawyer/Miller Group. David Sawyer and Scott Miller—the firm's principals—handled much of the television advertising for the Dukakis presidential campaign. At the same time, according to records filed with the Justice Department, they were active foreign agents. Their firm had a $2 million contract with the government of Colombia, plus contracts with the Philippine government and the exiled government of Panama.

George Bush's campaign press secretary, Sheila Tate, worked as a registered foreign agent for the French firm Thomson S.A. immediately after leaving First Lady Nancy Reagan's staff in February 1985. During the campaign, Richard Fairbanks, formerly Assistant Secretary of State, chaired Bush's Asia-Pacific Task Force while he also worked as a foreign agent for Fujitsu (one of Japan's leading computer companies) and the government of Iraq. He now represents Japanese auto parts manufacturer Koito in its battle with T. Boone Pickens to keep Pickens off the Koito board of directors.

Another foreign agent in the Dukakis camp was Andrew Manatos, Assistant Secretary of Commerce in the Carter Administration. Manatos, a major Dukakis fund-raiser, worked for the government of Greece.

In spoils politics, lobbying contracts for Japan and other foreign interests are among the most lucrative rewards. In the 1980s, one of the biggest winners was the political consulting firm of Black, Manafort, Stone & Kelly, which played a key role in the last three Republican presidential victories. Over the past decade, the firm has parlayed its political clout into unexcelled lobbying power. It provides a perfect example of how politics and commercialism are now seamlessly merged in Washington.

Formed in 1980 as Black, Manafort & Stone, the firm was originally a Republican campaign consulting group. In the 1980 presidential campaign, Charles Black was political director of the Reagan for President Committee. Paul Manafort oversaw the Reagan campaign's "southern strategy." Roger Stone was Reagan's campaign director for the northeastern United States.

Once Reagan was elected, the three political advisers played key roles in forming the Reagan Administration. Manafort was personnel director for the Reagan transition; Stone was deputy political director of the personnel office, where he and Manafort screened candidates for all presidential appointments; Black served as a political adviser during the staffing of the administration. Needless to say, few people knew the top officials of the Reagan Administration better than Manafort and Stone.

In the 1984 election, Black, Manafort, and Stone were again deeply involved in the Reagan campaign. Black was the campaign political director; Manafort was political director for the Republican convention; Stone again served as campaign director for the Northeast.

After Reagan won reelection, the firm expanded its operations. It recruited Peter Kelly, the Democratic National Committee's finance chairman, and James Healey, another Democrat, who had been chief of staff to the chairman of the Ways and Means Committee and special assistant to Speaker of the House Tip O'Neill. In December 1984, the firm changed its name to Black, Manafort, Stone & Kelly.

In the 1988 presidential campaign, Charles Black was a senior political adviser to George Bush and his platform negotiator at the Republican convention. Paul Manafort was Bush's campaign scheduler. Roger Stone was co-director of the Bush campaign in California. Lee Atwater, another partner in the firm, was George Bush's campaign manager. Peter Kelly was a fund-raiser for Michael Dukakis. In early 1989, George Bush named Atwater chairman of the Republican National Committee.

But the partners of Black, Manafort collected far more than political spoils in the 1980s. They used their White House connections to go after high-paying clients. In the process, the firm has become one of the leading lobbyists for American companies and foreign organizations. Between 1981 and 1984, they signed up many U.S. corporations and trade associations, plus four foreign governments as clients. Sixteen more foreign clients were added after the 1984 and 1988 victories. Among the firm's more notable past and present clients are the military dictator and government of Nigeria; Filipino businessmen with close ties to Ferdinand Marcos; the government of the Bahamas; Angolan rebel leader Jonas Savimbi; and the governments of—or private interests in—Korea, Peru, Portugal, Lebanon, and Somalia.

James Lake presents another prominent example of someone who advises the President on politics while lobbying on behalf of the Japanese. Lake was George Bush's press adviser in the 1988 presidential campaign. During Lake's tenure on the campaign, he was also a lobbyist on the payrolls of Mitsubishi Electric, the Japan Auto Parts Industries Association, and Suzuki.

Lake was an integral cog in the Republican campaign machine in 1980, 1984, and 1988. More important to his success as a lobbyist, however, is his intimate friendship with Clayton Yeutter, U.S. Trade Representative from 1985 to 1989 and now Secretary of Agriculture.

In 1988, a veteran investigative journalist from Japan noted that it was common wisdom in Tokyo business and government circles that one of the surest ways to gain access to and influence with Yeutter was to hire

James Lake. And in case after case, that's just what the Japanese did.

In 1987, during a critical moment in the market-oriented, sector-selective (MOSS) auto parts negotiations, for instance, Lake was hired to represent the interests of the Japan Auto Parts Industries Association. Lake and his staff worked closely with the Senate and the Commerce Department to ensure Japan's success in persuading the American government to adopt its weak MOSS proposals.

When the U.S. government found that Mitsubishi Electric and other Japanese companies were dumping semiconductors on the U.S. market, Lake gave Mitsubishi the uncontested access it needed to persuade the USTR and the rest of the Reagan Administration to lift the sanctions that had been placed upon Japanese electronics companies.

The clout that Lake offers his clients is illustrated by the entrée he sold to Mitsubishi—the world's largest electronics conglomerate—when he signed on as their lobbyist in a battle against Fusion Systems, a tiny high-tech firm in Rockville, Maryland. Then Lake showed America how effective a true politician's politician can be.

In the 1970s, Fusion Systems invented and produced a unique kind of commercial ultraviolet curing equipment. Mitsubishi soon began a major effort to wrench this proprietary technology away from Fusion Systems. Fusion sought help from the American government. Lake was hired by Mitsubishi to see that Fusion did not get it.

The story begins with Don Spero, a prototypical American entrepreneur. Spero—a tall, slim former athlete—is the last American to win a world championship in single sculling. Spero first traveled to Japan in 1964, when he competed in the Tokyo Olympics. He holds a Ph.D. in plasma physics from Columbia University.

Fusion's production facility, located in a suburban Washington office park, looks more like the most advanced high-technology Japanese plant than it does a typical American factory. Its employees resemble graduate students more than factory workers.

Fusion's principal product is a high-power microwave lamp system used in industrial production. The core of that system is an ultraviolet (UV) lamp. When bombarded with microwaves, the lamps emit UV rays that instantly dry special inks, adhesives, and other materials. Once twenty to thirty hours were needed to dry the inks on plastics. Fusion's UV system can do the same job in a matter of seconds.

Spero and his colleagues developed their system for a wide variety of commercial uses and carved out a niche in a highly specialized market. Today, Fusion lamps are used in the production of semiconductor chips, optical fibers, graphic arts films, and printed circuit boards.

Unlike most small U.S. companies, Fusion markets its products extensively in foreign countries. Almost one-third of its sales are exports; half of these are to Japan. Fusion's conflict with Mitsubishi began with one of these Japanese sales.

In 1977, Mitsubishi Electric bought a Fusion lamp. Over the next decade, Mitsubishi flooded Japan's Patent Office with some 257 applications surrounding the technology in the Fusion lamp. If successful in obtaining these patents, Mitsubishi could actually prevent Fusion from selling its own products in Japan.

Mitsubishi was using a common Japanese tactical maneuver called "patent flooding." Japanese companies file enormous numbers of patent claims on such generic technologies as screws, clamps, or other features that surround or support an invention. At a Senate hearing in June 1988, Maureen Smith, Deputy U.S. Assistant Secretary of Commerce for Japan, explained how this tactic is used against foreign inventors:

> It is common practice for a Japanese company to learn of an invention that it would like to have, and to surround the patent applications for that invention with its own applications. These applications may cover what are, taken individually, relatively insignificant aspects of the new invention. However, if enough of these "nuisance" patents are filed, the inventor of the original product may discover that he is unable to produce his [own] product if these [nuisance] patents are granted.

Once a Japanese company files these nuisance patents, Smith added, it will "offer not to apply them against the original inventor of the product, but at a price. The price is generally a licensing or cross-licensing arrangement that gives the Japanese company rights to the technology in question."

Time after time, Japanese companies have used this tactic to force foreign firms to share their best technology—often leaving them with nothing more than token royalty payments. Frequently, when this occurs, the Japanese firm adds a secrecy clause to the contract, thereby prohibiting the U.S. firm from revealing either the deal or the practice of patent flooding. This has enabled the Japanese to use this scheme— largely unnoticed—for years. Regis McKenna, an adviser to Apple Computers, estimates that between 1950 and 1978, Japan paid $9 billion for 32,000 technology licenses that were actually worth $1 trillion. (In other words, they paid less than one cent on the dollar.) Most of these licenses were acquired from small, innovative American firms.

Only a handful of American companies have the financial resources to fight a large Japanese company in Japan's parochial legal system. To contest each initial application in a patent-flooding case costs $3,000 to $5,000. To appeal applications can cost as much as $100,000 and take five to ten years. For Fusion, the cost of litigating the case from start to finish could easily have come to $25 million—or as much as the firm's revenues for one year.

Mitsubishi's patent siege on UV microwave lamp technology placed an impossible financial drain on Fusion's limited resources. In 1985, Spero approached Mitsubishi with an offer: "Why don't we just agree that, in Japan, you will not assert your patents against us? In exchange, we will agree not to challenge your applications, and together we'll just compete for the market." Mitsubishi agreed. Its price: a royalty-free, worldwide cross license to Fusion's core technology.

It was a counteroffer Spero had to refuse. He explains: "If we gave Mitsubishi the unlimited right to use our proprietary technology, Fusion would be out of business in five years."

So Spero began a long-term struggle to defeat the most important patent applications Mitsubishi had filed to "surround" the UV lamp. Spero claims he knew the early cases would be legal "slam dunks" for his company. After all, the technology under dispute was virtually identical to that in the lamp Mitsubishi Electric bought from Fusion in 1977. And sure enough, when the first two applications were reviewed two years later, the Japanese patent examiner found in Fusion's favor and denied the issuance of Mitsubishi's patents. Still, the matter was far from settled.

Mitsubishi demanded a review by a three-person tribunal from the Japanese Patent Office. Conveniently for Mitsubishi, MITI—which is charged with helping Japanese firms acquire advanced foreign technologies—is also responsible for Japan's patent system and its tribunal reviews. In January 1987, the MITI/Patent Office tribunal overturned the rulings favoring Fusion. It ordered the challenged patents to be issued to Mitsubishi. At the same time, Fusion learned, Mitsubishi officials had contacted some of Fusion's largest customers, saying that they were considering a patent infringement suit against Fusion. Spero knew he could not win without the help of the U.S. government.

Like many American entrepreneurs, Spero was reluctant to ask for help. But unlike most American businessmen, he was located just outside Washington and knew something about politics. By chance, he had a friend who worked in the Geneva office of the USTR.

When they were ten years old, Spero met Michael Samuels at summer camp. They had stayed in touch over the years. In 1985, Samuels was appointed Deputy U.S. Trade Representative. At Samuels' swearing-in party, Spero met Clayton Yeutter. In what Spero describes as a two-minute cocktail conversation, Yeutter learned that Fusion did business in Japan and suggested that Spero meet Joseph Massey, the Assistant U.S. Trade Representative for Japan and China. Later that year, Spero met with Massey and discussed how Fusion could expand its distribution system in Japan.

Two years later, when Fusion's patent rulings were overturned by the Japanese Patent Office, Spero went to Massey again. Fusion's difficulties with Japan's patent system were similar to those experienced by dozens of other U.S. companies. But because many feared that criticisms of the Japanese system would jeopardize their business ties with Japan, few American CEOs would ask for help. Massey thought Fusion's case should be used to highlight intellectual property rights as a trade issue between the United States and Japan.

At about this time, Spero learned that Mitsubishi was bringing in a heavyweight lobbyist to plead its case before the U.S. government: James Lake. Once he heard about the Lake-Yeutter friendship, Spero knew that his biggest battle would be getting his own government to take Fusion's side.

Fusion and Mitsubishi opened new negotiations in September 1987. The Japanese company made an oral offer to settle if Fusion would stop its opposition to Mitsubishi's patent applications in Japan. One month later, Mitsubishi reneged on this agreement and refused further negotiations.

Fusion stepped up its efforts with Congress. In December 1987, it persuaded Lloyd Bentsen, chairman of the Senate Finance Committee, to write on Fusion's behalf to the Japanese Ambassador in Washington. Bentsen's letter stressed that if Japan would not take action to help Fusion, then Congress would. As an added measure, Fusion hired Paula Stern, former chairwoman of the International Trade Commission, to help make its case to Yeutter.

Lake and Mitsubishi pursued a very different tack. They portrayed the issue as a simple commercial dispute. It was, they said, an issue for technicians—not for politicians. The argument worked. In January 1988, a Mitsubishi executive told *Inside U.S. Trade* that Yeutter had agreed that their conflict with Fusion was simply a private commercial affair. Mitsubishi "was assured the Administration would not get involved and 'put their arm' on a Japanese company for commercial reasons."

Spero increased pressure on the USTR and Mitsubishi. He gave an interview to *Frontline*, the national news show. Then he saw to it that Fusion's story made *The Wall Street Journal*, the *National Journal*, and the Washington *Post*.

Though Yeutter had, in effect, assured the Japanese that the U.S.

government would stay out of the matter, Deputy U.S. Trade Representative Michael Smith, a career civil servant and trade negotiator, decided to get involved. Like Massey, Smith had become an advocate for using the Fusion-Mitsubishi conflict to highlight trade difficulties between the two countries over matters of intellectual property. In April 1988, Smith raised the issue with the Japanese in biannual trade talks. He also met with Mitsubishi officials in Tokyo, and demanded that they settle the case, lest it cause a political flap. Mitsubishi clearly took him seriously enough to resume negotiations with Spero.

The Japanese government also took Smith seriously. Japanese officials were furious that he had involved himself in the matter, and voiced their complaints to the State Department and the USTR.

Though the efforts of Smith, Massey, and others held promise, time was working against Fusion. In addition to the costs of lawyers, lobbyists, and patent experts, Spero was devoting much of his own time, and that of his senior staff, to the fight with Mitsubishi.

In a May 1988 article in the *National Journal*, James Lake offered an update on the Fusion-Mitsubishi case. Lake said, "Spero has done everything he can to solve this politically or through the press. I have tremendous respect for his efforts to try to make this more than a commercial issue. Every time we think we have this tamped down, it pops up somewhere else."

Keeping the issue tamped down, of course, was the Lake-Mitsubishi strategy. One way that the Japanese company did so was to open negotiations with Fusion whenever there was political pressure, only to end them whenever the pressure was removed. Needless to say, these talks never produced an agreement.

In June 1988, Mitsubishi quickly reopened negotiations after the Senate announced hearings to examine U.S. problems with the Japanese patent system. After three days of intensive negotiations, Spero thought an agreement was in sight. A key sticking point was an insistence by Mitsubishi's Washington legal counsel—the firm of Baker and McKenzie—that neither Spero nor anyone else at Fusion Systems could ever reveal the settlement, discuss the Japanese patent system, or publicize Fusion's experiences. The final straw was a demand that Spero refuse to testify before a June Senate Commerce Committee hearing on U.S.-Japan patent conflicts. Spero was outraged. He rejected the offer and testified.

In June 1988, Lake became the media adviser to the Bush presidential campaign. Meanwhile, he continued to represent Mitsubishi.

In late 1988, several members of Congress showed a renewed interest in the Fusion case, prompting Mitsubishi to reopen its negotiations yet again. In January 1989, following still another negotiating session, Spero asked Takeshi Sakurai, Mitsubishi Electric's top representative in Washington, why Mitsubishi had raised the settlement stakes so high during their talks the summer before—high enough to kill the talks. Sakurai told Spero that he personally had upped the settlement demands when it became clear that "your government will not help you."

Fusion's case against Mitsubishi remains "tamped down"—both in Japan and in the United States. USTR Carla Hills raised the issue with the Japanese in October 1989. Spero has testified again before Congress. Mitsubishi continues to file patents in Japan. For now, Fusion remains the market leader even in Japan but operates under the growing threat of Mitsubishi's mounting pile of patent filings. Spero has nothing but praise for the career USTR negotiators who have supported his company's efforts. But he never heard from James Lake's good friend Clayton Yeutter, despite all the congressional letters and public attention.

Spero's wisdom, in retrospect: "Japan's political power in Washington is awesome. Mitsubishi and its lobbyists are just sitting there laughing at us. If they can continue to pick off the little guys like me, you can just wave goodbye to America's creative power."

Chapter Nine

GRASS-ROOTS
POLITICKING

I N T H E F A L L of 1988, a Japanese consulting firm presented twenty
of Japan's largest electronics manufacturers with a detailed blueprint for
influencing the European Community's effort to create a single market
in 1992.

Japanese firms were advised to join every local industry association
they could; to hire lobbyists and public relations personnel in each of
the EC's twelve nations; to establish an intelligence-gathering network
in each country; to spread their facilities across the EC; to hire European
lawyers and financial experts who could monitor local developments; and
to appoint a local political-establishment figure as a figurehead chairman—someone who would be willing to open doors and lay the ground-
work for the systematic lobbying of national officials and politicians.

Every element of this strategy was first employed by the Japanese in
America. But Japan's penetration of the American political system goes
far deeper than hiring lobbyists and advisers and joining trade associations.

In recent years, the Japanese government and major business organizations, such as the Electronics Industries Association of Japan (EIAJ),
have mounted an extensive grass-roots political campaign throughout
America. In 1985, Akio Morita, then chairman of EIAJ, explained to its
members that they needed to broaden their political activities beyond
Congress and federal agencies in Washington. Morita argued that only
by establishing close ties at state and local levels could Japanese firms
hope to gain a foothold in American politics and economic policymaking—
particularly since, he said, the "top priority of the . . . Congress, [S]enate

and federal government agencies quite naturally is placed on U.S. interests."

To change these priorities, the Japanese are funneling at least $300 million a year (of the $400 million they spend all told) to create a pro-Japan constituency throughout America. Europe can expect an assault of similar magnitude in the near future.

In May 1989, Senator Max Baucus (D-Mont.) spoke to a hundred of his business constituents in the city of Bozeman, Montana. He denounced Japanese protectionism. He advocated tough U.S. actions to open Japan's markets. As anticipated, Baucus' audience became angry. The big surprise was that their anger was directed at him rather than the Japanese. Why? Many of the attendees were selling to Japan; others hoped to. Most were afraid that a tough American approach to Japan would jeopardize their own business opportunities.

Throughout America, Japan is now able to mobilize local interests and put pressure on elected officials like Baucus to sacrifice broad national interests for narrow local concerns.

In 1986, Eddie Mahe, Jr., a leading Republican political consultant and adviser to the Japanese Embassy in Washington, went to Tokyo to tutor Japanese businessmen on how they could best create a grass-roots "pro-Japan" constituency in America. In his talk, Mahe suggested that any new Japanese offensive follow a few simple principles.

The first principle: America's economy is driven by American politics. In America, most politics are local. And the most important local issue is always jobs. Thus, couch all issues in terms of jobs.

The second principle: Just as politics are local, so are matters of trade. While most national trade debates are fought over abstract theories of "free trade" versus "protectionism," few Americans really understand the pros and cons of the arguments. In practice, North Carolinians think that trade policy means textiles. Iowans think it means beef or corn. In Michigan, trade means automobiles. As Mahe told the Japanese:

[I]f individual Japanese businessmen go into communities around the United States opening up new plants and creating jobs you have a significant opportunity to affect [American] politics.

Mahe also gave the Japanese some shrewd advice on the bewitchment of American politicians. When choosing a plant site, the Japanese should meet with as many elected officials from as many communities as possible.

Why? Because even those officials whose communities are not selected will remain friendly and hope to have better luck next time.

When meeting with members of Congress, Mahe counseled, don't go to Washington: go to their district offices. By meeting in the district office, the member will come to think of them as constituents, and treat them accordingly.

Mahe also tutored the Japanese on how to transform a governor into a lobbyist for Japan. He told them that a governor would be delighted to meet with any Japanese executive who was thinking about putting a new facility in that state. Once a relationship was established between the Japanese firm and state officials, the governor would gladly lobby in Washington for the Japanese company if Congress were considering "some kind of trade bill that would affect you as a businessman."

Actually, the Japanese have little need to solicit the favors of governors, since most governors now devote much of their energies to wooing the Japanese. More states now have offices in Tokyo than in Washington. One of the basic missions of these offices is to attract Japanese investment. And one of the biggest lures is their state's congressional clout in Washington.

Foreign investors—particularly the Japanese and Koreans—have added some of their own political wrinkles to facility-siting. They systematically try to muzzle congressional critics by directing companies to invest in their districts. To begin with, facilities are often placed in the district of a powerful member of Congress who sits on a trade committee, particularly one who is a critic of Japan. Japanese companies, for instance, have placed seven facilities in the district of Georgia congressman Ed Jenkins, a persistent critic of Japanese protectionism. Another tactic is to locate a facility across the street from a principal U.S. competitor or in the same congressional district. By "sharing" the same member of Congress with its competitor, the foreign company is often able to dilute or neutralize its rival's Washington influence.

Employing this elementary political arithmetic, Japanese automobile manufacturers have carefully spread their new factories across the nation. Chrysler's Lee Iacocca comments, "With each plant, the Japanese have tried to get two senators." Conversely, Japan now threatens elected officials if they hesitate to adopt a position that Japan views as "correct." When Florida legislators considered the state's unitary tax in the mid-1980s, for example, Japanese executives threatened to remove their existing facilities—and blackball the state for any future investment—unless the tax was repealed. And so it was.

Overseas asset-holders also exploit the eagerness of local officials to ingratiate themselves with potential investors. When Congress was de-

bating legislation on federal monitoring of foreign investment, for instance, one member after another went to the microphone to oppose the
bill—because, they said, their constituents and local business organizations had been told that the legislation threatened foreign investment
in their communities.

When Congressman Wes Watkins (D-Okla.) indicated his support for
the legislation, he was rebuked editorially by the largest paper in his
state for risking the state's chances to attract foreign factories.

As Mahe pointed out, the Japanese now have the power to set much
of America's trade agenda. Noting that there were 700 new or expanding
Japanese facilities in the United States, he observed:

> [I]f those 700 individual businesses thought through what it is they
> could do at the local level in the communities in which they are
> active in the United States, you could do a great deal about "trade
> policy" between the two countries in both countries.

Mahe's only mistake was to understate Japan's business presence in
the United States, and thus its potential political influence. In 1989, the
Japan External Trade Organization (JETRO) reported there were more
than 6,900 companies in the United States and Canada in which the
Japanese have stock ownership of at least 10 percent—the level that the
Securities and Exchange Commission defines as "a controlling interest."
By any measure, this is a massive potential political base for Japan.

The Electronics Industries Association of Japan (EIAJ), made up of 600
of Japan's largest electronics concerns, has spearheaded Japan's grass-
roots politicking in America.

EIAJ's American campaign began modestly in 1972, when the association created its first public relations program. The goal: to deflect
American criticism of Japan's assault on the U.S. television industry. By
the late 1970s, however, EIAJ's members had come under bitter criticism
for dumping semiconductors onto the American market. At the same
time, the Japanese government was being attacked for protecting its
home semiconductor market from U.S. exports, and the United States
was beginning to insist that Japan open its closed telecommunications
market.

EIAJ's solution? Help top industry and government officials to "understand" (or to accept) the Japanese position. To "educate" America,
EIAJ hired a New York public relations firm and sponsored five U.S.
seminars—one each in New York and Palo Alto in 1979 and three once-

a-year meetings in Washington, D.C. Each of the Washington meetings focused on a generic topic. In 1980, EIAJ's seminar on quality control drew 200 people. A 1981 seminar on Japanese management had 350 attendees, as did a 1982 seminar on high-tech management.

At bottom, the substance of these seminars was irrelevant to the Japanese. What they wanted, and what they got, were Washington contacts. Akio Morita puts it this way:

> During these seminars, we gained some irreplaceable assets, namely, the many contacts in Washington with whom we were able to directly exchange opinions. We deeply felt the significance of these contacts, and were able to correct the misunderstandings set forth in [the Semiconductor Industry Association of America's] criticism of Japan.

Dozens of other Japanese organizations sponsored similar U.S.-Japan forums in the 1980s. The Japanese readily admit that the purpose of these exchanges is not to resolve issues, but to establish personal relationships between U.S. and Japanese opinion leaders. For Japan, the "big political idea" is based on a fundamental, but effective, public relations maneuver: If you befriend a wide array of U.S. elites, you can use your new "friends" to defuse criticism.

After EIAJ seminars had substantially achieved this goal, the organization set out on its next task—targeting key members of Congress. In March 1983, it arranged a meeting in Tokyo among its member companies and the congressmen who served on the House Ways and Means Subcommittee on Trade. This exchange opened up a dialogue that continues today.

In February 1985, EIAJ also flew six influential congressional staff aides to Japan for an eight-day, all-expenses-paid stay. Again, the purpose was to help the staffers "understand" Japanese business practices.

By 1985, electronics and semiconductor issues had become such serious political matters in the United States that EIAJ's seminars, breakfast meetings, and trips—even its lobbyists—were no longer enough. The Japanese had also become openly disdainful of their high-priced American apologists and the "endless political games" they played.

Suguo Kagehira, chairman of EIAJ's Overseas Public Relations Committee, puts it bluntly: "In working with lobbyists, once a 'case' is closed, everything is over. The personal contacts that had been cultivated up to that point are often terminated." Kagehira adds, "Although we consider such [lobbying] activities 'unavoidable,' we certainly do not consider them desirable." Rather, he says, "the people that we need to 'appeal'

-MAY 20 1977

His Excellency
Fumihiko Togo
Ambassador Extraordinary and
Plenipotentiary of Japan
Embassy of Japan
Washington, D.C.

Excellency:

I wish to confirm the following position of the Office
of the Special Representative for Trade Negotiations in
response to the concerns of the Government of Japan on the
current investigation under Section 337 of the Tariff Act of
1930, as amended, and other pending issues on television
receivers imported from certain firms in Japan expressed at
the time of our recent negotiation:

In regard to the concerns of the Government of Japan on
the current Section 337 investigation on television receivers
imported from certain firms in Japan, I can assure the
Government of Japan that the Office of the Special Representative for Trade Negotiations will urge the USITC to confine
its investigation to allegations of practices that are
clearly not within the scope of the Antidumping Act of 1921
and the countervailing duty law. I intend to convey to the
USITC our view that those segments of the complaint which
involve unresolved questions under those laws should be
referred to the Treasury Department for further consideration should any further action be warranted by that Department.

In regard to the conspiracy and monopolization charges
added to the complaint, the Department of Justice has
stated in respect to this particular case that to hold the
Japanese Government liable for sovereign conduct relating to
normal policies involving domestic taxation, domestic
investment and Japanese commerce, or to hold Japanese firms
acting pursuant to governmental directives implementing

IOOO01

The 1977 secret side letter on the television negotiations
from then–Special Trade Representative Robert Strauss
to the Japanese government (letter continues).

such policies within sovereign Japanese territory, liable under Section 337, would raise serious problems of sovereign immunity, act of state and comity. With regard to the issue of predatory pricing, the Department of Justice is of the view that this issue is not separable from an antidumping complaint and is within the jurisdiction of the Treasury Department. I fully concur and will reiterate that opinion to the USITC.

It is our view that Section 337 investigations should not duplicate other existing remedies under law and should avoid any harassment that might occur to those parties under investigation. We strongly believe that the fostering of duplicative legal investigations by separate agencies was not the intent of the Congress under the Section 337 statute. I can further assure the Government of Japan that I will strongly urge the USITC to consider the adverse effect of this investigation in its current form upon the international trading relations of the United States, pointing out that the potential for harassment in such an investigation is clear and should be avoided.

I will recommend to the USITC that they limit their present investigation to matters not falling within the scope of the Antidumping Act and the countervailing duty law, and that if it would be determined that matters falling within those two statutes constitute necessary elements in a broader investigation of unfair practices, the USITC rely upon the determination of the Secretary of the Treasury to establish those particular unfair trade practices, rather than conduct a separate independent investigation on these matters.

We are deeply concerned about the ruling of the Customs Court that found, in Zenith Radio Corporation v. the United States, that the remission or rebate of consumption taxes by the Government of Japan on consumer electronic exports is a "bounty or grant" and that the Secretary of the Treasury should levy countervailing duties. The Department of Justice has already filed an appeal which will be pursued quickly and vigorously. I can assure you that it is the belief of the Executive Branch of the Government of the United States of America that the exemption or remission on exports by the Government of Japan of such domestic commodity taxes is in accord with international trading rules and that countervailing duties should not be applied because of such exemption or remission. Should it become necessary I would urge that the decision be appealed to the Supreme Court.

With respect to pending antidumping duties, the Treasury Department has assured me that it will make a special effort to liquidate promptly all entries on which appraisement has been withheld in administering the antidumping law, the Treasury Department will attempt to resolve promptly all outstanding issues relating to the appraisement of exports from Japan in order to reduce uncertainty. We recognize that it is in the best interest of all parties to such action that this case be resolved expeditiously. The Treasury Department also has assured me that it will promptly inform the Government of Japan of any significant developments that may arise from such investigations. If requested, the Treasury Department will provide information on such developments and will receive any information that the Government of Japan wishes to provide. The Treasury Department will carry out these efforts in strict conformity with the International Antidumping Code.

Sincerely,

Robert S. Strauss

Former President Reagan and Mrs. Reagan arrive
in Tokyo on a plane chartered by Fujisankei
Communications for the ex-President's 1989 public
relations tour of Japan. *AP/Wide World Photos*

The partners of the Blackstone Group advertised their U.S. merger and acquisitions services in a 1988 Japanese daily newspaper. Below is an unofficial translation of the advertisement. *Advertisement reprinted with permission of the Blackstone Group*

Nihon Keizai Shimbun
(Japanese Economic News)
Friday, June 17, 1988
(a full-page advertisement)

A NEW ERA IN M&A
(Merger and Acquisition)

In recent years there has been a significant change in the world economy, beginning with the problem of currency. At the same time, there has been an increase in M&A activity. In the midst of these changes, there has been a need for increased M&A among Japanese enterprises, and we hear demands for M&A know-how. The advantages that M&A bring are more than one might assume. For example: a business may launch into a new field, strengthen and expand in an existing field, and, additionally, experience increased success in penetrating foreign markets. However, the image of merger and acquisition still has the quality of a "money game" in Japan.

"We want to realize a new concept of M&A based on a truly friendly relationship between one business and another that brings mutual profits."

We, the Blackstone Group, are an investment bank which helps you, the management of Japanese business, materialize such desires. Our organization is a partnership. Each partner is active in his specialization on the front line of the world economy. If you are thinking about developing a new business or an investment strategy that will be effective in the U.S., by all means, consult us! We, the Blackstone Group, are proud of our accomplishments and resources and we promise to deliver all of it to you for new M&A.

LAWRENCE D. FINK
General Partner of the Blackstone Group; Chairman of Blackstone Financial Management. He was active in First Boston and in 1981 became a Managing Director at age 29. Elected as a member of the Board of Management in 1984. Specializes in mortgage-backed securities. Also known by the fact that First Boston developed new financial products such as LBO under his direction.

STEPHEN A. SCHWARZMAN
President of the Blackstone Group. Started his career as an investment banker at Lehman Brothers; became a Managing Director at a young 31 years. Later belonged to the M&A department of the same company (1977–84); also worked as the Chairman of the M&A Committee (1983–84). He is active as an advisor to such top enterprises as Chrysler, Goodyear, Litton Industries, and RCA Records.

PETER G. PETERSON
Chairman of the Blackstone Group. He was a Presidential Aide for international economic problems under Nixon (1971). He was the U.S. Secretary of Commerce (1972–73) and later Chairman of Lehman Brothers Kuhn Loeb (1973–83). Recently he succeeded David Rockefeller as Chairman of the Council on Foreign Relations. He is active as an officer in various organizations, including being a director of the Japan Society. He has also been given honorary doctorates by a number of universities.

DAVID A. STOCKMAN
General partner of the Blackstone Group. He was Director of the Budget for five years under Reagan, and the youngest member of the cabinet in this century. Later entered Salomon Brothers (1986) where he was in charge of the Department of Corporate Finance. He was also elected as one of the ten best young businessmen by the All-American Junior Chamber of Commerce.

ROGER C. ALTMAN
Vice-Chairman of the Blackstone Group. Started his career as an investment banker at Lehman

Brothers (1969), soon he became a partner (1974), and that year he was selected as one of the ten best young bankers in the U.S. Dealt with domestic finance as an Assistant Secretary under Carter. Later returned to Lehman Brothers (1981) and managed the Department of Investment Banking.

THE BASE OF THE BLACKSTONE GROUP'S WORK IS FRIENDLY TRANSACTIONS. RECENTLY WE TIED THE KNOT BETWEEN "SONY & CBS RECORDS" AND ALSO "BRIDGESTONE & FIRESTONE."

CORPORATE ADVISORY SERVICES

For example, CBS Records' friendly M&A by Sony is one of our accomplishments.

1. We are an investment bank specializing in M&A, restructuring, corporate financial advisory services, etc. We give confidential advice which is based on long-term strategy, of course, paying attention to the United States' legal and political environment. Our advice is highly reliable because our group's management, which has broad experience and close relationships with the top management of the large corporations of the U.S., will directly participate.

2. We only recommend transactions that are truly friendly and the most profitable to our customers. We are earning high respect by accomplishing such acquisitions as CBS Records' purchase by Sony (2 billion dollars), E. F. Hutton's purchase by Shearson Lehman Brothers (960 million dollars), Firestone's acquisition by Bridgestone (2.6 billion dollars), etc. We are still providing advisory services after the M&A of Firestone and Bridgestone.

3. Our customer list has a lineup of the top enterprises of the world whose business covers the U.S., Japan, and Europe. For example, American International Group, AAMCO, Chrysler, Inland Steel, Mead Corporation, Nestlé, Primerica Corporation, Search & Search, Sony, Squibb Corporation, etc.

4. We can help accomplish global transactions according to each customer's need, since we have close ties with the top enterprises and financial organizations of the U.S., Japan, and Europe, such as Nikko Securities.

5. A consultative committee consisting of management from leading enterprises in the U.S. backs up our strategies on investments. They include management which represents American industries such as those listed below:

Michael W. Blumenthal (Chairman of UNISYS; former Secretary of the Treasury)

Anthony M. Solomon (Chairman of S. G. Warburg; former Chairman of the Federal Reserve Bank in New York)

Charles R. Lazarus (Chairman of Toys Я Us)

John A. Young (President of Hewlett-Packard; Chairman of President's Advisory Committee concerning industrial competitive power)

Alan J. Zakon (Chairman of Boston Consulting Group)

6. Peter G. Peterson and David A. Stockman are world-known financial authorities who believe that an improvement in the U.S. trade deficit will benefit specific businesses or industries. Japanese customers can fully utilize their knowledge on the subject.

BLACKSTONE CAPITAL PARTNERS L.P.

We are highly trusted. Our equity capital, which amounts to 700 million dollars, is one of the reasons for that trust.

1. We have 700 million dollars as capital and we have more than 5 billion dollars of additional funds available in order to provide services such as restructuring, leveraged buy-out (LBO), bridge finance, etc., in a fast, confidential, and effective manner. Soon our equity capital will grow to 1 billion dollars. We welcome the participation of Japanese institutional investors.

2. This fund enables us to respond to various M&A needs of Japanese enterprises, such as a joint venture investment. Also, it makes it possible for us to purchase a department of a company if it differs from the customer's need at the time of the purchase.

3. Our investors are first-rate financial organizations and annuity companies, such as Prudential Insurance, Nikko Securities, Metropolitan Life Insurance, CE Financial Services, Imperial Savings, American General, American Savings & Loan, Mitaui Trust & Banking Corporation, etc.

BLACKSTONE FINANCIAL MANAGEMENT

One of our resources is affiliated companies for asset management.

1. We established Blackstone Financial Management as a link in our industrial strategy. We provide services concerning asset management, finance, and investment to financial institutions all over the world.

2. Laurence D. Fink, who is the Chairman of Blackstone Financial Management and also General Partner, was a Managing Director of First Boston. Our president, Ralph L. Schlosstein, also has had a brilliant career, including the fact that he was responsible for the Department of Mortgage-Backed Securities at Shearson Lehman Hutton. These two people are leading a group of professionals who have broad experience and accomplishments. And they will give you advice. Presently Blackstone Financial Management is planning a fund for Japanese industrial investors.

Watch for it!

Translated by Kumiko Sakai & Associates

Ryoichi Sasakawa, founder of a right-wing, ultra-nationalist political party in Japan, conferred with Benito Mussolini in 1939. *Courtesy of Addison-Wesley Publishers*

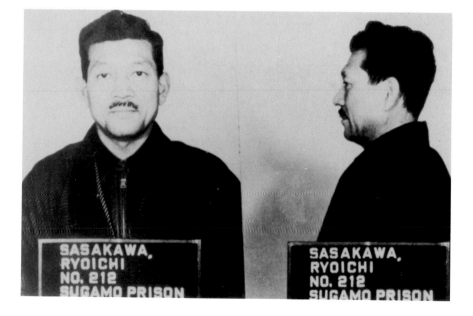

Sasakawa was arrested by Allied Occupation
forces in 1945 for alleged Class A war crimes
and detained in Sugamo Prison. *Courtesy
of Addison-Wesley Publishers*

Former President Jimmy Carter jogs with Ryoichi
Sasakawa, a major contributor to Carter's post-
Presidential policy programs, 1984. *AP/Wide
World Photos*

to are not politicians or lobbyists, but rather ordinary Americans. . . . We should emphasize direct dialogue with them, as in a local election." And that's just how EIAJ's campaign is being directed.

In 1985, Japanese electronics companies charted a new direction for their American politicking—one that would concentrate on what they termed "long-term lobbying." Americans call it the grass-roots approach.

The man who set EIAJ on its new course was Akio Morita, a co-founder of Sony Corporation and Japan's best-known businessman. He once lived in America, speaks fluent English, has many American friends in business and politics, keeps an apartment in New York City, and is wickedly humorous. His business peers in Japan consider him an expert on American politics. In the early 1980s, Morita helped lead Japan's successful fight to repeal California's unitary tax. His U.S. subsidiary has donated heavily to the campaign chests of American politicians. In the late 1980s, Morita bought CBS Records and Columbia Pictures. In short, Morita is a formidable figure, here and in Japan, personally and politically.

In June 1985, Morita told the EIAJ membership that American criticism of Japan "is not due to a misunderstanding of and prejudice against Japan, but rather to certain political intentions." In response, Morita said, the Japanese electronics industry needed to mount a grass-roots political campaign in America. This campaign

> should not stop with PR within the electronics industry, but . . . should expand [its] PR activities to the mass media, consumer groups, and political groups on the state level.

In December 1985, Morita laid out an extraordinarily comprehensive approach for EIAJ's American politicking. His plan consisted of:

- Managing debates and seminars in states and localities.
- Staging local events with local Japanese factories and plants.
- Publishing local newsletters and magazines.
- Instituting exchanges with state universities and think tanks.
- Contacting state economic development bureaus, local chambers of commerce, and state offices of U.S. senators and representatives.
- Organizing exchanges with local consumer groups.
- Contacting local press representatives.
- Operating student exchange programs.

Morita proposed that all facets of the campaign be integrated into a single program. In this way, what might otherwise be an ineffective series of random and unrelated efforts by individual companies and Japanese agencies would be concentrated into a strong, unified message. According to Morita, EIAJ's grass-roots message would have four parts: (1) that Japanese investment creates jobs in America; (2) that Japanese companies help to rebuild depressed American communities; (3) that Japanese companies provide products that satisfy American consumers; (4) that the U.S. and Japanese economies are deeply interdependent.

As with any effective propaganda, this message contains an element of truth. It also omits some important realities, such as the fact that the investment opportunities open to the Japanese in America are largely denied to potential U.S. investors and other foreigners in Japan. Nor does it dwell on what kinds of jobs are being created by Japanese companies or who gets them. What level of displacement of American companies results? What kind of interdependence does Morita contemplate? Perhaps the one-way dependence by the United States on Japan, as alluded to by Shintaro Ishihara in the book he co-authored with Morita?

In the late 1980s, the EIAJ message was hammered home time after time by Morita, other EIAJ members, Japanese government officials, and Japan's American agents. Presidents Reagan and Bush were among many who picked up and echoed the message. Whenever U.S. policymakers, policy analysts, reporters, editors, or critics questioned the mounting investment of Japanese companies or Japanese business practices, they were met with the same message from dozens of supposedly independent sources.

While EIAJ's propaganda was effective on a national scale, the ultimate goal of its program was to forge a pro-Japan constituency among state and local opinion leaders. Before going nationwide with this effort, EIAJ decided to do a trial run in one state. Matt Reese & Associates, a political consulting firm specializing in grass-roots campaigns, was hired to identify several states where such a program could be tested.

The leading candidate was Tennessee. By 1987, Japan had a major economic presence in the state. Its 47 facilities employed 10,000 Tennesseans. In fact, Japanese assets in Tennessee represented 10 percent of its total manufacturing investment in the United States.

Tennessee was an attractive test site for another reason as well. Japan had already done extensive public relations and education work there. In the early 1980s, several universities had established Japan centers. The University of Tennessee at Chattanooga had created a broad-based, off-campus program to increase general public awareness about Japan.

By 1987, school districts in all four of the state's major cities had special education programs on Japan.

Most of the state's cultural organizations had also sponsored Japan-related events. Four of the state's television stations had broadcast weekly programs about Japan. Many other stations had presented special documentaries on Japan. One, in fact, aired a sixteen-part series on Japanese history and culture. In 1986, a Japan-Tennessee Society was formed. Its forty-five members, most of whom were Japanese or American business people, held their first meeting at the governor's residence. In March 1986, Tennessee celebrated Japan Week. That same year, Governor Lamar Alexander published a book, *Friends: Japanese and Tennesseans,* which was distributed throughout the state.

Despite all this outward goodwill, Tennesseans still had apprehensions about Japan. A January 1987 report on Tennessee-Japan relations by the Japan Center for International Exchange in Tokyo reveals:

One concern in late 1986 by some Tennessee policymakers is that current Japanese investment in the state is so great that future investors might go elsewhere.

Once the Japanese picked Tennessee for their new experiment, state officials were contacted and a new local organization was created—the Tennessee-Japan Friends in Commerce (TJFC). To prevent any impression that this was just a Japanese front, three co-sponsors were recruited: the state government, an academic organization (the Japan Center of Tennessee), and the Japan-Tennessee Society. Still, two-thirds of the financing for Friends in Commerce came from the EIAJ and its member companies—particularly Toshiba, Sharp, and Matsushita.

A "local political-establishment figure"—former lieutenant governor Frank Gorrell—was chosen and paid to chair the organization, after former Governor Ned McWherter refused to head it. Matt Reese & Associates was commissioned to identify several thousand Tennessee opinion leaders. These leaders were then invited to become a part of the new organization.

In its first public initiative, TJFC sponsored three heavily subscribed forums. The topic: the importance of "friendship" between the people of Tennessee and Japanese businesses. To reach opinion leaders throughout the state, forums were held in Nashville, Knoxville, and Memphis. Among the attendees were the governor, leading Tennessee business leaders, academics, the press, and other state officials. The keynote address was given by Morita. Most of the other speakers were from Japanese subsidiaries located in Tennessee.

At the time of the forums, Congress was considering sanctions against Toshiba for selling defense equipment to the Soviet Union. Tennessee's congressional delegation was pressed by the governor and many of Toshiba's local supporters to oppose all sanctions. As one Tennessee congressman says: "My arm was twisted so hard that I feel lucky to still have it."

As with all experiments, a few glitches occurred in these forums. One was some low-level grumbling about Japan having too much political influence in Tennessee. Another embarrassment arose when a speaker at one of the forums—Fred Smith, founder and CEO of Federal Express—broached the issue of Japanese protectionism. Smith mentioned that his company had been denied access to the Japanese market, while his Japanese competitors had open access to the U.S. market. Though Smith's speech was conciliatory, he pointed out that the Japanese had not done enough in real terms to counter the impression "that Japan expects more here than it is willing to give there."

For the most part, however, the experiment was deemed a success. The meetings established contacts for EIAJ with state opinion leaders which could be developed further, and they conveyed to these leaders an important message about the benefits that would come to Tennessee from Japanese investment.

The forums also addressed state officials' concern about future Japanese investment in Tennessee. The blunt message they got was that their continuing "friendship" with Japan was the key that "would allow Tennessee to continue to lead the United States in attracting Japanese investment."

This message, of course, put into practice Eddie Mahe, Jr.'s principles of grass-roots politicking.

By 1990, the Japanese had established a formidable grass-roots political infrastructure throughout the United States. Part of this infrastructure is a formal part of the government of Japan. MITI has eight offices in the United States (in New York, San Francisco, Chicago, Los Angeles, Houston, Atlanta, Denver, and Puerto Rico), which operate as the Japan External Trade Organization (JETRO).

While JETRO provides some help for U.S. exporters and information about Japan, its primary mission is to help Japanese businesses in America. The preponderance of its work consists of collecting economic and political intelligence in the United States and sending that information back to Tokyo. Much of the more than $11 million that JETRO spends in America each year goes to hire Washington lawyers, lobbyists, research firms, and "insiders." JETRO registered with the Justice Department in 1969; its propaganda and political activities made it a "foreign agent" by Justice's standards.

The Japanese Foreign Ministry has nine consulates in the United States (in Boston, Chicago, Houston, Kansas City, Los Angeles, New Orleans, New York, San Francisco, and Seattle). In addition to providing a convenient contact between Americans and the Japanese government and serving Japanese companies, the consuls general and their staffs devote much of their time to local public relations activities.

Japan's grass-roots political network is comprised of a large number of private and quasi-public organizations. While there is no common organizational design, these groups do tend to share certain features.

One common denominator is that much of their work is centered on local, state, and regional organizations. Local organizations and Japanese transplants are expected to pay any administrative costs that are incurred. By early 1990, a majority of the states had their own Japan-America Societies. Most of the country is also blanketed by regional PR groups, such as the Japan–U.S. Southeast Association and the Japan–U.S. Midwest Association, which limit their membership to state government officials and Japanese corporations.

These regional, state, and local organizations are usually created under the sponsorship of the governor or some other local political figure, generally with Japanese encouragement. Thus, Japan's political connections are established up front.

Most often, these organizations are chaired by a "local political-establishment figure" who is able to open doors. Often, they are well-connected lawyers or people who do business with the Japanese. Membership consists primarily of the employees of Japanese companies, local opinion leaders and politicians, and those with Japanese business connections, such as lawyers, builders, shippers, bankers, exporters, and suppliers.

The Japanese government provides some money to help finance the work of these organizations. In this way, it gains access to influential Americans whose business interests might make them natural local political allies of Japan. To help American participants "understand" Japanese positions, they are often provided with carefully structured trips to Japan. Upon their return, they are encouraged to write articles and give lectures about what they saw and learned. Most of these organizations have a full program of guest speakers, many of whom are provided by the Japanese government. Needless to say, few critics of Japanese business practices are invited to speak—or even permitted to participate.

A clear indication of the priority that Japan now assigns to developing a pro-Japan grass-roots political constituency in America came in April 1988, when the leading companies in the Keidanren formed the Council for Better Investment in the United States—later renamed the Council for Better Corporate Citizenship in the United States (CBCCIUS). The stated purpose of CBCCIUS is to help Japanese companies become fully integrated "into American society."

The Keidanren is the premier business organization in Japan. As of September 1988, its membership included 120 associations and 921 corporations. The chairman of CBCCIUS is Akio Morita, who is also the Keidanren's vice chairman.

In his book *The Japan That Can Say "No,"* Morita is quite explicit about the political nature of CBCCIUS. He says:

> The Keidanren has established a "Council for Better Investment in the United States." . . . What we mean by "better investment" is the type of investment which will get Americans on Japan's side. If the number of Americans who view things the way Japan does increases [sic], then bashing Japan will cause lower vote counts. That would probably make politicians stop bashing Japan.

Working in combination, the Keidanren and Morita will take Japan's U.S. grass-roots politicking into high gear during the 1990s. As Craig Smith of *Corporate Philanthropy Report* notes, Japan is "buying enough time here to shift from a trade to an investment orientation. The aim is to become multifaceted players in our domestic economy ('If the protectionist gates swing shut, we'll be safely inside')."

Nissan, for instance, rapidly gained acceptance in Nashville's old-boy network by having its local CEO devote half his time to chairing the Nashville area United Way campaign. Nissan also gave more than $3 million to nearly 200 Tennessee community organizations.

Nissan's activities are merely a foretaste of how Japan intends to buy local goodwill in the 1990s. Smith estimates that Japanese foundations gave away $85 million in 1987 and $145 million in 1988. He says this was done with a "modestly-funded infrastructure of giving." For the 1990s, he says, "they're now talking about big bucks."

What makes these donations so troubling is this: Japanese companies have no tradition of charitable giving—either at home or abroad. They generally combine charity and political donations into one accounting line on their balance sheet. Now, they are being pressured by the Japanese government to give even more for the explicit purpose of defusing the mounting hostility toward Japanese trade protectionism.

In February 1990, the Foreign Ministry summoned 300 of Japan's leading business executives to a meeting at which they were summarily instructed to increase their local donations in the United States. To provide added inducement, the government announced that it would give large tax deductions to those Japanese corporations that contributed money in America.

About the same time, the Japanese Chamber of Commerce released a book containing suggestions on how Japanese companies could improve their local public relations in America. One key piece of advice: "take credit for good works accomplished."

4.
JAPANESE PROPAGANDIZING

Chapter Ten

JAPAN'S SIX EXCUSES

WHEN HE RETURNED from an extended trip to Japan in 1989, Alan Webber, managing editor of the *Harvard Business Review*, reported:

> The world has changed and Japan is different. On both sides of the Pacific, the old, entrenched interests are hard at work denying these conclusions, pretending that business as usual will do, and silencing the observers and analysts who call attention to the new situation. Japan's motives are not hard to fathom; after all, every day the country gains in wealth, economic power, and global momentum. The longer Japan successfully confounds U.S. leaders into thinking that all the old rules still apply, the longer the transfer of wealth and power can continue unimpeded. It is not *Japan's* job to inform *us* of our blind stupidity.

Just how does Japan confound America's leaders and the American people? In part, through one of the best-organized, least visible propaganda machines in the world. While the United States and the Soviet Union use propaganda to gain a military/strategic advantage over each other and their geopolitical rivals, Japan employs propaganda to capture an economic/strategic advantage over its industrial rivals.

The technique is simple: Japan persuades foreigners, particularly Americans, to adopt views that are favorable to Japan. Through propaganda, Japan has been able to ward off American criticism about its protectionist economic policies and has actually shaped the prevailing American view of the Japanese.

To aid in this process, Japan has hired a host of American tutors. One of them, political consultant Eddie Mahe, Jr., advises Japanese businessmen that, in American politics, "Perception is reality. If enough people believe something to be true, it has the same impact as being true whether it is a fact or not." The practical implication of Mahe's advice is this: shape the opinions of the American people, and you control the actions of their government.

Once Japanese leaders agree on the perceptions of Japan they want Americans to hold, a propaganda message is disseminated throughout the United States by hundreds of official and unofficial spokesmen. Dutch journalist Karel van Wolferen observes:

> It often seems as if all Japanese spokesmen are hooked up to the same prompter with the same message recorded on a loop of tape. . . . the essence of the message is almost always the same and is predictable down to the finer details. . . . The propaganda is all the more convincing because many informants believe these explanations.

What these spokesmen are delivering is the "official line"—or, in propaganda terms, the "theme." Over the years, Japan has advanced hundreds of propaganda themes, most of which are developed in what experts call a "capillary" decision process. Lower-level staff comes up with an idea, mid-level management discusses and modifies the proposal, and top managers approve it. Once a theme is adopted, it is diffused in a systematically integrated campaign.

Because the process of devising propaganda is difficult, lengthy, and expensive, there is great resistance to changing a line once it is adopted. Consequently, the Japanese find it much easier to vary a propaganda theme than to adopt a new one.

Although Japan has dozens of excuses to justify its closed markets, they can be grouped into six general themes. (1) "Japan creates jobs for Americans." (2) "Japan's critics are racists." (3) "It's America's fault." (4) "Globalization." (5) "Japan is unique." (6) "Japan is changing its ways."

Each theme has countless variations, all of which were encountered by Americans in the 1980s. Most are little more than rationalizations that give Americans the means to deceive themselves.

EXCUSE NO. 1: JAPAN CREATES JOBS FOR AMERICANS

When Japan began to be criticized in the late 1980s for its rapidly expanding investment in the United States, the propaganda theme most widely disseminated by its spokespersons—official, unofficial, and unaware—was that Japanese investment created new jobs for Americans.

But the theme is betrayed by the facts. The number of *new jobs* created by all foreign investment in the United States, including Japan's, is quite low. Of the 677,000 jobs that foreign investors claim to have created in 1988, only 34,000—a mere 5 percent—were created by the establishment of *new* foreign-owned operations in the United States. The other 95 percent were made up of *existing* jobs in U.S. companies that were taken over by foreign investors. Moreover, when we take into consideration the liquidation- or cutback-related layoffs in foreign firms' newly acquired U.S. affiliates, the *net* number of new jobs created by all foreign investment is nominal at best. In fact, it may actually be negative.

The "jobs" propaganda theme also glossed over the fact that many Japanese investments have been little more than inexpensive ways to acquire advanced U.S. technology. For instance, when Kubota, Ltd., Japan's largest manufacturer of agricultural machinery, decided to enter the computer business, it bought five small U.S. companies that specialized in software and supercomputer technology. Less than two years after Kubota's first U.S. acquisition in 1986, the company began manufacturing a mini-supercomputer. The Kubota example has been replicated in dozens of other fields by other Japanese companies.

Another overlooked economic fact is that Japanese foreign investment is actually worsening the American trade deficit. In their book *Foreign Direct Investment in the United States*, economists Paul Krugman and Edward Graham observe that foreign companies in the United States typically import more than two and a half times as many components as do comparable U.S. firms. Japanese corporations import more than six times as many. This strongly suggests that many of Japan's U.S. plants are little more than "screwdriver" operations where components are assembled, while strategic decision making is left to the home offices in Japan.

Like most of Japan's basic propaganda themes, the "jobs" line has many faces. When the rapid pace of Japanese investment in America became a political issue in 1988, for instance, a new twist was developed:

"The British and Dutch have far more U.S. holdings than the Japanese do." The point: not to worry.

The fact that Britain and Holland had larger U.S. portfolios than the Japanese was soon repeated so often by so many that it became an economic cliché. But after the Commerce Department reported in late 1989 that Japan's total U.S. investments had jumped ahead of those held by Canadians (until then the third-ranking cumulative foreign owner in America) and those held by the Dutch, this particular propaganda theme quickly disappeared.

Another powerful variant of the jobs theme is: "Japan is satisfying consumers with better products." Certainly, Japanese companies manufacture competitive products. But so do many American companies. From a political perspective, the issue is not whether American consumers will buy Japanese products; clearly they do. Nor is it an issue of whether Japanese consumers are permitted by Japan's many internal economic arrangements to buy competitive American products; usually they are not. Rather, the issue is whether American policymakers have the political option of closing the U.S. market to Japanese imports as a means of opening Japan's closed market to American exports.

The goal of Japan's "consumer" propaganda theme is to neutralize that option. It's no great challenge. Many Washington policymakers believe— accurately or not—that Americans "want it all, and want it now." Consequently, few politicians have the courage to advocate the sacrifices in consumption needed to increase savings, investment, and productivity. Still fewer appear willing to support crucial industries and technologies through tough-minded trade policies.

Japan's "consumer" propaganda theme exploits that political cowardice. During the midst of the congressional deliberations on the 1988 Trade Act, for instance, a delegation of leading Japanese business officials met privately with members of the House Ways and Means Committee. One congressional participant recalls:

> The Japanese sat on one side of a long table. We sat on the other. They spoke English, but had everything translated so that they could have a lag time before responding. When a member of Congress said that he favored closing the U.S. market to Japanese imports as long as Japan kept its markets closed to American exports, one of the Japanese businessmen began a long response. He would speak for a couple of minutes and stop to see if the translators had gotten it all written down, then he would continue. After a long, concluding statement in Japanese, his final words were, "Ralph Nader." "What the hell is this?" I thought. The translation was,

"You in Congress just think you can close the U.S. market to Japanese goods. If you do, you will be forced to answer to American housewives by Ralph Nader."

"Ralph Nader," of course, was an all-purpose euphemism for politically active American consumer organizations. The Japanese businessmen might also have pointed out that this was no idle threat: the Japanese help finance many of these groups.

EXCUSE NO. 2: JAPAN'S CRITICS ARE RACISTS

"Criticism of Japan is racism" has long been a mainstay of Japanese propaganda. With no apparent hesitation, Japanese propagandists automatically label critics "racists." Variations include calling critics "Japan bashers," "Jap bashers," or even "Japanophobes." These ad hominem attacks are so common that examples are superfluous. By contrast, critics of German trade policies are never labeled "racist" or "German bashers." And critics of, say, Latin American trade practices are rarely labeled "Hispanophobes."

Of course, some Americans are racist and some Japan bashing does occur. But the vast majority of the accusations of racism and Japan bashing are little more than cynical gambits by the Japanese to weaken legitimate American complaints, silence Japan's critics, and forestall U.S. actions that would advance American interests ahead of Japan's.

Japan's habit of smearing its opponents as "racist" is a potent political weapon. In a March 1990 article in the *National Journal* Bruce Stokes points out that although 45 percent of the U.S. trade deficit is with Japan, Democrats find it difficult to speak up about what can or should be done about Japanese protectionism because "attacking Japan for its trade and foreign investment practices exposes the party to charges of racism." Producing self-censorship, of course, is the prime objective of this propaganda theme.

In large part, the "racism" propaganda theme reflects Japan's own obsession with race, foreigners, and its national "uniqueness." Even sophisticated Japanese spokesmen praise their country's racial homogeneity and support policies to maintain it.

One consequence of Japan's race/culture fixation is that foreigners in Japan frequently encounter social barriers. For example, Japan persistently refuses to grant citizenship to more than 700,000 of its residents who were born in Japan because their ancestry is Korean. Similarly, though the Japanese government promised in the late 1970s to accept 10,000 Asian boat people as refugees, it has so far admitted fewer than 7,000. By contrast, America has welcomed more than 1 million Southeast Asian refugees since 1975.

In an October 1989 speech before a hundred Japanese businessmen in the prefecture of Yamagata, Minister of Foreign Affairs Taro Nakayama explained his country's attitude in this way:

> If foreign workers were let into Japan on a large scale, Japanese society would face a problem of accommodating racially mixed off-spring resulting from intermingling between foreign men and Japanese women.

Minister Nakayama's attitude is hardly unique. A 1989 *Business Week* poll revealed that 42 percent of the Japanese blame America's economic problems on the size of its minority population.

Still another example of Japanese race-consciousness: the sudden outbreak and rapid growth of anti-Semitism. According to the Simon Wiesenthal Center, more than forty strongly anti-Semitic books were published in Japan in 1988–89. As one American Japan watcher observes:

> It says quite a bit about the innate race-consciousness of Japan—a non-Western, non-Christian, non-Arab country with no native Jewish population and no history of conflict with Israel—that it is now reaching out into other cultures to find new categories and new outlets for its own racist impulses. But then, the Japanese tend to think that *all* non-Japanese are inferior. That's one reason they feel free to behave towards foreigners—including foreign governments and foreign corporations—in ways that would be deemed dishonorable if directed towards a fellow Japanese.

Atlantic Monthly editor James Fallows, who has lived in Japan, says that because the Japanese are so preoccupied with the matter of race, they naturally assume that others are similarly obsessed. So adverse foreign actions and criticism are often attributed to racial motives.

When the late Japanese businessman Ginji Yasuda could not obtain American financing to remodel his decaying Las Vegas casino, he wondered aloud to reporters whether his difficulties pointed to "some inference of racism." Shintaro Ishihara, co-author of *The Japan That Can Say "No,"* claims American criticism of Japanese trade practices is the result of racial prejudice. Akio Morita, the book's other author, tends to agree. Morita commented on the 1988 Toshiba sanctions: "When something can become this emotional, perhaps Mr. Ishihara is right in his contention that racial problems lie at the root of the problem."

What Ishihara refuses to consider is that much of America's "Japan problem" stems from the simple lack of Japanese trade reciprocity. And Morita ignores the fact that Americans might be legitimately angry that an inadequately supervised Toshiba subsidiary had severely damaged Western military security by illegally transferring restricted military technology to the Soviet Union.

In the summer of 1989, University of South Carolina professor Robert Angel predicted that criticism of Japan would soon be labeled "McCarthyism." Angel showed extraordinary prescience. But then, America's all-purpose political slur has long been used to fight other political battles. In 1981, for example, lawyers who represented terrorist organizations like the Baader-Meinhof Gang called the formation of a Senate Subcommittee on Security and Terrorism "McCarthyism." In 1989, critics of the federal Drug Enforcement Agency (DEA) called its new program to stop indoor marijuana production "marijuana McCarthyism."

In their 1989 book, *Destructive Generation*, Peter Collier and David Horowitz call the term "McCarthyism" "a spell that creates . . . self-censorship." As they explain:

> Thirty years after Joe McCarthy's death, "McCarthyism" has become an omnibus synonym for sinister authority. . . . Individuals and parties compete to brand each other with the scarlet M, using the term as the moral trump card which automatically terminates arguments.

This smear is now being used against not only those who question Japan's actions but also those concerned about how the Japan Lobby operates in Washington. In a 1988 Washington *Post* book review, for instance, American Enterprise Institute fellow John Makin attempted to dismiss Martin and Susan Tolchin's book *Buying Into America*, which analyzed the growth of foreign direct investment in the United States, by linking it to the late Senator McCarthy and his notorious congressional investigations.

In October 1989, George R. Packard of Johns Hopkins University wrote scathingly in the Washington *Post* denouncing articles on Japan written by the group of men the Japanese call "the Gang of Four"— Clyde Prestowitz, James Fallows, Karel van Wolferen, and Chalmers Johnson. In his closing paragraphs, Packard linked all four with the late Senator McCarthy:

The United States lost a generation of China experts to the attacks of Sen. Joseph McCarthy and the "China Lobby." It would be a real tragedy if the new critics were to somehow succeed in making it appear un-American to speak and read Japanese, or to have studied the history, politics and economic institutions of Japan.

The absurdity of Packard's accusation is underscored by the fact that each of the four has studied and lived in Japan. Each believes that current U.S. policies toward Japan are misguided. Each has argued for changes in these policies. Packard's reference to McCarthy, in effect, made the *critics*—rather than the substance of what they had to say—the issue.

In like manner, criticism of the Japan Lobby was linked with "McCarthyism" after *New York Times* journalist Clyde Farnsworth reported in December 1989 that Japan expert Gary Saxonhouse, a paid consultant to the President's Council of Economic Advisers (CEA), also served as an unpaid adviser to Japan's Ministry of International Trade and Industry (MITI). When questioned by the press about his dual advisory role, Saxonhouse accused those who criticized him of being "McCarthyite." Japan's lobbyists quietly spread the same line to the press and politicians.

The "those who criticize Japan revive McCarthyism" theme also found its way into print after House Majority Leader Richard Gephardt asked the White House legal counsel to determine whether Saxonhouse's dual advisership constituted a conflict of interest. On December 24, 1989, Washington *Post* columnist Hobart Rowen responded to Gephardt's inquiry this way:

> In my opinion, it would be downright stupid to deny the American government the guidance of experts who know something about Japan because of some innocent academic connection. It smacks of the same McCarthyism that provoked the Cold War effort to discourage the exchange of scientific information between American and Russian academics.

The problem with this attempt at a directed acquittal is simply this: MITI is no academic organization and Gephardt's question was not about Saxonhouse's patriotism. Gephardt merely asked about the propriety of Saxonhouse advising both governments *simultaneously* on the same topic: U.S.-Japan economic relations. Still, Rowen's charge of "McCarthyism" made Gephardt's actions the issue—not Saxonhouse's.

EXCUSE NO. 3: IT'S AMERICA'S FAULT

The "it's America's fault" excuse promotes the perception that America's trade problems are entirely homegrown. If this were true, America would be hard put to blame the Japanese for any bilateral trade frictions.

Certainly, America has many economic shortcomings. Too many American companies have a short-term view. Poor quality still plagues many American goods. Americans save too little and consume too much. Drug abuse is a national problem. The American educational system often performs abysmally. Many American workers are ill equipped to compete in an advanced industrial economy.

Still, these inadequacies do not explain why U.S. products that are competitive in both price and quality are kept out of Japan's market. Hundreds of American companies produce goods and services that are the best in the world by any measure—price, quality, service, innovation, marketing. The firms that make these products hire salespeople who speak Japanese. They work hard. They take a long-term view of their relationship with Japanese customers. Yet most make only a token penetration into the Japanese market. By contrast, these products compete with great success against Japanese goods in Europe and other markets. In 1989, the Office of the U.S. Trade Representative helped to explain this phenomenon when it listed, in its review of foreign trade barriers, some seventeen pages of governmental, corporate, and cultural barriers in Japan that keep out foreign goods.

But Japan's propagandists prefer to ignore these barriers. Instead, they point their fingers at America. A complex variant of the "it's America's fault" theme is that almost all of America's trade deficit with Japan is due to America's large federal budget deficit—that 85 to 90 percent of the trade deficit with Japan would remain even if all Japanese barriers were removed. This 10 to 15 percent estimate has been quoted so often that its validity is never questioned. Japanese negotiators use it as proof positive that their trade barriers are nominal at best. Both the Reagan and Bush administrations have cited the estimate to justify opposition to tougher trade legislation.

Yet work by many scholars and trade analysts suggests that Japanese protectionism, in all its forms, is now responsible for a significant portion of the bilateral U.S. deficit with Japan. As long ago as 1985, the Commerce Department compiled a short list of U.S. products—such as supercomputers, satellites, citrus, and soda ash—that are excluded by Japanese protectionism. These products alone were worth some $17 billion (then equal to about half the bilateral trade deficit) to U.S. exporters.

When the value of the dollar dropped dramatically, boosting the price competitiveness of its exports, the trade deficit with Europe fell and ultimately disappeared. By contrast, the deficit with Japan remained stubbornly high. This defies all economic logic—unless we consider one critical factor: Japan's markets are far more closed than are America's or those of any of its major trading partners. And that's *Japan's* fault.

Another variant of the "it's America's fault" theme is that "Americans don't try hard enough." An often cited example is the claim that American manufacturers refuse to build a car with right-sided steering for the Japanese market. But the example, much like the point it seeks to prove, is simply inaccurate. Ford and General Motors build more than 1 million cars each year with right-sided steering for the British and other markets. If the Japanese market was truly open, these models could be sold in Japan.

But Japan has long kept foreign cars out of its market. Of the 4.2 million cars sold in Japan in 1989, fewer than 200,000 were imported. A maze of Japanese protectionist nontariff "standards" and vehicle inspections greet would-be auto exporters. Insurance rates on a foreign car, for instance, are kept three times higher than those on domestic vehicles. (Several of the corporate groups that manufacture automobiles also own insurance companies that set the rates.) Japanese manufacturers also dominate domestic dealerships, preventing them from selling other makes. (In the United States, such practices are illegal.) In principle, there is a way around this distribution bottleneck: buy a Japanese manufacturer with an established dealer network. But that won't happen. Donald Petersen, who until the spring of 1990 was chairman of Ford Motor Company, points out that even if cash-rich Ford wanted to increase its current position in Mazda enough to control the company, Japan's Finance Ministry would never permit it to happen.

European governments have always taken a hard-nosed approach to Japan's protection of its automotive market. The government of Italy restricts Japanese vehicle exports to the precise number of Italian-made cars that Japan allows in. The European Community and Japan have established an arrangement that ties Japanese imports to Europe to Japanese reciprocity. Thus, Japan imported more than 120,000 expensive German-made cars in 1989 alone. Ironically, the European cars being sold in Japan have *left-sided steering*, as do the Honda Accords made in Marysville, Ohio, and exported to Japan.

EXCUSE NO. 4: GLOBALIZATION

Once Japanese investors began to buy large chunks of America in the mid-1980s, Japan's propaganda machine kicked back into high gear, this time promoting the themes of "globalization" and "internationalization." The Japanese sought to convey the idea that national borders are disappearing, along with such "outdated" concepts as national pride and national security. In their place was emerging a single global market, where dependence and allegiance have no place. The underlying message: policy sophisticates shouldn't worry about the Japanese purchases of American assets, or about Japan's quest for global domination of key industries.

Kenichi Ohmae, director of the Tokyo office of McKinsey & Co. and a leading promoter of this line, takes the argument one step further. He argues that corporations are no longer Japanese, American, or European. Rather, he says, they are entities separate from nations. "There are no longer any national flag carriers. Corporations must serve their customers, not [their] governments."

According to Ohmae's "globalization" thesis, the dollars Japan has accumulated are Japanese "immigrants"—they come back to America, where they are used to purchase productive holdings. In the process, an economic alchemy occurs: "[O]nce these dollars cross the U.S. border they are American, not Japanese. Dollars don't belong to the nation of their current owners, but to the nation in which they are invested . . . it's as if they become citizens of that country." Ohmae concludes that the "unfortunate and uneducated bashing [of Japan] will stop" once Americans understand that the money the Japanese make by selling their wares to Americans is reinvested in America when the Japanese buy buildings, factories, securities, land, and other assets.

But Ohmae and others pushing the "globalization" thesis ignore the possibility that the dollars held by Japan could be used to buy American *exports* rather than American *assets*. They also ignore the fact that by selling its appreciating capital stock (real estate and companies) to buy depreciable foreign-made consumer goods (cars, VCRs, and other home electronics), America is sure to be a poorer nation in the long run. For after the consumables are gone and forgotten, foreign investors will still be taking profits and rents from their ownership of equity.

The globalization theme also glosses over that fact that ownership of U.S. companies is equal to economic control over such basic decisions as where jobs will be created. As Jodie Allen and Hobart Rowen point out in a 1989 Washington *Post* article: "[J]obs don't float across national borders as easily as capital. . . . Fair or not, the impression persists that Japanese targeting of U.S. markets, whether for autos or semiconductors, has cost us jobs."

The Japanese understand that it *does* matter who owns a nation's capital stock—and where companies do their research, production, and service work. Indeed, MITI's basic purpose is to help Japan in this process. Other countries also recognize the link between ownership, economics, and politics. The European Community, for instance, requires foreign firms to locate much of their research and manufacturing in Europe as a condition of market access. Consequently, many American companies are shifting major portions of their operations to Europe, often under duress; others are voluntarily transferring production and jobs to Europe. Why? Because the U.S. government is largely indifferent to the longer-term fate of American industry. European governments take a very different view. In Europe, the governments have firm prohibitions against the predatory industrial schemes—such as dumping—that the Japanese have used to undermine competitors in America. Europeans value their indigenous companies for the jobs, wealth, and taxes that they create.

The globalization line has worked well for the Japanese in the United States. Not only does it offer an excuse for the U.S.-Japan equity-for-consumables swap; it dismisses Japanese protectionism and the consequent destruction of American companies as irrelevant—so long as Americans are spoon-fed a continuous stream of consumer goods.

America's acceptance of the globalization argument allows Japan to deploy the full political force of the United States against Europe. When the Europeans demand market reciprocity from the Japanese, and refuse to permit the Japanese to circumvent this requirement through low-value-added assembly operations in Europe, Japan responds by building these "screwdriver" operations (so called because all the workers do is put together kits manufactured in Japan) in the United States. They then persuade the U.S. government that these are "American" products and use the political muscle of the U.S. government to get them into Europe. This tactic has met with considerable success. In February 1990, the USTR announced that products from Japanese-owned facilities in the United States were *American* products and the U.S. government would aggressively resist European efforts to exclude them.

Still, for all of the Japanese arguments that national borders are evaporating, Japan's own borders remain substantially closed to the rest of the world. Foreign investors have been so restricted that they own less than 1 percent of Japan's national assets. That figure stands in stark contrast to comparable numbers in the United States (9 percent) and West Germany (17 percent). Japan is notorious for admitting fewer imported manufacturing goods than other nations—importing raw materials and unfinished products instead. In the 1980s, the ratio of manufactured imports to GNP was less than 3 percent in Japan compared with roughly 7 percent in America and well over 10 percent for most European countries.

American policymakers and opinion leaders have yet to grasp the nature of the profound economic shifts now under way in the world. They still cannot fathom Japan's economic objectives. Guided by a laissez-faire ideology, beguiled by the fuzzy concept of "globalization," and confronted by Japan's American agents of influence, our policy elites remain studiously neutral in the struggle of American corporations with their Japanese competitors. But then, passive acceptance of Japan's growing role in the U.S. economy—together with the use of American muscle to fight Japan's political battles—is precisely the goal of the "globalization" line.

EXCUSE NO. 5: JAPAN IS UNIQUE

Tennessee entrepreneur John R. Latendresse produces cultured pearls that are exported around the world. When Latendresse was getting started in the early 1980s, he went to Tokyo, where, he says, the chairman of Japan's cultured pearl export association asked whether he "was aware that the cultured pearl business really belongs to Japan—that it was part of their history, their culture, and their heritage."

Latendresse replied, "Henry Ford is part of our culture and part of our past—and look what the hell you people have done with his idea!"

The "Japan is unique" line is a staple of Japanese propaganda. It reflects an attitude among many Japanese that is reinforced by a large body of popular literature called *Nihonjin-ron*—writing that elaborates how Japan is "different" and the Japanese are "special."

Repeatedly and successfully, Japan has used the "uniqueness" theme as a ploy in its trade negotiations with America. For many years, the Japanese have argued that their country is a "small, poor island with no resources that must export to survive."

Between the late 1950s and the early 1980s, the Japanese succeeded with a different version of the theme: they persuaded Americans that the Japanese "can't invent, they can only copy." While far from true, this line's widespread acceptance helped Japan forestall political criticism about the massive, debilitating transfer of American technology to Japan.

Still another variant on this theme is that Japanese consumers "don't want foreign goods." Those who argue this line are in effect saying that *even if there were no trade barriers* Japan still would not buy what American companies have to offer. But the facts tell a different story: Japanese consumers will buy low-priced, high-quality foreign products— if they have the opportunity. Japanese tourists regularly return home loaded with foreign goods superior to those found in Japan. Many also bring back Japanese goods that are sold abroad at prices dramatically lower than in Japan.

EXCUSE NO. 6: JAPAN IS CHANGING ITS WAYS

In his 1864 State of the Union message to Congress, Abraham Lincoln wrote:

Owing to the peculiar situation of Japan, and the anomalous form of its government, the action of that empire in performing treaty stipulations is inconstant and capricious. Nevertheless, good progress has been effected by the western powers, moving with enlightened concert. . . . There is reason to believe that these proceedings have increased rather than diminished the friendship of Japan towards the United States.

Now, as in Lincoln's time, the American hope is that, with a little patience and understanding, the characteristics that set Japan apart from the rest of the world will recede into insignificance and Japan will become more like other nations. From the beginning of America's relationship with Japan, a central objective of the U.S. government has been to increase the feelings of "friendship" in Japan toward the United States. These American hopes are kept alive by a constantly changing cast of cosmopolitan Japanese spokesmen, all of whom continue to assert that change in Japan is imminent.

As Karel van Wolferen observes, in the 1960s experts predicted that Japan would change once its youth came into positions of influence. In the 1970s, Japan was supposed to change once enough Japanese tourists and businessmen had been exposed to other nations and other cultures. In the 1980s, the alleged agent of change was the "internationalization" of Japan's financial market and the rising expectations of other countries toward the world's richest nation. In 1989, the promised stimulus for change was the Recruit political scandal, which many felt would produce a Japanese government less beholden to its corporations and more concerned about its consumers.

Beguiled by the prospect of "imminent change" for more than thirty years, America has been extraordinarily patient about Japanese protectionism. When Japan's trade surplus with America ballooned in the 1980s, for instance, the Japanese government began to pound out the message that it was finally opening its markets to American imports.

In the first package of measures, Japan announced that it would reduce sixty-seven assorted trade barriers. It promised to create an office to help potential importers and listen to foreign grievances. But as the USTR drily reported, the promised steps "largely reflected a compilation of measures that had already been undertaken by various Japanese government agencies."

Time and again, Japanese officials have trumpeted "new" market-opening steps—ones that had already been taken. In the spring of 1984, the U.S.-Japan Trade Study Group—comprised of businessmen from both countries—reported that many of the allegedly new undertakings had "been previously announced." Even the Reagan Administration viewed the proposed tariff changes as "too little, too late."

Still, Japan's market-opening assurances worked to vent American political pressures for four years. By the time policymakers in the first Reagan Administration lost patience, they had been replaced by a new team of officeholders.

In late 1989, Japan responded to renewed American demands to open its market by announcing a new package of measures. The Japanese proposals and the accompanying public relations campaign were hauntingly familiar. The Japanese announced that they were now ready and willing to reverse the very programs that had made Japan an exporting powerhouse. MITI said that it would eliminate tariffs on 1,004 goods and reduce levies on four others. Masahisa Naito, director general of MITI's International Trade Administration Bureau, claimed that these measures were a "180-degree turnaround from the old export-oriented policies." He said that they would eliminate the vast differentials between the price of goods in Japan and those abroad; that they would open the Japanese distribution system to foreigners; and that they would break down the *keiretsu* system, by which Japan's tightly clustered companies do business exclusively with each other.

Naito predicted that the new measures would reduce Japan's trade surplus from $81 billion in 1989 to $78 billion in 1990. He said, "This reflects how sincere and convinced we are of the effects these measures will generate. They are unprecedented in any part of the world and are very major." Naito's message was not a new one. He wanted to convince federal officials that Japan was changing and that they needn't continue U.S. efforts to open Japan's closed markets.

For all America's anticipation of change, Japan remains by far the most closed industrial economy in the world. And it is reasonable to ask: Do Japan's policymakers really want to change?

Japan has the world's largest accumulation of savings; the world's most advanced commercial technology; the world's most productive manufacturing capacity; and the world's lowest unemployment rate. Japanese society is stable. Japan has little crime and few problems with drugs or alcoholism. Japan—with an economy half the size of that of the United States—is investing at twice the rate we are, which virtually guarantees that it will be even more productive and competitive in the 1990s. In the late 1980s, Japan ran an annual trade surplus with the United States of almost $50 billion—and the prospect is for similar surpluses for the indefinite future. Whenever it wishes, Japan has more than enough wealth to improve its quality of life without denting its global competitiveness.

Why would Japan want to abandon an economic and social system that serves its interests so well? Why would it adopt an economic system that offered disproportionate benefits to America? Japan's behavior, considered in its totality, strongly suggests that Japan wants to keep the existing system in place at all costs—regardless of the future consequences for the "special U.S.-Japan relationship." Japan just wants us to think that it is changing.

Chapter Eleven

THE JAPANESE WURLITZER

JAPAN'S ECONOMIC PROPAGANDA techniques are re-markably similar to America's political propaganda techniques. A quick way to understand how Japan spreads its propaganda in America is to look at how America spreads its own propaganda elsewhere.

America operates two propaganda programs—one is overt, the other is covert. The *overt* program is operated by the U.S. Information Agency (USIA), which diffuses information about American culture, history, and political positions. USIA employs all the standard public relations techniques—hosting lunches, arranging interviews, distributing literature, providing American guest speakers, stocking libraries, arranging cultural exchanges, sponsoring conferences, and financing trips to America for students, academics, and foreign opinion leaders.

America's *covert* propaganda program is directed by the Central Intelligence Agency. By any measure, this is a massive undertaking. Loch Johnson estimates that fully 40 percent of CIA secret operations are propaganda programs.

The substance of this covert propaganda is carefully monitored to ensure that it reflects the nuances of the government's current policies. Policy papers describing the intended message are prepared by the CIA and reviewed by the State Department—even the White House. To spread its propaganda, the CIA has recruited several hundred members of the foreign media. Johnson says:

> The CIA secretly provides a flood of supportive propaganda distributed through its vast, hidden network of "media assets": reporters, newspaper and magazine editors, anchormen, television

163

producers, cameramen, broadcast technicians—the whole range of
media personnel. Whatever foreign policies or slogans the White
House may be pushing at the time . . . (there have been hundreds
of such propaganda "themes" over the years) . . . the CIA will likely
be advancing these same ideas through its covert channels.

In most cases, the CIA's message will appear under the byline of a
foreign media asset: "The end result in each case is that a native citizen,
ideally one with respected media credentials, endorses the U.S. position
in his or her native tongue and through the country's own news outlets,"
Johnson says.

In addition to advancing specific U.S. themes, the CIA also uses its
media assets to boost politicians and opinion leaders in other countries whose positions are favorable to the United States and to tarnish
those whose positions are not. Other nations do the same, including
Japan.

Why do foreign journalists free-lance as CIA propaganda promoters?
Money is generally the biggest incentive. Most work for a regular CIA
salary or on a piece/rate basis. Others volunteer. Ideology, patriotism,
personal affinity for Americans, social ties, and entrapment have each
served as bonds. Some work for America as a means of professional
advancement: in return for their assistance, the CIA, the Defense Department, and the State Department give them privileged access to
officials, scoops, and inside information. Others are unaware that they
are being used. Regardless of the reason, the end result is the same.

Japan's propaganda techniques are similar to those used by America.
Much like an enormous Wurlitzer organ, Japan pumps out a steady flow
of propaganda through thousands of outlets—books, speeches, reports,
conferences, television, editorials, articles, and whisper campaigns.

The overt propaganda largely is concerned with providing foreigners
a better understanding of Japanese history and culture. It is managed
by government agencies like the Japan External Trade Organization
(JETRO) and Japan's Foreign Ministry, and surfaces in an array of official
government publications.

Japan's covert propaganda, on the other hand, has little to do with
history and culture. Not surprisingly, it aims to develop the Japanese
economy, its industries and its exports. MITI and a slew of Japanese
agencies, foundations, companies, and trade associations work quietly to
further this end. Often, they see to it that others—including Americans
in the pay of Japan—further it for them.

A representative example of how the Japanese Wurlitzer works is its
program to blunt criticism of Japan's rapidly growing, highly visible in-

vestments in many of America's most productive and most critical industries.

After the Reagan Administration began its radical devaluation of the dollar in 1985, Japan used its newfound purchasing power to acquire undervalued American assets. The Japanese acquisition of such prominent properties and companies as Rockefeller Center, CBS Records, and the Firestone tire company generated sharp but generally unfocused political criticism.

The foreign investment issue crystallized in February 1988 with the publication of the Tolchins' *Buying Into America*. The Tolchins found themselves regularly in the press, and they appeared on many national news programs.

One of the book's findings is that federal data on foreign investment are so incomplete that national policymakers have only the vaguest idea of which American assets are owned by foreign investors, or the extent to which foreigners control those assets. This lent support to those in Congress who favored the Bryant Amendment—legislation that would have forced foreign investors to provide the federal government with basic information about their U.S. acquisitions. Not surprisingly, Japan fiercely opposed this proposed new law.

Soon after the Tolchin book was published, one of Japan's key American advisers, Richard Whalen, crafted a public relations strategy that showed his clients how to help deflect the criticism that followed the release of the book. Whalen was well qualified for his task: A speechwriter and phrasemaker for many prominent politicians, he ran a firm—Worldwide Information Resources, Ltd., or WIRES—through which he had advised the Pinochet-led government of Chile in the early 1980s about improving its access to U.S. military assistance, rescheduling its foreign debt, and countering criticisms about human rights abuses. Since Whalen went into the political consulting business, his major foreign clients have included the government of Japan and Toyota Motor Sales U.S.A., Inc.

As the head of WIRES, Whalen advises his foreign clients on matters of U.S. policy, analyzes U.S. media coverage of relevant events, and orchestrates strategies for disseminating "important (but unreported) documents and statements." Whalen and his staff draft letters on behalf of their foreign clients. When appropriate, they write and submit op-ed pieces or letters to various publications. Whalen also uses his contacts to open doors to high-level federal officials for his clients.

The strategy for deflecting criticism about Japanese investment in America was based on Whalen's observation that the issue of foreign investment will "ultimately be decided by the American public's perceptions, not by objective facts." Whalen and his staff concluded that, in the 1990s, political and congressional concern would focus on four principal aspects of the foreign investment issue:

- Foreign control of major U.S. corporations and industries.
- Foreign speculation in real estate.
- Control of U.S. banks and financial firms.
- The overall, cumulative impact of foreign investment across industry and geographic lines (the "national sovereignty" question).

In a report prepared before the 1988 elections on public opinion and the policy and political environment for foreign investment issues, WIRES described the strengths and weaknesses of the Tolchins' book and outlined possible lines of attack. The report also profiled the positions of those members of Congress—Congressman John Bryant (D-Tex.), Senator Tom Harkin (D-Iowa), Congressman Bart Gordon (D-Tenn.), Congressman Charles E. Schumer (D-N.Y.), Senator Ernest F. Hollings (D-S.C.), Senator Barbara A. Mikulski (D-Md.), and Senator Steven D. Symms (R-Idaho)—who had been particularly outspoken on the issue.

WIRES compared the likely foreign investment attitudes of a Republican Administration with those of a Democratic Administration in 1989–93. It concluded that a Bush-led Administration "would support free entry of new capital while attempting to appease growing public reaction to foreign involvement in the U.S. economy." By contrast, the report said a Democratic Administration "would be more likely to pursue nationalist policies to control foreign investment, such as requiring more review and approval of foreign takeovers of a certain size or in sensitive industries."

Most telling about the WIRES report, however, were three political points that Whalen and his staff emphasized:

- "America's political leadership has not accepted—or told the public—that the United States had lost a significant measure of autonomy in its economic policymaking and political-economic decision making."
- "America is being sold cheap," a senior MITI official noted for his blunt candor told WIRES in Tokyo not long ago. "This is the painful part of devaluation."
- "At the peak of their wealth, the oil-rich Arabs never approached the scale of Japanese wealth. Nor did they have the business acumen and skills to deploy their dollars without American assistance. The Japanese do, and they have the ability to compound their wealth

and their political and economic influence far into the future. This
is what worries thinking Americans."

To counter the vocal worries of "thinking Americans," the WIRES
report recommended that the Japanese mount an educational campaign
directed toward American interests with a stake in international investment. Specifically, the report proposed:

> Japanese private sources (such as think-tanks and foundations)
> should co-sponsor with American counterparts, such as the Brook-
> ings Institution and the American Enterprise Institute, seminars
> and conferences on the benefits of international trade.

A second recommendation was that discussions be encouraged between prominent leaders of the private sectors in both countries, who
could discuss the notion of a Japan-U.S. free trade agreement.

WIRES also recommended that Japanese companies demonstrate their
intent to be a "constructive, long-term" force in America. It urged the
Japanese to take steps to lower barriers to American investment, particularly in sectors that claimed high visibility, such as financial institutions.

Other WIRES recommendations focused on what Japan could do to
improve its public image in America. Among these were that Japanese
companies in America should present an "American face" (hire Americans
as their local managers and spokesmen) and be more aggressive in their
dealings with the press.

WIRES told its clients that their Japanese spokesmen should emphasize that their companies expect "national treatment" for investment
disclosures—that is, they do not expect to have to disclose any more
information to the U.S. government than American firms are required
to disclose.

But if the Japanese companies were *really* given national reciprocity—
if their U.S. operations were treated in the same manner that American
firms are treated in Japan—they would have been forced to disclose much
more information to the federal government.

The report's final point echoed a key to success for Japan's Wurlitzer:
"The message will have to be repeated many times, in imaginative ways,
in an atmosphere of rising political tensions."

In mid- and late 1988, conferences on foreign investment became an
American growth industry. Many were conducted by think tanks that
were funded—in part or whole—by Japanese sponsors. Others were

organized by accounting and law firms that had hefty Japanese client bases or by trade associations with extensive Japanese membership. Japanese companies urged still other policy organizations to hold foreign investment symposia. Lawrence Baer, president of the Global Economic Action Institute (GEAI), a think tank funded largely and initially by the Unification Church, says a Japanese trading company approached him in 1988 and encouraged GEAI to sponsor a conference on foreign investment. The group complied. The roster of forum participants featured leading Wall Street bankers, most of whom were helping the Japanese buy more American assets.

All of these conferences were strikingly similar. For the most part, the speakers were well-known investment bankers, lawyers, ex-officials, or academics with personal or professional ties to Japan. Two of the most prominent speakers on this conference circuit were Elliot Richardson and Peter Peterson. Besides being founder, general counsel, and head of the Association for International Investment, Richardson is a senior partner in the law firm of Milbank, Tweed, Hadley & McCloy. One of his firm's clients is the government of Japan. Peterson, once Secretary of Commerce, is chairman of the Blackstone Group, a well-known Wall Street investment bank that is partially owned by Japanese investors.

Usually, the organizers of these conferences invited a token critic to play "bad guy," someone like Clyde Prestowitz, Susan Tolchin, or Congressman John Bryant. The balance of the program was devoted to discussing how foreign investment created jobs, explaining how the Bryant Amendment would deter foreign investment, stressing that Britain and the Netherlands had more cumulative holdings in America than Japan, and detailing how America needed foreign capital to finance its budget deficit and rebuild its industries.

Concurrent with these conferences, a flood of op-ed pieces in support of foreign investment were submitted to national and local newspapers. Most printed these pieces without revealing that their authors had financial relationships with the Japanese.

After the 1988 election, President Bush said that Americans should mute their criticism of foreign investment, lest foreign investors refuse to finance the federal budget deficit. The Administration also passed the word that it would veto the Bryant legislation if Congress approved the measure.

Japan got the Administration's message. Soon after Bush's announcement, a Japanese diplomat reported that his embassy had concluded that the foreign investment issue was no longer a pressing political problem, and that the embassy staff once assigned to work on the matter had been reassigned. The push to hold conferences and print articles about the benefits of foreign investment came to an abrupt halt. So did the conferences and articles.

In the spring of 1989, MITI contacted Japanese investors and "suggested" that they be "sensitive" about making conspicuous purchases in America. The warning came at a propitious moment. The Bush Administration was considering whether to declare Japan an unfair trader. When the Administration decided to give Japan a simple slap on the wrist, Japanese purchases of prestigious American assets soon began surging again.

In the fall of 1989, Japanese investors bought Columbia Pictures, then New York's Rockefeller Center. At the same time, ex-President Reagan was paid a well-publicized $2 million for making a speaking tour of Japan. In combination, these three events put Japanese investment back into the public spotlight. The Japanese Wurlitzer went back to work.

On November 1, 1989, Richard Whalen's firm WIRES sent a twenty-three-page foreign investment report to America's newspaper editors, columnists, and foreign editors. It looked like an official news release or wire report. The report's principal message: "In an increasingly interdependent world economy, investment across borders is both inevitable and beneficial to the U.S."

The balance of the report argued that Japanese and other foreign investment was good for America, and that the Exon-Florio Amendment to the 1988 Trade Act—which gave the President the authority to investigate and block foreign acquisitions that threaten national security—is bad. Americans with ties to Japan echoed the same message in op-ed pieces, interviews, and speeches.

Japan's propaganda is effective because it is delivered systematically by thousands of credible spokespersons. While some are Japanese, most are Americans. The motivation of the Japanese is obvious. The incentive for most Americans is, too: money. Still, some Americans reinforce Japan's positions out of a sincere conviction that Japan's positions are right and Japan's critics are wrong. Regardless of their motivation, Japan's American assets help tilt much of the debate about U.S.-Japanese relations in Japan's favor.

The Soviets have long attempted to smooth their relationships with foreigners by using spokespersons who serve as what van Wolferen calls "buffers"—people who speak the language of the foreign country; are familiar with that country's culture, politics, and current thinking; and can present the Soviet propaganda lines convincingly. One of the best-known Soviet buffers is the ubiquitous Georgi Arbatov, director of the

Institute for the Study of the USA and Canada. People like Arbatov are disarmingly frank, often witty, sometimes sympathetic, and always knowledgeable. Most are also affable, which gets them far with many Americans.

Japan's buffer system is far larger and far more effective than that of the Soviets, which reflects the fact that buffers have had a long-standing role in Japan's foreign relations effort. Like Arbatov, many of Japan's buffers operate government or corporate institutes. Some are academics and editors from leading Japanese publications. Others are officials of the Keidanren. A few—like former MITI Vice Minister Makoto Kuroda— are retired Japanese diplomats and government officials. Still others are leading Japanese business leaders.

The best of these buffers spend much of their time abroad advancing Japan's positions with the foreign press, at conferences, and in meetings with foreign opinion leaders. At nearly every symposium on U.S.-Japan relations held in the United States, the same people from this small cast of buffers are put forward as the "face of Japan."

Within Japan, most foreign visitors are introduced to a surprisingly small universe of people who constitute what could be called the "buffer class"—Japanese notables from business, academia, politics, and government whose task it is to "handle" foreigners. Often, foreign visitors are "matched" to meet with members of the buffer class who have attended the same schools or have lived in the same countries.

Alan Webber observes that the Japanese carefully approach these meetings. Their agendas include: (1) preparing for the discussion; (2) having the discussion; (3) reviewing tapes or notes from the discussion; (4) following up the discussion; and (5) preparing for a subsequent discussion. Japanese in positions of power talk to each other constantly about ongoing or anticipated debate between Japan and its trading partners. "They practice their arguments and their own logic," he says, "in ways that we don't even begin to imagine." Webber adds:

> When you go to meet with someone in power, they will test you early on to see how well-prepared you are. They have been rehearsing among themselves for months. They are debaters who enter a meeting prepared to win, to convince you of their point of view. Americans go into these meetings for a conversation and in that sense we are disarmed and unprepared.

The arguments that the power elite buffers make to foreigners are reinforced by many other Japanese who may not be aware that what they are arguing is simply Japan's propaganda line. According to Webber, the unaware Japanese propagandists "really believe what they say and are wonderfully innocent. They are only describing what they know. The fact that what they know is only half the story is not their fault." Still, it reflects the fact that the Japanese people are fed much of the same propaganda that is exported to America and the rest of the world.

Since the end of World War II, the most influential advocacy of the Japanese point of view in the United States has come from a small co-alition of America's Japan experts and insiders. Colloquially, their critics call them the Chrysanthemum Club—after the floral symbol of Japan's Imperial family.

Membership in this club consists primarily of those Americans with an intellectual, personal, or business stake in the present course of U.S.-Japan relations. First among equals in this club are those members of America's foreign policy establishment who deal with Japan. They try to preserve "the relationship" by defending Japan to Americans. A clear example of this is found in a twelve-page special advertising section published in the February 1990 *Atlantic Monthly*, entitled "Ambassador Mansfield Talks to America." The supplement features advertisements by seven Japanese companies, but the focal point is a long essay by Mike Mansfield, U.S. Ambassador to Japan from 1977 to 1989.

Mansfield's essay is little more than a sustained apology for Japan. In some detail, he describes America's satisfaction with the existing U.S.-Japan security arrangements, how Japan has rapidly moved to reduce its dependence on an export-driven economy, Japan's vast foreign aid pro-gram, the jobs and benefits created by Japanese investment in America, the importance of Japanese imports to U.S. exporters, how helpful the regular inflow of capital from Japan is in financing the federal debt, and how "the Japanese market is no longer as closed as many people like to think; 'Japan Inc.,' as we used to perceive it, no longer exists." Mansfield notes that "perhaps only 25 percent of our deficit with Japan is caused by Japanese market restrictions." The balance, he says, is due to a "com-placent and self-indulgent" America.

Mansfield's criticisms of Japan's role in creating any trade imbalance are few and oblique. Even those critical remarks are softened by his observation that Japanese leaders now understand that they must take action to preserve the world trade system because Japan "takes from the system without giving enough in return."

Just as American diplomats want to preserve the U.S.-Japanese re-lationship, many Defense Department officials wish to retain the status quo of American military bases in Japan. To these officials, any other aspect of the U.S.-Japan relationship is merely a bargaining chip to be employed in negotiations over these facilities.

The overwhelming majority of America's Japan experts in universities and think tanks depend on the Japanese for hard-to-get access—and often funding—to conduct writing and research about Japan and U.S.-Japan relations. Glen Fukushima, formerly the USTR's top expert on Japan, notes "the strange propensity among American Japanologists to feel one-sidedly positive about Japan. . . . If you're a foreigner who is too critical about Japan, your sources of information, funding, and friends dry up." Needless to say, the Japanologists provide positive talk.

Other Chrysanthemum Club members are ideologues devoted to the philosophy of anti-Communism or the tenets of "free trade." To them, changes in current U.S.-Japan relations might push Japan out of the American sphere of influence and away from a free trade regime. Still others simply admire Japan—or enjoy criticizing the United States. More than a few are executives of American companies with a special niche in the Japanese market, who doubtless feel that change could threaten their economic standing.

Regardless of their motivations, the Chrysanthemum Club plays a key role in Japan's propaganda scheme: it puts an American face on many of Japan's positions. Such advocacy is highly effective because of the obvious expertise of the advocates themselves. Yet as Kevin L. Kearns, an American diplomat who served in Tokyo during the late 1980s, reported in the *Foreign Service Journal* in December 1989, the Chrysanthemum Club's members

> somehow fail to see the trail from predatory Japanese policies, to lost markets, to destroyed industries, to large outflows of wealth in the form of trade deficits, and finally to the resultant decline of American power and influence. . . . Chrysanthemum members seem to see their function not as representing U.S. interests but as balancing the demands of both sides . . . to make the increasing Japanese domination of the U.S. economy as painless a process as possible for our institutions and the American people.

Japan has thousands of spokesmen who distribute its propaganda. When those who are Japan's employees are clearly identified, journalists and policymakers can fairly balance their judgment of the facts and arguments presented to them, because they know that the spokespersons are in the pay of Japan.

But the financial ties of the many Americans who speak for Japan are usually far less visible. And Congress, federal officials, and the public are usually unaware of these links when they hear these people's comments on U.S.-Japan relations.

Since the mid-1970s, for instance, ex-trade official Harald Malmgren has advised Japanese corporations and the government of Japan. Over the past fifteen years, dozens of journalists have cited Malmgren as an expert on American trade policies and U.S.-Japan relations. But the journalists who quote him rarely identify Malmgren's money ties to Japan.

In the midst of Zenith's fight against Japan's television cartel, for instance, Malmgren criticized Zenith CEO John Nevin in a Chicago *Tribune* story. To the story's readers, Malmgren was just an impartial Washington analyst who had no personal interest in the particulars of the Zenith case. But this impression was as incorrect as Malmgren was interested. Though the *Tribune* piece never mentioned it, Malmgren was paid $300,000 by Japanese television manufacturers to broker a political deal with the Carter Administration. The *Tribune* story also overlooked Malmgren's contract with the Japanese, in which he said he might be "engaged in the preparation and dissemination of political propaganda" on behalf of his clients.

The Zenith affair was only one of many forums in which Malmgren has been able to advance his views. A search by NEXIS, a computerized database of news stories, reveals that during the 1980s Malmgren was cited or quoted in seventy-six stories about trade and economic issues. As Congress was drafting tough new trade legislation in 1987 and 1988, Malmgren's views on the trade bill and its implementation were printed by many of America's leading news organizations. In many of these stories, Malmgren denigrated the legislation, particularly those elements that would have strengthened America's ability to pry open Japan's closed markets. He called the legislation "technical protection" and "vigilante-style unilateral retaliation." And while he was lambasting American trade legislation, Malmgren was working for Japanese trade interests. He earned $51,250 in 1987 and $104,500 in 1988 as an adviser to the Japan External Trade Organization (JETRO) in New York.

The articles that cited Malmgren identified him as a "former deputy U.S. trade negotiator [and] now a consultant," or "former trade negotiator," or "a trade consultant in Washington," or "a leading international trade specialist," or "president of Malmgren, Inc., and former trade negotiator." None of them mentioned that Malmgren was working for the Japanese.

Like Harald Malmgren, dozens of former U.S. trade officials in the pay of Japan, as well as hundreds of academics whose work is supported by Japanese funding and access, write and are regularly quoted on trade matters without their financial links being revealed. Most often, these financial links are not revealed because they are not known. Gaps in this sort of information largely are attributable to serious loopholes in federal reporting requirements for foreign agents. Malmgren, for instance, canceled his foreign agent registration statement with the Justice Department in September 1985. He is not even listed in *Washington Representatives*, the standard reference source on lobbyists, lawyers, and consultants in the capital.

To find a record of Malmgren's relationship with the government of Japan in 1987 and 1988, a reporter would have to guess that JETRO might be one of his clients. Then the reporter would have to read through all of JETRO's foreign agent activity filings with the Justice Department. If he was simply providing advice and counsel to Japanese companies, no public record of his relationship would exist for the reporter to cite, for the Foreign Agents Registration Act (FARA) does not require Malmgren to keep registering if he is not actively and directly lobbying or attempting to influence public policy. Nor does it require him to maintain a registration if his only job is to advise foreign interests or to conduct research for them. Perhaps few, if any, of Malmgren's public views have a connection with the source of his livelihood. The point remains: readers need and deserve such information to weigh, interpret, and finally judge comments by Malmgren and others who work for Japan.

Just as vocal advocates often conceal financial ties to Japan, other trade experts are frequently bullied into a pernicious form of self-censorship. An executive producer of an influential weekly public affairs program says that since the early 1980s fewer and fewer American trade experts are willing to criticize Japanese policies on the record. One former U.S. negotiator explains why:

> Many of the best-known names [of trade experts] are those of people on Japan's payroll. They would be risking their fees with public criticism. Many others remain silent because they seek Japanese clients or are afraid of being labeled a "Japan basher" or "racist."

As they do with former trade officials, the press and federal policymakers often call upon Wall Street financiers for comments and policy advice on U.S.-Japan economic relations. For the most part, these Wall Street experts reinforce Japan's point of view.

It's not surprising. Japanese investors provide much of the new money on which Wall Street depends. And Japanese investors now own an extensive financial stake in many of America's leading investment firms. Nomura Securities, for instance, owns 20 percent of Wasserstein, Perella, the prominent merger and acquisition (M&A) specialists. Yamaichi Securities holds 20 percent of the Lodestar Group, which is led by the ex-vice chairman of Merrill Lynch & Company and former chairman of Morgan Stanley & Company. Sumitomo Bank bought a 12.5 percent share in Goldman, Sachs for $500 million in 1986. Former Federal Reserve chairman Paul Volcker works for Fuji-Wolfensohn, a joint venture to which Fuji Bank contributed $52.5 of the $55 million start-up capital. Volcker says most of the firm's clients are Japanese companies that want to expand their presence in America.

When a Wall Street executive reinforces the Japanese point of view—in print, in public debate, on Capitol Hill, or elsewhere—the important money relationships that exist between the executive, his firm, and the Japanese are seldom acknowledged.

One of the most prominent Wall Street firms that broker Japanese purchases of American assets is the Blackstone Group, which is 20 percent owned by Nikko Securities. Blackstone has been the investment banker for many Japanese acquisitions of prestigious American companies, including the Sony buyout of CBS Records and Columbia Pictures. In the process, Blackstone has prospered. *Financial World* reports that Blackstone chairman Peter Peterson earned at least $15 to $25 million in 1988.

To attract more business, Blackstone ran a full-page advertisement in Japan's largest daily business journal, *Nihon Keizai Shimbun*. The ad, written in Japanese, encouraged Japanese companies to continue their acquisitions of American firms. It extolled the economic advantages of such investments—entry into a new field, increased capacity in an existing field, and greater penetration of a foreign market (America). As the ad makes clear, Blackstone also offers the Japanese political advice about how to keep these acquisitions "friendly" ones.

The promise is not hollow. Three of the firm's key officers give Blackstone its political leverage: Peterson, Secretary of Commerce under President Nixon and onetime head of Lehman Brothers; David Stockman, who directed OMB in the first Reagan Administration; and Roger Altman, Assistant Secretary of the Treasury in the Carter years and an economic adviser to presidential candidate Michael Dukakis in 1988.

Not surprisingly, Peterson and Stockman are two of the nation's strongest advocates for keeping America's markets open to Japanese exports and investment. Both men write articles, address conferences, and advise policymakers on the topic. At the same time, Peterson heads both the prestigious Council on Foreign Relations and the Institute for International Economics—a Washington think tank that has been most effective in enforcing a rigid "free trade" orthodoxy over the past decade.

In 1988, *Business Week*'s William Holstein asked Peterson whether

Blackstone's lucrative financial relationship with the Japanese affected his views on Japan or his role as head of two of America's most influential policy organizations. Peterson responded, "I've been for open trade and open investment since the 1950s, at a time when it hurt my short-term interests."

The Japanese are naturally drawn to such laissez-faire advocates as Peterson, Stockman, and Altman. They are also attracted by the prestigious links such men have had with the government, their unsurpassed access in Washington, and their commanding influence in prominent policy organizations. As William Gleysteen, president of the Japan Society in New York, says, the Japanese "think the Council on Foreign Relations is made of gold."

The Blackstone Group uses its connections to attract Japanese clients. It publicizes its relationships with the Council on Foreign Relations and other prominent U.S. policy organizations. The *Nihon Keizai* ad prominently featured a group picture of Stockman, Altman, Peterson, and two other partners. The biographies of the three financiers emphasized their political connections and influence with America's key opinion leaders. Peterson, for example, was described this way:

> He was a Presidential Aide for international economic problems under Nixon (1971). He was the U.S. Secretary of Commerce (1972–73) and later chairman of Lehman Brothers Kuhn Loeb (1973–83). Recently he succeeded David Rockefeller as chairman of the Council on Foreign Relations. He is active as an officer in various organizations, including being a director of the Japan Society. He has also been given honorary doctorates by a number of universities.

The message is obvious: Blackstone has connections in Washington, has influence in America's most exclusive foreign policy circles, and is a part of the powerful American establishment in which Japan needs well-placed friends.

A number of former Presidents have engaged in post-presidential commercialism. Until recently, though, no former President has ever rented out the prestige of the office or provided a foreign entity with public endorsements.

In October 1989, Reagan hired himself out—for $2 million—to do public relations work for Japan's Fujisankei Communications. The Fujisankei conglomerate, headed by a controversial and conservative tycoon, owns Japan's largest radio network, a national newspaper, and the country's most successful television chain.

For two of the nine days that Reagan was in Japan, he was an official guest of the Japanese government. Emperor Akihito and Empress Michiko hosted a lunch for the Reagans at the Akasaka Palace in Tokyo. A State Guest House banquet was hosted by Prime Minister Toshiki Kaifu and attended by three former Prime Ministers. The Japanese government presented Reagan with Japan's highest honor, the Grand Cordon of the Supreme Order of the Chrysanthemum.

For the remainder of his trip, the ex-President worked for Fujisankei. He made two twenty-minute speeches and attended company-sponsored events. He gave exclusive interviews to Fujisankei's television stations and newspapers. He presided over a concert for 17,000 guests in Yokohama to raise money for the Reagan Presidential Library. He also solicited additional library contributions from wealthy Japanese industrialists.

While privately seeking Sony Corporation funds for his library, Reagan defended Sony's controversial October 1989 purchase of Columbia Pictures. The ex-President proclaimed, "I'm not too proud of Hollywood these days with the immorality that is shown in pictures, and the vulgarity. . . . I just have a feeling that Hollywood needs some outsiders to bring back decency and good taste to some of the pictures that are being made."

As for the growing Japanese investment in America, Reagan said, "The United States still is the widest investor in the other countries. . . . So how can we complain if someone wants to invest in us?"

Most important, Reagan used his tour as an opportunity to blame America for the U.S.-Japan trade deficit. At a Fujisankei-sponsored banquet for Japanese industrialists, he said trade frictions between the two countries had been caused by "trade protectionists" in Washington—the people he "had to fight every day I was there." It was a perfect recitation of the "it's America's fault" propaganda line that Japan had peddled throughout the 1980s.

Reagan concluded his trip with a brief talk aired on Fujisankei's national television network. With "America the Beautiful" softly playing in the background, the ex-President thanked Fujisankei Communications for making his trip possible. He congratulated Fujisankei for its efforts to improve U.S.-Japan relations.

It is difficult to imagine Kakuei Tanaka, Helmut Kohl, François Mitterand, or Margaret Thatcher providing a similar paid endorsement of an American firm.

Though with less pomp and circumstance, Jimmy Carter has also used his prestige on behalf of the Japanese—specifically, to promote the public career of Japanese billionaire Ryoichi Sasakawa. On November 7, 1989, Carter praised Sasakawa and the Sasakawa foundations in a full-page advertisement placed in *The Wall Street Journal*. The ad featured an enormous picture of the ex-President in the center of the page. In the accompanying text, Carter described how Sasakawa's foundations had provided financial backing for Global 2000, the ex-President's agricultural aid project for Africa, through the Atlanta-based Carter Center. Global 2000 consumes much of Carter's time and has helped rehabilitate his once less than popular image with the American public.

Sasakawa's friendship and close association with the former President has done much for his personal prestige. Sasakawa and Carter travel together and have made several joint appearances. In 1985, Carter and his wife made an unpublicized trip to Japan to attend a memorial service for Sasakawa's mother.

What is far less publicized is Sasakawa's "unsavory political history," as one State Department document describes it. In the pre-World War II period, he gained notoriety as a rich Japanese ultranationalist who had made his fortune in rice speculation in the late 1920s. In 1931, he founded the 15,000-member Kokusui Taishuto, Japan's Fascist National Essence Mass Party. Members of the group donned black shirts, in frank imitation of Benito Mussolini's Italian fascists. In fact, Sasakawa conferred in Rome with Mussolini, the man he called his political idol—the "perfect dictator and fascist"—in the early days of Kokusui Taishuto. According to de-classified government records, moreover, Sasakawa flew to Italy and Germany before W.W. II to urge the consummation of the Axis military alliance.

Less than four months after the Japanese surrender in 1945, Sasakawa was imprisoned as a Class A war criminal for his "crimes against peace, namely, participation in a conspiracy for the preparation of aggressive war." American authorities—to whom Sasakawa admitted using his personal wealth to disseminate nationalist Japanese propaganda—reported that Sasakawa "was active in the war and grew rich off ill-gotten gains." He was accused of plundering strategic materials from China for the Imperial Navy, and rebuked:

He has been squarely behind Japanese military policies of aggression and anti-foreignism for more than twenty years. He is a man of wealth and not too scrupulous about its use. He chafes for continued power. He is not above wearing any new cloak that opportunism may offer.

Sasakawa was released from prison in 1948. He soon emerged as an influential, behind-the-scenes political broker, and was the first big funder of Japan's ruling Liberal Democratic Party.

Using his superb political connections, Sasakawa founded the Japan Motorboat Racing Association, which was soon given an exclusive government concession for pari-mutuel gambling on speedboat races. In 1980 alone, Sasakawa's gambling revenues grossed $7.4 billion. Of this amount, local governments received 11 percent, Sasakawa got 9 percent, and 1 percent went to his Japan Shipbuilding Industry Foundation.

Through his purse, Sasakawa has ingratiated himself with Carter and other world leaders. The Sasakawa foundations—with close to $500 million in donations outstanding—underwrite a great deal of the research and policy analysis on Japan that is carried out in American think tanks, universities, and other institutes. Many Japanese say that Sasakawa's contributions are merely a vain attempt to spend his way to a Nobel Peace Prize. But much of his money buys nothing more than propaganda that is aimed at helping Americans "understand" Japan's point of view. Carter's endorsement of Sasakawa gives credibility to the man as well as his activities.

In recent years, Sasakawa and other Japanese industrialists have cultivated incumbent Presidents by funding their pet projects. The *Japan Economic Journal* reports that Shigeru Kobayashi, a Japanese real estate mogul worth an estimated $6 billion, "donated more than $1 million to Reagan projects in 1987 and 1988, including $100,000 to Nancy Reagan's anti-drugs program and $1 million to the Reagan Historical Library in California." When the departing President held a small farewell White House party for his friends in January 1989, Kobayashi and his son were among the select group of guests.

In the 1980s, Japanese individuals and companies provided major contributions to build both the Reagan and Carter presidential libraries. At $100 per person, ticket sales from Reagan's "friendship concert" in Yokohama, for instance, netted him more than $1 million for his library. The Japanese government contributed an additional $2 million to the project. The Carter Presidential Library in Atlanta has also received considerable support from Japan. Together, the donations of Sasakawa's Japan Shipbuilding Industry Foundation and YKK, the Japanese zipper company, totaled more than $1 million.

Although it is disturbing to consider, future incumbent Presidents are certain to take note of the extent to which the Japanese funded their predecessors' pet projects. They are certain to recognize how rewarding Japan's friendship might be when they themselves retire. Someday they themselves will need generous friends to help them support their presidential libraries and museums, the only archives for their presidential records and monuments to their presidency.*

The architects of the U.S. Constitution were worldly men. They anticipated that foreign powers would attempt to sway the views and decisions of the President. The Constitution therefore forbids incumbent Presidents from accepting gifts from foreign interests.

But the Founding Fathers did not anticipate that sitting Presidents would seek foreign money to fund their private projects. They certainly could not have foreseen that ex-Presidents might turn to blatant commercialism after leaving office. Nor could they have imagined that ex-Presidents would seek funds from foreign powers to support their post-retirement activities.

Until recently, former Presidents were expected to comport themselves with the dignity befitting America's highest and most honored position. For almost two centuries, their behavior met that expectation. But now former Presidents of the United States are available to do public relations stints for America's biggest trade competitors.

---

* While the Presidential Libraries Act of 1955 authorizes the National Archives to maintain an ex-President's library out of federal funds, fees paid by visitors, and the sale of reproductions and documents, money for the land and the construction of the facilities must be obtained from private sources.

Chapter Twelve

JAPAN ON JAPAN

JAPAN'S MOST AMBITIOUS propaganda program to date is aimed at American educators and the U.S. media. Its goal is to control and shape what successive generations of Americans know and think about Japan.

Japan's effort is made far easier by the fact that most Americans know very little about Japan—or the rest of the world, for that matter. A recent survey by the Gallup Organization found that one in seven Americans cannot find their own country on a world map. One in two cannot spot Central America. Two in three cannot identify Vietnam. Three in four cannot locate the Persian Gulf.

Most Americans know equally little about the history of their country, about world history, about economics, about the social sciences, or about foreign languages. A survey commissioned by the National Endowment for the Humanities revealed that 40 percent of respondents answered incorrectly when asked in which half of the nineteenth century the Civil War was fought.

Even well-educated Americans know very little about such things, because most of them were not required to study these subjects in school. Indeed, 38 percent of American colleges and universities do not even require students to take a history course. So it is hardly surprising that American schools teach their students almost nothing about Japan—culturally, geographically, or economically. Nor is it really surprising that Japan is taking advantage of this intellectual vacuum, filling it systematically with its own views.

Certainly there is nothing wrong with Japan wanting to promote a favorable image of itself in America. After all, we are Japan's largest market and principal ally. What *is* wrong is the manner in which Japan is reshaping American education. What is also wrong is that American media coverage of U.S.-Japan relations too often serves as a forum to broadcast Japan's own propaganda, cloaked in a coat of "objective" information.

Since the late 1970s, the Japanese government has exerted increasing control over the content of what American elementary and high school students are taught about Japan. Japan's agenda is simple: to influence the views of the next generation of Americans about trade, history, and other aspects of Japan when students are young and most impressionable. Japan reaches these students through their American teachers.

Most American teachers know very little about Japan. (Little wonder. Most were not taught about Japan when they were students.) Moreover, federal, state, and local government agencies generally fail to provide teachers with an adequate opportunity to increase their knowledge or acquire up-to-date teaching materials on Japan.

The efforts of the Japanese government to fill this knowledge gap began in 1978, when it commissioned California-based consultant Charles von Loewenfeldt to develop a strategy to shape what American elementary and high school students are taught about Japan. As a first step, von Loewenfeldt, who has been registered as a foreign agent for Japan since the mid-1950s, conducted a national survey on how American schools teach the subject of Japan. His study's most important finding was that individual classroom teachers, and not school administrators, play the key role in deciding whether and to what extent students learn about Japan. Von Loewenfeldt's obvious conclusion: if the Japanese government wanted to shape what American children learn about Japan, it first had to convince classroom teachers that the topic was an important one, and if it wanted to influence what was taught, it then had to "teach" the teachers.

Soon the government of Japan began its U.S. education program by offering elementary and secondary social studies teachers all-expenses-paid tours of Japan. The purpose of the indoctrination trips—what the Japanese call "invitational diplomacy"—was to present a carefully structured view of Japan for important first-time visitors. The concept was simple: if the teachers' first impressions of Japan were favorable, the impressions were likely to be lasting ones. For decades Japan has successfully conducted this type of "invitational diplomacy" for American journalists, business and labor leaders, elected officials, government staff, and other well-known U.S. opinion leaders. The Japanese were confident that their "invitational diplomacy" would work on America's elementary and high school teachers. As one of the Americans who helps organize the teachers' trips explained:

> [T]he results [were] always the same. The Americans returned feeling affection for the Japanese as human beings, as well as expressing admiration for their many accomplishments. . . . We were sure it would be even more worthwhile to take American teachers to Japan—because the effects of their positive response to the Japanese people they would meet, and the things they would see, would be transmitted to America's children and go on for many, many years.

The teacher trips are carefully planned by the Japanese government and its American agents. Tours typically begin with a visit to the historic city of Kyoto, where the teachers are exposed to old-style Japan and put up in a small Japanese inn. Next, they go to Shikoku, one of the main islands, where they stay with selected local families for three or four nights to absorb the "personal touch" of Japan. Then the teachers are taken to Hiroshima Peace Park, where the dropping of the atomic bomb in 1945 is retold from a Japanese perspective. From there it is on to Osaka, where they are shown modern Japanese industry. Finally, the teachers go to Tokyo, where they visit the famous "cram schools."

The prospect of a free trip to Japan has stimulated an enormous interest among teachers to include Japan as a subject in their classrooms. Indeed, thousands have applied for slots on these indoctrination trips. Over the past decade, more than 300 elementary and high school educators have taken part.

But the visits are only the beginning of Japan's propaganda program. A requirement placed on participants is that, on their return, they write reports or prepare other materials that describe their experiences. The process of writing the report is intended to reinforce the teachers' positive impression of their tour, and the reports are often converted into articles for the teachers' school or community newspapers. Teachers who participate are also encouraged to spread their newfound knowledge by giving speeches in local schools and churches and to civic organizations in which they "explain" Japan to others.

A calculated part of Japan's invitational diplomacy strategy is to exploit the enthusiasm of returning teachers. One of Japan's American agents puts it bluntly:

> One teacher who has visited Japan can infect hundreds, even thousands, of other teachers with his or her enthusiasm. This positive

feeling, added to the sharing of new knowledge, materials, and practical ideas about how to incorporate Japan into the curriculum, makes for exceedingly effective results.

To help trip alumni "infect" other teachers, the Japanese government has financed the production and distribution of a special teachers' guide-book—*Planning a Teachers' Workshop on Japan*—as well as several related videotapes and instructional materials. In addition, Japanese officials and their representatives regularly attend social science conventions. There, they court teachers and operate a "Japan Hospitality Suite," from which they dispense sake, sushi, and teaching materials about Japan.

The Japanese government maintains close contact with the alumni of their "invitational diplomacy" through a communications network operated by von Loewenfeldt. His network enables teachers to keep in touch with each other and to receive regular supplies from the Japanese—lesson plans, videotapes, handbooks, magazine articles, and assorted other items.

Much of the information Japan filters to American teachers is generic, like descriptions of its geography, climate, wildlife, and population. But other items echo many of Japan's standard propaganda themes: "Japan is a resource-poor island that must export to survive." "Japan is unique, because it has four seasons." "The globalization of the world economy means that who owns and operates companies within national boundaries is irrelevant." And, of course, "Japan is changing."

Many of these teaching materials present history and economics from a Japanese perspective. One widely distributed workbook funded in large part by the Japanese explains that Japan's military invasion of China was a response to European and American insults after World War I—in essence, to racism. Another guide glosses over Japan's subjugation of Korea and Taiwan and its military occupation of China, much as Japan's own school textbooks do. The atrocities Japan committed against the Chinese, Koreans, Filipinos, Dutch, Americans, British, and others who came under Japan's control in World War II are conspicuously omitted—just as they are in Japan's own schoolbooks.

On the other hand, these texts pay substantial attention to America's role in "creating" the war in the Pacific, U.S. actions that are said to have influenced Japan's decision to attack Pearl Harbor, and Japan's perspective on America's dropping the atomic bomb on Hiroshima and Nagasaki. The way the Japanese government, which controls the education curriculum in its own country, presents much of this information is deeply disturbing. It is as if one sought to teach about Germany's role in World War II without mentioning its conquests, its brutal occupations, or the Holocaust.

Not surprisingly, most of the U.S. teaching guides sponsored by Japan minimize or rationalize Japan's role in the U.S.-Japan trade imbalance. Either the trade deficit is dismissed as a matter of little importance or it is blamed on American business, workers, and government. One widely used guide explains that Japan's markets are relatively more closed than other countries' because the Japanese need assured sources of rice and coal, cash reserves to buy necessities should prices rise in world markets, and reliable domestic and international sources of essential goods. Just why other countries have no similar need is not mentioned.

As part of the educational ripple effect that Japan seeks to achieve through this program, trip alumni are encouraged to prepare and distribute their own teaching guides. Sadly, many of these lesson plans merely parrot what their authors have been taught by the Japanese. One alumni-produced lesson plan deals with the landmark Omnibus Trade Act of 1988 by having students read two documents published by the Keidanren—"Protectionist Moves in America" and "A Request to the Prime Minister on the Eve of His Trip to the United States." Both pieces are highly critical of the landmark American law. The guide offers no reading materials or other information in support of the Trade Act. On related issues of foreign investment in America, this guide never mentions that such ownership could have adverse consequences for the United States. Instead, it teaches that "direct investment [by Japan] helps strengthen the economy of the target country [in this case, America], which helps to increase employment with the building of new companies." This is, of course, Japan's long-standing line that "Japanese investment creates jobs in America."

In the 1980s, the Tokyo government's financing of the program was supplemented with funds from Japanese corporations, their American subsidiaries, and Japanese-funded foundations. A principal source of additional money for the "Program for Teaching about Japan" is the U.S.-Japan Foundation. This organization was created in 1981 with a $44.8 million donation from the Japan Shipbuilding Industry Foundation, which is controlled by Ryoichi Sasakawa.

The foundation says Sasakawa is not responsible for its operations. Rather, it is administered by twenty trustees, nine of whom are Japanese, one of whom is Sasakawa's son. The chairman of this group is William Eberle, once the U.S. Trade Representative, who later became Nissan Motors' principal foreign agent in Washington. Eberle, who was recently appointed to the USTR's elite and influential Advisory Committee for

Trade Policy and Negotiations, still represents Nissan's interests through his New England consulting firm, Manchester Associates.

The U.S.-Japan Foundation says that from its inception it has accepted the primary importance of addressing bilateral economic issues in its programs. To do so, it has created a nationwide public affairs infrastructure to encourage mutual understanding between Japanese interests and the American people.

The principal way the foundation achieves this mutual understanding is by spending more than $2 million annually on its "Program for Teaching about Japan." The program concentrates on social studies—economics, history, trade, and U.S.-Japan relations. As part of its outreach program, the foundation pays for regional colleges and universities to provide summer training for "in-service" teachers, to arrange for Japan "experts" to lecture through these schools, and to distribute instructional materials—including lesson plans, sample lessons, primary source documents, videotapes, and student handouts. A goal of this program is to make it extraordinarily easy for teachers to offer lessons on Japan by providing them virtually everything they need.

The foundation established its first regional university outreach center for teacher training in pre-college Japanese studies at Stanford University in the early 1980s. By 1990, the program had become a national network of eleven regional centers that serve forty-four states. The foundation says these centers reach "thousands of educators around the country through programs in teacher training, curriculum development, resource services and community outreach."

In 1990, the foundation announced it would expand its program beyond the training of "in-service" teachers to

> focus on "pre-service" training in Japanese studies for prospective teachers while they are still undergraduates. By providing appropriate training and guidance at the undergraduate level, the next generation of teachers will be equipped with the knowledge and skills to teach about Japan at the outset of their careers.

Ironically, Japan's proselytizing of American social science teachers— its dissemination of teaching materials and its efforts to "educate" the next generation of teachers—is happening in the absence of public comment. Meanwhile America's school systems are convulsed in debates over "creation science" versus evolution and both parents and politicians are pondering the consequences of allowing firms like Whittle Communications to broadcast commercials in the daily television program that it beams to schoolchildren. While the public and its representatives

are not paying attention, the Japanese government, Japanese corporations, a foundation funded by an ultranationalist billionaire, and a cadre
of Japan's foreign agents are well along in their program to shape what
American children think about Japan and the U.S.-Japan political/eco-
nomic relationship.

Japan's ambitions to educate Americans do not end in the twelfth grade.
The Tokyo government has created a complex network of American economists, policy analysts, and Japan specialists. This hierarchy of involve-
ments ranges from monitoring to full funding.

At the first level, the Japanese merely follow the writings and other
work of those whose actions may affect Japan. A personal example illus-
trates how thorough the Japanese are. My earlier book *The High-Flex
Society* contained several recommendations for legislation that could create a more competitive environment for American business. Within six
weeks after the book was released in 1986, senior MITI officials in Tokyo
were initiating discussions of those proposals with visiting members of
Congress (most of whom had not yet read the book). Two years later,
executives in the Tokyo office of my corporate employer were contacted
by MITI officials who noted that several provisions in the over one-
thousand-page Trade Act then being considered by Congress were similar
to recommendations in the book. MITI wanted to know if there was a
connection. The Japanese government did all of this using the English-
language edition of the book: an updated Japanese translation was not
published until the spring of 1989. My experience with careful Japanese
scrutiny is not unique.

At the second level of involvement, Japan's Ministry of Finance runs
an informal council of international advisers, which includes more than
a hundred of the world's leading trade experts, fifty-two of whom are
American. The Finance Ministry's council essentially operates as an academic exchange and includes critics of Japan's policies. MITI, too, has
a foreign advisory corps, which, by contrast, is smaller and more formal,
meets annually, and excludes critics of Japanese trade practices.

Lastly, Japan helps fund the work of most American academic organizations and Washington think tanks that study U.S.-Japan relations
(336 American colleges and universities offer Japanese studies programs).
Professor Chalmers Johnson estimates that more than 80 percent of all
American studies about Japan are financed by the Japanese. Other knowledgeable observers believe Johnson's estimate is too low. Regardless of
whether the actual figure is as high as 90 percent or as low as 50 percent,
the reality is that a major portion of America's policy-related thinking

about U.S.-Japan relations is being supported by Japanese interests—
who are far from disinterested parties.

Why does Japan endow university chairs and help finance some of
Washington's most influential think tanks? It knows that the people from
these organizations craft many of the ideas and much of the public debate
on American trade and economic policy. Think-tank fund-raisers boldly
advertise the influence they wield to potential contributors, domestic as
well as foreign. For a number of years, the Heritage Foundation has
even printed its promotional brochures in several foreign languages.

Without question, the views of those whose work is funded by the
Japanese are genuinely held. These individuals would surely make the
same arguments without Japanese or other foreign support. The effect
of the foreign funding is to amplify their particular perspectives, sustain
their work, and give them a sharp advantage in the enormously competitive American and global marketplace of ideas.

Almost without exception (and not surprisingly), Japanese and other
foreign funders give financial support to scholars and organizations who
advocate open-door trade policies. Invariably, the studies these advocates
produce minimize the role of Japanese protectionism in the U.S.-Japan
trade deficit. Even when their studies promote the need for a more open
Japanese market, they also argue against reciprocal actions by the United
States to reduce that protectionism. In essence, theirs is criticism without
a "bite."

Among the most frequently cited examples of this painless sting is the
joint report on U.S.-Japan relations issued in late 1989 by Japan's Keizai
Doyukai, the Japan Association of Corporate Executives, and America's
Committee for Economic Development (CED). The report places most
of the blame for the U.S.-Japan trade deficit on Washington's budget
deficit. While it says that Japan must open its markets, it also warns
against any retaliation by the United States. The Japanese have used this
report to back their claim that America has created most of its trade
deficit with Japan.

The Japanese team for this study was led by Takashi Ishihara, the
chairman of Nissan Motors. The American delegation was led by William
Eberle, who has been a consultant and lobbyist for Nissan since 1979.
Eberle's Japanese connection was revealed neither in the report nor at
the press conference where the study was released. A CED representative says that Eberle was one of the strongest critics of Japan on the
American team and that the other committee members were well aware
of his connection to Nissan. Yet the audience for the report—Congress,
American business, and the U.S. media—were not.

This example is not unique. In 1988, Eberle co-authored a report issued by the Aspen Institute that made many of the same points as the CED report. As with the CED report, Eberle's Japan connections were not revealed.

A subtle but critical consequence of Japanese funding of U.S. policy thinking is that it often induces self-censorship, not only among those who receive funding but also among those who simply seek it, who are aware that Japan punishes its critics by withholding support and pressuring their employers. In the early 1980s, for instance, Robert Angel, then director of the Japan Economic Institute (JEI), resigned his post over an argument with the Japanese government following his refusal to publish as news the propaganda offered up by the Foreign Ministry. One leading American university has been informed by the representative of a major Japanese automaker that the school has been blackballed for funding so long as a prominent academic and critic of Japanese trade practices remains a faculty member. In April 1990, the acting director of the JEI "banned" Washington free-lance researcher Mindy Kotler from using its library and interacting with its personnel because she had written an article that criticized the organization. The Japanese government rescinded its ban only after the Washington *Post* reported the incident.

The message the Japanese convey is clear: scholars and institutions that desire funding and access from them risk both when they criticize Japan. Thus, many academics watch what they say—at least in public. Fusion Systems CEO Don Spero says that when he went to America's leading universities looking for physicists who would testify for him in his company's patent fight against Mitsubishi Electric, he was repeatedly rebuffed by academics who claimed they were afraid that their testimony would threaten their funding from Japan. Little wonder, then, that the most widely circulated academic studies on the politics of U.S.-Japan economic relations tend to focus on U.S. protectionism or the conflict between the U.S. executive and legislative branches over America's trade agenda. Japan's industrial policies, cartels, and money politics remain largely unexamined by those funded with Japanese money.

Conversely, those who rely on Japanese funding and access are often the foremost critics of the advocates of changes in U.S. trade policies and U.S.-Japan relations. They don't alter their views to get foreign money; they get the money because of the views they hold. Thus, their credibility far exceeds that of paid publicists. Some of the strongest opposition to the works of Karel van Wolferen, Clyde Prestowitz, and James Fallows, for instance, comes from George R. Packard, the dean of the Johns Hopkins University's School of Advanced International Studies (SAIS)—one of America's preeminent academic centers for U.S.-Japan studies and a regular recipient of Japanese funding. Packard has publicly labeled van Wolferen a hoax; he calls the works of Fallows and Prestowitz a threat to the U.S.-Japan relationship.

Not surprisingly, the Japanese exploit American academic views that support their official point of view. A good example is found in a sixteen-page advertising supplement printed in the February 1989 issue of the *Atlantic Monthly*. The ad was paid for by Japanese companies and featured a long essay by Packard. In it, he mainly argued that whatever trade differences exist between America and Japan are outweighed by the many other benefits of the bilateral "relationship." In a telling passage about the importance he places on the bilateral "relationship," Packard notes that he has many long-standing friendships in Japan, and that

> [i]t would be unrealistic in the extreme to imagine that all of these personal friendships could have been formed and would continue to survive were there serious differences in the national interests of our two nations.

Packard's point: tough U.S. action on the trade deficit risks both the all-important bilateral "relationship" and the many existing personal and financial ties between leading figures in both countries. Japan repeatedly makes trade issues just such a test of the "relationship." It is, therefore, happy to publicize views such as Packard's.

Ironically, such views also often reinforce the views that the Japanese have of themselves. When leading academics say that America is primarily at fault for the bilateral trade imbalance, Japanese politicians have a perfect excuse to do nothing to correct it. Likewise, ad hominem attacks by respected scholars on writers who expose the reality of Japan's economic and political practices make it easier for the Japanese to ignore the substance of that analysis, regardless of its merits. A classic example is an October 1989 *Japan Times* article written by John Makin, a fellow at the American Enterprise Institute and the current director of the Japan-U.S. Friendship Commission, a federal agency. Makin attacks James Fallows' views on Japan with this allegation:

> Writer James Fallows has struck a rich vein by revealing to Americans in a lengthy series of articles in *Atlantic* magazine that he has lived in Japan for a number of years, and, in fact, doesn't like Japanese people very much.

Fallows responds, "Outrageous." But the damage is done. A wide audience in Japan is left with the false impression that James Fallows' political and economic views are shaped by a personal dislike of the Japanese people.

Virtually alone among established American think tanks is the Hudson Institute, which does not seek foreign funding. Mitchell Daniels, the past president of Hudson and former political director in the Reagan White House, says:

> Most organizations, including ours, are small and a dependency relationship grows up around a large grant. At a time when contributors are hard to come by in this country, major foreign contributors can put subtle pressures on the content of studies. We are not dogmatic about taking foreign money, but we have turned down some offers. I question whether large foreign contributions come without strings, so we intend to be very careful about taking foreign funds.

Since most Americans form their impressions about Japan from what they read, see, and hear through the American media, the Japanese have a strong, obvious interest in shaping the media's coverage of Japan—and they spend millions to do just that. While some of Japan's media effort in the United States simply tries to provide information and promote better mutual understanding between the two nations, much more is designed to reinforce Japan's propaganda themes; deflect potential criticisms; and isolate Japan's critics. The difficulty, of course, lies in distinguishing between media presentations that aim to promote mutual understanding and those that strive to reinforce Japan's economic and political objectives.

Japan influences the American media's coverage of Japan in two basic ways. The first is to finance the programs that are presented to Americans. The second is to influence the content of the reporting by independent journalists.

Japanese sponsorship of radio and television public affairs programs in America began in the early 1980s. In January 1990, John B. Judis reported in the *Columbia Journalism Review* that Telejapan produced shows for the Christian Broadcasting Network in 1983, for the USA Cable Network in 1984, and for public television stations in 1986. In 1984, Cable News Network (CNN) began showing *This Week in Japan*, a show paid for by the Japan Center for Information and Cultural Affairs (JCICA). Both Telejapan and JCICA have direct links with the Japanese government agencies that are primarily responsible for disseminating Japan's economic and trade propaganda—Telejapan with MITI and JCICA with the Ministry of Foreign Affairs.

The American producers of these shows insist that they have total control over their editorial content. But according to Judis, "representatives of the Center for Information and Cultural Affairs can make suggestions for what should appear on the show and participate in conferences reviewing a previous week's show. They also helped set the original guidelines for the show—emphasizing 'what is common between the U.S. and Japan.' " In effect, the sponsors of the show do have some say over the management of their investment.

In 1989, NHK, Japan's national public broadcasting system, initiated *Japan Today*, a nightly television news program, in America. The program, which is paid for by the Japanese electronics conglomerate NEC, is a special "news" production created for the American audience. As Judis explains, "American viewers are not necessarily getting to see how the Japanese view the world; what they see instead is how the Japanese want Americans to think the Japanese view the world."

The Sasakawa-funded U.S.-Japan Foundation began underwriting radio and television programs about Japan in the mid-1980s. The centerpiece was the Japan Project, operated out of WNET, New York's public television station. The basic goal of the Japan Project was to increase U.S. television programming dealing with Japan. Through a public broadcast consortium, the Japan Project aimed to raise American "awareness" about Japan. Foundation publications say that it had "extensive consultations" with the producers of "influential public affairs programs" to develop special programs or segments relating to Japan. Specifically, the foundation tried to get airtime on programs like *The MacNeil/Lehrer Newshour, Adam Smith's Money World,* and *Frontline.*

The Japan Project proposed to raise major funding from Japanese corporations. This money would then be used to underwrite television programs aired on the cash-poor Public Broadcasting System (PBS) and its affiliated stations. To guide this effort, the Japan Project established a U.S.-Japan Public Television Program Council, which included representatives of PBS and several of the nation's other leading public television stations—WQED (Pittsburgh), WNET (New York), WGBH (Boston), WETA (Washington, D.C.), WTTW (Chicago), KUON (Lincoln, Nebraska), KCET (Los Angeles), and KCTS (Seattle). The Public Television Program Council enabled the Japan Project team to develop a collegial link with those broadcast media organizations across the country that control American public television and influence U.S. public opinion.

In May 1987, the Japan Project sponsored a ten-day trip to Japan for seven representatives of U.S. public television stations. The group met in Tokyo with 200 representatives from major Japanese corporations who, according to the foundation, were "active in the U.S. press, media and advertising." Eventually, the Japan Project raised enough funds to produce three programs and a WGBH-TV series on U.S.-Japan relations. The foundation gave Nebraskans for Public Television $50,000 to underwrite two additional thirty-minute television programs and produce accompanying print materials.

The U.S.-Japan Foundation has also funded a number of radio programs. In 1988, it gave the Cambridge Forum in Massachusetts $10,000 to develop a radio series called *Understanding Japan Today.* Every year since 1987, the foundation has provided $100,000 per year to National Public Radio (NPR) to support its Tokyo reporting for the influential news programs *Morning Edition* and *All Things Considered.*

Public television and radio shows like those funded by the U.S.-Japan Foundation are taken seriously by viewers and listeners because they present views that are considered to be objective and untainted by commercial considerations. By underwriting "soft" programs that concentrate on improving U.S.-Japan relations and increasing Americans' "understanding" of Japan, Japanese sponsors are able to project a highly credible, favorable impression of their country. This, of course, is the nature— and the goal—of good propaganda, and the reason that Japan puts up the money.

Even the prospects of Japanese funding can influence the media and preempt potential critics. One independent producer of public affairs programs puts it bluntly:

> In the last half of the 1980s, the Japan Project had a chilling effect on those of us who wanted to do programs that might be critical of Japan. The participating stations were reluctant to offend potential Japanese sponsors. Consequently, Japan was able to buy a half-decade of inattention.

While Japan directly funds some media programs, its principal efforts concentrate on influencing the reporting by the American media. Sometimes, this influence takes the form of cash.

One scheme involved Ryoichi Sasakawa and a secret program operated out of the United Nations. Beginning in the late 1970s, Sasakawa provided $1.25 million to a UN fund. Sasakawa says that his donation was made at the request of Genichi Akatani, then UN Under Secretary General for Public Information, and only after consultation with Japan's Transport Ministry. The program was administered by Japanese diplomats at the UN.

In this program, leading newspapers in fifteen countries—including

Japan's *Asahi Shimbun* and France's *Le Monde*—were given up to $48,000 to publish news supplements that expressed the UN's views but did not identify the funding source. Editors from the participating newspapers and UN officials met quarterly in European cities where they discussed future issues. *The New York Times*, which uncovered this scheme and its funding source, cited a confidential UN document describing the program as one that aimed to create "a direct collegial link with newspapers, including editors, that would lead to stronger cooperation between the United Nations system and newspapers, which were so influential in guiding public opinion." Getting close to editors, of course, is a prime objective of a propaganda effort such as this.

In 1986, MITI went a step further by establishing a $200,000 fund to pay moonlighting American reporters directly. Initially, MITI officials proposed to put on its payroll one reporter, editor, or local chamber of commerce director in each of ten states. If the plan worked, it would be expanded to include more states and reporters. Two of the states chosen to begin the Moonlighter Project were Missouri and Michigan, the home states of four of the most influential congressional critics of Japanese trade policies—Congressmen Richard Gephardt and John Dingell and Senators Donald Riegle and John Danforth. According to a report in Japan's *Mainichi Shimbun*, "the Japanese side is aiming at collecting information about local enterprises while making use of their [American] 'faces.' " *Mainichi Shimbun* also reported that MITI had prepared a list of those journalists in each of the ten states that it would try to recruit.

MITI proposed that, through the Moonlighter Project, American journalists would collect information that would help Japanese companies expand their operations in America. MITI also intended to have these reporters "conduct PR on Japan's market-opening measures."

MITI's program collapsed only after Congress learned of it. Senators John Heinz (R-Pa.), Riegle, and Frank Murkowski (R-Alaska) wrote scathing letters to the U.S. Secretary of State, the U.S. Attorney General, Japan's Prime Minister, and the Japanese Ambassador in Washington. MITI responded with a bland public statement that the purpose of its program was simply to obtain views and opinions at the local level for "furthering the programs to expand Japanese exports of U.S. products and to increase Japanese investment in this country." MITI asserted that it was "entirely untrue to say, as Senator Heinz has done, that JETRO plans to 'manipulate American attitudes' through employment of U.S. reporters, or that JETRO is 'trying to buy a position image by buying American journalists and opinion makers.' "

In an off-the-record interview, a former employee of the Japanese government noted with a trace of condescension that MITI had been clumsy even to propose such a scheme. This person explained that Japan can get its point across to the American press in far less risky ways.

One of those ways has already been discussed—namely, establishing a professional tie or a money relationship with key trade experts on whom the media depend for information and quotes. A representative example occurred on January 24, 1990, when *New York Times* columnist Peter Passell wrote about the breakup of U.S. Memories, the failed attempt by American companies to jointly produce dynamic random access memory chips (DRAMs).

Passell claimed that Japanese control of global DRAM production did not make American corporations vulnerable to a Japanese power play. Nor did it pose an economic threat to the United States. The authority Passell quoted to legitimize his argument was Gary Saxonhouse. Passell's identification of Saxonhouse as "a specialist on the Japanese economy at the University of Michigan" gave the impression that an impartial academic expert thought the failure of U.S. Memories was of no consequence to America.

But Saxonhouse was not really neutral. In 1989, he was a part-time consultant to the President's Council of Economic Advisers (CEA). In that capacity, he was a principal opponent of federal support for advanced technology projects like U.S. Memories and high-definition television (HDTV). He also played a key role in formulating the CEA's position on Japan, as well as the U.S. government's trade policies with Japan. All the while, however, Saxonhouse had been an unpaid adviser to MITI— a relationship, ironically, that was first reported by *The New York Times* in December 1989.

Had Passell fully identified Saxonhouse's role at the CEA and his outside connection with MITI, the entire effect of his column would have been spoiled. When asked whether he knew of Saxonhouse's relationship with MITI, Passell responded, "I'm fully aware. But the relationship is so fragile as to be irrelevant. I've known Gary since graduate school. He is an unbiased scholar who did his Ph.D. thesis on Japanese industrial policy and knows Japan very well. His affiliation with MITI is academic. It involves only one trip to Japan a year. His integrity is certainly not going to be compromised by an academic trip to Japan."

Passell has a point—no serious scholar's views can be compromised with a single trip to Japan. But Saxonhouse's involvement with MITI runs far deeper than that. According to MITI itself, the purpose of its twenty-two-person advisory board (officially called the Research Institute on International Trade and Industry, or RIITI) is to "aid MITI in its policy-formation process." Members of the advisory board have special access in Japan, and they are paid to speak at institute functions. Saxonhouse himself spoke at institute functions twice in 1988, in Tokyo and in Osaka, and participated in the institute's spring 1989 meeting.

Saxonhouse never hid his MITI connection. He revealed it to CEA chairman Michael Boskin when he signed on as the council's Japan expert. (Boskin himself had been on an advisory board of Japan's Finance Ministry but had resigned the position when he went to work for the President.) Boskin thought that Saxonhouse's relationship with MITI was irrelevant, and did not ask him to resign. One week after *The New York Times* revealed Saxonhouse's Japan connection, the White House announced his departure from the CEA.

One of the most subtle ways the Japanese influence American media coverage is their attempt to shift the responsibility for U.S.-Japan relations onto the shoulders of American journalists. To prevent critical reports about Japan, the Japanese tell journalists that such reportage will certainly harm the special bilateral "relationship." In much the same way, the Japanese also try to make American journalists responsible for saving free trade. As one editorial writer explains, this is not a hard sell: "It's always easy to take a free trade position. You get few complaints, and it's not hard to write."

In their zeal to save free trade and defend the "relationship," some journalists—like *The Wall Street Journal*'s Paul Gigot and the Washington *Post*'s Hobart Rowen—go a step further and regularly defend Japan against those who criticize its economic and political practices.

In Gigot's January 12, 1990, column, for instance, he alleged that critics of the Japan Lobby—including this author—were engaged "in a campaign to discredit American free-traders." Gigot claimed the "real intention" of those who question the workings of the Japan Lobby was "to taint and discredit any American who doubts the wisdom of picking trade fights with Japan." By Gigot's account, critics of Japan's politicking in America pose a threat to free trade and the U.S.-Japan relationship.

By virtue of his association with the Washington *Post*, Rowen is one of the most prominent—not to mention prolific—chroniclers of macroeconomic policy in the United States. His column regularly advocates 1960s-style solutions to America's economic woes. In the mid-1980s, for example, Rowen argued that a weak dollar would reverse most of America's trade deficit, and repeatedly defended the notion that only a tiny fraction of the bilateral deficit was due to Japanese protectionism. Rowen has regularly opposed actions by the United States to use market access as leverage to open the Japanese market for American exports. Many traditional economists, of course, share his views.

In his support of economic orthodoxy, however, Rowen mentions or defends Japan's economic and political practices in most of his articles. A computerized search of all news articles listed on the database NEXIS revealed that Rowen wrote 573 pieces between 1985 and 1989 that directly referred to Japan—56 percent of his articles during that period. In these articles, Rowen repeatedly condemned any views other than those that advocated hard-line free trade, calling them "protectionist." Conversely, he labeled critics of Japanese protectionism "Japan bashers." According to the NEXIS records, in fact, Rowen was one of the first American journalists to employ that phrase. Six percent of Rowen's columns that mention Japan cited that phrase or another variation—"Japan bashing" or "Japan bash." The central thrust of most of his writing on the U.S.-Japan trade problem is that it's America's fault.

Many of the sources that Rowen cites are ex-officials who subsequently went to work as foreign agents. Time and again, Rowen has identified these ex-officials' prior public positions but has failed to mention that they now work as agents of influence. In October 1987, Rowen lambasted unilateral U.S. actions to roll back "trade barriers established by the Europeans, Koreans, Japanese and Taiwanese" with a scathing quote from "former trade negotiator Harald Malmgren." Rowen failed to note Malmgren's extensive lobbying activities for both Japanese and European interests.

In a March 1990 article, Rowen attacked those who had expressed concern over growing foreign investment in the United States. He said, "Let's look at the facts, as gathered and announced last week by the Association for International Investment (AFII). . . ." What Rowen did not tell his readers was that the news release he quoted came from an organization that is funded by foreign companies and that exists to keep America open to foreign investors.

Later in this same article, Rowen wrote, "Now, what should be deduced from a calm analysis of these numbers? First, as the AFII's chairman, Elliot Richardson, said . . ." Rowen failed to note that Richardson is paid by AFII, or that Richardson's law firm in Washington—Milbank, Tweed, Hadley & McCloy—represents the governments of Japan, Kuwait, and Mexico. Certainly none of these clients are impartial when it comes to U.S. foreign investment policies.

One of Rowen's principal sources on Japan is also one of Japan's principal spokesmen. In a column published in the Washington *Post* on February 25, 1990, Rowen wrote:

> When I want to know what is really going on in Japan, I've found it instructive over the past dozen years to talk to [Tadashi] Yamamoto, a graduate of Marquette University in Milwaukee, who has

a keen understanding of what makes the American political machine work.

Yamamoto is the head of the Japan Center for International Exchange. According to one Japan expert, Yamamoto is Japan's "King of Buffers." Another refers to him as the leader of Japan's "mutual understanding" industry. During the 1980s, Rowen quoted Yamamoto repeatedly. While Yamamoto is doubtless an honorable man, one of his primary responsibilities is to promote Japan's point of view in America. What is extraordinary about Rowen's stating that he depends on the head of a Japanese organization for information about "what is really going on in Japan" is that his own newspaper's Tokyo bureau provides some of the most respected reportage in the world about Japan.

When other media tactics do not work, the Japanese wield a stick on those journalists who write about topics that Japan's power holders do not want analyzed. Soon after *Foreign Affairs* published an article by Karel van Wolferen that preceded his 1989 book, *The Enigma of Japanese Power*, Japan's Foreign Ministry waged a campaign to discredit the article among representatives of the European Community in Japan. The Japanese also sent representatives to speak with high officials in the Dutch government and van Wolferen's chief editor. Their message was that van Wolferen was undermining the Dutch-Japanese relationship.

Soon after the article was published, a Dutch journalist who worked for the same newspaper as van Wolferen went to Tokyo. Japan's Foreign Ministry arranged for the reporter to meet with twenty-one high-ranking Japanese officials. In seventeen of these meetings, Japanese officials criticized van Wolferen's article, saying essentially the same things that had already been said to Dutch government officials and van Wolferen's editor. The visiting reporter subsequently learned that their comments were based on "talking points" that had been prepared and distributed by the Foreign Ministry.

After van Wolferen's book was published in 1989, Japanese authorities, especially those from the Foreign Ministry and the Keidanren, waged a campaign to discredit the book by casting doubts about the author's qualifications and motivations. Fred Barnes, a senior editor at *The New Republic*, says that as late as April 1990 four high-ranking Japanese officials he interviewed on separate occasions in Tokyo volunteered criticism about van Wolferen and the so-called "revisionists." Barnes says that most of this criticism seemed to come from the same talking points.

It should be no surprise that Japan's Foreign Ministry also pays careful attention to what American journalists and authors write about Japan. If a book or an article criticizes Japan, or if the ministry does not agree with what it says, the writer will receive a call from Japanese officials or someone else with a link to Japan. The purpose of these calls is to maintain what the Japanese refer to as "quality control" over foreign media accounts on Japan. Actually, it is a form of intimidation.

As one journalist puts it, the more effective this type of media intimidation is in undermining their critics and preventing negative publicity, the more the Japanese will use it. As he explains it: "Countries are basically people, and people are basically children. If they scream or complain and it works once, they do it again and again—as long as it works." He concludes:

> [Y]ou cannot make a legitimate criticism [about Japan] and not have it be considered an insult. There is the unstated impression . . . that if you write a piece criticizing Japan, you are a Japan basher. . . . That kind of [impression] builds a certain sensitivity. So you tend to hold back [from writing stories you might otherwise report].

Self-censorship, of course, is one of the main goals of Japan's media "quality control" program.

CONCLUSION

THE COLD WAR is over, and many of the policies and attitudes that it spawned are obsolete. In years ahead, America's influence in the world will be shaped more by economics, science, and technology than by the tools of war.

To meet this new challenge, America urgently needs new policies. Before the United States can chart a new national direction, however, some fundamental issues require attention.

- Should America's trade and economic interests be elevated to the same national priority as its defense and foreign policy concerns?
- Should U.S. antitrust laws be applied to the affiliates of foreign corporations operating in the United States?
- Should foreign access to the U.S. market be conditioned on American access to foreign markets?
- Should conditions be placed on foreign investment in America?
- Should America be concerned that foreign banks may hold as much as 50 percent of U.S. financial assets within ten years?
- Should American government and business establish more cooperative relationships?
- Should the U.S. government provide assistance in developing the technologies that will shape American industries and jobs in the twenty-first century?
- Are some industries and technologies so critical to America's economic and military security that they warrant special federal policies?

The answers to these and similar questions will determine America's future. Today, much of the current policy and political debate over these issues is fundamentally dishonest. Too many of the leading participants have a financial stake—often undisclosed—in advocating foreign points of view. When American and foreign interests are consistent, the actions of these agents of influence are of no real importance. It is only when U.S. interests are played against foreign interests that this power game becomes truly threatening to the United States. Today, this is the prevailing nature of the game.

Both the game and its rules require basic reform. Here are eight relatively modest proposals that would do much to reduce the influence of foreign interests over American affairs.

1. STOP WASHINGTON'S REVOLVING DOOR

The revolving door is a chronic problem in Washington. In recent years, it has begun to spin faster and with greater frequency. Partly this is due to the fact that relatively low federal salaries discourage many talented people from entering public service. But there is another, equally important reason: during the Carter and Reagan years, public service was made an object of contempt. Neither Reagan nor Carter seemed to understand that they could not denigrate government without denigrating public service.

As a consequence, the top positions in agencies and government now go to a small cadre of insiders who shift from public office to lobbying and back again. For them, public service is a sabbatical from working for the very same special interests they are supposed to hold in check as federal officials. When the revolving door involves trade matters, many of those special interests are foreign-based and the nature of the conflict pits American interests against foreign.

To stop the Washington revolving door—or at least to slow it—three actions are required:

First, those who hold the top federal positions, including the Director of the CIA, USTR, and Secretary of State, should be prohibited *permanently* from becoming a foreign agent or a lobbyist for domestic companies. Those who would refuse to serve in government because of such a limitation certainly are not the kind needed to tend the public's affairs.

Second, a longer "cooling-off" period is required for lower-level federal officeholders. Federal law stipulates that as of January 1991, ex-officials will have to wait one year before they can lobby, counsel, or advise on trade matters. This short time period cannot possibly guarantee the integrity of trade policymaking and administration. A period of five to ten years would slow the movement between public service and influence peddling and help assure the integrity of federal decision making.

Given these tighter rules, American corporations need to make a concerted effort to hire former federal officials with trade expertise. One of Japan's principal political advantages is that those who craft and administer American trade policies know that their best post-government job opportunities lie with the Japanese—largely because U.S. companies do not hire them. In theory, this should not be important. In reality, it is.

Lastly, the federal program for career public servants needs to be strengthened to encourage more talented people to work in government and to stay longer. Japan and other nations have a distinct advantage in trade negotiations because their side is always represented by a handful of political appointees and a staff of competent civil servants. Because America fills dozens of ambassadorships and hundreds of key policy positions with political amateurs, negotiations with other nations have become akin to a baseball game between the Oakland A's and a sandlot club. Guess which is America's Team.

2. REQUIRE FULL DISCLOSURE OF FOREIGN AGENTS

In politics, sunshine is the best disinfectant. Although the Foreign Agents Registration Act of 1938 requires those who represent foreign principals to report in some detail their client relationship to the Attorney General, the act has many loopholes. Lobbyists who work for an American affiliate of a foreign company, for example, are exempted. So are lawyers who perform legal chores on their clients' behalf, even when the same work might be considered lobbying when done by nonlawyers. Foundations funded by foreign companies and governments but incorporated in the United States are similarly excluded.

If American officials and the public are to possess the information they need to balance what they read and hear from foreign interests, much greater, more stringent disclosure requirements are needed. The first step is to require that all those who represent foreign clients—lawyers, lobbyists, foundations, and others—provide full disclosure to the Justice Department. No exemptions.

The second step is to increase the Justice Department's capacity to monitor compliance with this law. Today, a staff of fewer than fifteen people is responsible for monitoring 3,500 registered foreign agents. The Foreign Agents Registration Act division of the Justice Department is so understaffed that years often pass before reports are audited for accuracy.

Many foreign agents know this, and exploit the situation by failing to provide all the required information.

3. PROHIBIT FOREIGN PARTICIPATION IN AMERICAN ELECTIONS

Today, foreign companies participate in American politics by making major financial contributions to national political parties, state political parties, and state and local campaigns, and by operating PACs through U.S. affiliates and trade organizations over which they have effective control. Japanese and other foreign contributions to American political parties and campaigns constitute blatant interference in America's domestic affairs. A flat prohibition on such contributions is long overdue. Money politics is bad enough; foreign money politics is out of the question.

4. PROVIDE FULL FEDERAL FUNDING FOR PRESIDENTIAL LIBRARIES

Franklin D. Roosevelt was the only President in modern times who did not want a physical monument to his presidency. Presidential libraries serve that purpose for Roosevelt's successors. The responsibility for raising private funding for these libraries has forced American Presidents to become supplicants to monied contributors. Japan and other foreign interests have ingratiated themselves with a succession of Presidents by providing large donations to build these libraries. The surest way to stop this backdoor politicking is for the federal government to fully fund their construction. The cost is trivial compared to what is at risk.

5. PROHIBIT FOREIGN GIFTS OR COMPENSATION TO EX-PRESIDENTS

The Constitution prohibits incumbent Presidents from accepting gifts or other compensation from foreign interests. But it says nothing about ex-Presidents. The post-presidential commercialism of ex-Presidents demeans the presidency itself. By holding out the promise of multimillion-dollar speaking fees or other remuneration, foreign interests have a very real means of exerting undue influence on a President. The most direct way to eliminate this potential abuse is to prohibit ex-Presidents from accepting pay or valuable gifts from foreigners, perhaps at the risk of their pensions.

6. LIMIT STATE AND LOCAL SUBSIDIES
TO ATTRACT CORPORATIONS

For many years, states and localities have competed strenuously to lure investment and facilities that create jobs. Given the importance of the U.S. market, the issue for most foreign companies is never whether to invest but where.

As the level of competition increases among states and localities, so does the ability of foreign investors to gain increasingly generous state and local tax breaks and other valuable handouts. These subsidies can be extremely costly for state and local governments. In the 1980s, the state of Kentucky gave Toyota more than $325 million in taxpayer-financed incentives to locate a manufacturing facility there. Other Japanese companies sit back and wait while states fight among themselves to offer better deals.

To gain the favor of prospective investors (domestic as well as foreign), many governors and mayors constantly lobby Washington and their state congressional delegations on these investors' behalf. During the Toshiba affair, some of Toshiba's most effective political advocates were governors and mayors who either had one of its facilities or wanted one for their region. The Japanese government and Japanese businesses take advantage of state and local officials' intense desire to attract facilities and jobs.

This political problem is not unique to America. To keep it under control, the European Community limits how much member states can bid to attract investment. Similarly, Japan also limits how much local governments can offer potential corporate investors. America needs the same restrictions, and it needs them for both foreign and domestic investment.

7. REDUCE AMERICA'S DEPENDENCE
ON FOREIGN CAPITAL

Foreign lenders finance a significant portion of America's budget deficit. As a result, the United States is losing much of the flexibility and independence it needs to craft its own domestic, trade, and foreign policies.

Each upcoming Treasury auction prompts a new round of jitters among U.S. Treasury officials. They fear that the Japanese government and Japanese institutional investors will decide not to participate. In their anxiety, Treasury and other cabinet officials spend much of their time between auctions pressuring their colleagues in the executive branch not to take tax, regulatory, trade, or other policy measures that might offend

Japanese and other foreign investors and cause them to boycott a Treasury bond sale.

Similarly, the ability of the Federal Reserve to set interest rates is greatly limited by America's need to attract foreign capital. This results in an upward pressure on the exchange rate and on domestic interest rates, and reduces the Federal Reserve's flexibility to respond to domestic economic downturns.

The deficit continues because both Republicans and Democrats have put partisan advantage above national interest. They have refused to cut spending or raise taxes. The longer this stalemate persists, the more vulnerable America becomes to foreign political pressures.

8. INCREASE BUSINESS INVOLVEMENT WITH GOVERNMENT

Twenty years ago, American business began to take serious note of the skill with which the Japanese plied the American market. Almost overnight, Japan watching became a cottage industry. Books and articles about the Japanese style of management, manufacturing processes, quality assurance, resource allocation, employment practices, strategic planning, and training techniques became must reading for American managers.

In the end, we came to understand that one secret of Japan's success was that the Japanese had adopted fundamental American management techniques and then applied them more rigorously and skillfully than we.

Likewise, American businesses have long used a full range of public affairs skills to strengthen their position in the domestic market. The Japanese and other foreign interests have studied us closely and now understand these techniques. They operate in the same forums as American companies, abide by the same rules, and bid for the same talent to guide and represent them. They have demonstrated that they can match their American competitors in this critical art at every step—and outstep them at many turns.

Prowess in molding public opinion—gaining the credibility to blunt negative sentiments or to advance longer-term goals—is the newest, and perhaps most powerful, advantage in the hands of foreign competitors. It is an advantage that American firms hand them on a platter. By remaining largely disengaged from their own government, American firms create a domestic political vacuum that the Japanese and other foreign interests gladly fill.

If American companies intend to succeed in the 1990s and the twenty-first century, they must pay at least as much attention to public affairs as a mainstay of competition as they do to producing first-class goods and services. Indeed, of the many important lessons the Japanese have taught American businesses, one stands out: the political dimension of competition is as consequential as the economic.

In sum, other nations' campaign for America is completely legal. It plays the American economic game by American rules. It uses the campaign tactics and methods of American politics. It hires Americans to lobby, educate, and influence other Americans. It is the highest stakes political-economic game in the world today, affecting whole industries, billions of dollars, millions of jobs, and ultimately, the wealth and power of nations.

It is also deeply corrosive of America's political and economic system. The revolving door of Washington, D.C., breeds cynicism and mistrust, and represents a virulent strain of political corruption—completely legal, completely unethical. The problem, of course, is not in Tokyo or any other foreign capital, but in Washington, D.C.

Americans have all but lost sight of some of the most basic lessons of civics—chief among them the guiding concept of civic virtue. The value of national service—for an individual to be of service to the country and to work on behalf of the country's interests—has been cheapened by a more mundane coin of the realm: personal advancement, self-interest, big money. As a consequence, the United States is not only selling corporate assets and real estate to foreign bidders; also for sale is American integrity and national honor.

It is up to the American people to demand a higher standard of conduct from their elected and appointed representatives. The manipulation of America's political and economic system by foreign interests with the willing and eager participation of Americans-for-hire threatens our national sovereignty. It threatens our future. It continues only because we tolerate it.

APPENDIX A

APPENDIX B

NOTES

ACKNOWLEDGMENTS

INDEX

APPENDIX A

Former Federal Officials Who Later Represented Foreign Interests

(A Partial List of Officeholders, 1980–1990)

AGENT[1]	GOVERNMENT BRANCH	PUBLIC POSITION	FIRM OF EMPLOYMENT	FOREIGN CLIENT	COUNTRY	FEES AND EXPENDITURES PAID TO FIRM[2] (1980–1990)
Alberger, William R.	Intl. Trade Cmsn.	Chairman	Garvey, Schubert and Barer	Japan Deep Sea Trawler	Japan	$ 174,827
				SONATRACH	Algeria	53,860
				China Ocean Shipping	China	38,847
				Japan Fisheries Assn.	Japan	50,983
				Kidd Creek Mines	Australia	— na —
				Energy Resources	Australia	— na —
			Bishop, Cook	Sugino Cycle, Inc.	Japan	— na —
				Sakai Ringyo Co.	Japan	— na —
				Cotia Comerc. Imp./Exp.	Brazil	— na —
Aldonas, Grant	Dept. of State	Spec. Asst. to Under Secy. for Econ. Affairs	Miller & Chevalier	Government of Canada	Canada	506,299
Aldridge, Diana	U.S. Senate	Senate Aide	Hill & Knowlton	Hyundai Motor America	South Korea	435,081
				Intl. Reporting and Info.	Intl.	— na —

Name	Agency	Position	Firm	Client	Country	Amount
Allen, Richard V.	White House	Natl. Security Adviser	Richard V. Allen Company	Prince Talal	Saudi Arabia	— na —
				Republic of Korea	South Korea	— na —
				Government of Canada	Canada	— na —
				Govt./Repub. of Turkey	Turkey	— na —
				Seoul Olympic Org. Cmte.	South Korea	972,059
				Chinese Assn. Ind. and Comm.	Taiwan	1,580,000
				Panama Canal Study Grp.	Japan	556,822
				Alitalia	Italy	62,736
				Baden-Württemberg Dev.	W. Germany	56,944
				Korean Overseas Information Service	South Korea	— na —
Allison, Thomas	Dept. of Transp.	General Counsel	Preston, Thorgrimson	Government of Nauru	Nauru	522,278
Altschuler, Irwin	Dept. of Treasury	Atty., Off. of Reg. Counsel, U.S. Customs Service	Brownstein, Zeidman	Camara de la Industria de Transformación	Mexico	88,297
				Vitrocrisa Cristalería	Mexico	— na —
Amerine, David	Dept. of Commerce	Atty., Off. of Gen. Counsel	Brownstein, Zeidman	Camara de la Industria de Transformación	Mexico	88,297
Anderson, Jean	Dept. of Commerce	Chief Counsel, Intl. Trade	Weil, Gotshal and Manges	Noranda	Canada	— na —

Note: All those listed in Appendix A have submitted signed registration statements—now form OMB 1105-0013—or other personally signed contracts for representation with the Foreign Agent Registration Act/Public Office of the United States Department of Justice.

In some cases, the names of several firms may appear with the name of a single individual. This indicates that the individual worked for more than one firm after leaving public office. In these cases, the receipts shown were received by the firm with which the individual was associated only during the period the individual worked with that firm, and only for the time the agent was registered to represent that client. For each agent who worked with multiple firms, the firms are listed in reverse chronological order.

[1] This list includes only those federal officials who left office between the years 1980 and 1990.

[2] Public records do not reveal how much individual foreign agents receive from clients they represent. Figures shown here reflect the amount paid by the client *to the firm* during the period the agent was registered to represent that client.

AGENT[1]	GOVERNMENT BRANCH	PUBLIC POSITION	FIRM OF EMPLOYMENT	FOREIGN CLIENT	COUNTRY	FEES AND EXPENDITURES PAID TO FIRM[2] (1980–1990)
Appelbaum, Judith	Fed. Trade Cmsn.	Adviser to Cmsnr.	Reichler, Choate, Appelbaum & Wippman	Republic of Nicaragua / United Coconut Assn.	Nicaragua / Philippines	$ 1,811,672 / 149,000
			Powell, Goldstein	Republic of Nicaragua	Nicaragua	474,780
Arky, M. Elizabeth	House of Reps.	Staff, Telecomm. and Finance Subcmte.	Winthrop, Stimson	Norsk Forsvarsteknologi / Kongsberg Vaapenfabrikk	Norway / Norway	33,657 / — na —
Armstrong, Philip	Dept. of Ed.	Dep. Asst. Secy. for Pub. Affairs	Hill & Knowlton	Palm Oil Reg. and Licensing / Seibulite Intl.	Malaysia / Japan	308,970 / 110,317
Bafalis, Louis A.	House of Reps.	Member of Cong.	Evans Group	Republic of Cyprus	Cyprus	156,171
Bailey, Norman A.	White House	Spec. Asst./Pres.	Kaplan, Russin and Vecchi	Govt. of Venezuela	Venezuela	176,049
			KRV Intl.	Presidential Campaign of Fidel Chavez Mena	El Salvador	33,920
			Colby, Bailey	ADICAL	Brazil	60,000
				Latin Amer. Iron & Steel	Chile	11,652
				Monetary Auth./Singapore	Singapore	122,989
				Embassy of Japan	Japan	12,000
				Companhia de Tubarão	Brazil	86,889
				Emb. of Repub. of Korea	South Korea	60,250

Name	Body	Title	Firm	Clients	Country	Amount
Bailey, Pamela G.	White House	Spec. Asst./Pres.	Michael K. Deaver Associates	Royal Emb. of Saudi Arabia Intl. Cult. Soc./Korea Daewoo Corporation CBI Sugar Group, Inc. Min. Comm. and Ind. Devlt. Embassy of Canada	Saudi Arabia South Korea South Korea Latin America Mexico Canada	375,000 357,642 192,773 300,000 62,500 100,290
Bannerman, M. Graeme	U.S. Senate	Staff Director, For. Rels. Cmte.	Bannerman and Associates	Govt. of Bangladesh Govt. of Tunisia Govt. of Philippines Embassy of Lebanon Philipp. Coconut Auth. Arab Repub. of Egypt	Bangladesh Tunisia Philippines Lebanon Philippines Egypt	252,625 166,314 136,523 124,641 49,189 — na —
Bario, Patricia	White House	Dep. Press Secy.	Burson-Marsteller	Saudi Basic Industries Sultanate of Brunei Petróleos de Venezuela INTELSAT Stern Magazine	Saudi Arabia Brunei Venezuela Intl. W. Germany	640,122 370,569 41,952 31,765 33,819
Barnds, William	House of Reps.	Staff Director, Asia/Pacif. Subcmte.	Japan Econ. Inst.	Government of Japan	Japan	— na —
Barnes, Michael	House of Reps.	Member of Cong.	Arent, Fox	Outokumpu Oy Potash Corp./Saskatch Intl. Computers Toyota Motor Corp. Uranerzbergbau GmbH Sony Corporation Neptune Orient Line	Japan Canada Gr. Britain Japan W. Germany Japan Singapore	347,246 523,423 2,500 — na — — na — — na — — na —
Bayh, Birch E.	U.S. Senate	Senator	Rivkin, Radler	NYK Line	Japan	185,815

[1] This list includes only those federal officials who left office between the years 1980 and 1990.

[2] Public records do not reveal how much individual foreign agents receive from clients they represent. Figures shown here reflect the amount paid by the client *to the firm* during the period the agent was registered to represent that client.

AGENT[1]	GOVERNMENT BRANCH	PUBLIC POSITION	FIRM OF EMPLOYMENT	FOREIGN CLIENT	COUNTRY	FEES AND EXPENDITURES PAID TO FIRM[2] (1980–1990)
Bayless, James	Dept. of Commerce	Dep. Asst. Secy., Cong. Affairs	Akin, Gump	INTELSAT Embassy of the PRC	Intl. China	$ 621,440 171,860
Beall, James A.	House of Reps.	Staff Coord., Ways and Means Cmte.	Ball, Janik & Novack	Fujitsu Microelec.	Japan	48,035
Bello, Judith H.	Dept. of Commerce	Policy Dep./Off. of Dep. Asst. Secy., Import Adm.	O'Melveny & Myers	Assn. Téléph./Télégr. Inds.	France	11,889
Bennett, Alan R.	U.S. Senate	Couns./Govt. Affairs	Kaye, Scholer	Elsevier Sci. Publrs.	Netherlands	699,230
Berger, Samuel R.	Dept. of State	Deputy Director, Policy Planning	Hogan & Hartson	Underwriters at Lloyd's Comwlth. of Bahamas Intl. Cmte. Pass. Lines Daimler-Benz AG Embassy of Japan Government of Poland Cncl. Eur./Jap. Shipowners	Gr. Britain Bahamas Intl. W. Germany Japan Poland Intl.	43,990 32,628 27,176 5,727 — na — — na — — na —
Bickwit, Leonard	Nuclear Reg. Cmsn.	Gen. Counsel	Miller & Chevalier	Republic of France	France	89,369
Bircher, John E.	Dept. of State	Dir. Near East/ South Asian Affairs	Neill & Co.	Arab Repub. of Egypt Government of Kenya Kingdom of Morocco Kingdom of Jordan	Egypt Kenya Morocco Jordan	738,000 707,250 600,000 440,000

Name	Former Office	Position	Firm	Client	Country	Amount
Bliss, Julia Christine	White House	Asst. Gen. Counsel, Off. of U.S. Trade Rep.	Madge, Rose	Islam Repub. of Pakistan	Pakistan	320,000
				Government of Guinea	Guinea	150,000
				Government of Jamaica	Jamaica	75,000
				Government of Liberia	Liberia	— na —
				China Trade Devlt. Cncl.	China	— na —
				Govt. of Côte d'Ivoire	Côte d'Ivoire	— na —
				African Devlt. Bank	Intl.	— na —
				Rossing Uranium Ltd.	Namibia	— na —
				Korea Free Trade Assn.	South Korea	— na —
				Toshiba Corporation	Japan	11,106,514
				Govt. of Hong Kong	Hong Kong	916,778
				Japan Lumber Importers	Japan	55,125
				Sovcomflot	USSR	— na —
Blum, Barbara	EPA	Deputy Admin.	Direction International	AB Volvo	Sweden	— na —
				TRE Konsulter AB	Sweden	— na —
Bockorny, David	White House	Spec. Asst. to Pres. for Leg. Affairs	Bergner, Boyette and Bockorny	Coord. Cncl., N. Amer. Affairs	Taiwan	153,000
				Republic of Korea	South Korea	39,240
Bode, Denise A.	U.S. Senate	Senate Aide	Goll & Liebengood	Thomson-CSF, Inc.	France	327,840
				Fiat, SpA	Italy	715,398
				Ricoh	Japan	54,245
Bondurant, Amy	U.S. Senate	Couns., Comm. Cmte.	Verner, Liipfert	Matra Aérospace	France	293,838
Bor, Robert M.	House of Reps.	Chf. Couns., Agr. Cmte.	Bishop, Cook	CSR, Ltd.	Australia	182,676
Boyette, Van R.	U.S. Senate	Senate Aide	Bergner, Boyette	China Exter. Trade	Taiwan	— na —

[1] This list includes only those federal officials who left office between the years 1980 and 1990.

[2] Public records do not reveal how much individual foreign agents receive from clients they represent. Figures shown here reflect the amount paid by the client *to the firm* during the period the agent was registered to represent that client.

AGENT[1]	GOVERNMENT BRANCH	PUBLIC POSITION	FIRM OF EMPLOYMENT	FOREIGN CLIENT	COUNTRY	FEES AND EXPENDITURES PAID TO FIRM[2] (1980–1990)
Brady, Lawrence	Dept. of Commerce	Asst. Secy., Trade Adm.	Hill & Knowlton	N.H. Ball Bearings/Minebea	Japan	$ 250,997
				Airbus Industrie N. Amer.	European Comm.	487,147
				Republic of Turkey	Turkey	1,815,254
				Elec. Inds. Assn./Japan	Japan	311,158
				Korean Airlines	South Korea	356,884
				Seibulite Intl.	Japan	110,317
				NEC Corporation	Japan	898,610
				Republic of Korea	South Korea	233,441
				Brother, Inc.	Japan	21,362
Breglio, Vincent	U.S. Senate	Exec. Dir., Rep. Campaign Cmte.	Susan Davis Intl.	Arab Repub. of Egypt	Egypt	80,000
Brock, William E.	White House	U.S. Trade Rep.	The Brock Group	Bd. For. Trade/Repub. of China	Taiwan	240,000
				Airbus Industrie N. Amer.	European Comm.	75,000
	Dept. of Labor	Secretary		Panama Trade Devlt. Cmte.	Panama	— na —
Brown, Ronald	U.S. Senate	Senate Aide	Patton, Boggs & Blow	Sultanate of Oman	Oman	— na —
				Duty Free Shoppers, Ltd.	Hong Kong	— na —
				Hampton-Windsor	Zaire	— na —
				Republic of Gabon	Gabon	— na —
				Japan Air Lines	Japan	— na —
				Asoc. de Azucaderos	Guatemala	— na —
				E. Palicio y Cia	Venezuela	— na —
				Republic of Haiti	Haiti	— na —
Burke, Kelly H.	U.S. Air Force	Lieut. Gen. (Ret.)	Stafford, Duke and Hecker	Sumitomo Corporation	Japan	480,000
				Oerlikon-Buhrle Mach.	Switzerland	43,750

Name	Former Agency	Position	Firm	Client	Country	Amount
Bushong, David W.	U.S. Senate	Minor. Counsel, Intelligence Cmte.	Gold & Liebengood	Fiat, SpA	Italy	426,937
				Beretta USA Corp.	Italy/Belgium	139,638
				Thomson-CSF, Inc.	France	237,503
				Ricoh	Japan	34,794
				BAA, plc	Gr. Britain	47,829
Calhoun, Michael	Intl. Trade Cmsn.	Commissioner & Vice Chairman	Laxalt, Washington	Asoc. de Empresas RENFE	Spain	485,793
				Govt. of Antigua/Barbuda	Antigua/Barbuda	868,366
				Henri Sfeir	Lebanon	45,000
			Finley, Kumble	Hangdok Tire Manuf.	South Korea	— na —
				Kor. Musical Instrument Assn.	South Korea	— na —
Cannon, William Stephen	Dept. of Justice	Dep. Asst. Atty. Gen./Antitrust	Wunder, Ryan, Cannon & Thelen	Industrial Equity (Pacific) Ltd.	New Zealand	— na —
Canzeri, Joseph W.	White House	Dep. Asst. Chf. of Staff	Joseph W. Canzeri	New National Party	Grenada	— na —
			Canzeri Company	Curaçao Intl. Trust	Netherlands Antilles	30,937
				Inst. of Financial/Fiscal Studies	Netherlands Antilles	— na —
Cartwright, Suzanne	House of Reps.	House Aide	Verner, Liipfert	Consol. Grain and Barge	Japan	89,326
Casey, Thomas J.	Fed. Commun. Cmsn.	Dep. Chf./ Common Carrier Bureau	Mintz, Levin	Commun. Ind. Assn./Japan	Japan	705,315

[1] This list includes only those federal officials who left office between the years 1980 and 1990.

[2] Public records do not reveal how much individual foreign agents receive from clients they represent. Figures shown here reflect the amount paid by the client *to the firm* during the period the agent was registered to represent that client.

AGENT[1]	GOVERNMENT BRANCH	PUBLIC POSITION	FIRM OF EMPLOYMENT	FOREIGN CLIENT	COUNTRY	FEES AND EXPENDITURES PAID TO FIRM[2] (1980–1990)
Cassidy, Robert	White House	Gen. Couns., Off. of U.S. Trade Rep.	Wilmer, Cutler and Pickering	Lufthansa AG	W. Germany	$ 7,764,535
				Cmsn. of Eur. Comm.	European Comm.	455,697
				Govt./Fed. Repub. of Germany	W. Germany	— na —
			Kaye, Scholer	Elsevier Sci. Publrs.	Netherlands	606,793
				Cmsn. of Eur. Comm.	European Comm.	— na —
Castillo, A. Mario	House of Reps.	Agr. Cmte. Staff	Arter & Hadden	Union of Agr. Coops./ZENCHU	Japan	605,181
Chapoton, John E.	Dept. of Treasury	Asst. Secy./Tax Policy	Vinson & Elkins	Attys. Liability Assur. Soc.	Bermuda	15,400
				Canadian Banknote Co.	Canada	27,210
				Canadian Security Printers	Canada	— na —
			John E. Chapoton	Paribas Asset Mgmt.	France	30,672
Church, Frank	U.S. Senate	Senator & Chmn., For. Rel. Cmte.	Whitman & Ransom	Japan Ext. Trade Org.	Japan	27,944
				Daiwa Steel Tube Inds.	South Korea	8,388
				Govt./Repub. of China	Taiwan	— na —
Chwat, John	House of Reps.	House Aide	Chwat/Weigend	Eduardo M. Cojuangco, Jr.	Philippines	— na —
Cohen, Edward B.	White House	Dep. Spec. Asst./Pres.	Davis Wright Tremaine	American Honda Motor Co.	Japan	31,721
Cohen, Scott	U.S. Senate	Staff Dir., For. Rel. Cmte.	Gilbert A. Robinson, Inc.	INTELSAT	Intl.	37,221

Name	Former Position	Agency/Dept.	Firm	Client	Country	Amount
Cooper, Doral S.	Asst. U.S. Trade Rep., Bilateral Affairs	White House	Crowell & Moring International	Bd. For. Trade/Repub. of China	Taiwan	527,813
				Samsung Electronics	South Korea	196,620
				Sing. Trade Devlt. Bd.	Singapore	185,000
				Government of Thailand	Thailand	84,279
				Wacker Siltronic Corp.	Israel	32,386
				UN Conf. on Trade	Intl.	10,000
				Korea For. Trade Assn.	South Korea	78,225
				Mfrs. Assn. of Israel	Israel	1,000
				Industrial R&D Corp.	Israel	— na —
				Ministry of Ind./Trade	Israel	— na —
			Michael K. Deaver Associates	CBI Sugar Group, Inc.	Latin America	300,000
				Government of Canada	Canada	100,290
Copeland, James M., Jr.	Dep. Asst./Pres., Cong. Rel.	White House	McAuliffe, Kelly, Raffaelli & Siemens	Emb. of Repub. of Turkey	Turkey	— na —
Cople, William J. III	Atty., Off. of Secy./Gen. Couns.	Dept. of Defense	King & Spalding	Agie Holding, AG	Switzerland	— na —
				Elox Corporation	Switzerland	— na —
				Ind. Elektronik Agie	Switzerland	— na —
				Agie USA, Inc.	Switzerland	— na —
Cowan, Mark D.	Asst. Leg. Couns.	Central Intelligence Agency	Jefferson Group	Lebanese Info. & Research Center	Lebanon	— na —
				Mgmt. Planning/Research	Bahrain	— na —
				Siciliana Appalti Costruz.	Italy	— na —
	Chf. of Staff to Secy. Ray Donovan	Dept. of Labor	Hill & Knowlton	Republic of Turkey Min./For. Affairs; Govt. of Iceland	Turkey	31,295
					Iceland	600,000
Cram, M. Victoria	Leg. Asst., Dem. Study Grp.	U.S. Congress	Ball, Janik & Novack	Fujitsu Microelec.	Japan	48,035

[1] This list includes only those federal officials who left office between the years 1980 and 1990.

[2] Public records do not reveal how much individual foreign agents receive from clients they represent. Figures shown here reflect the amount paid by the client *to the firm* during the period the agent was registered to represent that client.

AGENT[1]	GOVERNMENT BRANCH	PUBLIC POSITION	FIRM OF EMPLOYMENT	FOREIGN CLIENT	COUNTRY	FEES AND EXPENDITURES PAID TO FIRM[2] (1980–1990)
Culver, John C.	U.S. Senate	Senator	Arent, Fox	Toyota Motor Corp.	Japan	$ 1,103,059
				Outokumpu Oy	Japan	941,306
				Sitmar Cruises	Australia	229,106
				Uranerzbergbau GmbH	W. Germany	89,112
				Lars Krogh & Co.	Norway	48,033
				Verein. Edelstahlwerke	W. Germany	37,858
				Patton & Morgan Corp.	Gr. Britain	3,189
Cutler, Lloyd N.	White House	Counsel to Pres.	Wilmer, Cutler and Pickering	Lufthansa AG	W. Germany	8,711,499
				Hapag-Lloyd	W. Germany	213,763
				AEG-Kanis Turbinenfabrik	W. Germany	151,789
				Cmsn. of the Eur. Comm.	European Comm.	122,648
				Kingdom of Netherlands	Netherlands	90,662
				Govt. of Tibet in Exile	Tibet	30,167
				Govt./Fed. Repub. of Germany	W. Germany	— na —
Dabaghi, William	Dept. of Transp.	Dir., Cong. Affairs	Arter & Hadden	Union of Agr. Coops./ZENCHU	Japan	957,384
Dalley, George A.	Dept. of State	Dep. Asst. Secy., Intl. Affairs	Neill & Co.	Government of Kenya	Kenya	235,960
				Arab Repub. of Egypt	Egypt	189,000
				Kingdom of Jordan	Jordan	110,000
				Government of Guinea	Guinea	75,000
				Kingdom of Morocco	Morocco	— na —
				Government of Jamaica	Jamaica	— na —
				Govt. of Côte d'Ivoire	Côte d'Ivoire	— na —
				China Trade Devlt. Cncl.	China	— na —
				Government of Liberia	Liberia	— na —
				African Devlt. Bank	Intl.	— na —
				Rossing Uranium Ltd.	Namibia	— na —
				Korea Free Trade Assn.	South Korea	— na —

Name	Agency	Title	Firm	Client	Country	Amount
Danzig, Richard	Dept. of Defense	Dep. Asst. Secy.	Latham & Watkins	Daewoo Industrial Co.	South Korea	1,341,403
Davis, Mendel J.	House of Reps.	Member of Cong.	Davis, Whitner	Akzo, NV	Netherlands	40,000
Deaver, Michael K.	White House	Asst. to Pres. and Dep. Chf. of Staff	Michael K. Deaver Associates	Intl. Cult. Soc./Korea	South Korea	476,770
				Royal Emb. of Saudi Arabia	Saudi Arabia	375,000
				CBI Sugar Group, Inc.	Latin America	300,000
				Embassy of Canada	Canada	100,290
Denvir, James P.	Dept. of Justice	Chf. Atty./ Antitrust	Akin, Gump	INTELSAT	Intl.	28,840
Denysyk, Bohdan	Dept. of Commerce	Dep. Asst. Secy.	Global USA	Komatsu Corporation	Japan	932,986
				Fanuc, Ltd.	Japan	864,403
				Hitachi, Ltd.	Japan	825,683
				All Nippon Airways	Japan	756,992
				Mazak, Ltd.	Japan	741,135
				Japan Aircraft Devlt. Co.	Japan	697,293
				Kyocera Corporation	Japan	602,503
				Repub. of Bophuthatswana	Bophuthatswana	112,500
				Voest-Alpine	Austria	— na —
				Ind. Coop. and Devlt.	Austria	— na —
Diefenderfer, William	U.S. Senate	Chf. of Staff, Finance Cmte.	Wunder, Ryan, Cannon & Thelen	Ad Hoc Insur. Group	Bermuda	175,356
Dolan, Michael W.	Dept. of Justice	Dep. Asst. Atty. Gen., Off. of Leg. Affairs	Winthrop, Stimson	Ironmasters' Assr.	Sweden	246,712
				Uddeholms AB	Sweden	77,736

[1] This list includes only those federal officials who left office between the years 1980 and 1990.

[2] Public records do not reveal how much individual foreign agents receive from clients they represent. Figures shown here reflect the amount paid by the client *to the firm* during the period the agent was registered to represent that client.

AGENT[1]	GOVERNMENT BRANCH	PUBLIC POSITION	FIRM OF EMPLOYMENT	FOREIGN CLIENT	COUNTRY	FEES AND EXPENDITURES PAID TO FIRM[2] (1980–1990)
Donnelly, Thomas R., Jr.	White House	Spec. Asst./ Pres., Legislation	Pagonis & Donnelly	Stelco/Dofasco/Algoma Steel Corp.	Canada	$ 23,018
				Govt./Repub. of Transkei	Transkei	72,284
Dowley, Joseph K.	House of Reps.	Chf. Couns., Ways and Means Cmte.	Dewey, Ballantine	Emb. of Repub. of Turkey	Turkey	129,676
Downen, Robert L.	Dept. of State	Dir. of Spec. Proj., E. Asia/ Pacif. Affairs	Neill & Co.	Government of Kenya	Kenya	235,960
				Arab Repub. of Egypt	Egypt	189,000
				Kingdom of Jordan	Jordan	110,000
				Government of Guinea	Guinea	75,000
				Kingdom of Morocco	Morocco	— na —
				Government of Jamaica	Jamaica	— na —
				Govt. of Côte d'Ivoire	Côte d'Ivoire	— na —
				China Trade Devlt. Cncl.	China	— na —
				African Devlt. Bank	Intl.	— na —
				Rossing Uranium Ltd.	Namibia	— na —
				Korea Free Trade Assn.	South Korea	— na —
Durant, Andrew G.	House of Reps.	Press Secy., Rep. Coleman	Hill & Knowlton	Ferruzzi Finanziaria	Italy	763,375
				Asia Sat. Telecomm.	Hong Kong	— na —
Eizenstat, Stuart	White House	Asst. to Pres./ Domestic Policy	Powell, Goldstein	Hitachi, Ltd.	Japan	1,021,404
				INTELSAT	Intl.	506,791
				Soc. Gén. de Surveillance	Switzerland	171,565
				Embassy of Morocco	Morocco	9,101
				Repub. of Nicaragua	Nicaragua	5,468
Elliott, Richard	Dept. of State	Atty./Adviser	Paul, Weiss	NEC Corp./NEC America	Japan	4,646,701
				Korea Fed. of Textile Ind.	South Korea	214,292

Name	Agency	Position	Firm	Client	Country	Amount
				Korea Iron and Steel Assn.	South Korea	37,626
Erb, Guy Feliz	Agency for Intl. Devlt.	Deputy Dir.	GFE, Ltd.	Consejo/Asuntos Intl.	Mexico	27,268
				DESC Comercio Exterior	Mexico	47,992
				Direcspicer, SC	Mexico	— na —
Evans, Billy Lee	House of Reps.	Member of Cong.	Hecht, Spencer and Associates	Hong Kong Trade Devlt. Cncl.	Hong Kong	1,064,397
				Govt./Repub. of Panama	Panama	309,647
				Freedom and Justice/Cyprus	Cyprus	115,000
Evans, Thomas B.	House of Reps.	Member of Cong.	Evans Group	Republic of Cyprus	Cyprus	156,171
				Fed. Repub. of Nigeria	Nigeria	128,436
				Former President Majluta	Dominican Republic	20,000
				Republic of China	Taiwan	— na —
			Manatt, Phelps	Republic of Cyprus	Cyprus	613,355
				NEC Corporation	Japan	226,622
				Government of Jamaica	Jamaica	189,000
			O'Connor & Hannan	U.K. Mutual Assn.	Bermuda	— na —
				CKLW Radio Broadcasting	Canada	— na —
				W. Eng. Shipowners Mutual	Gr. Britain	— na —
				Government of Jamaica	Jamaica	— na —
Fairbanks, Richard M. III	Dept. of State	Asst. Secy.; Spec. Negotr., MidEast Peace Process; and Amb.-at-Large	Paul, Hastings	Koito Manufacturing	Japan	286,082
				Embassy of Iraq	Iraq	334,885
				Fujitsu Microelec.	Japan	66,479

[1] This list includes only those federal officials who left office between the years 1980 and 1990.

[2] Public records do not reveal how much individual foreign agents receive from clients they represent. Figures shown here reflect the amount paid by the client *to the firm* during the period the agent was registered to represent that client.

AGENT[1]	GOVERNMENT BRANCH	PUBLIC POSITION	FIRM OF EMPLOYMENT	FOREIGN CLIENT	COUNTRY	FEES AND EXPENDITURES PAID TO FIRM[2] (1980–1990)
Farrell, J. Michael	Dept. of Energy	Gen. Counsel	Global USA	Komatsu, Ltd.	Japan	$ 313,500
				Fanuc, Ltd.	Japan	300,000
				Mazak Corporation	Japan	200,000
				Kyocera Corporation	Japan	200,000
				Repub. of Bophuthatswana	Bophuthatswana	187,490
				All Nippon Airways	Japan	100,000
				Japan Aircraft Devlt. Co.	Japan	87,500
Fein, Bruce	Fed. Commun. Cmsn.	Gen. Counsel	Hill & Knowlton	Republic of Turkey	Turkey	750,000
				Liberal Democratic Party	Japan	246,000
				Kingdom of Morocco	Morocco	297,605
				Govt. of Cayman Islands	Cayman Islands	158,114
				Government of Angola	Angola	20,000
				Korean Airlines	South Korea	76,863
				Côte d'Azur Develt.	France	11,689
				N. H. Ball Bearings/Minebea	Japan	— na —
Feith, Douglas J.	Dept. of Defense	Dep. Asst. Secy./Negotns. Policy	International Advisers, Inc.	Emb. of Repub. of Turkey	Turkey	875,000
Feldman, Mark B.	Dept. of State	Legal Adviser	International Advisers, Inc.	Emb. of Repub. of Turkey	Turkey	875,000
Ferris, Charles	Fed. Commun. Cmsn.	Chairman	Mintz, Levin	Commun. Ind. Assn./Japan	Japan	705,315
Fielek, Henrietta	U.S. Senate	Senate Aide	McAuliffe, Kelly	Emb. of Repub. of Turkey	Turkey	— na —

Name	Position	Firm	Client	Country	Amount
		Heron, Burchette	CBI Sugar Group, Inc.	Latin America	205,233
			NovAtel Communications	Canada	243,036
			Thai Steel Pipe Assn.	Thailand	116,981
			St. Lawrence Cement	Canada	45,654
			AgroQuímicas de Guatemala	Guatemala	30,713
			Intl. Maritime Satellite	Intl.	20,000
			Yamaichi Securities	Japan	10,000
			Canada Cement Lafarge	Canada	15,619
			Inland Cement	Canada	13,493
			St. Mary's Cement	Canada	3,832
			Asia Satellite Telecomm.	Hong Kong	5,898
			Daiwa Securities	Japan	2,348
Finley, Michael	House of Reps.	Staff Dir., Intl. Oper. Subcmte.			
		Hemisphere Assoc.	Embassy of El Salvador	El Salvador	13,300
			C.R. Assn. Bus./Entrep.	Costa Rica	— na —
Fortune, Terence	Dept. of State	Asst. Legal Adviser			
		Paul, Weiss	NEC Corp./NEC America	Japan	4,646,701
			Consol. Gold Fields	Gr. Britain	9,464,676
			Korea Fed. Textile Ind.	South Korea	214,293
			Repub. of Botswana	Botswana	51,314
			Korea Iron and Steel Assn.	South Korea	37,626
			Hyundai Heavy Ind.	South Korea	1,261
Fox, J. Edward	Dept. of State	Asst. Secy./Leg. Affairs			
		Mintz, Levin	Commun. Ind. Assn./Japan	Japan	80,000
Frank, Richard A.	Natl. Oceanic & Atmospheric Agency	Administrator			
		Richard A. Frank Law Offices	Japan Fisheries Assn.	Japan	82,685

[1] This list includes only those federal officials who left office between the years 1980 and 1990.

[2] Public records do not reveal how much individual foreign agents receive from clients they represent. Figures shown here reflect the amount paid by the client *to the firm* during the period the agent was registered to represent that client.

AGENT[1]	GOVERNMENT BRANCH	PUBLIC POSITION	FIRM OF EMPLOYMENT	FOREIGN CLIENT	COUNTRY	FEES AND EXPENDITURES PAID TO FIRM[2] (1980–1990)
Frank, Richard A. (cont'd)	Natl. Oceanic & Atmospheric Agency	Administrator	Ginsburg, Feldman and Bress	Kingdom of Morocco	Morocco	$ 250,000
			Wald, Harkrader	Japan Fisheries Assn.	Japan	216,719
Freedman, Matthew	Dept. of State	Spec. Asst., Program and Policy Coord.	Black, Manafort	Govt. of St. Lucia	St. Lucia	— na —
				Govt. of Barbados	Barbados	— na —
				Govt. of Dominican Republic	Dominican Republic	— na —
Freiberg, Ronna	White House	Cong. Liaison	Hill & Knowlton	Republic of Turkey	Turkey	3,207,822
				Côte d'Azur Devlt.	France	27,204
				Kingdom of Morocco	Morocco	297,605
				Government of Angola	Angola	20,000
				Govt. of Cayman Islands	Cayman Islands	204,230
				Palm Oil Reg. and Licensing	Malaysia	450,838
				Airbus Industrie N. Amer.	European Comm.	259,344
				Assn. Advmt. Human Rights	Japan	60,000
				Hambros/Sharps, Pixley	Gr. Britain	— na —
Furman, Harold W.	Dept. of Interior	Dep. Asst. Secy.	Heron, Burchette	Asoc. Export de Flores	Colombia	1,031,596
				St. Lawrence Cement	Canada	1,002,294
				CBI Sugar Group, Inc.	Latin America	433,659
				Genstar Cement	Canada	76,897
				Japan Tobacco	Japan	101,616
				Mitsubishi Electric	Japan	109,624
				Lake Ontario Cement	Canada	74,048
				Canada Cement Lafarge	Canada	182,999
				St. Mary's Cement	Canada	46,280
				Assn. Advmt. Human Rights	Japan	14,000

Name	Agency	Position	Firm	Client	Country	Amount
Gibbons, Clifford	White House	Spec. Asst. to U.S. Trade Rep.	Hogan & Hartson	RSV Mining Equipment	Netherlands	10,364
				All Nippon Airways	Japan	9,554
				Commwlth. of Bahamas	Bahamas	844,411
				Government of Ontario	Canada	471,520
				Underwriters at Lloyd's	Gr. Britain	401,992
				Aermacchi	Italy	206,309
				Embassy of Japan	Japan	181,765
				Intl. Cmte. Pass. Lines	Intl.	176,181
				Cncl. Eur./Jap. Shipowners	Intl.	3,224
Gifford, Dawn	U.S. Senate	Senate Aide	Swidler & Berlin	Hyundai Motor Co.	South Korea	353,765
Gold, Martin B.	U.S. Senate	Senate Aide	Gold & Liebengood	Intl. Gold Corp.	South Africa	51,189
				Fiat, SpA	Italy	788,933
				Ricoh	Japan	— na —
Gold, Peter F.	U.S. Senate	Senate Aide	Winthrop, Stimson	Kongsberg Vaapenfabrikk	Norway	7,643
Goldfield, H. P.	Dept. of Commerce	Asst. Secy./Trade Devlt.	Wellford, Wegman	Embassy of Canada	Canada	407,249
			Swidler & Berlin	Hyundai Motor Co.	South Korea	353,765
Gould, Rebecca	House of Reps.	Assoc. Minor. Couns., Energy and Comm. Cmte.	Verner, Liipfert	Consol. Grain and Barge	Japan	89,326
				Matra Aérospace	France	293,838
Grisso, Michael	House of Reps.	House Aide	Pagonis & Donnelly	Govt./Repub. of Transkei	Transkei	72,284

[1] This list includes only those federal officials who left office between the years 1980 and 1990.

[2] Public records do not reveal how much individual foreign agents receive from clients they represent. Figures shown here reflect the amount paid by the client *to the firm* during the period the agent was registered to represent that client.

AGENT[1]	GOVERNMENT BRANCH	PUBLIC POSITION	FIRM OF EMPLOYMENT	FOREIGN CLIENT	COUNTRY	FEES AND EXPENDITURES PAID TO FIRM[2] (1980–1990)
Hardee, David W.	U.S. Senate	Minor. Tax Couns., Finance Cmte.	Akin, Gump	Fujitsu, Ltd.	Japan	$ 977,875
				Hoylake Investments	Bermuda	417,680
				Fujitsu America	Japan	142,386
				Grand Metropolitan PLC	Gr. Britain	96,178
				Bank of Nova Scotia	Canada	89,627
				Fujitsu Microelec.	Japan	76,963
				Salgad International	Israel	13,865
				Plessey Co. PLC	Gr. Britain	— na —
				Tate & Lyle PLC	Gr. Britain	— na —
Hathaway, Michael	U.S. Senate	Staff Dir., Energy and Nat. Resources Cmte.	United Intl. Consultants	Embassy of S. Africa	South Africa	1,856,878
Hawkins, Edward	U.S. Senate	Chf. Tax Couns., Finance Cmte.	Squire, Sanders and Dempsey	Embassy of Belgium	Belgium	38,951
Heiman, Bruce	U.S. Senate	Senate Aide	Preston, Thorgrimson	Inst. Lat. del Fiero/Acero	Chile	— na —
Helmke, Mark	U.S. Senate	Senate Aide	Robinson, Lake, Lerer & Montgomery	Hoylake Investments	Bermuda	430,412
				Friends/Democ. in Pakistan	Pakistan	121,000
				Islam Dem. Alliance	Pakistan	16,500
Hessler, Curtis	Dept. of Treasury	Asst. Secy./ Economics	Paul, Weiss	Nippon Electric Co.	Japan	145,845
Hildenbrand, William	U.S. Senate	Secy. of Senate	Gold & Liebengood	Fiat, SpA	Italy	788,933
				Intl. Gold Corp.	South Africa	51,189

Name	Former Office	Position	Firm	Client	Country	Amount
Hirschhorn, Eric	Dept. of Commerce	Dep. Asst. Secy./Export Adm.	Bishop, Cook	CSR, Ltd.	Australia	258,019
				BAT Industries	Gr. Britain	55,227
				Volvo Car, BV	Netherlands	38,211
				Patson PTY, Ltd.	Australia	4,204
				Prof. Alfred Zehe	E. Germany	4,209
Horlick, Gary	Dept. of Commerce	Dep. Asst. Secy./Import Adm.	O'Melveny & Myers	CRA, Ltd.	Australia	150,235
				Government of Canada	Canada	480,622
				Broken Hill Proprietary	Australia	336,534
				Perisco Pizzamiglio	Italy	129,979
				Brewers Assn. of Canada	Canada	76,161
				Eur. Chem. Ind. Fed.	Intl.	42,878
				German Chem. Ind. Assn.	W. Germany	19,970
				Assn. Téléph./Télégr. Inds.	France	11,908
				Nippon Steel	Japan	— na —
Huddleston, Walter	U.S. Senate	Senator	Hill & Knowlton	Republic of Turkey	Turkey	— na —
Hymel, Gary	House of Reps.	House Aide	Hill & Knowlton	Natl. Devlt. Info. Off.	Indonesia	3,255,400
				Côte d'Azur Devlt.	France	27,204
				Republic of Korea	South Korea	233,441
				Hyundai Motor America	South Korea	283,479
				Soc. Gén. de Surveillance	Switzerland	220,172
				Palm Oil Reg. and Licensing	Malaysia	450,838
				Govt. of Cayman Islands	Cayman Islands	204,230
				Airbus Industrie N. Amer.	European Comm.	551,519
				Nintendo of America	Japan	492,773
				Sanwa Bank, Ltd.	Japan	375,054
				Marubeni America Corp.	Japan	136,796
				Assn. Advmt. Humar Rights	Japan	60,000
				Korean Airlines	South Korea	294,802

[1] This list includes only those federal officials who left office between the years 1980 and 1990.

[2] Public records do not reveal how much individual foreign agents receive from clients they represent. Figures shown here reflect the amount paid by the client *to the firm* during the period the agent was registered to represent that client.

AGENT[1]	GOVERNMENT BRANCH	PUBLIC POSITION	FIRM OF EMPLOYMENT	FOREIGN CLIENT	COUNTRY	FEES AND EXPENDITURES PAID TO FIRM[2] (1980–1990)
Hymel, Gary (cont'd)	House of Reps.	House Aide	Hill & Knowlton	Government of Angola	Angola	$ 20,000
				Martin Baker Aircraft	Gr. Britain	— na —
				Kuwait Petrol/Santa Fe	Kuwait	— na —
				Embassy of Venezuela	Venezuela	— na —
				Prince Talal	Saudi Arabia	— na —
				Republic of Turkey	Turkey	— na —
				INTELSAT	Intl.	— na —
				Portals, Inc.	Gr. Britain	— na —
				Salen Dry Cargo	Sweden	— na —
				Liberal Democratic Party	Japan	— na —
Janka, Leslie A.	White House	Spec. Asst./Pres. and Dep. Press Secy.	Neill & Co.	Kingdom of Morocco	Morocco	1,290,000
				Kingdom of Jordan	Jordan	1,220,000
				Arab Repub. of Egypt	Egypt	1,820,483
				Islam Repub. of Pakistan	Pakistan	560,000
				Government of Kenya	Kenya	531,708
				Government of Gabon	Gabon	187,500
				Government of Guinea	Guinea	75,000
				Govt./Dem. Repub. of Sudan	Sudan	60,000
				Govt. of El Salvador	El Salvador	5,000
				INTELSAT	Intl.	— na —
				Government of Jamaica	Jamaica	— na —
Jarvis, Patricia	Dept. of Health and Human Svces.	Spec. Asst., Off. of Legis.	Gold & Liebengood	Beretta USA Corp.	Italy/Belgium	139,638
				Fiat, SpA	Italy	426,937
				Thomson-CSF, Inc.	France	279,330
				Ricoh	Japan	34,794
Jennings, Horace	U.S. Senate	Senate Aide	Neill & Co.	Kingdom of Morocco	Morocco	— na —
				Government of Kenya	Kenya	— na —
				Government of Guinea	Guinea	— na —

Name	Agency	Title	Firm	Client	Country	Amount
				Government of Jamaica	Jamaica	— na —
				Govt. of Côte d'Ivoire	Côte d'Ivoire	— na —
				China Trade Devlt. Cncl.	China	— na —
				African Devlt. Bank	Intl.	— na —
				Rossing Uranium Ltd.	Namibia	— na —
				Korea For. Trade Assn.	South Korea	— na —
				Kingdom of Jordan	Jordan	— na —
Jollie, Susan B.	Civ. Aero. Bd.	Assoc. Gen. Couns., Antitrust and Litigation	Galland, Kharasch	Air Jamaica	Jamaica	405,867
				Orient Airlines Assn.	Philippines	130,363
				Wallenius Lines	Sweden	122,821
				H.K. Aircraft Engineering	Hong Kong	31,721
				Israel Aircraft Ind.	Israel	27,218
				Soule, SA	France	8,990
			SMC International	All Nippon Airways	Japan	39,689
Jones, James R.	House of Reps.	Member of Cong.	Dickstein, Shapiro & Morin	Toshiba Corporation	Japan	158,505
Kabel, Robert J.	White House	Spec. Asst. to Pres. for Leg. Affairs	Manatt, Phelps	Republic of Cyprus	Cyprus	574,465
				NEC Corporation	Japan	470,444
Kamm, Linda Heller	Dept. of Transp.	Gen. Counsel	Foley & Lardner	Holland Sweetener Co.	Netherlands	— na —
Kassinger, Theodore W.	U.S. Senate	Intl. Trade Couns., Finance Cmte.	Vinson & Elkins	Vitro, SA	Mexico	2,201,443
			Theodore Kassinger	Belg. Endive Mktg. Bd.	Belgium	8,143

[1] This list includes only those federal officials who left office between the years 1980 and 1990.

[2] Public records do not reveal how much individual foreign agents receive from clients they represent. Figures shown here reflect the amount paid by the client *to the firm* during the period the agent was registered to represent that client.

AGENT[1]	GOVERNMENT BRANCH	PUBLIC POSITION	FIRM OF EMPLOYMENT	FOREIGN CLIENT	COUNTRY	FEES AND EXPENDITURES PAID TO FIRM[2] (1980–1990)
Kirschenbaum, Bruce	White House	Dep. Spec. Asst. to Pres. for Intergovt. Affairs	Stroock & Stroock	Chemolimpex For. Trade/Chinoin Pharm. and Chem.	Hungary	$ 32,080
				Bank Ha'poalim	Israel	— na —
Kopp, George S.	House of Reps.	Chf. Couns., Subcmte. on Nat. Resources	Global USA	Hitachi, Ltd.	Japan	458,014
				All Nippon Airways	Japan	252,728
				Fanuc, Ltd.	Japan	258,369
				Hyundai Motor America	South Korea	250,000
				Jap. Fed. Constr. Contr.	Japan	225,616
				Japan Aircraft Devlt. Co.	Japan	253,807
				Komatsu Corp.	Japan	357,986
				Kyocera Corp.	Japan	226,354
				Mazak, Ltd.	Japan	276,634
Kurman, Michael	Dept. of Interior	Spec. Asst. to Solicitor	Arent, Fox	Outokumpu Oy	Japan	941,306
				Toyota Motor Corp.	Japan	1,103,059
				Sitmar Cruises	Australia	229,106
				Uranerzbergbau GmbH	W. Germany	89,112
				Verein. Edelstahlwerke	W. Germany	36,035
				Lars Krogh & Co.	Norway	48,033
				Patton & Morgan Corp.	Gr. Britain	3,189
				Nova Scotia Resources	Canada	— na —
Lachter, Stephen	Dept. of Transp.	Spec. Aviation Counsel	Patton, Boggs & Blow	Govt./Sultanate of Oman	Oman	509,653
				Duty Free Shoppers, Ltd.	Hong Kong	311,805
				Nakajima All Co.	Japan	406,807
				Government of Iceland	Iceland	177,227
				Fiart Cantieri Italiani	Italy	51,873
				Beckett Packaging	Canada	38,465
				Minerals Marketing Corp.	Zimbabwe	17,238

Name			Firm	Client	Country	Amount
Lande, Stephen	White House	Asst. U.S. Trade Rep.		Fundac./Def. Comercio Ext.	Costa Rica	12,650
				Govt./Repub. of[2] Marshall Isl.	Marshall Isl.	9,039
				Buini e Grandi, SpA	Italy	1,134
				E. Palicio y Cia	Venezuela	— na —
				Unitary Tax Campaign	Gr. Britain	— na —
				Government of Spain	Spain	— na —
			Manchester Trade	Korea For. Trade Assn.	South Korea	96,808
				Sidermex International	Mexico	43,498
				Hylsa	Mexico	29,807
				Tubos de Acero de Mex.	Mexico	18,959
				Asoc. de Export/Textiles	Costa Rica	10,346
				Wiresteel	Mexico	5,705
				Mexinox SA de CV	Mexico	— na —
			Manchester Assoc.	Korean Traders Assn.	South Korea	95,252
				Inst. de Comerc:o Ext.	Mexico	41,854
				Natl. Invest. Cncl./Panama	Panama	38,408
				Tubos de Acero de Mex.	Mexico	20,179
				Sidermex International	Mexico	18,163
				Embassy of Israel	Israel	18,467
				Kitan Consolidated	Israel	15,000
				Hylsa	Mexico	16,600
				Barbados Export Prom.	Barbados	2,177
				Canacero	Mexico	2,500
Laxalt, Paul	U.S. Senate	Senator	Laxalt, Washington	Asoc. de Empresas RENFE	Spain	485,793
				Govt. of Antigua/Barbuda	Antigua/Barbuda	868,366
				Henri Sfeir	Lebanon	45,000
Lazarus, Simon	White House	Assoc. Dir., U.S. Domestic Policy	Powell, Goldstein	INTELSAT	Intl.	506,791
				Soc. Gén. de Surveillance	Switzerland	171,565

[1] This list includes only those federal officials who left office between the years 1980 and 1990.

[2] Public records do not reveal how much individual foreign agents receive from clients they represent. Figures shown here reflect the amount paid by the client *to the firm* during the period the agent was registered to represent that client.

AGENT[1]	GOVERNMENT BRANCH	PUBLIC POSITION	FIRM OF EMPLOYMENT	FOREIGN CLIENT	COUNTRY	FEES AND EXPENDITURES PAID TO FIRM[2] (1980–1990)
Lehman, Bruce A.	U.S. Senate	Couns., Jud. Cmte.	Swidler & Berlin	Hyundai Motor Co. China Trade Devlt. Cncl. Government of Bermuda	South Korea Taiwan Bermuda	$ 353,764 38,000 — na —
Lenahan, Walter	Dept. of Commerce	Dep. Asst. Secy. for Textiles/ Apparel	Mudge, Rose	Asoc. Nacl. Industriales China Textile Imp./Exp. Hong Kong Trade Dept. Sovcomflot	Colombia China Hong Kong USSR	50,600 — na — — na — — na —
Levine, Kenneth	Fed. Energy Reg. Cmsn.	Dir., Cong. Affairs	Wunder, Ryan, Cannon & Thelen	Ad Hoc Insur. Group Government of Bermuda	Bermuda Bermuda	— na — — na —
Libby, I. Lewis	Dept. of State	Dir. Spec. Proj., Bur. of E. Asia	Dickstein, Shapiro & Morin	Embassy of Malaysia Falconbridge	Malaysia Gr. Britain	267,131 140,686
Liebengood, Howard S.	U.S. Senate	Sergeant at Arms	Gold & Liebengood	Fiat, SpA Thomson-CSF, Inc. Beretta USA Corp. Intl. Gold Corp. BAA, plc Ricoh	Italy France Italy South Africa Gr. Britain Japan	788,933 327,840 157,934 51,189 47,829 34,794
Lighthizer, Robert	White House	Dep. U.S. Trade Representative	Skadden, Arps	Hoylake Investments British Airports Auth. Government of Jamaica Min. Ind. and Comm./Sugar and Alc.	Bermuda Gr. Britain Jamaica Brazil	2,480,013 233,397 62,249 44,302
Lipsky, Abbott B.	Dept. of Justice	Dep. Asst. Atty. Gen./Antitrust	King & Spalding	Agie Holding AG Elox Corporation	Switzerland Switzerland	— na — — na —

Name	Agency	Position	Firm	Client	Country	Amount
				Ind. Elektronik Agie	Switzerland	— na —
				Agie USA, Ltd.	Switzerland	— na —
Long, C. Thomas	Fed. Home Loan Bank Board	Dep. Gen. Counsel	Jones, Day, Reavis & Pogue	Morgan Grenfell & Co.	Gr. Britain	1,214,461
				Heron International	Gr. Britain	966,422
				Konica USA	Japan	142,674
				Embassy of the PRC	China	115,000
				Govt. of Costa Rica	Costa Rica	— na —
				London Chamb. Comm./Ind.	Gr. Britain	— na —
MacDonald, David	White House	Dep. U.S. Trade Representative	Teeley-MacDonald	Govt./Repub. of Seychelles	Seychelles	90,000
			Baker & McKenzie	Textile/Garment Mfrs.	Uruguay	— na —
Manatos, Andrew	Dept. of Commerce	Asst. Secy./Cong. Affairs	Manatos & Manatos	Embassy of Japan	Japan	36,000
				Government of Greece	Greece	306,048
Marcuss, Stanley	Dept. of Commerce	Asst. Secy./Ind. and Trade	Milbank, Tweed	People's Repub. of China	China	35,000
Martin, Guy R.	Dept. of Interior	Asst. Secy./Land and Water	Perkins, Coie	Krupp Atlas Elektronik	W. Germany	— na —
Massey, Donald F.	U.S. Senate	Dep. Sgt. at Arms	Hill & Knowlton	Republic of Turkey	Turkey	3,207,822
				Natl. Devlt. Info. Office	Indonesia	2,205,400
				Hitachi, Ltd.	Japan	1,254,813
				Kingdom of Morocco	Morocco	821,964
				Airbus Industrie N. Amer.	European Comm.	487,147
				Republic of Korea	South Korea	233,441
				Hyundai Motor America	South Korea	435,081
				Soc. Gén. de Surveillance	Switzerland	220,172

[1] This list includes only those federal officials who left office between the years 1980 and 1990.

[2] Public records do not reveal how much individual foreign agents receive from clients they represent. Figures shown here reflect the amount paid by the client *to the firm* during the period the agent was registered to represent that client.

AGENT[1]	GOVERNMENT BRANCH	PUBLIC POSITION	FIRM OF EMPLOYMENT	FOREIGN CLIENT	COUNTRY	FEES AND EXPENDITURES PAID TO FIRM[2] (1980–1990)
Massey, Donald F. (cont'd)	U.S. Senate	Dep. Sgt. at Arms	Hill & Knowlton	Palm Oil Reg. and Licensing	Malaysia	$ 450,838
				Govt. of Cayman Islands	Cayman Islands	204,230
				Mazda Motor Corp.	Japan	994,704
				Nintendo of America	Japan	492,773
				N.H. Ball Bearings/Minebea	Japan	165,151
				Marubeni America Corp.	Japan	136,796
				Assn. Advmt. Human Rights	Japan	60,000
				Asbestos Institute	Canada	76,821
				Martin Baker Aircraft	Gr. Britain	18,407
				Côte d'Azur Devlt.	France	27,204
				Liberal Democratic Party	Japan	— na —
				Adnan Khashoggi	Saudi Arabia	— na —
Mathias, Charles	U.S. Senate	Senator	Jones, Day, Reavis & Pogue	Embassy of the PRC	China	127,845
McElheny, Richard L.	Dept. of Commerce	Asst. Secy. for Trade Devlt.	The Brock Group	Airbus Industrie N. Amer.	Switzerland	75,000
			Hill & Knowlton	Kingdom of Morocco	Morocco	821,964
				Republic of Korea	South Korea	233,441
				Brother, Inc.	Japan	73,006
				Elec. Inds. Assn./Japan	Japan	610,613
				Govt. of Cayman Islands	Cayman Islands	362,344
				Korean Airlines	South Korea	356,884
				Airbus Industrie N. Amer.	European Comm.	424,842
				Daewoo Electronics Corp.	South Korea	32,500
				Liberal Democratic Party	Japan	246,000
				Hyundai Motor America	South Korea	435,081

Official	Agency	Position	Firm	Client	Country	Amount
				Hitachi, Ltd.	Japan	612,029
				Can. Asbestos Info. Ctr.	Canada	60,150
				Côte d'Azur Devlt.	France	27,204
				Elec. Inds. Assn./Korea	South Korea	276,960
				Soule, SA	France	41,582
				Soc. Gén. de Surveillance	Switzerland	222,672
				Bur. National du Cognac	France	845,804
				Yucatán Dept. Econ./Devlt.	Mexico	202,832
				Iceland Min. For. Affairs	Iceland	45,603
				NEC Corporation	Japan	510,212
				Palm Oil Reg. and Licensing	Malaysia	417,608
				Nihou Kotsu Bunka Kyodai	Japan	241,379
				Marubeni America Corp.	Japan	116,399
				Seibulite Intl.	Japan	44,188
				Asoc. Nat. Papel/Celulcse	Brazil	— na —
				Makita USA	Japan	— na —
				Asoc. Export de Flores	Colombia	— na —
McGovern, John J.	Secur. and Exch. Cmsn.	Asst. to Chmn.	Wunder, Ryan, Cannon & Thelen	Aermacchi	Italy	347,206
				Airship Industries	Gr. Britain	117,200
				Mirabella	Italy	32,062
				Intermarine SpA	Italy	17,390
			Akin, Gump	Airship Industries	Gr. Britain	27,668
Mentz, J. Roger	Dept. of Treasury	Asst. Secy./Tax Policy	Cadwalader, Wickersham & Taft	Mercedes-Benz	W. Germany	— na —
Moffett, A. Toby	House of Reps.	Member of Cong.	A. Toby Moffett	Government of Lebanon	Lebanon	25,000

[1] This list includes only those federal officials who left office between the years 1980 and 1990.

[2] Public records do not reveal how much individual foreign agents receive from clients they represent. Figures shown here reflect the amount paid by the client *to the firm* during the period the agent was registered to represent that client.

AGENT[1]	GOVERNMENT BRANCH	PUBLIC POSITION	FIRM OF EMPLOYMENT	FOREIGN CLIENT	COUNTRY	FEES AND EXPENDITURES PAID TO FIRM[2] (1980–1990)
Morgan, Lance Ian	U.S. Senate	Press Secy./ Select Cmte., Secret Mil. Asst. for Iran and Nicaraguan Opposition	Robinson, Lake, Lerer & Montgomery	Hoylake Investments Japan Auto Pts. Inds. Assn. Friends/Democ. in Pakistan Islam Dem. Alliance Komatsu Elec. Metals	Bermuda Japan Pakistan Pakistan Japan	$ 430,412 175,567 121,000 16,500 21,000
Morris, William	U.S. Senate	Gen. Counsel, Finance Cmte.	Rogers & Wells	Paribas Corporation	France	565,441
Morris, William H., Jr.	Dept. of Commerce	Asst. Secy./ Trade	Global USA	Fanuc, Ltd. All Nippon Airways Hitachi, Ltd. Japan Aircraft Devlt. Co. Komatsu Corporation Kyocera Corporation Mazak, Ltd. Repub. of Bophuthatswana Voest-Alpine Samsung Semiconductor Hyundai Motor America Murata Machinery Korea For. Trade Assn. Ind. Coop. and Devlt.	Japan Japan Japan Japan Japan Japan Japan Bophuthatswana Austria South Korea South Korea Japan South Korea Austria	864,403 756,992 938,183 697,293 932,986 602,503 741,135 112,500 137,084 278,592 328,350 — na — — na — — na —
Moyer, Homer E.	Dept. of Commerce	Gen. Counsel	Miller & Chevalier	Government of Canada Republic of France	Canada France	506,299 89,369
Murdock, J. E. III	Fed. Aviation Adm.	Chief Counsel	Heron, Burchette	St. Lawrence Cement Asoc. Export de Flores	Canada Colombia	839,195 664,722

Name	Service	Position	Firm	Client	Country	Amount
				CBI Sugar Group, Inc.	Latin America	356,159
				AgroQuímicas de Guatemala	Guatemala	115,376
				Canada Cement Lafarge	Canada	127,850
				Intl. Maritime Satellite	Intl.	58,296
				St. Mary's Cement	Canada	21,076
				Genstar Cement	Canada	36,465
				RSV Mining Equipment	Netherlands	— na —
				Assn. Advmt. Human Rights	Japan	— na —
Murphy, Daniel J.	U.S. Navy	Admiral (Ret.); Chf. of Staff/ Vice Pres. George Bush	Murphy & Demory	Korea Tacoma Marine	South Korea	120,718
				Government of Haiti	Haiti	84,000
				PCI, Inc.	Canada	99,211
				PACO Enterprises	Japan	50,000
				Pen Holdings	Taiwan	— na —
			Hill & Knowlton	Republic of Turkey	Turkey	2,208,568
				Government of Haiti	Haiti	790,290
				Republic of Korea	Korea	233,441
				Kingdom of Morocco	Morocco	821,964
				Airbus Industrie N. Amer.	European Comm.	227,803
				Elec. Inds. Assn./Japan	Japan	477,094
				Govt. of Cayman Islands	Cayman Islands	362,344
				Martin Baker Aircraft	Gr. Britain	18,407
				Korean Airlines	South Korea	356,884
				Brother, Inc.	Japan	71,488
				Côte d'Azur Devlt.	France	38,892
				Liberal Democratic Party	Japan	246,000
				Daewoo Electronics Corp.	South Korea	32,500
				Hyundai Motor America	South Korea	435,081
				Government of Angola	Angola	20,000
				Can. Asbestos Info. Ctr.	Canada	60,150
				Hitachi, Ltd.	Japan	368,834

[1] This list includes only those federal officials who left office between the years 1980 and 1990.

[2] Public records do not reveal how much individual foreign agents receive from clients they represent. Figures shown here reflect the amount paid by the client *to the firm* during the period the agent was registered to represent that client.

AGENT[1]	GOVERNMENT BRANCH	PUBLIC POSITION	FIRM OF EMPLOYMENT	FOREIGN CLIENT	COUNTRY	FEES AND EXPENDITURES PAID TO FIRM[2] (1980–1990)
Murphy, Daniel J. (cont'd)	U.S. Navy	Admiral (Ret.); Chf. of Staff/ Vice Pres. George Bush	Hill & Knowlton	Soc. Gén. de Surveillance	Switzerland	$ 222,672
				Soule, SA	France	41,582
				Elec. Inds. Assn./Korea	South Korea	191,230
				Iceland Min. For. Affairs	Iceland	31,295
				Bur. National du Cognac	France	408,314
				City of Krefeld	W. Germany	— na —
				Baden-Württemberg Dev.	W. Germany	— na —
				German Natl. Tourist Off.	W. Germany	— na —
				Asoc. Export de Flores	Colombia	— na —
				Government of Canada	Canada	— na —
				Embassy of Japan	Japan	— na —
				Royal Emb. of Saudi Arabia	Saudi Arabia	— na —
Muskie, Edmund S.	Dept. of State	Secretary	Chadbourne & Parke	Mfrs. Life Insur.	Canada	— na —
				Amalgamated Metal Corp.	Gr. Britain	— na —
Nimetz, Matthew	Dept. of State	Under Secy. for Secur. Asstce.	Paul, Weiss	NEC Corp./NEC America	Japan	4,453,812
				Korea Fed. Textile Ind.	South Korea	166,457
				Korea Iron and Steel Assn.	South Korea	32,064
O'Connell, K. Michael	Dept. of Commerce	Sr. Policy Analyst, Intl. Trade Adm.	Collier, Shannon & Scott	Petróleos de Venezuela	Venezuela	1,584,951
				Siemens AG	W. Germany	547,033
				Petrojam, Ltd.	Jamaica	333,720
Oglesby, M. B.	White House	Dir., Off. of Cong. Affairs	Hecht, Spencer and Associates	H.K. Trade Devlt. Cncl.	Hong Kong	599,828
				Govt./Repub. of Panama	Panama	159,647
				Freedom and Justice/Cyprus	Cyprus	115,000
Olmer, Lionel	Dept. of Commerce	Under Secy. for Intl. Trade Adm.	Paul, Weiss	NEC Corp./NEC America	Japan	— na —
				Government of Poland	Poland	— na —

Name	Office	Position	Firm	Client	Country	Amount
Perry, William	White House	Dir., Latin Amer. Affairs/ Natl. Secur. Cncl.	Neill & Co.	Kingdom of Morocco	Morocco	900,000
				Government of Kenya	Kenya	707,250
				Islam Repub. of Pakistan	Pakistan	440,000
				Arab Repub. of Egypt	Egypt	739,043
				Government of Gabon	Gabon	187,500
Perugino, Roxanne	House of Reps.	Staff, For. Affairs Cmte.	Bannerman and Associates	Government of Tunisia	Tunisia	160,314
Popkin, Richard	Dept. of Commerce	Dep. Asst. Secy./Trade Adm.	Swidler & Berlin	Hyundai Motor Co.	South Korea	353,765
Printz, Albert C.	Agency for Intl. Devlt.	Envir. Coord.	Neill & Co.	Arab Repub. of Egypt	Egypt	919,043
				Kingdom of Jordan	Jordan	670,000
				Government of Gabon	Gabon	187,500
				Islam Repub. of Pakistan	Pakistan	560,000
				Government of Kenya	Kenya	1,055,172
				Kingdom of Morocco	Morocco	900,000
				Government of Guinea	Guinea	75,000
				Government of Jamaica	Jamaica	150,000
				Korea For. Trade Assn.	South Korea	— na —
				Rossing Uranium Ltd.	Namibia	— na —
				African Devlt. Bank	Intl.	— na —
				China Trade Devlt. Cncl.	China	— na —
				Govt. of Côte d'Ivoire	Côte d'Ivoire	— na —
Pruitt, Steven L.	House of Reps.	Exec. Dir., Hse. Budget Cmte.	Heron, Burchette	CBI Sugar Group, Inc.	Latin America	205,233
				NovAtel Communications	Canada	243,036
				Thai Steel Pipe Assn.	Thailand	116,981
				AgroQuímicas de Guatemala	Guatemala	30,713
				Canada Cement Lafarge	Canada	15,619
				Intl. Maritime Satellite	Intl.	20,000

[1] This list includes only those federal officials who left office between the years 1980 and 1990.

[2] Public records do not reveal how much individual foreign agents receive from clients they represent. Figures shown here reflect the amount paid by the client *to the firm* during the period the agent was registered to represent that client.

AGENT[1]	GOVERNMENT BRANCH	PUBLIC POSITION[1]	FIRM OF EMPLOYMENT	FOREIGN CLIENT	COUNTRY	FEES AND EXPENDITURES PAID TO FIRM[2] (1980–1990)
Pruitt, Steven L. (cont'd)	House of Reps.	Exec. Dir., Hse. Budget Cmte.	Heron, Burchette	St. Mary's Cement	Canada	$ 3,862
				Asia Satellite Telecomm.	Hong Kong	5,898
				St. Lawrence Cement	Canada	45,654
				Inland Cement	Canada	13,493
				Yamaichi Securities	Japan	10,000
				Daiwa Securities	Japan	2,348
				Asoc. Export de Flores	Colombia	— na —
			Laxalt, Washington	Air China International	China	— na —
				Asoc. de Empresas RENFE	Spain	— na —
				Govt. of Antigua/Barbuda	Antigua/Barbuda	— na —
				Govt. of Angola	Angola	— na —
				Operaciones Turísticas	Honduras	— na —
				Institut de la Vie	France	— na —
Raffaelli, John	U.S. Senate	Senate Aide	McAuliffe, Kelly, Raffaelli & Siemens	Emb. of Repub. of Turkey	Turkey	— na —
Ratchford, William R.	House of Reps.	Member of Cong.	Gold & Liebengood	Fiat, SpA	Italy	788,933
				Thomson-CSF, Inc.	France	313,444
				Beretta USA Corp.	Italy	139,638
Reuss, Henry S.	House of Reps.	Member of Cong.	Rose, Schmidt, Hasley & DiSalle	Mex. Lead Oxide Producers	Mexico	237,077
				Inst. Mex. de la Fluorita	Mexico	27,797
				Industrias Penoles	Mexico	— na —
				Minera de las Cuevas	Mexico	— na —
Rhodes, John J.	House of Reps.	Member of Cong.	Hunton & Williams	INTELSAT	Intl.	38,718

Ribicoff, Abraham	U.S. Senate	Senator	Kaye, Scholer	Elsevier Sci. Publrs.	Netherlands	699,230
				Japan Ctr. Info./Cult.	Japan	90,914
Richardson, Elliot	Dept. of State	Amb.-at-Large	Milbank, Tweed	Embassy of Iceland	Iceland	41,633
				People's Repub. of China	China	35,000
				Government of Kuwait	Kuwait	36,895
				JDS Intl. Consulting	Angola	— na —
Richmond, Marilyn	U.S. Senate	Couns., Comm. Cmte.	Heron, Burchette	Asoc. Export de Flores	Colombia	1,031,596
				St. Lawrence Cement	Canada	1,002,294
				CBI Sugar Group, Inc.	Latin America	433,659
				Mitsubishi Electric	Japan	109,624
				Japan Tobacco	Japan	101,616
				Canada Cement Lafarge	Canada	183,999
				Genstar Cement	Canada	76,897
				St. Mary's Cement	Canada	46,280
				Lake Ontario Cement	Canada	74,048
				RSV Mining Equipment	Netherlands	10,364
				Assn. Advmt. Human Rights	Japan	14,000
Robertson, Mark	U.S. Senate	House Aide	Hill & Knowlton	Palm Oil Reg. and Licensing	Malaysia	308,970
				Kingdom of Morocco	Morocco	297,605
				Government of Canada	Canada	— na —
Robinson, Phillip	White House	Staff, Off. of Tech. Assessment	Patton, Boggs & Blow	Nakajima All Co.	Japan	152,409
				Duty Free Shoppers, Ltd.	Hong Kong	146,977
				Government of Iceland	Iceland	128,165
				Sultanate of Oman	Oman	90,302
				Royal Trust Co.	Canada	85,296
				Cargolux Airlines	Luxembourg	58,240
				Fund Pro-Image/Exterior	Colombia	37,500
				Olympic Fibers, SA	Costa Rica	65,816
				Beckett Packaging	Canada	11,472

[1] This list includes only those federal officials who left office between the years 1980 and 1990.
[2] Public records do not reveal how much individual foreign agents receive from clients they represent. Figures shown here reflect the amount paid by the client *to the firm* during the period the agent was registered to represent that client.

AGENT[1]	GOVERNMENT BRANCH	PUBLIC POSITION	FIRM OF EMPLOYMENT	FOREIGN CLIENT	COUNTRY	FEES AND EXPENDITURES PAID TO FIRM[2] (1980–1990)
Robinson, Phillip (cont'd)	White House	Staff, Off. of Tech. Assessment	Patton, Boggs & Blow	Fiart Cantieri Italiani	Italy	$ 7,985
				Fund./Def. Comercio Ext.	Costa Rica	7,150
				Govt./Repub. of Marshall Isl.	Marshall Isl.	— na —
				Minerals Marketing Corp.	Zimbabwe	— na —
Rose, Jonathan	Dept. of Justice	Asst. Atty. Gen., Legal Policy	Jones, Day, Reavis & Pogue	Embassy of the PRC	China	127,845
				Morgan Grenfell Ltd.	Gr. Britain	1,392,632
				London Chamb. Comm/Ind.	Gr. Britain	— na —
				Govt. of Costa Rica	Costa Rica	— na —
Rosendahl, Jennifer	House of Reps.	House Aide	Neill & Co.	Government of Kenya	Kenya	1,055,172
				Kingdom of Morocco	Morocco	1,590,000
				Arab Repub. of Egypt	Egypt	2,180,483
				Kingdom of Jordan	Jordan	1,330,000
				Government of Gabon	Gabon	437,500
				Islam Repub. of Pakistan	Pakistan	560,000
				Government of Jamaica	Jamaica	150,000
				Government of Guinea	Guinea	75,000
				Govt./Dem. Repub. of Sudan	Sudan	60,000
				Govt. of El Salvador	El Salvador	5,000
				Korea For. Trade Assn.	South Korea	— na —
				Rossing Uranium Ltd.	Namibia	— na —
				African Devlt. Bank	Intl.	— na —
				China Trade Devlt. Cncl.	China	— na —
				Govt. of Côte d'Ivoire	Côte d'Ivoire	— na —
Rousselot, John	White House	Spec. Asst./Pres.	Alcalde and Rousselot	Brit. Assn./Invest. Trust	Gr. Britain	— na —
Salmon, John J.	House of Reps.	Chf. Couns., Ways and Means Cmte.	Dewey, Ballantine	The Dee Corp., PLC	Gr. Britain	44,591
				Hanschell Inniss, Ltd.	Barbados	11,748

Name	Office	Position	Firm	Client	Country	Amount
Samolis, Frank	House of Reps.	Staff, Ways and Means Subcmte. on Trade	Patton, Boggs & Blow	Sultanate of Oman	Oman	509,653
				Nakajima All Co.	Japan	406,807
				Government of Iceland	Iceland	177,227
				Duty Free Shoppers, Ltd.	Hong Kong	311,805
				Fiart Cantieri Italiani	Italy	51,873
				Beckett Packaging	Canada	38,465
				Fund./Def. Comercio Exter.	Costa Rica	12,650
				Minerals Marketing Corp.	Zimbabwe	17,238
				Govt./Repub. of Marshall Isl.	Marshall Isl.	9,039
				Buini e Grandi, SpA	Italy	1,134
				Unitary Tax Campaign	Gr. Britain	— na —
				E. Palicio y Cia	Venezuela	— na —
				Government of Spain	Spain	— na —
Sandifer, Myron G. III	U.S. Senate	Senate Aide	Jack McDonald Co.	Hitachi Sales/America	Japan	155,839
				Soc. Gén de Surveillance	Switzerland	85,745
				Minorco SA	Luxembourg	10,906
Santos, Leonard	U.S. Senate	Chf. Trade Couns., Sen. Finance Cmte.	Perkins, Coie	Krupp Atlas Elektronik	W. Germany	— na —
			Verner, Liipfert	Oerlikon-Buhrle Military	Switzerland	53,697
				J. D. Irving, Ltd.	Canada	20,574
				Matra Aérospace	France	17,468
				Déambinox, SA	France	— na —
Satterfield, David	House of Reps.	Member of Cong.	Bishop, Cook	BAT Industries	Gr. Britain	513,597
				CSR, Ltd.	Australia	218,177
				Patson PTY, Ltd.	Australia	11,404
Saunders, Stephen	White House	Asst. U.S. Trade Representative	Saunders and Co.	Mitsubishi Electric	Japan	234,328
				Embassy of Japan	Japan	220,000

[1] This list includes only those federal officials who left office between the years 1980 and 1990.

[2] Public records do not reveal how much individual foreign agents receive from clients they represent. Figures shown here reflect the amount paid by the client *to the firm* during the period the agent was registered to represent that client.

AGENT[1]	GOVERNMENT BRANCH	PUBLIC POSITION	FIRM OF EMPLOYMENT	FOREIGN CLIENT	COUNTRY	FEES AND EXPENDITURES PAID TO FIRM[2] (1980–1990)
Saunders, Stephen (cont'd)	White House	Asst. U.S. Trade Representative	Saunders and Co.	Seiko-Epson Corp.	Japan	$ 141,411
				Taiwan Textile Fed.	Taiwan	93,428
				Ohbayashi Corporation	Japan	78,426
				Bd. For. Trade/Repub. of China	Taiwan	18,000
				Elec. Inds. Assn./Japan	Japan	— na —
				Government of Canada	Canada	— na —
Scruggs, John F.	Dept. of Health and Human Svces.	Asst. Secy./ Legis.	Gold & Liebengood	Fiat, SpA	Italy	788,933
				Thomson-CSF, Inc.	France	313,443
				BAA, plc	Gr. Britain	34,055
				Ricoh	Japan	56,772
				Beretta USA Corp.	Italy	60,046
Simons, Lawrence	Fed. Housing Adm.	Commissioner	Powell, Goldstein	Embassy of Morocco	Morocco	9,101
Sittman, William	White House	Spec. Asst./Pres.	Michael K. Deaver Associates	Intl. Cult. Soc./Korea	South Korea	476,770
				Daewoo Corporation	South Korea	255,273
				CBI Sugar Group, Inc.	Latin America	300,000
				Embassy of Canada	Canada	100,290
				Min. Comm. and Ind. Devlt.	Mexico	62,500
				Royal Emb. of Saudi Arabia	Saudi Arabia	375,000
				Govt. of Singapore	Singapore	— na —
				Korea Broadcast./Adv.	South Korea	— na —
Small, Karna	Natl. Secur. Cncl.	Dir. Pub. Affairs	Hill & Knowlton	SGS North America	Switzerland	220,172
				Republic of Turkey	Turkey	2,237,447
				Govt. of Cayman Islands	Cayman Islands	362,344
				Elec. Inds. Assn./Korea	South Korea	311,960
				Hyundai Motor America	South Korea	126,807
				Elec. Inds. Assn./Japan	Japan	344,816
				Palm Oil Reg. and Licensing	Malaysia	450,838

Name	Agency	Position	Firm	Client	Country	Amount
Smith, Michael B.	White House	Dep. U.S. Trade Representative	Steptoe & Johnson	Can. Sugar Institute	Canada	— na —
Stern, Paula	Intl. Trade Cmsn.	Chairwoman	Winthrop, Stimson	Metallverken Nederlande■	Sweden	1,268,871
Stone, Richard B.	U.S. Senate	Senator	Richard B. Stone	Republic of China	Taiwan	92,000
			Proskauer, Rose, Goetz & Mendelsohn	Bd. For. Trade/Repub. of China / Government of Guatemala	Taiwan / Guatemala	170,000 / 110,000
Talmadge, Herman E.	U.S. Senate	Senator	Barnett & Alagia	Thai Food Proc. Assn.	Thailand	390,000
Tate, Sheila B.	White House	Press Secretary	Burson-Marsteller	Thomson, SA	France	384,119
Thompson, Robert	White House	Exec. Asst./Vice Pres. George Bush	Thompson and Co.	Mitsubishi Elec./Amer. / Suzuki of America Auto / Emb. of Repub. of Turkey / Reed Telepublishing	Japan / Japan / Turkey / Gr. Britain	308,614 / 317,802 / 100,000 / 22,412
Topelius, Kathleen E.	Fed. Home Loan Bank Board	Atty., Off. of Gen. Counsel	Morgan, Lewis and Bockius	Banco de Santander	Spain	4,445
Urbanchuk, John	U.S. Army	Desk Officer, Polit./Mil. Div., Off. of Dep. Chf. of Staff	Hill & Knowlton	Ferruzzi Finanziaria	Italy	763,375

[1] This list includes only those federal officials who left office between the years 1980 and 1990.

[2] Public records do not reveal how much individual foreign agents receive from clients they represent. Figures shown here reflect the amount paid by the client *to the firm* during the period the agent was registered to represent that client.

AGENT[1]	GOVERNMENT BRANCH	PUBLIC POSITION	FIRM OF EMPLOYMENT	FOREIGN CLIENT	COUNTRY	FEES AND EXPENDITURES PAID TO FIRM[2] (1980–1990)
Valdez, Abelardo	Dept. of State	Chief of Protocol	Laxalt, Washington	Govt. of Antigua/Barbuda	Antigua/Barbuda	$ 868,366
				Asoc. de Empresas RENFE	Spain	485,793
				Henri Sfeir	Lebanon	45,000
				Government of Angola	Angola	749,000
				Operaciones Turisticas	Honduras	75,000
				Institut de la Vie	France	— na —
				Air China International	China	— na —
Vanik, Charles A.	House of Reps.	Member of Cong./Chm., Ways and Means Cmte.	Squire, Sanders and Dempsey	Embassy of Belgium	Belgium	44,951
Verstandig, Lee	Dept. of HUD	Under Secretary	Verstandig and Associates	Assn./Hops Prod. and Dealers	W. Germany	110,000
			Michael K. Deaver Associates	Daewoo Corporation	South Korea	192,773
				Intl. Cult. Soc./Korea	South Korea	357,642
				Royal Emb. of Saudi Arabia	Saudi Arabia	375,000
				Min. Comm. and Ind. Devlt.	Mexico	62,500
				Embassy of Canada	Canada	25,000
				CBI Sugar Group, Inc.	Latin America	— na —
Vicario, Joseph	Intl. Trade Cmsn.	Sr. Atty./Adviser, U.S. Customs	Heron, Burchette	Asoc. Export de Flores	Colombia	1,351,646
				St. Lawrence Cement	Canada	1,208,078
				CBI Sugar Group, Inc.	Latin America	433,659
				Canada Cement Lafarge	Canada	183,999
				RSV Mining Equipment	Netherlands	52,166
				Mitsubishi Electric	Japan	109,624
				Genstar Cement	Canada	76,897
				Lake Ontario Cement	Canada	74,048

Name	Former Position	Agency	Firm	Client	Country	Amount
				Intl. Maritime Satellite	Intl.	— na —
				St. Mary's Cement	Canada	46,280
				Daiwa Securities	Japan	— na —
				AgroQuímicas de Guatemala	Guatemala	8,097
				Agora Centro/Estud. Intl.	Argentina	2,000
				Yamaichi Securities	Japan	— na —
				Thai Steel Pipe Assn.	Thailand	— na —
Waldmann, Raymond	Asst. Secy., Intl. Econ. Policy	Dept. of Commerce	TransNational	ADICAL	Brazil	20,000
			Global USA	Fanuc, Ltd.	Japan	100,000
				Mazak Corporation	Japan	50,000
				Komatsu, Ltd.	Japan	62,500
				Repub. of Bophuthatswana	Bophuthatswana	37,500
			Raymond Waldmann	Taiwan Dir. Gen. Telecomm.	Taiwan	13,770
Watkins, Robert E.	Dep. Asst. Secy., Automotive Affairs	Dept. of Commerce	Weatherly & Co.	Kia Motors Corporation	South Korea	45,000
Wegman, Richard	Chf. Couns./Staff Dir., Govt. Affairs Cmte.	U.S. Senate	Garvey, Schubert and Barer	Embassy of Canada	Canada	— na —
				Government of Canada	Canada	— na —
				Province of Manitoba	Canada	— na —
				Province of Ontario	Canada	— na —
			Wellford, Wegman	Embassy of Canada	Canada	646,783
				Province of Manitoba	Canada	301,619
				Province of Ontario	Canada	132,319

[1] This list includes only those federal officials who left office between the years 1980 and 1990.

[2] Public records do not reveal how much individual foreign agents receive from clients they represent. Figures shown here reflect the amount paid by the client *to the firm* during the period the agent was registered to represent that client.

Appendix A

AGENT[1]	GOVERNMENT BRANCH	PUBLIC POSITION	FIRM OF EMPLOYMENT	FOREIGN CLIENT	COUNTRY	FEES AND EXPENDITURES PAID TO FIRM[2] (1980–1990)
Wellford, W. Harrison	White House	Exec. Assoc. Dir., Off. of Mgmt. and Budget	Wellford, Wegman	Embassy of Canada	Canada	$ 646,783
				Province of Manitoba	Canada	306,619
				Sakhalin Oil Devlt. Coop.	Japan	— na —
Whitfield, Dennis	Dept. of Labor	Dep. Secretary	The Brock Group	Bd. For. Trade/Repub. of China	Taiwan	240,000
Wides, Burton	U.S. Senate	Couns., Jud. Cmte.	Arent, Fox	Sitmar Cruises	Australia	— na —
Winnick, Jeanne	White House	Asst./Press Secy.	Susan Davis Intl.	Honduran National Party	Honduras	— na —
Witeck, Robert	U.S. Senate	Senate Aide	Hill & Knowlton	Republic of Turkey	Turkey	1,383,568
				Côte d'Azur Devlt.	France	38,892
				Liberal Democratic Party	Japan	246,000
				Hyundai Motor America	South Korea	435,081
				Kingdom of Morocco	Morocco	297,605
				Korean Airlines	South Korea	294,802
				Government of Angola	Angola	20,000
				Govt. of Cayman Islands	Cayman Islands	204,230
				Asbestos Institute	Canada	— na —
				NEC Corporation	Japan	— na —
				Soc. Gén. de Surveillance	Switzerland	— na —
				Arab Women's Council	Intl.	— na —
				Prince Talal	Saudi Arabia	— na —
				Brother, Inc.	Japan	— na —
				Can. Asbestos Info. Ctr.	Canada	— na —
				Salen Dry Cargo	Sweden	— na —

				Client	Country	Fee
Wunder, Bernard	Dept. of Commerce	Asst. Secy., Commun./ Info.	Wunder, Ryan, Cannon & Thelen	INTELSAT	Intl.	— na —
				Airbus Industrie N. Amer.	European Comm.	— na —
				Republic of Korea	South Korea	— na —
				Kingdom of Morocco	Morocco	— na —
				Ad Hoc Insur. Group	Bermuda	— na —
				Industrial Equity (Pacific) Ltd.	New Zealand	— na —

[1] This list includes only those federal officials who left office between the years 1980 and 1990.

[2] Public records do not reveal how much individual foreign agents receive from clients they represent. Figures shown here reflect the amount paid by the client *to the firm* during the period the agent was registered to represent that client.

APPENDIX B

Japan's Registered Foreign Agents in America
(March 1990)

JAPANESE ORGANIZATION	AMERICAN AGENT	DATE FIRST REGISTERED
All Nippon Airways Co.	Global U.S.A., Inc.	9/13/84
Assn. for the Advancement of Human Rights	Hill & Knowlton, Inc.	4/11/88
Bank of Japan	Wilbur F. Monroe Assoc.	9/21/78
Brother Industries, Ltd.	Hill & Knowlton, Inc.	5/15/87
The Central Union of Agricultural Cooperatives (ZENCHU)	Donald G. Lerch, Jr., & Co. Arter & Hadden	1/8/87 3/3/87
Chiyoda Chemical, Engineering & Construction Company, Ltd.	Hori & Bunker, Inc.	7/17/89
Communications Industry Assn. of Japan	Anderson, Hibey, Nauheim & Blair Mintz, Levin, et al.	2/12/82 2/2/87
Consolidated Grain & Barge Co.	Verner, Liipfert, et al.	9/19/88
Consulate General of Japan	Whitehouse Assoc. Michael Klepper Assoc. Bernhagen & Assoc. Philip Van Slyck, Inc.	2/24/70 9/9/87 6/15/87 9/29/66
Eitaro Itoyama	Black, Manafort, et al.	8/23/89
Electronics Industries Assn. of Japan	H. William Tanaka Baron/Canning & Co. Hill & Knowlton, Inc. Anderson, Hibey, et al. Mudge, Rose, et al.	12/9/77 6/14/72 5/27/83 1/31/86 10/2/87
Embassy of Japan	Charles von Loewenfeldt, Jr. H. William Tanaka Philip Van Slyck, Inc. Hogan & Hartson Mike Masaoka Assoc.	9/16/71 4/24/56 5/4/71 5/7/71 1/26/84

JAPANESE ORGANIZATION	AMERICAN AGENT	DATE FIRST REGISTERED
Embassy of Japan (cont'd)	Dechert, Price & Rhoads	4/27/77
	Walter H. Evans III	5/15/79
	Saunders & Co.	3/8/83
	Washington Resources & Strategy	6/8/87
	Law Offices of Paul H. Delaney, Jr.	10/25/88
	North American Precis Syndicate	12/20/89
Export-Import Bank of Japan	Dechert, Price & Rhoads	4/27/77
Fanuc, Ltd.	Global U.S.A., Inc.	6/29/83
The Fasteners Inst. of Japan	H. William Tanaka	11/15/89
Federation of Japan Salmon Fisheries	Jay Donald Hastings	5/24/82
Federation of Japan Tuna Fisheries	Jay Donald Hastings	9/14/83
Fuji Electric Co., Ltd.	Myron H. Nordquist	1/5/90
	Kelley, Drye & Warren	11/3/88
Fuji Heavy Industries, Ltd.	Willkie, Farr & Gallagher	7/24/86
	Piper Pacific Intl.	10/26/89
Fujitsu America, Inc.	Akin, Gump, Strauss, et al.	8/7/87
	Victor Atiyeh & Co.	4/22/88
Fujitsu, Ltd.	Akin, Gump, Strauss, et al.	4/17/86
	Michael Solomon Assoc.	10/2/87
	Morrison & Foerster	8/23/89
Fujitsu Microelectronics	Ball, Janik & Novack	3/28/89
	Akin, Gump, Strauss, et al.	4/17/86
Government of Japan	Japan Economic Inst. of America	1/25/56
	Wilbur F. Monroe Assoc.	5/4/78
	Orrick, Herrington & Sutcliffe	6/15/89
Guam Oranao Development Co., Ltd.	Gerard F. Schiappa	9/1/89
Hitachi America, Ltd.	Jack H. McDonald Co.	9/29/87
	Powell, Goldstein, Frazer, et al.	9/25/87
Hitachi, Ltd.	Powell, Goldstein, Frazer, et al.	10/24/85
	Hill & Knowlton, Inc.	3/30/87
	Global U.S.A., Inc.	9/5/85
Hitachi Research Inst.	Hill & Knowlton, Inc.	5/31/89
Hitachi Sales Corp. of America	Powell, Goldstein, Frazer, et al.	4/10/87
	Jack H. McDonald Co.	4/10/87
Hokuten Trawlers Assn.	Jay Donald Hastings	5/24/82
	Garvey, Schubert & Barer	8/9/79
The Industrial Bank of Japan	Wilbur F. Morse Assoc.	9/28/79

JAPANESE ORGANIZATION	AMERICAN AGENT	DATE FIRST REGISTERED
Intl. Public Relations Co., Ltd.	TKC International Inc.	9/10/81
	Civic Service, Inc.	6/28/82
Intl. Telecom Japan, Inc.	Debevoise & Plimpton	11/5/87
Japan Aero Engines Corp./Japan Aircraft Development	Global U.S.A., Inc.	9/13/84
Japan Air Lines	Law Offices of John P. Sears	5/9/84
	West Glen Communications	11/23/88
	Charles von Loewenfeldt, Inc.	1/5/54
Japan Auto Parts Industries Assn.	Robinson, Lake, et al.	6/12/87
Japan Automobile Mfrs. Assn.	H. William Tanaka	6/9/77
	Law Offices of John P. Sears	5/9/84
	Jellinek, Schwartz, et al.	2/23/90
Japan Automobile Tire Mfrs. Assn.	H. William Tanaka	6/13/84
Japan Bearing Industrial Assn.	H. William Tanaka	11/12/81
Japan Deep Sea Trawlers Assn.	Jay Donald Hastings	5/24/82
	Garvey, Schubert, et al.	8/9/79
Japan Economic Inst.	Donald G. Lerch, Jr., & Co.	10/22/70
Japan Electronic Industry Development Assn.	Graham & James	1/12/90
Japan Export Metal Flatware Industry Assn.	H. William Tanaka	10/8/81
Japan External Trade Organization (JETRO)	The International Marketing Center, Ltd.	6/15/76
	Dentsu Burson-Marsteller	8/11/86
	The Klein Partnership	8/27/86
	Michael Solomon Assoc.	1/6/87
	Productions by Hirahara	3/8/88
	TransPacific Communications Research Co.	8/26/88
	Hill & Knowlton, Inc.	5/31/89
Japan Fair Trade Center	Arnold & Porter	9/11/87
Japan Federation of Construction Contractors	Global U.S.A., Inc.	7/10/87
Japan Fisheries Assn.	Jay Donald Hastings	11/16/78
	Garvey, Schubert, et al.	2/22/82
	Richard A. Frank Law Offices	11/30/87
	Bernhagen & Assoc.	2/6/90
Japan Foundation	Modern Talking Pictures Service, Inc.	7/30/81
	Charles von Loewenfeldt, Inc.	2/10/87

JAPANESE ORGANIZATION	AMERICAN AGENT	DATE FIRST REGISTERED
Japan Galvanized Iron Sheet Exporters' Assn.	Willkie, Farr & Gallagher	12/26/85
Japan Inst. for Social & Economic Affairs	Charles von Loewenfeldt, Inc.	11/14/79
Japan Iron & Steel Exporters' Assn.	Charles E. Butler & Assoc. Willkie, Farr & Gallagher Steptoe & Johnson	12/29/83 12/26/85 4/19/89
Japan Lumber Importers' Assn.	Mudge, Rose, et al.	2/1/85
Japan Machine Tool Builders Assn.	Anderson, Hibey, et al.	7/14/83
Japan Machinery Exporters' Assn.	Anderson, Hibey, et al.	7/14/83
Japan Metal Forming Machine Builders Assn.	Anderson, Hibey, et al.	7/14/83
Japan Pottery Exporters' Assn.	H. William Tanaka	8/3/81
Japan Society of Industrial Machinery Manufacturers	Paul A. London & Assoc.	4/5/88
The Japan Steel Works, Ltd.	Popham, Haik, et al.	4/28/89
Japan Telescopes Mfrs. Assn.	Mike Masaoka Assoc.	11/3/83
Japan Tobacco, Inc.	Daniel J. Edelman, Inc.	8/7/86
Japan Trade Center	H. William Tanaka Mike Masaoka Assoc. TKC International, Inc.	8/9/66 6/19/74 1/15/79
Japan Tuna Fisheries Co-op	Anderson & Pendleton, C.A.	6/13/86
Japan Whaling Assn.	Tele-Press Associates, Inc.	11/14/79
Japan Wire Products Exporters Assn.	Willkie, Farr & Gallagher	12/26/85
Japanese Information Service of the Japanese Consulate	Derus Media Service, Inc.	7/14/87
Japanese National Tourist Org.	Modern Talking Pictures Service	2/11/82
Japanese Tanner Crab Assn.	Jay Donald Hastings	5/24/82
Kinki Nippon Tourist Co.	Intermarketing, Inc.	3/15/89
Koito Manufacturing Co.	Paul, Hastings, et al. Kekst & Co.	7/7/89 2/21/90
Komatsu Ltd.	Global U.S.A., Inc. Arnold & Porter Ogilvy & Mather, et al. APCO Assoc.	7/22/83 2/12/90 2/13/90 2/14/90

JAPANESE ORGANIZATION	AMERICAN AGENT	DATE FIRST REGISTERED
Koyo Corp. of U.S.A.	Powell, Goldstein, Frazer, et al.	6/28/89
Koyo Seiko Co., Ltd.	Powell, Goldstein, Frazer, et al.	6/28/89
Kyocera Corp.	Global U.S.A., Inc.	3/24/84
Marubeni America Corp.	Hill & Knowlton, Inc.	2/24/88
Matsushita Electric Industrial Co.	Weil, Gotshal & Manges	8/4/86
Mazak Corp.	Global U.S.A., Inc.	7/11/83
Mitsubishi Electric Corp.	Robinson, Lake, et al.	12/1/86
Mitsubishi Electric Corp. through Universal Public	Saunders & Co.	7/28/87
Mitsubishi Electronics America Inc.	Thompson & Co.	2/25/88
Mitsubishi Motors Corp.	Ruder Finn	10/5/87
Mitsubishi Trust & Banking	Civic Service, Inc.	3/18/88
Murata Machinery, Ltd.	Global U.S.A., Inc.	1/24/90
Nakajima All Co., Ltd.	Patton, Boggs & Blow	9/26/86
NEC Corp.	Hill & Knowlton, Inc. Manatt, Phelps, et al. Paul, Weiss, Rifkind	5/20/87 4/10/87 5/10/85
New Hampshire Ball Bearings	Hill & Knowlton, Inc.	9/13/88
NHK	Anderson, Hibey, et al.	9/5/89
Nihon Agency, Inc.	Intermarketing, Inc.	11/20/87
Nintendo of America, Inc.	Hill & Knowlton, Inc.	5/30/89
Nippon Cargo Airlines Co.	Williams & Jensen, P.C.	10/24/85
Nippon Steel Corp.	Steptoe & Johnson	3/28/89
Nippon Telegraph and Telephone Public Corp. (NTT)	Civic Service, Inc.	6/15/83
Nippon Yusen Kaisha (NYK)	Pettit & Martin	4/17/86
Nissan Aerospace Division/Nissan Motor Co., Ltd.	International Technology & Trade Assoc., Inc.	2/21/90
Nissan Motor Co., Ltd.	Manchester Assoc., Ltd.	8/9/79
Nissho Iwai American Corp.	William E. Colby	5/12/88

JAPANESE ORGANIZATION	AMERICAN AGENT	DATE FIRST REGISTERED
Nissho-Iwai Co., Ltd.	Cove, Cooper & Lewis, Inc.	11/6/79
NKB Co. Inc.	Harry A. Savage	4/17/89
Nomura Research Inst.	Wilbur F. Monroe Assoc.	5/8/84
North Pacific Longline Assn.	Paul D. Kelly	4/20/88
North Pacific Longline Gillnet Assn.	Jay Donald Hastings	5/24/82
Ohbayashi Corp.	Graham & James Saunders & Co.	5/3/89 1/13/88
PR Service Co., Ltd.	Civic Service, Inc.	5/2/88
Research Development Corp. of Japan	International Science & Technology Assoc.	6/22/87
Ricoh Electronics, Inc.	Fleishman-Hillard, Inc.	9/1/88
Sanwa Bank, Ltd.	Civic Service, Inc. Hill & Knowlton, Inc.	7/25/88 3/31/88
Seibulite International, Inc.	Hill & Knowlton, Inc.	9/13/88
Seiko-Epson Corp.	Saunders & Co. Victor Atiyeh & Co.	6/14/89 4/22/88
Shintaro Ishihara	Fleishman-Hillard, Inc.	1/12/90
Sony Corp.	Arent, Fox, et al. Debevoise & Plimpton	7/14/86 10/5/83
Sumitomo Corp.	Stafford, Burke, et al.	10/25/84
Suzuki of America Automotive Corp.	Thompson & Co.	2/25/88
Toa Nenryo Kogyo Kabushiki Kaisha	First Associates, Inc.	2/25/87
Tohoku Electric Power Co.	Washington Policy & Analysis Michael Solomon Assoc.	7/3/89 8/11/89
Tokyo Agency, Inc.	Fleishman-Hillard, Inc.	4/5/87
Tokyo Electric Co.	Kelley, Drye & Warren	7/24/87
Toshiba Corp.	Mudge, Rose, et al.	4/14/87
Toyo Kogyo, Ltd.	Hill & Knowlton, Inc.	2/16/87
Toyo Menka Kaisha, Ltd.	Sedam & Shearer, P.C.	10/14/87
Toyota Motor Corp.	Hill & Knowlton, Inc. Arent, Fox, et al.	5/31/89 5/4/83

Appendix B

JAPANESE ORGANIZATION	AMERICAN AGENT	DATE FIRST REGISTERED
Toyota Motor Corporate Services of North America	Schnader, Harrison, et al.	11/14/89
World Vision Travel Co.	Hori & Bunker	9/7/89
Yamaha Motor Co.	Willkie, Farr & Gallagher	4/28/86

NOTES

FOREWORD

PAGE   KEY WORDS

xii   **When Keynes:** Robert Skidelsky, *John Maynard Keynes: Hopes Be-*
        trayed, 1883–1920 (Viking Press, 1986), p. 379.

INTRODUCTION

xv   **Own \$285 billion:** *Survey of Current Business*, U.S. Department of
        Commerce, Bureau of Economic Analysis, June 1989, Table 1.
        Control more than \$329 billion: "Japanese Investment in the U.S.,"
        U.S. Department of State, Center for the Study of Foreign Affairs,
        October 1989, p. 6.

xvi   **Control more than 25 percent of California's:** "New Wave in Califor-
        nia," Washington *Post*, November 12, 1989.
        Possess more real estate holdings: *Survey of Current Business*, U.S.
        Department of Commerce, Bureau of Economic Analysis, June 1989,
        Table 4.
        Routinely purchase: "Mitsui Real Estate Chairman: Investment in U.S.
        Properties Will Continue to Soar," *Japan Economic Journal*, January
        13, 1990, p. 18.
        Trade up to 25 percent: "We Can't Do Without Their Money," *USA*
        Today, January 9, 1990.
        Nearly 20 percent of the semiconductors: Unpublished data, Instat
        Data Services (Arizona), March 1990.
        More than 30 percent of the automobiles: "Cooperation, A Bone of
        Contention for Unions," Washington *Post*, May 20, 1990.

xvii   **While Britain, Japan:** Calculated from unpublished data of the U.S.
        Department of Justice: "Pending Foreign Principals," March 1990.
        Paul Krugman, the prominent: Paul Krugman, *The Age of Diminished*
        Expectations (The Washington Post Company, 1990), p. 69.

xviii   **The cost is more than:** Interview with Craig Smith, Corporate Philan-
        thropy Report, May 25, 1990.

CHAPTER ONE: JAPAN'S POLITICAL VICTORIES

3   **Fewer than 30 percent:** "Public Policy Aspects of the A. T. Kearney
        Study on U.S. Manufacturing Competitiveness," A. T. Kearney, Inc.,
        1987.
        By contrast, the top executives: Interviews with European and Japa-
        nese executives.

4   **Altogether, 161 countries:** *Report of the Attorney General to the Congress of the United States on the Administration of the Foreign Agents Registration Act of 1938, as amended, for the Calendar Year 1987* (U.S. Department of Justice, 1989).

       Japan's American political machine: Calculated from unpublished data of the U.S. Department of Justice: "Pending Foreign Principals: Japan," March 1990.

5   **As von Raab notes:** Interview, March 1989.

8   **"We were outraged":** Confidential interview, December 1989.

9   **DuBois provided:** "CIA Confirms Toshiba Scandal," Statement of Congressman Duncan Hunter, March 9, 1988.

10   **Congress received a letter:** Letter from George P. Shultz, C. William Verity, and William H. Taft IV to the Hon. William Proxmire, March 29, 1988.

       Public records reveal: Supplemental Statements Pursuant to Section 2 of the Foreign Agents Registration Act of 1938, as amended, for Mudge, Rose, Guthrie, Alexander & Ferdon, Registration Number 3200, March 26, 1990, September 28, 1989, March 20, 1989, October 11, 1988, April 18, 1988, and October 9, 1987; Supplemental Statements Pursuant to Section 2 of the Foreign Agents Registration Act of 1938, as amended, for Dickstein, Shapiro & Morin, Registration Number 3028, January 6, 1989, July 20, 1988, January 11, 1988, and July 10, 1987.

11   **"Grave political problems":** Letter from Shintaro Abe, Masayoshi Ito, Michio Watanabe, et al., to President Ronald Reagan, September 29, 1988.

12   **American producers:** "How Japanese Growers Bested U.S. Rice Growers," *SAM TRADE*, November 1988, pp. 1–4.

       In fact, the heads of: Ibid., p. 2; letter from Ray Selbe, President, Colorado Wheat Administrative Committee, to Ambassador Clayton Yeutter, October 19, 1988; and letter from Willard Pedersen, Chairman, North Dakota Wheat Commission, to Ambassador Clayton Yeutter, October 20, 1988.

       To add insult to injury: "Rice Display Is Removed," *New York Times*, March 17, 1990.

       Japan's exclusionary practices: "Close Construction Ties Likely to Thwart U.S.," *Japan Economic Journal*, January 23, 1988, p. 4.

13   **Japan promised:** "Construction Contracts Still Elude U.S. Builders," *Japan Times*, April 21, 1990.

CHAPTER TWO: AMERICA THE VULNERABLE

16   **The lawyer-lobbyist:** Confidential interview, July 1989.

17   **"Although very few lawyers":** Confidential interview, January 1989.

       The same lawyer notes: Ibid.

The Washington attorney observes: Ibid.

18 **As Richard Harwood:** Richard Harwood, "A Shilling from the King," Washington *Post*, February 22, 1989.

Abbell's new job: Michael Isikoff, "Cartel Defendants' D.C. Lawyer: Ex-Prosecutor Angers Former Justice Dept. Colleagues," Washington *Post*, October 2, 1989.

19 **A 1986 General Accounting Office:** "Foreign Representation: Former High-Level Federal Officials Representing Foreign Interests," United States General Accounting Office, July 1986.

20 **Bush's response:** Art Pine, "Bush Hits Fears of Foreign Investing," Los Angeles *Times*, February 22, 1989.

Ishihara advocates: Akio Morita and Shintaro Ishihara, *The Japan That Can Say "No": The New United States–Japan Relations Card* (Kobunsha/Kappa-Holmes, 1989). The quote is based on a translation of this book published in the *Congressional Record*, November 14, 1989, p. E 3783. The author bought a Japanese-language version of this book to protect Mr. Morita's and Mr. Ishihara's intellectual property rights.

21 **In 1986, Japan's government:** Side letter, Office of the U.S. Trade Representative, Arrangement Between the Government of Japan and the Government of the United States Concerning Trade (Washington, D.C., September 1986).

Alan Wolff, counsel for: Interview, February 1989.

Senator Pete Wilson said: "Wilson Threatens New Sanctions Against Japan Unless Artificial Chip Shortage Removed and Blackmail Tactics Stop," Press Release, March 21, 1988.

In March 1988, Wilson announced: Ibid.

22 **Mesa officials say:** Interview with T. Boone Pickens, November 1989, and an internal memorandum from W. Mark Womble to Sidney L. Tassin, "Union Bank of California ('UBC')," May 4, 1989.

Economist David Hale: Interview, February 1990.

According to the *Far Eastern:* "Banking Practices," *Far Eastern Economic Review*, October 26, 1989, p. 8.

23 **A 1988 American Enterprise:** Kanji Nishio, cited in Kenneth B. Pyle, "The Burden of Japanese History," in John H. Makin and Donald C. Hellman, eds., *Sharing World Leadership? A New Era for America and Japan* (American Enterprise Institute, 1989), pp. 61–62.

24 **In 1989, Herbert Stein:** Herbert Stein, "Don't Worry about the Trade Deficit," *Wall Street Journal*, May 16, 1989.

In 1990, Stein: Herbert Stein, "Who's Number One? Who Cares?" *Wall Street Journal*, March 1, 1990.

Only now is a new: Marc Levinson, "Is Strategic Trade Fair Trade?" *Across the Board*, June 1988, p. 8.

MIT's Paul Krugman: Paul R. Krugman, "Is Free Trade Passé?" *Economic Perspectives*, Fall 1987, p. 132.

25   **Muraoka's maneuver:** "Japan May Ask for Probe of U.S.," *Washington Times*, June 5, 1989.

26   **Clyde Prestowitz, formerly:** Clyde V. Prestowitz, Jr., *Trading Places* (Basic Books, 1988), p. 256.
      As it turns out, NTT: Ibid.

27   **"What we lobbyists want":** Confidential interview, October 1989.

CHAPTER THREE: JAPAN'S POLITICAL MIND-SET

28   **Hayasaka recalls:** Interview with Shigezo Hayasaka, Washington, D.C., November 2, 1989.
      The Keidanren alone: "Japan's $3 Billion Election," *The Economist*, February 3, 1990, p. 31.

29   **In the 1990 elections:** Steven R. Weisman, "Despite Year of Scandal, 'Money Politics' Seems As Strong As Ever in Japan," *New York Times*, January 29, 1990.
      Official reports from: Ibid.
      By contrast, in the United States: Calculated from "FEC Final Report on 1988 Congressional Campaigns Shows $459 Million Spent," October 31, 1989; "FEC Releases Final Report on 1988 Presidential Primary Campaigns," August 25, 1989; and unpublished data, May 2, 1990, for 1987–88 election cycle spending by Michael S. Dukakis and George Bush; Federal Election Commission, Washington, D.C.
      In the 1990 election, the LDP: Weisman, "Despite Year of Scandal."

30   **The Recruit affair:** Karel van Wolferen, *The Enigma of Japanese Power* (Alfred A. Knopf, 1989); James Fallows, *More Like Us* (Houghton Mifflin, 1989); Clyde Prestowitz, *Trading Places*; and Chalmers Johnson, *MITI and the Japanese Miracle* (Stanford University Press, 1982).
      Recruit is unusual: Fred Hiatt and Margaret Shapiro, "Will Takeshita's Resignation Be Enough?" Washington *Post*, National Weekly Edition, May 1–7, 1989.

31   **Consider the network:** Mark G. Chalpin, "Hostile Takeover—Japanese Style," *The Construction Lawyer*, January 1989.
      More than 88 percent: Van Wolferen, *The Enigma of Japanese Power*, p. 111.

32   **What gives the *zoku-giin*:** Hayasaka interview, November 1989.

33   **For example, the Japanese:** Keiko Hitotsuishi, "The Art of Politics: The Japanese Way" (unpublished), Tokyo, 1990.
      Business buys favors: Charles Smith, "More Money Politics: How the LDP Amassed a Huge War Chest for Elections," *Far Eastern Economic Review*, February 22, 1990.
      That very same evening: Chalpin, "Hostile Takeover—Japanese Style," p. 4.
      As one Japanese politician: Hayasaka interview, November 1989.

Van Wolferen reports: Van Wolferen, *The Enigma of Japanese Power*, p. 120.

Two high officials: Margaret Shapiro, "Scandal Escalates in Japan," Washington *Post*, March 9, 1989.

The line between gifts: "Nakasone Apology to Japan," *The Times* (London), May 26, 1989, and Fred Hiatt, "2 Top Legislators Indicted in Japan," Washington *Post*, May 23, 1989.

34 **Japanese prosecutors report:** Shapiro, "Scandal Escalates in Japan."

One prominent Japanese: Hayasaka interview, November 1989.

35 **"Although there is":** Van Wolferen, *The Enigma of Japanese Power*, p. 405.

36 **According to Meyer:** Herbert E. Meyer, *Real-World Intelligence* (Weidenfeld and Nicolson, 1987), p. 58.

37 **Bob Woodward:** Bob Woodward, *Veil: The Secret Wars of the CIA 1981–1987* (Simon & Schuster, 1987), pp. 368–69.

The real purpose: Confidential interview, November 1988.

In 1988, during the: Interview with Richard Gephardt, April 1989.

38 **One week prior:** Confidential interview, January 1989.

Japanese interests have: *Washington Representatives 1989* (Columbia Books, 1989), pp. 719–20.

39 **One former U.S. trade:** Confidential interview, December 1989.

40 **Clyde Prestowitz reports:** Interview with Clyde Prestowitz, February 1990.

The story of Japan's: Confidential interview, October 1989.

As one senior congressional: Confidential interview, November 1989.

The construction executive: Confidential interview, October 1989.

Indeed, in a remarkable outburst: Carla Rapoport, "Japan Says U.S. Trade Bill Is Racist and Protectionist," *Financial Times*, April 23, 1988.

41 **Former Tanaka aide:** Interview with Shigezo Hayasaka, Tokyo, April 1989.

42 **So Yasu called Ron:** Clyde H. Farnsworth, "U.S. Heeded Nakasone Plea in Air-Cargo Dispute," *New York Times*, May 8, 1986.

In April 1986: Ibid.

43 **In the Nixon Administration:** Henry Kissinger, *White House Years* (Little, Brown, 1979), p. 332.

In the Carter Administration: Letter from Robert S. Strauss, U.S. Special Representative for Trade Negotiations, to Fumihiko Togo, Ambassador Extraordinary and Plenipotentiary of Japan, May 20, 1977; confidential minutes, "Meeting of 8 June 1979 on Understandings in the Area of Subsidies and Countervailing Measures" (subsequently known as "The Hufbauer Agreement").

In the Reagan Administration: Office of the U.S. Trade Representative, "Arrangement Between the Government of Japan and the Government of the United States Concerning Trade," September 1986; Office of the U.S. Trade Representative, "Record of Understanding

Between the United States and Singapore at Bilateral Consultations for the GSP General Review on 22nd–23rd September 1986" (unpublished); and confidential letter from Clayton Yeutter, U.S. Trade Representative, to the Honorable Kyung-Won Kim, Ambassador of the Republic of Korea, August 28, 1986.

43   **In 1978, the Japanese:** Interview with William C. Triplett II, Senior Professional Staff Member, United States Senate Foreign Relations Committee, April 29, 1990.
In 1986, foreigners: Ibid.
That same year: Clyde Haberman, "The Presumed Uniqueness of Japan," *New York Times Magazine*, August 28, 1988.
In 1987, American garbage: "Adachi Ward to Ban Use of Disposers Which Can Flush Garbage Down Drain," *Yomiuri*, October 15, 1987.
Also that year, American beef: Stuart Auerbach, "Japanese Aide Cites Health, Religious Reasons for Slackening U.S. Beef Imports," *Washington Post*, December 18, 1987.

44   **The Japanese official:** Interview with Clyde Prestowitz, July 1989.
That same summer: Telephone interview with Alan Webber, July 1989.

45   **In 1987 alone:** *Report of the Attorney General to the Congress of the United States on the Administration of the Foreign Agents Registration Act of 1938, as amended, for the Calendar Year 1987* (U.S. Department of Justice, 1989).

CHAPTER FOUR: WASHINGTON'S REVOLVING DOOR

49   **The British writer:** Robert Byron, *The Road to Oxiana* (Oxford University Press, 1937), p. ix.

50   **Yet an informal Department:** Confidential interview, March 1988.
These ex-officials often provide: Stuart Auerbach, "U.S. to Protest Taping of Trade Talks in Seoul," *Washington Post*, September 15, 1989.

51   **Edmund Muskie:** Short-Form Registration Statements, Under the Foreign Agents Registration Act of 1938, as amended, for Edmund S. Muskie, Registration Number 3490, February 15, 1989, and June 15, 1983.
Another former Secretary of State: Jeff Gerth and Sarah Bartlett, "Kissinger and Friends and Revolving Doors," *New York Times*, April 30, 1989; Walter Pincus, "Kissinger Says He Had No Role in China Mission," *Washington Post*, December 14, 1989; and Elaine Sciolino, "Committee Backs State Depart. Pick," *New York Times*, March 17, 1989.
For whatever reason: Elaine Sciolino, "Eagleburger Won't Disclose Kissinger's Client List," *New York Times*, November 12, 1989.

52   **In May 1988:** John J. Fialka, "Former Defense Official Creates Firm to Lobby in Washington for Turkey," *Wall Street Journal*, February

19, 1989; Greg Rushford and Judy Sarasohn, "Talking Turkey," *Legal Times*, February 20, 1989.

Admiral Daniel Murphy: "Foreign Representation: Former High-Level Federal Officials Representing Foreign Interests," United States General Accounting Office, July 1986, Appendix IV, pp. 22–27.

Former Air Force generals: Ibid.

One of the best-connected: Gene Marlowe, "U.S. Generals Find New Careers at Foreign Firms," Richmond *Times-Dispatch*, September 19, 1989.

Between 1973 and 1990: Compiled from Short-Form Registration Statements, Under the Foreign Agents Registration Act of 1938, as amended, U.S. Department of Justice, January 1973 to April 1990, and *Washington Representatives*.

53 **In 1989, the top three:** (Carla Hills) Exhibit B to Registration Statement, Under the Foreign Agents Registration Act of 1938, as amended, U.S. Department of Justice, May 10, 1985. Eleanor Kerlow, "Giant Trade Lumber Case Ends in Win for Dewey, Ballantine," *Legal Times*, January 19, 1987. (S. Linn Williams) Form DJ-305, Short-Form Registration Statement, Under the Foreign Agents Registration Act of 1938, as amended, March 10, 1975. (Julius Katz, as chairman of the Government Research Corporation) Registration Statement Pursuant to Section 2 of the Foreign Agents Registration Act of 1938, as amended, for the Government Research Corporation, August 18, 1988; and Pamela Brogan, "Revolving Door Spins at USTR," *Legal Times*, April 10, 1989.

54 **They proposed a reorganization:** Separate and confidential interviews with three USTR officials: January 1988, August 1988, October 1989.

One former employee: Confidential interview, August 1988.

He told the Baltimore *Sun*: Mark Matthews, "Access in Washington: A Case Study," Baltimore *Sun*, May 19, 1986.

By contrast, Lake spoke: Stuart Auerbach, "Foreigners Hiring Reagan's Ex-Aides; Clients Pay Millions for Efforts to Block Administration Policies," Washington *Post*, February 16, 1986.

One former USTR official: Confidential interview, October 1989.

55 **Minchew's career:** *United States of America* v. *Daniel Minchew*, Criminal No. 79-00363, U.S. District Court, District of Columbia, Filed July 30, 1979; Waiver of Indictment, signed by Daniel Minchew, July 30, 1979; Judgment and Probation/Commitment Order, United States District Court for District of Columbia, *United States of America* v. *Daniel Minchew*, October 10, 1979; and Timothy S. Robinson, "Talmadge Ex-Aide Minchew Sentenced to Four Months on Fake Voucher Count," Washington *Post*, October 11, 1979.

Between 1973 and 1990: First Amended Short-Form Registration Statement, Under the Foreign Agents Registration Act of 1938, as amended, for William R. Alberger, Registration Number 3047, April

18, 1983; (Italo Ablondi) Supplemental Statement Pursuant to Section 2 of the Foreign Agents Registration Act of 1938, as amended, for Ablondi & Foster, p.c., Registration Number 3235, August 4, 1989; Short-Form Registration Statement, Under the Foreign Agents Registration Act of 1938, as amended, for Paula Stern, Registration Number 3873, February 10, 1989; (Michael J. Calhoun) *Washington Representatives 1985* (Columbia Books, 1985), pp. 57, 202, and *Washington Representatives 1986* (Columbia Books, 1986), pp. 58, 114.

56 **Goldfield left office:** Supplemental Statement Pursuant to Section 2 of the Foreign Agents Registration Act of 1938, as amended, for Swidler & Berlin, Chartered, Registration Number 4079, August 5, 1988.

57 **Later, Watkins actually:** Letter from Robert E. Watkins to foreign automakers proposing the creation of an organization named American Manufacturers Committed to Investment in the United States, September 23, 1987.

As Clyde Prestowitz notes: *Trading Places*, p. 267.

In the spring of 1989: "List Reveals Possible FTA Panelists to Review Dumping, Subsidies Cases," *Inside U.S. Trade*, January 6, 1989, p. 11, and *Washington Representatives 1989*.

58 **While some are competent:** Raymond Vernon, "Can the U.S. Negotiate for Trade Equality?" *Harvard Business Review*, May–June 1989, p. 336.

A less charitable Washington: Confidential interview, February 1989.

59 **One former Japanese Embassy:** Confidential interview, July 1989.

Journalist James Fallows: James Fallows, "The Japan Handlers," *Atlantic Monthly*, August 1989, pp. 18–19.

60 **Longtime Washington attorney:** Interview with Harry McPherson, January 1989.

62 **He says that he:** Confidential interview, January 1989.

According to a knowledgeable USTR: Confidential interview, March 1990.

R. Michael Gadbaw: Quoted in Stuart Auerbach, "Fujitsu Hiring from State Spurs Debate on Lobbying," Washington *Post*, January 17, 1990.

CHAPTER FIVE: JAPAN BUYS WASHINGTON

65 **Historian Howard Schonberger:** Howard Schonberger, "The Japan Lobby in American Diplomacy, 1947–1952," *Pacific Historical Review*, Vol. 46, No. 3, August 1977, pp. 327–59.

66 **Using Kern as the voice:** John Roberts, "The Rebirth of Japan's Zaibatsu: Revealing the political machinations and secret powers of Harry Kern, a little known American newsman, who helped Japan's major trading houses survive post-war dissolution," *Insight*, July 1978.

67 **It is a relationship:** Kenneth Pyle, "The Burden of Japanese History," p. 59.

In his study of that period: John G. Roberts, "The 'Japan Crowd' and the Zaibatsu Restoration," *The Japan Interpreter*, Vol. 12, Nos. 3–4, Summer 1979.

69   **According to *The Wall Street Journal*:** Jonathan Kwitny, "Richard V. Allen Used White House Prestige Freely in Nixon Years," *Wall Street Journal*, October 28, 1980, and a telephone interview with David Fleming, November 1989.

70   **Among his prizes:** Short-Form Registration Statement, Under the Foreign Agents Registration Act of 1938, as amended, for Harald B. Malmgren (doing business as Malmgren, Inc.), Registration Number 2773, April 21, 1977.

In 1979, he landed: "Agreement: The Commission of the European Communities (EC) retains herewith the services of Harald B. Malmgren and Matthew J. Marks (M and M) for consultation with regard to U.S. implementation of the accords reached in the Multilateral Trade Negotiations (MTN), with special reference to the drafting of Legislation to give effect thereto," signed by Harald B. Malmgren and Matthew J. Marks on February 22, 1979, and Roy Denman for the Commission of the European Communities on August 2, 1979; Harald B. Malmgren, Exhibit B to Registration Statement, Under the Foreign Agents Registration Act of 1938, as amended, January 30, 1979.

That same year, Malmgren signed: Registration Number 2854, Malmgren, Inc., Supplemental Statement Pursuant to Section 2 of the Foreign Agents Registration Act of 1938, as amended, February 2, 1979, and the Agreement between International Public Relations Co., Ltd., and Malmgren, Inc., December 28, 1978.

71   **The Japanese government also:** Registration Number 2854, Malmgren, Inc., Supplemental Statement Pursuant to Section 2 of the Foreign Agents Registration Act of 1938, as amended, February 2, 1979, and Malmgren, Inc., Exhibit B to Registration Statement, Under the Foreign Agents Registration Act of 1938, as amended, January 29, 1979.

One former trade official: Confidential interview, October 1989.

David Osborne wrote: David Osborne, "Japan's Secret Agents," *The New Republic*, October 1, 1984.

This stream became a flood: "Foreign Representation: Former High-Level Federal Officials Representing Foreign Interests," Appendix IV, United States General Accounting Office, July 1986.

72   **One aide says:** Confidential interview, July 1989.

73   **Later, McElheny sent:** Letter from Richard L. McElheny, Senior Vice President, Gray and Company, to the Honorable Frank Horton, October 17, 1985.

The former official says: Confidential interview, July 1989.

74   **As a starting point:** *Role of the Congressional Staff in the U.S. Decision Making Process* (National Institute for Research Advancement, Tokyo), June 1984.

75 **A high-ranking Senate aide:** Confidential interview, November 1988.
Authors Kazutami Yamazaki and Masao Kanasashi: "Verification of
Japanese and U.S. Politics—Part I: Discovering U.S. Congress," a
thirteen-part series, *Nihon Keizai Shimbun*, January 1988.
One former senior congressional aide: Interview with Nancy A. Lea-
mond, January 1989.

CHAPTER SIX: JAPAN TAKES TELEVISION

78 **Japan's assault:** Brief of Appellants, Zenith Radio Corporation and
National Union Electric Corporation, *In Re: Japanese Electronic Products Antitrust Litigation*, D.C. Civ. No. 0000189 (3d Cir. 1981), pp.
35–36.
79 **The Stabilization Council:** Ibid.
80 **To administer its price fixing:** Ibid.
81 **In 1976, only 500:** Committee on Energy and Commerce, U.S. House
of Representatives, *Unfair Foreign Trade Practices: Criminal Components of America's Trade Problem*, April 1985, pp. 94–97.
82 **One of Matsushita's:** *Japanese Electronic Products Antitrust Litigation*,
p. 34.
84 **Treasury chose a third:** Confidential interview, March 1989.
One former U.S. trade negotiator: Ibid.
Kissinger himself recalls: Henry Kissinger, *White House Years*,
p. 329.
85 **In early 1972, Japan proposed:** "Japan Proposes Meeting with U.S.
on Anti-Dumping," *Japan Economic Journal*, January 25, 1972.
As is often the case: "Japan-U.S. Trade Issues Head for Another Flare-
Up," *Japan Economic Journal*, May 23, 1972.
86 **To prepare for the summit:** "Trade Talks with U.S. at Hakone End:
Japan Makes Concessions on Computers and Retail Chain," *Japan
Economic Journal*, August 1, 1972.
Many lawyers and former executives: Confidential interviews, Janu-
ary–March 1989.
87 **In 1977, five cartel members:** Short-Form Registration Statement,
Under the Foreign Agents Registration Act of 1938, as amended, for
Harald B. Malmgren (doing business as Malmgren, Inc.), Registration
Number 2773, April 21, 1977.
88 **As the *Japan Economic Journal*:** Stephen Bronte, "Japan Faces Need
to Intensify Lobbying If It Hopes to Check U.S. Protectionism," *Japan
Economic Journal*, June 10, 1980.
In a March 1977 *Newsweek*: Allan J. Mayer and Rich Thomas, "Hard
Times for Free Traders," *Newsweek*, March 14, 1977.
As part of the deal: Letter from Robert S. Strauss, U.S. Special Rep-
resentative for Trade Negotiations, to Fumihiko Togo, Ambassador
Extraordinary and Plenipotentiary of Japan, May 20, 1977.

89 **While still ITC chairman:** Agreement Between the Committee of Two Hundred Club Incorporated and Daniel Minchew, signed by Susumu Ogata (August 10, 1978) and Daniel Minchew (August 11, 1978), reprinted in *Investigation of Senator Herman E. Talmadge*, Proceedings of the United States Senate Select Committee on Ethics, Vol. 3, 1980, p. 771.

90 **Three days earlier:** Letter to Yoshio Kawahara, Minister (Commercial), Embassy of Japan, Washington, D.C., from Robert H. Mundheim, General Counsel of the Treasury, March 17, 1978.

91 **Nor did Treasury stop there:** "Meeting with Mr. Tanabe, 3:00 p.m., March 20, 1978," memorandum to the file from Jordan Luke.
   The meeting was held: "Meeting with Individuals & Companies Listed on Attached Sheet at 4:30 p.m., March 28, 1978," notes of the meeting at the United States Treasury between Mr. Tanabe of the Embassy of Japan, representatives of nine Japanese television manufacturers, Robert H. Mundheim, et al., March 28, 1978.

92 **Two weeks after:** "Assessment of Dumping Duties Against Televisions Imported from Japan—Problems Relating to Disclosure Conferences," memorandum to the Assistant Commissioner of Customs for Regulations and Rulings from Staff Attorneys of the Customs Service, Washington, D.C., April 18, 1978.
   In 1978, they tried: H.R. 8149 Conference Committee (Customs Procedural Reform Act), *Congressional Record*, S 9923, June 27, 1978, and Dan Morgan, "U.S. TV Makers See Threat in Customs Reform," Washington *Post*, June 25, 1978.

93 **The Japanese warned that:** "Note E-23," from the Embassy of Japan to the United States Department of State, April 13, 1978.
   The State Department sent: Letter to Michael Rodak, Jr., Clerk, Supreme Court of the United States, Washington, D.C., from Wade H. McCree, Jr., Solicitor General, April 14, 1978.
   The exchange between: Transcript of Oral Argument, in *Zenith Radio Corporation* v. *United States*, Sup. Ct. No. 77-539 (April 26, 1978).

94 **In a September 1978:** *Administration of the Antidumping Act of 1921*, Subcommittee on Trade, Committee on Ways and Means, United States Congress, September 21, 1978, p. 41.

95 **In a group memo:** " 'Estimated' Reduction of Dumping Duties Assessed Against Televisions Imported from Japan (T.D. 71-76); Adjustments to Foreign Market Value Due to Differences in Circumstances of Sale," memorandum to file from Staff Attorneys, Customs Service, March 2, 1979.
   In a March 19, 1979, letter: Letter to Robert Chasen, Commissioner, U.S. Customs Service, from Congressman Charles A. Vanik, March 19, 1979.

96 **On January 3, 1980, Hume:** "Japanese Televisions," memorandum to Robert C. Cassidy, Jr., from Ted Hume, January 3, 1980.

97 **On April 28, 1980, Homer Moyer:** "Settlement of the Dumping Case
on Japanese Television Imports," memorandum from Homer E.
Moyer, Jr., General Counsel of the Department of Commerce, to the
Secretary of Commerce, April 28, 1980.

Vanik agreed: Letter to John Greenwald, Deputy Assistant Secretary
for Import Administration, Department of Commerce, from Charles
A. Vanik, March 28, 1980.

98 **As one legal scholar notes:** Kevin C. Kennedy, *"Zenith Radio Corp.
v. United States:* The Nadir of the U.S. Trade Relief Process," *North
Carolina Journal of International Law & Commercial Regulation*, Vol.
13, No. 2, Spring 1988, p. 239.

In January 1979, Seymour Hersh: Seymour M. Hersh, "Inquiry Told
of Customs Fraud in Imports of Japanese TV Sets," *New York Times*,
January 24, 1979.

In March 1979, Alexander's, Inc.: United States District Court for the
Southern District of New York, File 79 Crim. No. 0194, March 29,
1979.

99 **The roster of unindicted co-conspirators:** "Government's Response to
the Court's Request for Further Information Concerning the Issue of
Single Versus Multiple Conspiracies: List of Un-Indicted Co-Conspirators," No. CR 80-183-RJK, *United States of America* v. *Sears, Roebuck
and Company, Incorporated*, United States District Court, Central
District of California, July 21, 1980.

Sears again petitioned: "Brief of Appellant United States," *United
States* v. *Sears, Roebuck and Company, Inc.*, United States Court of
Appeals for the Ninth Circuit, No. 88-5062.

100 **Among those items:** *Japanese Electronic Products Antitrust Litigation*,
pp. 1–4.

In late 1983, the Appeals Court: "Brief for the United States as Amicus
Curiae Supporting Petitioners," *Matsushita Electric Industrial Co.,
Ltd., et al., Petitioners* v. *Zenith Radio Corporation, et al.*, No. 83-
2004, Supreme Court of the United States, October Term, 1984.

102 **In a narrow 5–4 decision:** Al Kamen, "Supreme Court Won't Review
Dumping Case," Washington *Post*, April 28, 1987.

In 1989, New York Attorney General: "Panasonic to Refund Up to $16
Million in Nationwide Price Fixing Conspiracy," *News from Attorney
General Robert Abrams*, Department of Law, New York, January 18,
1989.

CHAPTER SEVEN: HIDDEN INTERESTS

109 **In July 1989, millionaire:** Michael Holmes and Scott Rothschild (Associated Press), "Chicken Processor's Checks Ruffle Feathers; Millionaire Hands Out $10,000 Gifts on Texas Senate Floor," Washington
Post, July 8, 1989.

111   **The American dealers:** Chuck Alston, "Imported-Car Dealers Show How to Leverage Funds," *Congressional Quarterly*, July 29, 1989.
MacKay lost: Interview with Buddy MacKay, February 6, 1989.
MacKay was referring to: Ibid.
While AUTOPAC has spent money: Calculated from "Committee Index of Candidates Supported/Opposed—(D) 1987–88: Auto Dealers and Drivers for Free Trade PAC," Federal Election Commission, February 9, 1989.

112   **In April 1989, Senators:** Kim Mattingly, " 'Independent' PAC Expenditures Blasted," *Roll Call*, April 17–23, 1989.
Tom Nemet, an auto-import dealer: Ibid.
A group called Friendship in Freedom: "A NATO Success: Arms Reductions," Advertisement by Friendship in Freedom, a German Initiative for European-American Relations, *New York Times*, June 20, 1989.

113   **As part of this arrangement:** Press release, Department of Justice, July 13, 1976, and memorandum, "To Recipients of Council Publications," from Noel Hemmendinger, Director, and Allen Taylor, Executive Secretary, United States–Japan Trade Council, September 10, 1976.

114   **In 1981,** *The New York Times* **revealed:** Clyde H. Farnsworth, "Japan Said to Infiltrate Consumer Group," *New York Times*, December 3, 1981.

115   **Although an officer of IEMCA says:** Unpublished notes from interview conducted by Mindy Kotler, Search Associates, September 9, 1988.

117   **In the end, the LSI official gave his speech:** Confidential correspondence, November 9, 1989.

118   **As one lobbyist associated with PTG:** Confidential interview, March 14, 1989.
The lobbyist notes: Ibid.

119   **In their place:** "S. 490," a position paper published by the Pro Trade Group, May 1987, and letter to members of Congress from the Pro Trade Group, March 16, 1987 (re-sent April 23, 1987).

120   **As the** *Japan Economic Journal* **pointed out:** Stephen Bronte, "Japan Faces Need to Intensify Lobbying If It Hopes to Check U.S. Protectionism."

CHAPTER EIGHT: THE POLITICIANS' POLITICIAN

121   **This attitude is reflected in an article:** Keitaro Hasegawa, "Japan's Business Community and the U.S. Presidential Election," *Chuo Koron*, August 1988 (translated from Japanese).
Investment banker Jeffrey Garten: Jeffrey E. Garten, "How Bonn, Tokyo Slyly Help Bush," *New York Times*, July 21, 1988.

122   **Through its American subsidiary:** "Anxiety Over Becoming Too Con-

spicuous," *Nihon Keizai Shimbun*, October 24, 1988 (translated from Japanese).

At the urging of Charles Manatt: Ibid.

Some party leaders lobby: James Lyons, "Party Time for Frank Fahrenkopf," *Legal Times*, August 22, 1988, and "Japan's Influence in U.S. Unrivaled," Jiji Press News Service, July 1, 1988.

When the Democratic National Committee held its election: *Washington Representatives 1988* and *Washington Representatives 1989.*

As Hedrick Smith observes: Hedrick Smith, *The Power Game: How Washington Works* (Random House, 1988), p. 122.

123 **Less than four months:** Clyde H. Farnsworth, "Washington Watch: New Lobbyists for Japanese," *New York Times*, May 11, 1981.

Stuart Spencer, for instance: Michael Isikoff, "Bush Aides' Lobbying Debated," Washington *Post*, September 9, 1988.

Former Ambassador to Costa Rica: David Hoffmann, "Noriega Drug Questions Ignored, Report Says," Washington *Post*, April 9, 1989.

Another politico: Isikoff, "Bush Aides' Lobbying Debated"; and Short-Form Registration Statement, Under the Foreign Agents Registration Act of 1938, as amended, for Joel West McLeary, Registration Number 3777, July 31, 1989.

124 **At the same time:** Agreement of Services and Fees: Memorandum to the Government of the Republic of the Philippines from the Sawyer/Miller Group, April 15, 1988, signed May 20, 1988, by Mark Malloch Brown for the Sawyer/Miller Group and Emmanuel N. Pelaez for the Philippine Government; Exhibit A to Registration Statement, Under the Foreign Agents Registration Act of 1938, as amended, for Sawyer/Miller Group, Registration Number 3777, to represent the Government of the Republic of Colombia, May 26, 1988; Agreement of Services and Fees: Memorandum to the Government of the Republic of Panama from the Sawyer/Miller Group, March 1, 1988, signed April 20, 1988, by representatives of the Government of Panama and the Sawyer/Miller Group.

George Bush's campaign press secretary: Short-Form Registration Statement, Under the Foreign Agents Registration Act of 1938, as amended, for Sheila B. Tate, Registration Number 2469, May 29, 1985, and Supplemental Statement Pursuant to Section 2 of the Foreign Agents Registration Act of 1938, as amended, for Burson-Marsteller, Registration Number 2469, November 25, 1985.

During the campaign, Richard Fairbanks: Short-Form Registration Statement, Under the Foreign Agents Registration Act of 1938, as amended, for Richard M. Fairbanks III, Registration Number 3763, and Supplemental Statement Pursuant to Section 2 of the Foreign Agents Registration Act of 1938, as amended, for Paul, Hastings, Janofsky & Walker, Registration Number 3763, December 16, 1987.

Another foreign agent in the Dukakis camp: Supplemental Statement

Pursuant to Section 2 of the Foreign Agents Registration Act of 1938, as amended, for Manatos & Manatos, Registration Number 3522, May 9, 1988.

125 **Sixteen more foreign clients:** Supplemental Statement Pursuant to Section 2 of the Foreign Agents Registration Act of 1938, as amended, for Black, Manafort & Stone, Inc., Registration Number 3415, May 6, 1985; Supplemental Statements Pursuant to Section 2 of the Foreign Agents Registration Act of 1938, as amended, for Black, Manafort, Stone & Kelly, Registration Number 3600, July 16, 1985, January 11, 1986, July 23, 1986; for period ending December 14, 1986 (date of filing illegible), August 19, 1987, January 14, 1988, and July 14, 1988; Supplemental Statement Pursuant to Section 2 of the Foreign Agents Registration Act of 1938, as amended, for Black, Manafort, Stone & Atwater, Inc., Registration Number 3710, February 25, 1986; Walter Shapiro et al., "Cashing In on Reagan: A New Breed of Access Peddlers Makes It Big," *Newsweek*, March 3, 1986.

126 **When the U.S. government found that Mitsubishi Electric:** Supplemental Statement Pursuant to Section 2 of the Foreign Agents Registration Act of 1938, as amended, for Robinson, Lake, Lerer & Montgomery, Registration Number 3911, March 10, 1988; Exhibits A and B to Registration Statement, Under the Foreign Agents Registration Act of 1938, as amended, for Robinson, Lake & Lerer, Inc., Registration Number 3911, November 12, 1986; and Short-Form Registration Statement, Under the Foreign Agents Registration Act of 1938, as amended, for James H. Lake, Registration Number 3911, November 18, 1986.

127 **At a Senate hearing in June 1988:** Testimony of Maureen Smith, Deputy U.S. Assistant Secretary of Commerce for Japan, U.S. Department of Commerce, before the Subcommittee on Foreign Commerce and Tourism of the Senate Commerce, Science, and Transportation Committee, June 24, 1988.

Regis McKenna, an adviser: John Hillkirk, "Hi-tech Battleground," *USA Today*, July 14, 1988.

130 **In a May 1988 article:** Bruce Stokes, "The Culture of Patents," *National Journal*, May 21, 1988.

In June 1988, Lake became: John E. Peterson, "Bush Aide to Retain His Japanese Clients," Detroit *News*, June 16, 1988; and "Bush Aide Lobbies for Japan," *UAW Washington Report*, Vol. 28, No. 22, 1988.

131 **In January 1989, following still:** Interview with Donald Spero, July 1989.

Spero's wisdom, in retrospect: Ibid.

CHAPTER NINE: GRASS-ROOTS POLITICKING

132   **Japanese firms were advised:** Guy de Jonquières, "Japanese Businesses Advised to Win Europe's Hearts and Minds," *Financial Times*, December 5, 1988.

133   **In May 1989, Senator Max Baucus:** T. R. Reid, "Made in Montana, Sold in Japan," Washington *Post*, National Weekly Edition, May 22–28, 1989.

       In his talk, Mahe suggested: Eddie Mahe, Jr., "The Local Angle: The Importance of U.S. Local-Level Politics for Japanese Business," delivered at the 55th International Economic Seminar, Tokyo, December 4, 1986.

134   **More states now have offices:** Linda M. Spencer, *American Assets: An Examination of Foreign Investment in the United States* (Congressional Economic Leadership Institute, 1988), p. 2.

       When Florida legislators: Confidential interview, December 1989.

135   **As Mahe pointed out, the Japanese:** Eddie Mahe, Jr., "The Local Angle."

       In 1989, the Japan External Trade Organization: Japan External Trade Organization, *1989–90 Directory: Japanese-Affiliated Companies in USA & Canada* (JETRO, 1990), p. 25.

       To "educate" America, EIAJ hired: Electronics Industries Association of Japan, "An Introduction to the Overseas Public Relations Activities of the Electronics Industries Association of Japan and a Look into the Future," June 1985, pp. 3–5 (translated from Japanese).

136   **Akio Morita:** Ibid., p. 4.

       In February 1985, EIAJ also flew: Ibid., p. 6.

       Suguo Kagehira: Suguo Kagehira, "From Washington to the State Level: Exchanges with the Local Community in Tennessee," Electronics Industries Association of Japan/Overseas Public Relations Committee, Keidanren Geppo, September 1988 (translated from Japanese).

137   **In June 1985, Morita told:** Electronics Industries Association of Japan, "An Introduction to the Overseas Public Relations Activities of the Electronics Industries Association of Japan and a Look into the Future," p. 4.

138   **According to Morita:** Electronics Industries Association of Japan, "Grassroots PR Campaign: The Needs and Substantial Activities," December 1985 (temporary translation).

139   **Most of the state's:** Richard Rice and Lucien Ellington, "Tennessee State: A Case Study," in *The Regional Underpinnings of the U.S.-Japan Partnership*, Vol. 3 (Japan Center for International Exchange, December 1986), p. 24.

       Despite all this outward goodwill: Ibid., p. 25.

140   **Tennessee's congressional delegation:** Confidential interview, March 1989.

      The forums also addressed state officials' concern: Remarks of Frank Gorrell, Chairman, Tennessee-Japan Friends in Commerce, printed in *Friends: A Success Story* (Tennessee-Japan Friends in Commerce, 1988), p. 3.

      MITI has eight offices: *Report of the Attorney General to the Congress of the United States on the Administration of the Foreign Agents Registration Act of 1938, as amended, for the Calendar Year 1987* (U.S. Department of Justice, 1989), pp. 421–27.

141   **Much of the more than $11 million:** Ibid.

142   **In his book *The Japan That Can Say "No"*:** Printed in the *Congressional Record*, November 14, 1989, p. E 3787.

      Working in combination, the Keidanren and Morita: Craig Smith, "Springtime in Tokyo," *Corporate Philanthropy Report*, Vol. 4, No. 7, April 1989, p. 6.

CHAPTER TEN: JAPAN'S SIX EXCUSES

147   **When he returned from an extended trip:** Alan Webber, *Harvard Business Review*, September-October 1989.

148   **Dutch journalist Karel van Wolferen:** Van Wolferen, *The Enigma of Japanese Power*, p. 12.

149   **The number of *new jobs* created:** Calculated from "Investment Outlays by Country of Each Ultimate Beneficial Owner, 1987–88," May 1989 Supplementary Tables, U.S. Department of Commerce, Bureau of Economic Analysis, June 1989, Table 10.

      Another overlooked economic fact: Edward M. Graham and Paul R. Krugman, *Foreign Direct Investment in the United States* (Institute for International Economics, 1989), pp. 55–56.

150   **Japan's "consumer" propaganda theme:** Confidential interview, May 1989.

151   **In a March 1990 article in the *National Journal*:** Bruce Stokes, "Running on Nationalism," *National Journal*, March 3, 1990, pp. 513–17.

152   **In an October 1989 speech:** Cited in Tim Johnson, "Nakayama on East Europe, PRC Aid, U.S. Trade," Kyodo News Service (English), October 24, 1989.

      Minister Nakayama's attitude is hardly unique: *Business Week*/Harris Poll of 1,000 adults conducted in Japan, November 10–14, published in Robert Neff, "Japan's Hardening View of America," *Business Week*, December 18, 1989.

      As one American Japan watcher observes: Confidential interview, April 1990.

      When the late Japanese businessman Ginji Yasuda: Robert Reinhold,

"Las Vegas Casinos Dull Japanese Success Image," *New York Times*, June 21, 1989.

152   **Shintaro Ishihara, co-author of:** Morita and Ishihara, *The Japan That Can Say "No,"* printed in the *Congressional Record*, November 14, 1989, pp. E 3785–86.

     Morita commented: Ibid., p. E 3788.

153   **In the summer of 1989, University of South Carolina:** Interview with John Judis, January 1990.

     In 1981, for example, lawyers who represented: Peter Collier and David Horowitz, *Destructive Generation: Second Thoughts About the '60s* (Summit Books, 1989), p. 182.

     In 1989, critics of the federal Drug Enforcement Agency: Peter Gorman, "Marijuana McCarthyism," *New York Times*, December 30, 1989.

     In their 1989 book *Destructive Generation*: Collier and Horowitz, *Destructive Generation*, pp. 167–84.

     In his closing paragraphs: George R. Packard, "The Japan-Bashers Are Poisoning Foreign Policy," Washington *Post*, October 8, 1989.

154   **The "those who criticize Japan revive McCarthyism" theme:** Hobart Rowen, "Government's Revolving Door Needs Slowing," Washington *Post*, December 24, 1989.

155   **In 1989, the Office:** *National Trade Estimate: Foreign Trade Barriers Report of the USTR*, Office of the U.S. Trade Representative, April 1989, pp. 97–114.

156   **Insurance rates on a foreign car:** Cristina Lee, "Japan's Insurance Rates Slow Auto Imports," *Journal of Commerce*, March 1, 1990.

     Donald Petersen, who until the spring of 1990: Interview with Donald Petersen, November 30, 1989.

157   **According to Ohmae's "globalization" thesis:** Kenichi Ohmae, "Global Village No Place for Japanphobia," *Wall Street Journal*, November 29, 1989.

     The globalization theme also glosses over: Hobart Rowen and Jodie T. Allen, "Brave New World, Inc.: To Superfirms, Borders Are Just a Nuisance," Washington *Post*, March 19, 1989.

158   **Foreign investors:** Graham and Krugman, *Foreign Direct Investment in the United States*, Table 1.8.

159   **In the 1980s, the ratio:** Peter Truell, "The Outlook: Why Reactions Differ to Japan and Germany," *Wall Street Journal*, February 26, 1990.

     Tennessee entrepreneur: "Not All the Cultured Pearls in the World Are Grown in Japan," *International Herald Tribune*, May 8, 1989.

161   **In the first package of measures:** Testimony of Pat Choate before the Senate Finance Committee, Washington, D.C., November 7, 1989.

CHAPTER ELEVEN: THE JAPANESE WURLITZER

163 **The substance of this covert propaganda:** Loch K. Johnson, *America's Secret Power: The CIA in a Democratic Society* (Oxford University Press, 1989), p. 22.

165 **Whalen was well qualified:** Letter of Understanding Between Richard J. Whalen, Chairman, Worldwide Information Resources, Ltd., and His Excellency Hernán Felipe Errázuriz, Chilean Ambassador to the United States, dated December 19, 1984; Supplemental Statement Pursuant to Section 2 of the Foreign Agents Registration Act of 1938, as amended, for Worldwide Information Resources, Ltd., Registration Number 3637, January 20, 1987; Report Pursuant to Federal Regulation of Lobbying Act for Worldwide Information Resources, Ltd., representing Toyota Motor Sales U.S.A., Inc., May 6, 1982 (subsequent filings through April 6, 1989); Supplemental Statement Pursuant to Section 2 of the Foreign Agents Registration Act of 1938, as amended, for JETRO (Japan External Trade Organization), New York, Registration Number 1643, Schedule D-4: Research Information Fees, August 4, 1989.

The strategy for deflecting criticism: "Foreign Investment: The Political Stakes," prepared by WIRES, Ltd., March 30, 1988, Preface.

168 **Lawrence Baer, president of:** Interview with Lawrence Baer, November 2, 1988.

Soon after Bush's announcement: Confidential interview, March 1990.

169 **On November 1, 1989:** Press release, "To: Editors, columnists and foreign editors; From: WIRES, Ltd.; Subject: Foreign direct investment in the United States—an update on recent trends," November 1, 1989, Worldwide Information Resources, Ltd.

170 **Alan Webber observes:** Telephone interview with Alan Webber, February 1990.

171 **Mansfield's essay is little more:** Mike Mansfield, "Ambassador Mansfield Talks to America," in "Special Advertising Section: Outlook on the U.S. and Japan," *Atlantic Monthly*, February 1990, pp. A2–A12.

172 **Yet as Kevin L. Kearns:** Kevin L. Kearns, "After FSX: A New Approach to U.S.-Japan Relations," *Foreign Service Journal*, December 1989.

173 **In the midst of Zenith's fight:** R. C. Longworth, "One Man Could Smash Trade System," Chicago *Tribune*, April 4, 1978.

He called the legislation: Hobart Rowen, "Reagan's Trade Problem," Washington *Post*, October 4, 1987.

He earned: Calculated from Supplemental Statements Pursuant to the Foreign Agents Registration Act of 1938, as amended, for JETRO (Japan External Trade Organization), New York, Registration Number 1643, January 1987 through December 1988.

174 **Malmgren, for instance, canceled:** Supplemental Statement Pursuant

to Section 2 of the Foreign Agents Registration Act of 1938, as amended, for Malmgren, Inc., Registration Number 3608, September 18, 1985, Termination Date: September 19, 1985.

174 **One former U.S. negotiator explains why:** Confidential interview, March 1990.

175 **Former Federal Reserve chairman:** Reuters, "Volcker to Work on Venture," *New York Times*, March 14, 1989.

Financial World **reports:** Shelley Liles, "Power Salaries on Wall Street," *USA Today*, June 22, 1989; and "Peterson Disputes 'FW,' " *USA Today*, July 17, 1989.

To attract more business: "A New Era in M&A," full-page advertisement in *Nihon Keizai Shimbun*, June 17, 1988.

In 1988, *Business Week*'**s:** William J. Holstein and Amy Borrus, "Japan's Clout in the U.S.: It's Translating Economic Might into Influence," *Business Week*, July 11, 1988, p. 65.

177 **While privately seeking Sony Corporation funds:** David Hoffman and Fred Hiatt, "Reagan Seeks Sony Donation; $1 Million for Video Equipment Discussed," Washington *Post*, October 28, 1989.

At a Fujisankei-sponsored banquet: Elisabeth Bumiller, "Sony May Restore 'Decency' to Hollywood, Says Reagan," Washington *Post*, October 26, 1989.

178 **On November 7, 1989:** *Wall Street Journal*, November 7, 1989.

What is far less publicized: Classified telegram from the American Embassy in Tokyo to the Secretary of State, "Subject: The Ubiquitous Mr. Sasakawa," September 21, 1977 (declassified September 20, 1982).

In 1931, he founded: Confidential memorandum (declassified) from ADCM—A. L. Seligmann to Ambassador Mansfield, memorandum on Ryoichi Sasakawa, October 4, 1979; and "SASAKAWA Ryoichi, Internee in Sugamo Prison," Legal Section of the Supreme Command of the Allied Powers, June 4, 1947, Document Number 185-39.

According to declassified: Case File 185: Dossier on Ryoichi Sasakawa, in Sugamo Prison, Records of Allied Operational and Occupational Headquarters, WWII, Document Number 185-43 (U.S. National Archives).

Less than four months after: Ibid.

American authorities: Ibid., p. 15.

He was accused of: Alec Dubro and David E. Kaplan, "Soft-Core Fascism: The Rehabilitation of Ryoichi Sasakawa," *Village Voice*, October 4, 1983.

179 **Through his purse:** *Ryoichi Sasakawa*, an autobiographical brochure, ca. 1981.

In recent years: "Donations Open U.S. Doors for Developer," *Japan Economic Journal*, March 25, 1989.

CHAPTER TWELVE: JAPAN ON JAPAN

181   **A recent survey:** *Geography: An International Gallup Survey,* Gallup
       Organization, 1988; "Americans Get Low Grades in Gallup Geography
       Test," press release from National Geographic Society, July 27, 1988;
       and Gilbert M. Grosvenor, "Those Panamanian Pandas," *New York
       Times,* July 31, 1988.
       A survey commissioned: Kenneth H. Bacon, "College Seniors Fail to
       Make Grade," *Wall Street Journal,* November 9, 1989.
       Even well-educated Americans: Ibid.

182   **As a first step:** Exhibit A to Registration and Exemption Statements,
       Under the Foreign Agents Registration Act of 1938, as amended, for
       Charles von Loewenfeldt, Registration Number 810, filed January 5,
       1954; Remarks by Susan Brossy Crosier, on behalf of Charles von
       Loewenfeldt, Incorporated, at the offices of the U.S.-Japan Founda-
       tion, New York, March 2, 1982.

183   **As one of the Americans:** Crosier Remarks.
       Tours typically begin: Ibid.; Exhibit B to Registration Statement, Un-
       der the Foreign Agents Registration Act of 1938, as amended, for
       Charles von Loewenfeldt, Inc., November 5, 1979; Letter of Under-
       standing Between Charles von Loewenfeldt, Incorporated, and Mr.
       Yoshiro Kurisaka, Managing Director, Japan Institute for Social and
       Economic Affairs, Ohtemachi Building, 1-6-1 Ohtemachi, Tokyo, Ja-
       pan, Signed October 30, 1979.
       Indeed, thousands have applied: Supplemental Statement Pursuant to
       Section 2 of the Foreign Agents Registration Act of 1938, as amended,
       for Charles von Loewenfeldt, Registration Number 810, July 31, 1989.
       One of Japan's American agents: Crosier Remarks.

184   **To help trip alumni "infect":** Ibid.
       The Japanese government maintains: Supplemental Statement Pur-
       suant to Section 2 of the Foreign Agents Registration Act of 1938, as
       amended, for Charles von Loewenfeldt, Registration Number 810, July
       31, 1989.

185   **A principal source of additional money:** "Setting New Objectives:
       USJF Precollege Program Advances into Second Phase," *Forum: News-
       letter of the United States–Japan Foundation,* Vol. 5, No. 2, Winter
       1990.
       This organization was created: *Report from January 1988 through
       December 1988,* United States–Japan Foundation, June 1989, Fore-
       word.
       The chairman of this group: Mark Hosenball, "Japan's Daddy War-
       Bucks: Why His Fund Has Trouble Giving Money Away," Washington

Post, January 21, 1990; Fred Hiatt and Paul Blustein, "U.S. Experts on Japanese Often Have Economic Ties," Washington *Post*, November 10, 1989.

185 **Eberle, who was recently appointed:** "Private Sector Advisory Committee—Membership Report by Committee: ACTPN, Advisory Committee for Trade Policy and Negotiations," Office of the Private Sector Liaison, Office of the United States Trade Representative, March 7, 1990.

186 **As part of its outreach program:** *Report from January 1988 through December 1988*, United States–Japan Foundation, June 1989, Foreword.

The foundation established its first: "Setting New Objectives: USJF Precollege Program Advances into Second Phase."

In 1990, the foundation announced: Ibid.

187 **At the second level:** *FAIR Fact Series: Japan's Financial Markets*, Foundation for Advanced Information and Research (Japan), Vol. 19, pp. 15–16.

336 American colleges and universities: Calculated from *Directory of Japan Specialists and Japanese Studies Institutions in the United States and Canada*, Vol. 2, Japan Foundation and the Association for Asian Studies (Japan Foundation, Tokyo, 1989).

Professor Chalmers Johnson estimates: Leslie Helm, Alice Z. Cuneo, and Dean Foust, "On the Campus: Fat Endowments and Growing Clout," *Business Week*, July 11, 1988, p. 70.

188 **For a number of years, the Heritage Foundation:** "Was Ist die Heritage Stiftung?," "Qué Es la Fundación Heritage?," "L'Institut Heritage Foundation," and Asian-language versions, Heritage Foundation.

The report places most: *Strengthening U.S.-Japan Economic Relations*, Council for Economic Development and Keizai Doyukai (CED, 1989).

The American delegation was led: Hiatt and Blustein, "U.S. Experts on Japanese Often Have Economic Ties."

A CED representative says: Telephone interview with Robert Holland, President, Committee for Economic Development, March 1990.

In 1988, Eberle co-authored: William D. Eberle and Richard N. Gardner, "As If the Future Mattered: Economic Policy in the New Administration—An Open Letter to the President-Elect," Aspen Institute, November 1988.

189 **In the early 1980s, for instance:** Holstein and Borrus, "Japan's Clout in the U.S.: It's Translating Economic Might into Influence," p. 66.

One leading American university: Confidential interview, May 1990.

In April 1990, the acting director: Stuart Auerbach, "Japan Group Punishes Writer for Article; Accused of 'Hatchet Job,' Researcher Was Banned from Library," Washington *Post*, April 5, 1990.

Fusion Systems CEO: Interview with Donald Spero, Zurich, August 1989.

Packard has publicly labeled van Wolferen: "Is the Trade Deficit with Japan a National Security Risk?" Transcript of *American Interests*, Show #914, Blackwell Corporation, Washington, D.C., air date December 30, 1989.

190   **He calls the works of Fallows and Prestowitz:** "The Japan-Bashers Are Poisoning Foreign Policy."

A good example: George R. Packard, "The U.S. and Japan: Partners in Prosperity," in "Special Advertising Section," *Atlantic Monthly*, February 1989.

Makin attacks James Fallows' views: John H. Makin, "Japan, U.S. Must Go Beyond Sniping: Trade Solutions—Some Starters," *Japan Times*, October 11, 1989.

Fallows responds: Telephone interview with James Fallows, May 1990.

191   **Mitchell Daniels:** Telephone interview with Mitchell Daniels, April 1990.

In January 1990, John B. Judis: John B. Judis, "A Yen for Approval: How the Japanese Are 'Helping' the U.S. Media Understand Japan," *Columbia Journalism Review*, January–February 1990.

192   **The American producers:** Ibid.

In 1989, NHK: Ibid.

The Sasakawa-funded U.S.-Japan Foundation: "USJF Supports National Awareness of Japan Through Public Television," *Forum: Newsletter of the United States–Japan Foundation*, Vol. 3, No. 1, Fall 1987.

193   **In 1988, it gave the Cambridge Forum:** "Schedule of Grants and Appropriations, Year Ending December 31, 1988," *Report from January 1988 through December 1988*, United States–Japan Foundation, June 1989, p. 10.

Every year since 1987: "Schedule of Grants," p. 15.

One independent producer: Confidential interview, February 1990.

Beginning in the late 1970s: Report from Kyodo News Service, May 29, 1981.

Sasakawa says: Ibid.

The program was administered: Report from Kyodo News Service, May 28, 1981.

In this program, leading newspapers: Bernard D. Nossiter, "U.N. Says Its Agencies Subsidize the Press," *New York Times*, June 11, 1981.

194   **In 1986, MITI went a step further:** Stuart Auerbach, "Japan Eyes U.S. Professionals as Lobbyists," Washington *Post*, October 22, 1986.

According to a report in Japan's: " 'Friction Reporters' to Be Assigned to US; MITI Planning 'Local Hire' in 10 States with Strong Criticism Against Japan," cited in the *Congressional Record*, October 17, 1986, p. S 17185.

194 **Senators John Heinz:** Letter to the Hon. Yasuhiro Nakasone, Prime Minister of Japan, from Senator Donald W. Riegle, Jr., October 16, 1986; letter to the Hon. George P. Shultz, Secretary of State, from Senator Donald W. Riegle, Jr., October 16, 1986; letter to His Excellency Nobuo Matsunaga, Ambassador of Japan to the United States, from Senator Frank H. Murkowski, October 16, 1986; letter to the Hon. Edwin Meese III, U.S. Attorney General, from Senator Frank H. Murkowski, October 28, 1986; and "Heinz: Japanese Plan to 'Buy American'; U.S. Reporters for Sale?," release from office of Senator John Heinz, October 16, 1986.

MITI responded: Unpublished MITI talking points, October 1986.

In an off-the-record interview: Confidential interview, July 1989.

195 **A representative example occurred:** Peter Passell, "U.S. Memories: Who is the Loser?" *New York Times*, January 24, 1990.

All the while, however: List of the Advisory Board of the Research Institute on International Trade and Industry (MITI/RI), 1989.

Saxonhouse himself spoke: John B. Judis, "Conflicting Japan Policy and a Conflict of Interest," *In These Times*, January 17–23, 1990.

196 **In Gigot's January 12, 1990, column:** Paul A. Gigot, "The Japanphobes Want Disclosure? OK, Let's Disclose," *Wall Street Journal*, January 12, 1990.

197 **In October 1987, Rowen lambasted:** Hobart Rowen, "Reagan's Trade Problem."

In a March 1990 article, Rowen attacked: Hobart Rowen, "Dispelling Some Myths about Foreign Investment," Washington *Post*, March 18, 1990.

In a column published: Hobart Rowen, "Japanese Voters Miss Opportunity for Reform," Washington *Post*, February 25, 1990.

198 **According to one Japan expert:** Confidential interview, March 1990.

Another refers to him as: Confidential interview, May 1990.

Soon after *Foreign Affairs* published: Interview with Karel van Wolferen, Tokyo, April 1990.

Fred Barnes, a senior editor: Interview with Fred Barnes, May 1990.

199 **As one journalist puts it:** Confidential interview, March 1990.

CONCLUSION

205 **Twenty years ago:** Interview with John P. Guttenberg, Jr., May 1990.

ACKNOWLEDGMENTS

Dozens of people have given me assistance and encouragement in writing this book. I am deeply in their debt. Many of them shared their wisdom and their experiences in confidence: some are in sensitive government positions, others are in sensitive private-sector posts. I am immensely grateful to them for their insights and their candor.

I have also benefited greatly from the efforts of the many journalists whose work is cited in this book. Their willingness to share information has been invaluable. It is a pity that they have not been given the airtime or print space to explore this topic more systematically. Hard scrutiny by the fourth estate remains one of the surest ways to safeguard the integrity of America's political processes.

Ashbel Green, my editor at Knopf, was a valued counselor. His enthusiasm and support for this project were vital. Jenny McPhee of Knopf kept the process moving with her talents and good nature.

I wish also to express my gratitude to Mary Williams, commander of the Foreign Agent Registration Act public office at the Department of Justice, who has been extraordinarily helpful, unusually patient, and a genuine pleasure to work with.

I am deeply grateful to Lloyd Hand and Martin Garbus for their meticulous review of this book and its documentation, and their wise suggestions.

Stephanie Epstein, my researcher and in-house editor, provided invaluable help. She located sources and people and materials that had long escaped the attention of others. She skillfully organized a massive set of files. Her editing was quick and sure. Her attention to detail continues to impress me. Her good spirit and uncompromising attitude about deadlines made a significant contribution to timely publication. Her many suggestions and discoveries made an important difference in the substance and style of this work.

Once again, I appreciate Diane Choate's encouragement and support. Surely those who are most pleased to see this book in print are the friends who tolerated my immersion (and theirs) in this topic for nearly three years. They were kind listeners and (on the whole) gentle critics. Their wit, good humor, and friendship are greatly prized.

INDEX

Abbell, Michael, 18
Abrams, Robert, 102–3
"access plus," 61–2, 123
ad hoc lobbying coalitions, 117–20
Admiral, 78
adversarial legal system, 16–17
aerospace industry, 44
agricultural cooperatives, 11
Agriculture, U.S. Department of, 26
Air Force, U.S., 44
airline industry, 42
Aitken, Bruce, 118–19
Akao, Nobutoshi, 77, 78
Akatani, Genichi, 193
Akihito, Emperor, 177
Alexander, Lamar, 139
Alexander's, Inc., 81, 98
Alfalfa Club, xv
Allen, Jodie, 157–8
Allen, Richard, 69–70
Altman, Roger, 175, 176
American Agricultural Movement, 12
American Bar Association, 18
American Business Conference, xx, 119
American Council on Japan (ACJ), 65–7
American Enterprise Institute, 23, 167
American International Automobile Dealers Association (AIADA), 111, 116, 118
American Telephone & Telegraph, 8
Anderson, Bette, 91
Anderson, Hibey, Nauheim & Blair, 72
Anderson, Stanton, 53, 72
Angel, Robert, 153, 189
anti-Communism, 23, 66, 172
Anti-dumping Act (1916), 100

anti-Semitism, 152
antitrust laws, 79, 83, 87, 90, 100–2, 200
Apple Computers, 8, 127
Arbatov, Georgi, 169–70
Armitage, Richard, 10
Army, U.S., 52
Asahi Shimbun, 194
Aspen Institute, 189
Association for International Investment (AFII), 51, 61, 168, 197
Astor, Vincent, 66
Atlantic Monthly, 171, 190
Atwater, Lee, 125
Auerbach, Stuart, 54
Australia, 102
Auto Dealers and Drivers for Free Trade PAC (AUTOPAC), 110–12
Automobile Importers of America, 119
automobile industry: ad hoc lobbying coalitions and, 119; components suppliers for, 57, 60; front groups for, 114–16; PAC of, 110–12; propaganda about, 156; state competition for plants, 134; tariff regulations and, 4–6

Baer, Lawrence, 168
Bahamas, 125
Baker, James, 61
Baker and McKenzie, 92, 130
Baldridge, Malcolm, 12
Bank of Tokyo, 21
banks: American, 65; foreign, U.S. assets held by, 200; Japanese, 22–3, 66–7, 175
Barnes, Fred, 198
Baucus, Max, 133
Belgium, 110

Bentsen, Lloyd, xv, 40–1, 129
Best Products, 102
Black, Charles, 124–5
Black, Manafort, Stone & Kelly, 124–5
Blackmun, Harry, 93
Blackstone Group, 168, 175–6
Boggs, Thomas, 112
Boren, David, 112
Boskin, Michael, 196
Brady, Nicholas, 6
bribery, 33–4
British Bank of Northern Commerce, xii
Brookings Institution, 167
Brooks, Jack, 12
Brown, Clarence ("Bud"), 57
Brown, Ron, 112, 122
Brown Brothers, Harriman, 66
Bryan, Richard, 112
Bryant, John, 166, 168
Bryant Amendment, 165, 168
budget deficit, 4, 188, 204–5; Japanese financing of, 20, 22–3, 121
buffers, 169–71
Burke, General Kelly, 52
Bush, George, xv, xx, 20, 23, 52, 138, 155, 166; foreign investment and, 168, 169; Hills appointed by, 38, 53; presidential campaign of, 54, 110, 123–5, 130; and Toshiba affair, 10
Business Roundtable, xx
Business Week, 152
Byron, Robert, 49

Cable News Network (CNN), 191
Cali cocaine cartel, 18
Cambridge Forum, 193
campaign financing: in Japan, 28–9, 33; in U.S., 109–12, 203
campaign officers, 121–5
Canada, xvi, xvii, 53, 62, 102, 135, 150; trade agreement with, 57–8

cartels, 13; of television manufacturers, 78–105
Carter, Jimmy, 8, 24, 51, 56, 71, 72, 124, 175, 201; Sasakawa and, 178, 179; and television cartel, 43, 87–9, 94, 95, 173
Cassidy, Robert, Jr., 75, 96
Caterpillar, 119
CBS Records, 137, 165, 175
Central Intelligence Agency (CIA), 9, 36, 70, 163–4
Chamberlain, Neville, 49
charitable donations, 142–3
Chasen, Robert, 95
Chiang Kai-shek, xvi
Chile, 165
China, 51, 66, 85, 153, 178, 184; Nationalist, xvi
China National Textiles Import & Export Association, 54
Christian Broadcasting Network, 191
Chrysanthemum Club, 171, 172
Chrysler Corporation, 4, 6, 134
Church, Frank, 71
Circuit City, 102
Colby, William A., 70
cold war, 23, 66, 200
Collier, Peter, 153
Colombia, 18, 124
Colorado Wheat Administrative Committee, 12
Columbia Pictures, 137, 169, 175, 177
Commerce Department, U.S., 12, 26, 27, 55–7, 59, 61, 96–7, 105, 126, 150, 155
Committee for Economic Development (CED), xx, 188–9
Committee to Preserve American Color Television (COMPACT), 87, 96–8
Communism, 23, 66
Compaq, 8
Congress, U.S., xix–xxi, 13, 26, 34, 38, 43, 50, 64, 68–76, 84, 112,

114, 115, 122, 132, 134–5, 150,
160, 173, 187, 188, 194; automobile industry and, 6; budget deficit
and, 23; computer chips and, 21;
dumping and, 86, 91, 94–7, 104;
EIAJ and, 136; ethics and, 16–18;
foreign investment and, 165, 166,
168; FSX and, 44; Fusion and,
129–31; ITC and, 55; PACs and,
111; Pro Trade Group and, 119,
120; rice exports and, 12; Toshiba
and, 7–10, 20, 139
congressional staff, 74–6, 136
Constitution, U.S., 180, 203
construction industry, 12–13, 31, 40
Construction Ministry, Japanese, 32
consumer electronics industry, 77,
102; public relations campaigns of,
137; *see also* television manufacturers
"consumer" propaganda theme,
150–1
Consumers for World Trade (CWT),
114, 118
corruption, political: in Japan, 29–30,
33; in U.S., 15–17
Council for Better Corporate Citizenship in the United States
(CBCCIUS), 142
Council for Better Investment in the
United States, 142
Council of Economic Advisors (CEA),
14, 24, 25, 60, 154, 195–6
Council on Foreign Relations, 60,
175, 176
Court of International Trade, 98
Culver, John, 71
Customs, U.S., xvii, 5, 6, 27, 81–3,
90–2, 94–6, 98, 104
Customs Court, 88, 90, 91
Czechoslovakia, 9

Daewoo conglomerate, 51, 53
Dai-ichi Bank, 22
Danforth, John, 194

Daniels, Mitchell, 191
Dannemeyer, William, 5
Defense Department, U.S., 26, 51,
61, 64, 164, 171–2
Defense Intelligence Agency, 9
Democratic Party, xix, 39, 71, 72,
88, 110–12, 122, 123, 125, 151,
166, 205
demonstration effect, 39
Dickstein, Shapiro & Morin, 10, 122
Diet, Japanese, 31–2, 73, 89
Dillon Reed, 66
Dingell, John, 194
disinformation, 44
Dole, Robert, 72
dollar, devaluation of, 156, 165
double-pricing schemes, 81–3, 86, 87
Drug Enforcement Agency (DEA),
153
drug trafficking, 18
DuBois, Guy, 9
Dukakis, Michael, 110, 111, 121,
123–5, 175
Dulles, John Foster, 66, 67
Dumont, 83
dumping, 21, 27, 68; laws against,
120; of semiconductors, 126, 135,
of television sets, 70, 82–3, 86,
89–98
Dyke, Gen. William, 52
dynamic random access memory
chips (DRAMs), 21, 195

Earle, Ronnie, 109
Earp, Gordana, 50
East Germany, 9
Eberle, William, 70, 86, 87, 185,
188–9
economic diplomacy, 41–3
economic propaganda, 43–5
educational propaganda, 181–7
Eizenstat, Stuart, 71
Electronics Industries Association of
Japan (EIAJ), 54, 81, 132, 135–40
Emerson, 78, 83, 87

Environmental Protection Agency
(EPA), 6
ethical standards, 15–19, 34; legal
profession and, 16–17; money and,
18–19
European Community (EC), xvi, xvii,
35, 58, 70, 132, 156, 158, 198, 204
Export-Import Bank, 26
Ezoe, Hiromasa, 30

factions: in Japanese politics, 32–3;
Madison on, 51
Fahrenkopf, Frank, 122
Fairbanks, Richard, 124
Fair Trade Commission, Japanese, 22
Fallows, James, 30, 45, 59, 152, 153,
189, 190
Far Eastern Economic Review, 22
Farnsworth, Clyde, 154
Farren, J. Michael, 13
Fascist National Essence Mass Party,
178
Federal Communications Commis-
sion, 104
Federal Election Commission, 110
Federal Express, 140
Federalist papers, 51
Federal Reserve, 175, 205
Federal Trade Adjustment Assistance
Act, 4n
Fiat, 51
Finance Ministry, Japanese, 22, 31,
67, 121, 156, 187, 196
Financial World, 175
Firestone tire company, 165
Fisk, Jim, 18
Fleming, David, 70
Ford, Gerald, 53, 54, 61, 70, 86, 87,
90
Ford Motor Company, 4, 6, 156
Foreign Agents Registration Act
(1938), 174, 202
foreign investment, 51, 120, 121,
197, 200; competition among states
for, 134–5, 204; globalization and,

157–8; Japanese restrictions on,
138; job creation and, 149–50;
propaganda on, 164–9
Foreign Ministry, Japanese, 31, 32,
73, 141, 143, 164, 189, 191, 198
foreign policy, 43; propaganda and,
171–2; Vietnam war and, 68
Foreign Service, 51
Forrestal, James, 66
Fortune, Terrence J., 50
France, 15, 102, 194
free trade, 23–5, 133, 172, 175,
196–7
Free Trade Agreement (FTA), 57–8
friendship gifts, 33–4
Friendship in Freedom, 112
front groups, 113–15
Frontline, 129
FSX jet fighter, 13, 44
Fuji Bank, 22, 175
Fujisankei Communications, 176, 177
Fujitsu, Ltd., 62, 71, 124
Fuji-Wolfensohn, 175
Fukuda, Takeo, 94
Fukuda Construction Company, 31
Fukushima, Glen, 172
Fusion Systems, 126–31, 189

Gadbaw, R. Michael, 62–3
Gallup Organization, 181
Gambles Import, 82
Garment, Leonard, 8, 10
Garten, Jeffrey, 121
General Accounting Office (GAO), 19
General Agreement on Tariffs and
Trade (GATT), 25, 70, 86, 87, 89,
93, 95, 119
General Dynamics, 44
General Electric, 78, 80, 88, 104
General Motors, 4, 6, 156
Gephardt, Richard, 154, 194
Germany, xvii, 6, 15, 112–13, 156,
158; Nazi, 49, 178, 184–5
Gigot, Paul, 196
Gison, Dunn & Crutcher, 53

Gleysteen, William, 176
Global Economic Action Institute
  (GEAI), 168
globalization, 157–9
Global 2000, 178
Global USA, 56
Goldfield, H. P., 56–7
Goldman, Sachs & Co., 175
Gordon, Bart, 166
Gorrell, Frank, 139
Gould, Jay, 18
Government Research Corporation
  (GRC), 53
Graham, Bob, 112
Graham, Edward, 149
Grant, Ulysses S., 18, 65
Gray, Robert, 72
Gray and Company, 72, 73
Great Britain, xvi, xvii, 6, 15, 49, 51,
  102, 110, 119, 149, 168
Greater East Asia Co-Prosperity
  Sphere, 68
Greece, xvi, 110, 124
Grew, Joseph Clark, 65
GTE/Sylvania, 87, 89

Hale, David, 22
Harkin, Tom, 166
Harriman, Averell, 66
Harriman family, 66
Harwood, Richard, 18
Hasegawa, Keitaro, 121
Hayasaka, Shigezo, 28, 41
Healey, James, 125
Hecht, Spencer & Associates, 123
Hecker, General Guy, 52
Heinz, John, 194
Hemmendinger, Noel, 113, 119
Heritage Foundation, 188
Hersh, Seymour, 98
Herzstein, Robert, 55
Hewlett-Packard, 8
high-definition television (HDTV),
  77–8, 103–5, 195
high-technology industries, 62;

HDTV and, 78, 105, 195; patent
  flooding and, 126–31; *see also*
  semiconductor industry
Hills, Carla, 13, 25, 38, 53, 59, 131
Hills, Roderick, 53
Hirohito, Emperor, 20
Hiroshima, atomic bombing of, 184
Hitachi, 53, 71, 82, 87
Hitotsubashi University, 31
Hollings, Ernest F., 166
Holstein, William, 175–6
Home Electric Appliance Market
  Stabilization Council, 78–9, 102
Honda, 57, 156
Hong Kong, 56; Trade Department,
  54
Horowitz, David, 153
Horton, Frank, 73
House of Representatives, U.S.,
  xviii, 5, 7, 19, 29, 109; Ways and
  Means Committee, 37–8, 89, 92,
  94, 110, 125, 136, 150
Housing and Urban Development,
  U.S. Department of (HUD), 15–
  16, 53
Hudson Institute, 191
Hume, Ted, 96–7
Hunter, Duncan, 9
Husak, A. Andrew, 99, 100

Iacocca, Lee, 6, 134
ideology: anti-Communist, 23, 66,
  172; free-trade, 23–5, 172; laissez-
  faire, 159, 176
industrial espionage, 37
industrial policy, 24, 25
influence networks, 60–1
Inhofe, James, 5
Inside U.S. Trade, 129
Institute for International Economics,
  175
Institute for the Study of the USA
  and Canada, 170
intelligence gathering, 36–8, 62, 70;
  on congressional staff, 74–5

Interior Department, U.S., 26
International Advisors, Inc., 52
International Electronics Manufacturers and Consumers of America, Inc. (IEMCA), 115, 116, 118
International Trade Administration (ITA), 55–6
International Trade Commission (ITC), 19, 27, 41–2, 55, 83, 86–90, 104, 129
Iraq, 124
Ireland, xvi
Ishihara, Shintaro, 20, 138, 152–3
Ishihara, Takashi, 188
Israel, xvi
Italy, 51, 156, 178
It's Your Business, 50–1

Japan Air Lines (JAL), 42
Japan Aluminum Federation, 54
Japan Association of Corporate Executives, 188
Japan Automobile Manufacturers Association (JAMA), 115, 123
Japan Auto Parts Industries Association, 54, 125, 126
Japan bashers, 9, 41, 44–5, 151, 197
Japan Center for Information and Cultural Affairs (JCICA), 71, 191–2
Japan Center for International Exchange, 139, 198
Japan Center of Tennessee, 139
Japan Economic Institute (JEI), 189
Japan Economic Journal, vii, 88, 117, 120, 179
Japanese Chamber of Commerce, 143
Japanese Fair Trade Commission (JFTC), 79, 100
Japanese Whaling Association, 71
Japan External Trade Organization (JETRO), 71, 135, 140–1, 164, 173, 174, 194
Japan Federation of Economic Organizations, *see* Keidanren

Japan Motorboat Racing Association, 179
Japan Project, 192–3
Japan Shipbuilding Industry Foundation, 179, 185
Japan Society, 176
Japan Tobacco Institute, 54
Japan Today, 192
Jenkins, Ed, 134
job creation, 149–50
Johns Hopkins University School of Advanced International Studies, 189
Johnson, Chalmers, 30, 45, 153, 187
Johnson, Loch, 163–4
Joint Chiefs of Staff, xv
Jones, Jim, 8, 10, 92, 122
journalists, propaganda by, 193–9
Judis, John B., 191, 192
Justice Department, U.S., 14, 18, 19, 50, 71, 81, 86, 87, 90, 92, 96–102, 104, 112, 113, 115, 120, 124, 140, 174, 202

Kagehira, Suguo, 136–7
Kaifu, Toshiki, 177
Kajima Construction, 31
Kanasashi, Masao, 75
Kansai Airport project, 12, 43, 56
Kato, Takashi, 33, 34
Katz, Julius, 53, 54
Kauffman, James Lee, 65
Kearns, Kevin L., 172
Keefe and Company, 72
Keidanren, 28–9, 142, 170, 185, 198
keiretsu, 66–7, 161
Keizai Doyukai, 188
Kelly, Peter, 125
Kennedy, John F., 74
Kern, Harry F., 65, 66
Keynes, John Maynard, xii
kickbacks, 68, 81–2, 98, 101
Kissinger, Henry, 51, 69, 84–6
Kobayashi, Shigeu, 179

Koito Manufacturing Company, 22, 124
Kokusui Taishuto, 178
Komatsu, 55–6
Kongsberg Vaapenfabrikk, 7
Korea, xviii, 15, 24, 43, 50, 51, 53, 57, 76, 102, 125, 134, 184, 197
Korea Iron and Steel Association, 54
Korean War, 66
Kostmayer Communications, 119
Kotler, Mindy, 189
Krugman, Paul, xvii, 24–5
Kubota, Ltd., 149
Kuroda, Makoto, 170
Kuwait, 197
Kwitny, Jonathan, 69–70
Kyoto University, 31

Labor Ministry, Japanese, 30
laissez-faire ideology, 159, 176
Lake, James, 54–5, 125–6, 129–31
Latendresse, John R., 159
Lebanon, 125
Lechmere, Inc., 103
legal ethics, 16–17
Lehman Brothers, 175, 176
Le Monde, 194
Lenahan, Walter, 56
Liberal Democratic Party (LDP), 11, 28–33, 72, 179
libraries, presidential, 177, 179–80, 203
Lincoln, Abraham, 160
lobbying, 19, 27, 45; by ad hoc coalitions, 117–20; by agricultural cooperatives, 11–12; by automobile industry, 5, 6; and congressional staff, 73–6; by construction industry, 12–13; by former U.S. government officials, 49–63, 69–73; full disclosure and, 202; grass-roots, 114, 132, 136–8; legal ethics and, 16–18; by Mitsubishi, 129–31; by political advisors, 123, 125; during postwar period, 64–8; by state and local governments, 204; by television cartel, 77–105; by Toshiba, 7–10; by trade associations, 115–17; by U.S. subsidiaries, 115
local governments, 132, 133, 204; public relations and, 138, 141
Lodestar Group, 175
Lovett, Robert, 66
LSI Logic, 117
LTV, 52
Luke, Jordan, 91
Luria and Sons, 103

MacArthur, General Douglas, 64–7
machine tool industry, 41–2
Mack, Connie, 111
MacKay, Buddy, 111
macro-economic policy, 196
Madison, James, 51
Magnavox, 78, 86
Mahe, Eddie, Jr., 133–5, 140, 148
Mainichi Shimbun, 194
Makin, John, 153, 190
Malmgren, Harald, 70–1, 86–8, 173–4, 197
Manafort, Paul, 124–5
management techniques, 136
Manatos, Andrew, 8, 124
Manatt, Charles, 122
Manchester Associates, 186
Mansfield, Mike, 171
Marcos, Ferdinand, 125
Marlowe, Gene, 52
Massey, Joseph, 129, 130
Matsushita, 53, 82, 83, 86, 102–3, 139
Matt Reese & Associates, 138, 139
Mazda, 156
McCarthyism, xiii, 41, 153–4
McCree, Wade, 93
McElheny, Richard, 72–3
McElwaine, Robert M., 111
McKenna, Regis, 127
McKinsey & Company, 157
McLeary, Joel, 123–4

McNeil, Francis, 123
McPherson, Harry, 60
McWherter, Ned, 139
Merrill Lynch & Company, 175
Mesa Petroleum, 21–2
Mexico, 197
Meyer, Herbert E., 36–7
Michiko, Empress, 177
microchips, *see* semiconductor
    industry
Mikulski, Barbara A., 166
Milbank, Tweed, Hadley & McCloy,
    168, 197
military technology, sales to Soviet
    Union of, 7–10
Miller, Scott, 124
Miller, William, 96
Minchew, Daniel, 55, 89
Ministry of International Trade and
    Industry, Japanese (MITI), 21, 32,
    37, 43, 79, 81, 85, 88, 89, 97, 128,
    140, 154, 158, 161, 164, 166, 169,
    170, 187, 191, 194–6; International
    Trade Administration Bureau, 161;
    Japan Trade Promotion Office, 113
Mitsubishi, 37, 52, 54, 64, 87, 92,
    125–31, 189
Mitsubishi Bank, 22
Mitsui, 64
Mitsui Bank, 22
Montgomery Ward, 102
Moonlighter Project, 194
Morgan Stanley & Company, 175
Morita, Akio, 20, 132, 136–9, 142,
    152–3
Morocco, 52
Morris, William, 56
Mosbacher, Robert, 44
Motorola, 78, 83, 86
Moyer, Homer, 97
Mudge, Rose, Guthrie, Alexander &
    Ferdon, 10, 56
Mundheim, Robert, 90–2, 94–6
Muraoka, Shigeo, 25
Murkowski, Frank, 12, 194

Murphy, Admiral Daniel, 52
Muskie, Edmund, 51
Mussolini, Benito, 178

Nagasaki, atomic bombing of, 184
Naito, Masahisa, 161
Nakasone, Yasuhiro, 20, 31, 34, 41–
    2, 121
Nakayama, Taro, 152
"name-brand" lobbyists, 69, 70
National Academy of Sciences, 77
National Archives, 180*n*
National Association of Manufactur-
    ers, xx, 66
National Endowment for the Human-
    ities, 181
National Grange, 119
National Intelligence Council, 36
National Journal, 129, 130
National Office of Machine Dealers
    Association, 115
National Public Radio (NPR), 193
National Security Agency, 37
National Security Council, 14, 52
National Union Electric Corporation
    (NUE), 83, 87, 90, 100–2
NEC, 119, 122, 192
Nemet, Tom, 112
Netherlands, xvi, xvii, 149, 150, 168,
    198
Nevin, John, 173
New Economic Policy, 85
New Republic, The, vii
newspapers, propaganda in, 193–9
Newsweek, 65–7
New York Stock Exchange, xvi
New York Times, The, 114, 194–6
NEXIS, 173, 197
NHK, 192
Nicaragua, 123
Nigeria, 125
Nihonjin-ron, 159
Nihon Keizai Shimbun, 75, 175, 176
Nikaido, Susumu, 72
Nikko Securities, 175

Nippon Telegraph and Telephone
(NTT), 26, 30, 34, 56
Nishio, Kanji, 23
Nissan, 52, 70, 142, 185–6, 188
Nixon, Richard, 8, 24, 43, 53, 68–70,
72, 84–7, 90, 175, 176
nokyo, 11
Nomura Securities, 174
Noriega, Manuel, 123
North Dakota Wheat Commission, 12
Northeast-Midwest Congressional
Coalition, 72–3
Norway, 7, 10
Nunn, Sam, 74
N. V. Philips, 86

O'Connor, Sandra Day, xv
Office of Management and Budget
(OMB), 14, 25, 175
Ohmae, Kenichi, 157
Okura Group, 80
Olive, David, 62
Olmer, Lionel, 56
Omnibus Trade and Competitiveness
Act (1988), 26, 119–20, 150, 169,
185, 187
O'Neill, Tip, 125
Orderly Marketing Agreement, 88
Osborne, David, 71
Overseas Private Investment Corpo-
ration (OPIC), 26, 53
Ozawa, Ichiro, 31

Packard, George R., 153–4, 189–90
Pakenham, Compton, 65
Palace Group, 80
Panama, 123, 124
Panasonic, 102–3
Passell, Peter, 195
patent flooding, 126–31
Patton, Boggs & Blow, 112, 122
Pearl Harbor, 184
Penney, J. C., 82, 115
Perle, Richard, 51–2
personal diplomacy, 41

Peru, 125
Petersen, Donald, 6, 156
Peterson, Peter, 168, 175–6
Philco, 78
Philippines, 124
Pickens, T. Boone, 21–2, 124
Pilgrim, Lonnie, 109
Pinochet, Augusto, 165
political action committees (PACs),
109–12, 203
political appointees, 59, 61–2
political consultants, 121–5
political contributions, *see* campaign
financing
Political Public Relations Center, 70
Portugal, 125
predatory practices, 13, 27, 69; of
television cartel, 78–105
presidential libraries, 177, 179–80,
203
President's Commission on Industrial
Competitiveness, 56
Prestowitz, Clyde, 26, 30, 40, 44–5,
57, 153, 168, 189, 190
price-fixing, 102–3
Project Omega, 90
propaganda, 35, 43–5, 112–13, 138,
147–8, 163–80; by American
spokesmen, 172–80; blaming
America, 155–6; buffers and, 169–
71; of change, 160–2; "consumer"
theme in, 150–1; foreign investment and, 164–9; and funding of
scholars and institutions, 187–90;
globalization theme in, 157–9; job
creation theme in, 149–50; media,
191–9; racism charges in, 151–4; in
schools, 181–8; "uniqueness"
theme in, 159–60
protectionism, 11; charges of, 25,
114, 177, 197; Japanese, 133, 135,
142, 155–6, 161, 196
Pro Trade Group (PTG), 117–20
Public Broadcasting System (PBS),
192–3

public relations campaigns, 135–6; charitable donations and, 142–3; of electronics industry, 137; in Tennessee, 138–40; *see also* propaganda
Pyle, Kenneth, 67

quality control, 135
Quayle, Dan, xv, 123

racism, Japanese charges of, 9, 40–1, 151–4
radio public affairs programs, 191, 193
RCA, 78, 80, 88, 103–4
Reagan, Nancy, 124, 179
Reagan, Ronald, 33, 36, 43, 56, 71, 97, 119, 122, 126, 138, 155, 161, 175, 191, 201; devaluation of dollar under, 165; and HUD scandal, 15; Nakasone and, 41–2, 121; 1989 trip to Japan, 34, 169, 176–7; presidential campaigns of, 54, 69, 123–5; presidential library of, 179; and Toshiba affair, 8–11
Real, Manuel L., 99
Recruit scandal, 29–31, 33, 34, 160
Rehm, John, 5, 99
Reid, Harry, 112
Republican Party, xix, 15, 33, 39, 54, 57, 72, 110–12, 121–5, 133, 166, 205
Research Institute on International Trade and Industry (RIITI), 195
Ribicoff, Abraham, 71
rice, Japanese barriers to imports of, 11–12
Richardson, Elliot, 50–1, 61, 168, 197
Riegle, Donald, 194
Rivers, Richard, 71, 75
Roberts, John G., 67–8
Rockefeller, David, 176
Rockefeller Center, 165, 169
Rodak, Michael, 93

Roosevelt, Franklin D., 203
Rostenkowski, Dan, 40–1, 92, 94–6
Rowen, Hobart, 154, 157–8, 196–7
Rumsey, Mary Harriman, 66

Saab, 119
Sakurai, Takeshi, 131
Samuels, Michael, 128–9
Sanwa Bank, 22
Sanyo, 87, 99
Sasakawa, Ryoichi, 178–9, 185, 192, 193
Sato, Eisaku, 85
Saudi Arabia, 67, 110
Savimbi, Jonas, 125
Sawyer, David, 124
Sawyer/Miller Group, 124
Saxonhouse, Gary, 154, 195–6
Schonberger, Howard, 65
schools, propaganda in, 181–7
Schultze, Charles, 24
Schumer, Charles E., 166
"screwdriver" operations, 149
Sears, John, 123
Sears, Roebuck & Company, 81, 82, 94, 98–101
Securities and Exchange Commission (SEC), 135
Semiconductor Equipment and Materials Industries (SEMI), 116–17
semiconductor industry, 20–1, 43, 59, 60, 62; dumping by, 126, 135; HDTV and, 78; trade association of, 116–17
Semiconductor Industry Association of America (SIAA), 21, 136
Senate, U.S., xviii, 5, 7, 19, 29, 37–8, 40, 44, 75, 109, 126, 127, 132; Commerce Committee, 130; Finance Committee, xv, 74, 110, 129; Foreign Relations Committee, 72, 123; Subcommittee on Security and Terrorism, 153
Sharp, 82, 87, 139
Shinto, Hisashi, 30

Shultz, George, 10, 42
side agreements, 43
Simon Wiesenthal Center, 152
Singapore, 43
Singer, 82
smear campaigns against critics,
    40–1, 151–4
Smith, Craig, 142
Smith, Fred, 140
Smith, Hedrick, 122
Smith, Maureen, 127
Smith, Michael, 130
Smith, Roger, 6
"soft" money, 110
Somalia, 125
Sony Corporation, 82, 109, 137, 175,
    177
Sorensen, Theodore, 74
Soviet Union, 7, 9, 10, 20, 38, 67,
    139, 147, 153, 170
Spain, 102
Spencer, Stuart, 123
Spero, Don, 126, 128–31, 189
Spitz, Erich, 77, 78
Stafford, Gen. Thomas, 52
Stanford University, 186
State Department, U.S., 13, 26,
    42–4, 50, 51, 53, 62, 64, 65, 67,
    69, 72, 92–3, 102, 104, 130, 163,
    164, 178
state politics, 132–5, 204; public re-
    lations and, 138–41
Stein, Herbert, 24
Stern, Paula, 129
Stockman, David, 175, 176
Stokes, Bruce, 151
Stone, Roger, 124–5
strategic trade theory, 25
Strauss, Robert, 88–90, 94, 97
Subaru, 114, 175
subsidized exports, 27, 84
Sumitomo Bank, 22
Sumitomo Corporation, 52, 64
Sun Microsystems, 8
supercomputer technology, 149

Supreme Court, U.S., xv, 84, 93–4,
    97–9, 101–2
Suzuki Corporation, 5, 54, 125
Switzerland, 110
Sylvania, 78
Symms, Steven D., 166

Taft, William H., IV, 10
Taiwan, xvii, 24, 76, 184, 197
Takase, Tamotsu, 69
Takeshita, Noboru, 29–31, 33, 34
Talmadge, Herman, 55
Tamura, Hajime, 40
Tanaka, Kakuei, 28, 29, 32, 41, 86,
    87
Tariff Commission, U.S., 100
Tate, Sheila, 124
tax laws, 43; state, 134
Taylor, Allen, 113
teachers, propaganda aimed at,
    182–6
Technics, 102–3
technology, 67, 200; investment as
    means of acquiring, 149; military,
    7–10; production capacity and, 20–
    1; television, 77–8, 79–80, 103–4;
    transfer of, 13, 21, 24, 44; *see also*
    high-technology industries
Tektronix, Inc., 8, 119
telecommunications, 50, 135
Telejapan, 191
Television Export Council, 80
Television Export Examination Com-
    mittee, 80
television manufacturers, 43, 70, 77–
    105, 135, 173
television public affairs programs,
    191–3
Tennessee, public relations campaign
    in, 138–40
Tenth Day Group, 80
textile industry, 43, 84–5
Thailand, 119
This Week in Japan, 191
Thompson, Robert, 5

Thomson CSF, 77, 104
Thomson SA, 124
Todai, 31
Tokyo Electric Power Company, 122
Tokyo University, 31
Tolchin, Martin, 109, 153, 165
Tolchin, Susan, 109, 153, 165, 168
Toshiba Corporation, 7–10, 20, 21, 53, 54, 82, 87, 92, 99, 122, 139–40, 152–3, 204
Toyota, 53, 71, 114, 119, 122, 165, 204
Trade Act (1974), 68, 86
Trade Act (1988), 120
Trade Adjustment Assistance Act (1990), 4n
Trade Agreements Act (1979), 95, 96
trade associations, 114–17
Trading with the Enemy Act (1917), 85
Transportation, U.S. Department of, 26, 42
Transport Ministry, Japanese, 31, 32, 193
Treasury Department, U.S., xvi, 4, 6, 14, 25–7, 60–1, 82–5, 87–92, 94–8, 100, 204
Truman, Harry S, 66, 74
Turkey, xvi, 51–2

Understanding Japan Today, 193
Union Bank of California (UBC), 21–2
United Nations, 193–4
U.S. Chamber of Commerce, xx, 66
U.S. Committee for Energy Awareness, 113
U.S. Electronics Industries Association, 82, 96
U.S. Information Agency (USIA), 163
U.S.-Japan Foundation, 185–6, 192, 193
U.S.-Japan Semiconductor Agreement (1986), 21, 59

U.S.-Japan Trade Council, 113–14, 119
U.S.-Japan Trade Study Group, 161
U.S. Memories, 195
U.S. Rice Council, 12
U.S. Trade Representative (USTR), 6, 11, 12, 25, 26, 52–5, 72, 75, 96, 120, 128–31, 155, 158, 161, 172; Advisory Committee for Trade Policy and Negotiations, 185–6
universities, Japanese endowments to, 187–90
Uruguay, 119
USA Cable Network, 191

Vanik, Charles, 92, 94–7
Verity, William, 10
Vernon, Raymond, 58
Vietnam war, 68
Volcker, Paul, 175
voluntary quotas, 4
Volvo, 119
von Loewenfeldt, Charles, 182, 184
von Raab, William, 5, 6

Walker, William, 10, 54
Walker family spy ring, 7
Wall Street Journal, The, 69, 129, 178
war criminals, 66, 178
Warwick Electronics, 86–7
Washington Post, The, 92, 129, 158, 189
Washington Representatives, 174
Wasserstein, Perella, 174–5
Watergate scandal, xxii, 86
Watkins, Robert, 57, 60
Watkins, Wes, 135
Watt, James, 16
Webber, Alan, 44–5, 147, 170–1
Westinghouse, 78, 80
Whalen, Richard, 165–6, 169
Whittle Communications, 186
Wides, Burton, 8
Williams, S. Linn, 53

Wilson, Pete, 21
Wolferen, Karel van, vii, 30, 33, 35, 44–5, 148, 153, 160, 169, 189, 190, 198
Wolff, Alan, 21
Woodward, Bob, 37
World Trade Forum, 119
World War II, 184–5
Worldwide Information Resources, Ltd. (WIRES), 165–7, 169

Yamaichi Securities, 175
Yamamoto, Tadashi, 197–8

Yamazaki, Kazutami, 75
Yasuda, 64
Yasuda, Ginji, 152
Yeutter, Clayton, 53–5, 125–6, 128–31
YKK, 179
Yoshida, Shigeru, 67

zaibatsu, 64–6
Zenchu, 11
Zenith, 78, 83–8, 90, 93–4, 97–8, 100–4, 173
zoku giin, 32

A Note About the Author

Pat Choate, a political economist, writes and lectures on competitiveness, management, and public policy. He is the author of numerous papers and reports, and his most recent book, The High-Flex Society, brought international attention to the decline of American competitiveness. He also co-authored America in Ruins, which documented the decay of the U.S. infrastructure, and Being Number One: Rebuilding the U.S. Economy, which addressed the problems in the American manufacturing and service sectors. He received his Ph.D. in economics from the University of Oklahoma. Mr. Choate lives in Washington, D.C.

A Note on the Type

This book was set in Caledonia, a typeface designed by W. A. Dwiggins (1880–1956). It belongs to the family of printing types called "modern face" by printers—a term used to mark the change in style of type letters that occurred about 1800. Caledonia borders on the general design of Scotch Roman, but is more freely drawn than that letter.
Composed by PennSet, Inc., Bloomsburg, Pennsylvania
Printed and bound by The Haddon Craftsmen, Scranton, Pennsylvania